To

Indie, Inc.

Texas Film and Media Studies Series
Thomas Schatz, Editor

Indie, Inc.

Miramax and the Transformation of Hollywood in the 1990s

ALISA PERREN

University of Texas Press ◆ Austin

Copyright © 2012 by the University of Texas Press
All rights reserved
Printed in the United States of America
First edition, 2012

Requests for permission to reproduce material from this work should be sent to:
Permissions
University of Texas Press
P.O. Box 7819
Austin, TX 78713–7819
www.utexas.edu/utpress/about/bpermission.html

♾ The paper used in this book meets the minimum requirements of ANSI/NISO Z39.48–1992 (R1997) (Permanence of Paper).

Library of Congress Cataloging-in-Publication Data

Perren, Alisa.
    Indie, Inc. : Miramax and the transformation of Hollywood in the 1990s / Alisa Perren. — 1st ed.
        p.   cm. — (Texas film and media studies series)
    Includes bibliographical references and index.
    ISBN 978-0-292-72912-4 (cloth : alk. paper) — ISBN 978-0-292-73715-0 (e-book)
    1. Miramax Films—History.   2. Independent filmmakers—United States.
I. Title.
    PN1999.M57P48   2012
    791.4302'3092—dc23   2011048530

For my parents

Contents

Acknowledgments

This book has undergone many changes from inception to its present form. Many, many people have offered intellectual and emotional support throughout the process. Gigi Durham, Richard Lewis, Neil Nehring, Horace Newcomb, Janet Staiger, Joe Straubhaar, Sharon Strover, and Craig Watkins provided early guidance. I could not have made it through the Austin phase of this project without margarita and movie breaks with Kyle and Lisa Barnett, Karen Gustafson, Lars and Aisha Hagen, Caroline Frick, Jennie Phillips, Gabe Rupertus, Lisa Hartenberger Toby, Valerie Wee, and Kate and Alex Wurm.

During the late 1990s and early 2000s, I spent my summers in Los Angeles, expanding my knowledge of Hollywood production and distribution practices. My personal and professional exchanges with several individuals enriched these trips. Particular thanks go to Tony Bacigalupi, Kevin and Anne Carney, Tanya and Don Chmielewski, Tom Cunha, Josh Hall, Rahbeka Harris, Tristan and Mark Hartmann, Jennifer Holt, Lucy Huang, Kuang Lee, Meika Loe, Chris Nance, Anh Nguyen, Sunny Nguyen, Dana Ritter, Lise and Shervin Samimi, Heidi Santillan, Karen Santillan, Mike and Carie Tolfo, and Tony Yee for much-needed lodging, friendship, and Ultimate Frisbee breaks during my California ventures.

My work has benefited from the array of viewpoints available in the Department of Communication at Georgia State University. I would especially like to thank David Cheshier, Kathy Fuller-Seeley, and Greg Smith for fielding numerous questions and offering helpful advice. In addition, I am appreciative of the assistance I received from a number of graduate students. Noel Kirkpatrick, Ian Peters, Karen Petruska, Eric Dewberry, and Shane Toepfer aided me on many an occasion by gathering images, checking citations, and performing many other vital tasks as I prepared to send this book to press. Jim Burr at the University of Texas Press has been a kind and generous editor, and I am thrilled to have had the chance to work with him on this project.

L. S. Kim, Christina Lane, P. David Marshall, Joanne Morreale, and Susan Dirks all have provided valued counsel over the years. Exchanges with Michael Newman, Yannis Tzioumakis, and Justin Wyatt helped me think through many of my arguments and ideas. I am grateful for Paul McDonald's attention to detail in reading the manuscript; his suggestions improved it immensely. No single person has had a bigger impact on my development as a scholar—and the shape of this project—than Tom Schatz. He has pushed me to be a better writer, thinker, and teacher. I cannot thank him enough for the mentorship and encouragement he has provided for well over a decade.

Jennifer Holt and Caroline Frick must be thanked (and then thanked again) for being such fantastic friends and colleagues. They have been there whenever I needed them, and I feel extremely lucky for that. I am incredibly fortunate to have had Cully Hamner come into my life as this project neared completion; he has stood by me patiently as I labored through the revision process. Finally, special thanks must go to my parents, Steve and Diane. They have always been there for me in every imaginable way, and thus I dedicate this book to them.

Indie, Inc.

CHAPTER ONE

Finding a Niche in the 1990s

The major studios are the big American Army. . . . If we went straight up against them, they would nuke us. We're the guerillas. We snipe and we hit and we win a few battles, then we retreat. We're good at being niche players. We don't want to grow up and be another Walt Disney.

Bob Weinstein, 1989

As moguls and minions awoke and rubbed the Oscar-party grit out of their eyes, the talk was about how Miramax had pulled it off. Talk, that is, and a whole lot of sniping.

Los Angeles Times, *March 1999*

In 1989, Miramax cochair Bob Weinstein employed military imagery to underscore his company's marginal position relative to the Hollywood studios. In 1999, the press mobilized similar imagery to present the company as an oppressive force in the film business. Nowhere was the dramatic shift in Miramax's image and industrial position more evident than on the morning after the 1999 Academy Awards ceremony. It was on this occasion that Amy Wallace of the *Los Angeles Times* reported on Miramax's surprising Best Picture Oscar win for *Shakespeare in Love* (1998). From the perspective of Wallace, along with many others in the industry and press, Miramax had effectively deployed its marketing acuity and the extensive resources of its parent company, Disney, to secure this award. In the process, however, Miramax had further fueled the growing antipathy toward its business practices. Wallace was not the only one to ask whether Miramax had "cynically shanghaied the academy, forever changing the way studios will have to play the game of Oscar pursuit."[1]

If anyone was feeling "shanghaied" on the day after the 1999 Academy Awards ceremony, it was DreamWorks SKG cofounders Jeffrey Katzenberg and Steven Spielberg. Initially everything seemed to be going in their young company's favor. It was only DreamWorks's second year distributing films, and the company had managed to garner a number of Academy Award nominations, including Best Picture and Best Director nods for *Saving Private Ryan* (1998). To many, the film looked to be a shoo-in for the awards; to Katzenberg and Spielberg, these awards would confer legitimacy on their nascent company. Yet, on the eve of the Oscars, DreamWorks faced the unpleasant possibility of Miramax's *Shakespeare in Love* taking home Best Picture honors. This could not help but sting Katzenberg in particular, since earlier in the decade he had been instrumental in his role as chairman of Walt Disney Studios in negotiating the acquisition of Miramax. This deal enabled the small independent film distributor to attain the resources it needed to produce, distribute, and market such Oscar-worthy fare as *Shakespeare in Love.*

Though brothers Bob and Harvey established Miramax in 1979, their company did not become an attractive acquisition target for Disney and other media conglomerates until more than a decade later. In fact, Miramax began its rapid ascent only after most other 1980s-era independent distributors declared bankruptcy. Following a string of critical and financial hits that included *Scandal* (1989), *sex, lies, and videotape* (1989), *My Left Foot* (1989), and *Cinema Paradiso* (1990), the company drew the interest of the press and industry. During the early 1990s, Miramax continued to build on its reputation and differentiate its product from that of the major studios through its North American distribution of such acclaimed films as *The Cook, the Thief, His Wife, and Her Lover* (1990), *Tie Me Up! Tie Me Down!* (1990), and *The Grifters* (1990).[2] Katzenberg was among those who took an interest in the company at this time. In the wake of Miramax's widely heralded marketing of the $62 million–earner *The Crying Game* (1992), he aggressively sought to make it part of the Magic Kingdom. Katzenberg convinced the Weinsteins to bring the company into the Disney fold, buying Miramax for what came to be considered a bargain-basement price of approximately $60 million.[3]

Over the next several years, Katzenberg's foresight was borne out, as Miramax distributed one hit after another with a release slate that included a range of edgy American indies, low-budget genre franchises, English-language imports, and foreign-language films. The company reaped hundreds of millions of dollars at the box office while also attracting critical acclaim, top awards, and creative talent. Films such as *Pulp Fiction* (1994), *Clerks* (1994), *Il Postino* (1995), *Scream* (1996), *The English Patient* (1996), *Good Will Hunting* (1997), and *Life Is Beautiful* (1998) were among the company's most profitable and high-profile investments. By the end of the 1990s, the Miramax-Disney relationship had helped alter the structure of the industry, the marketing of low-budget films, and motion picture aesthetics. Miramax peaked with *Shakespeare in Love*. This film's 1999 Oscar victory both reaffirmed Miramax's status as one of the key distributors of niche-targeted films in the 1990s and confirmed that the company had effectively honed its marketing skills. Indeed, that film's Best Picture nod reinforced Miramax's central role in reshaping the film industry and redefining production, distribution, and marketing practices throughout the decade.

Reassessing Miramax, Rethinking the Hollywood-Independent Relationship

Most prior examinations of Miramax have focused primarily on the company's role in distributing a certain strand of edgy, low-budget, "quality" American films, such as *sex, lies, and videotape*, *Clerks*, *Pulp Fiction*, *Sling Blade* (1996), and *Good Will Hunting*. This book takes a different approach. It is certainly the case that throughout the 1990s, Miramax was the most publicized and profitable distributor of low-budget, critically acclaimed indie films originating from the United States. It is also the case that the company was the most consistent in acquiring and releasing films that expanded beyond a core art-house crowd to attract a wider audience.[4] But such conceptualizations of Miramax prove far too limited. This book explores Miramax's economic, cultural, and creative impact on the film industry more broadly. Rather than seeing the company as simply making a narrow strand of "artier" movies accessible to a wider audience, *Indie, Inc.* illustrates how Miramax, under the ownership of Disney, played a major role in transforming Hollywood during the 1990s.

Though it began as an independent distribution company, Miramax quickly evolved to be far more than that. With the support of Disney, it developed into the preeminent contemporary specialty or indie division, involved in distributing niche-oriented films that appealed to demographic groups ranging from teenagers to baby boomers, African Americans to Latinos. When appropriate, Miramax certainly exploited discourses of independence that appealed to those possessing greater cultural capital. Indeed, employing such strategies aided the company as it cultivated one of the most recognizable brand identities in contemporary film. Though its roots may have been in the independent film world, and it readily tapped into those discourses as needed, the company should not be seen solely in terms of how it "made independent film mainstream." To do so is to minimize the company's more wide-ranging impact on film festivals, acquisitions, production budgets, distribution, marketing, exhibition, talent development, and multimedia exploitation, along with its influence on critical and cultural discourses about "independence" and the "mainstream." Through its business practices and press relations, Miramax contributed to ever-shifting notions about terms such as independence, indie, and Indiewood. These notions, in turn, fed into broader critical, journalistic, and scholarly discussions about the boundaries of both independent *and* Hollywood film.

As the first independent distributor to be acquired by a global media conglomerate in the 1990s, Miramax gained a head start on other companies. Disney's deep pockets, combined with the Weinsteins' aggressive behavior, enabled Miramax to play a dominant part in shaping the rapidly expanding specialty film business. Subsequently, every other major media conglomerate emulated—and responded to—Miramax's practices by launching their own specialty division or acquiring an existing independent distribution company. By the start of the new millennium, each major studio had developed at least one division modeled largely on Miramax's production and distribution strategies. This move signaled a major structural transformation, as indie divisions became the primary means through which conglomerates financed, produced, and distributed a diverse range of niche-oriented films. By 2000, News Corp. had Fox Searchlight, Vivendi Universal had Universal Focus,[5] Time Warner had New Line and Fine Line, Viacom had Paramount Vantage, and Sony had Sony Pictures Classics and Screen Gems.[6] Though the names and scope of these divisions shifted over time, all the major media corporations continued to allocate substantial resources to indie subsidiaries through most of the first decade of the 2000s. This investment indicated the conglomerates' recognition of the potential economic *and* cultural value of niche films. During this specific historical moment, such divisions came to be seen as vital sites in which to develop fresh talent, take creative risks, and experiment with new business models—much more so than the conglomerates' mass-market distribution arms.

To study the rise and fall of Miramax, then, is to study Hollywood in transition. Such an approach demands balancing an examination of Miramax with a discussion of developments taking place both with media conglomerates' motion picture divisions and with those distributors that remained unaffiliated with major corporations. Such an approach also necessitates blending an analysis of one company's business strategies and marketing practices with journalistic and critical discourses about that company and its films. Further, such an approach requires that one remain attentive to the most notable formal-aesthetic attributes of the films released both by Miramax and by its main competitors. In integrating industrial, discourse, and aesthetic analysis, my study can be situated within the emerging field of media industry studies.[7] This field blends political economy's critical approach to the production and distribution of culture with cultural studies' concern with the power struggles that occur over the value of and meanings within specific texts.[8] Media industry studies' call for historical specificity and its emphasis on empirical research make it a productive means through which to conduct an analysis of Miramax and its practices. The use of a media industry studies framework differentiates this book from others that have examined either contemporary Hollywood or independent film.

Most recent scholarship on Hollywood has taken a political economic approach; scholars such as Janet Wasko, Thomas Schatz, Paul McDonald, and Jennifer Holt have effectively mapped out broad changes in ownership and control in the media industries during the conglomerate era, especially in the film sector.[9] Such work helps to place Miramax's activities within a broader context, reinforcing that the Weinsteins were not "visionaries" who, through sheer force of will and a belief in the power of cinema, created new markets where none had existed before. As attractive as such romantic notions may be, political economists remind us that we must bear in mind that Miramax emerged out of specific industrial conditions. The company and its executives exploited these conditions quite effectively for a time. But the belief that they were immune to larger economic, technological, cultural, and institutional shifts contributed to the Weinsteins' departure from Miramax in 2005 and to the division's subsequent downsizing by Disney.

Research on the political economy of Hollywood reminds us that, even at its peak profitability in the late 1990s and early 2000s, Miramax remained a relatively small division within one of the largest media conglomerates in the world. For example, in 1998, the year that Miramax released such box office hits as *Halloween H2o* and *Rounders*, and *Good Will Hunting* and *Scream 2* completed their theatrical runs, the company grossed $393 million domestically and earned a 5.81 percent market share.[10] In comparison, Disney films such as *Armageddon*, *A Bug's Life*, *Mulan*, and *Enemy of the State* helped it gross more than $1.1 billion and lead the industry with a 16.37 percent market share that same year.[11]

Miramax's income may never have come close to that generated by Disney's primary film distribution arm, but this does not diminish the value of a case study of the subsidiary. Miramax, along with other indie divisions, had a substantive financial impact on both niche-oriented filmmaking specifically and Hollywood's business practices more generally. At the same time that conglomerates invested more heavily in indie divisions, their primary motion picture arms increasingly focused their efforts on releasing big-budget event films such as *Batman* (1989), *Jurassic Park* (1993), *Twister* (1996), and *Godzilla* (1998).[12] Thus the development and expansion of separate indie divisions, with their own distinct production, distribution, marketing, and exhibition practices, signaled the conglomerates' reassessment of their corporate structures and allocation of resources.

Though on the surface it might seem paradoxical, the rise of Miramax and other indie subsidiaries can be seen as intersecting with the global media conglomerates' increasing focus on producing and distributing niche products to specific demographic groups. This places Miramax's growth and expansion within the context of a shift from a model of mass production and consumption that dominated until the 1970s, and toward a late twentieth-century model of specialization and "just-in-time" production and consumption.[13] The shift in emphasis should not suggest that conglomerates ceased developing films for a mass audience—in fact, as the examples above show, quite the opposite is the case. Instead, the key point here is that these conglomerates restructured their operations in a way that shifted the production and distribution of a large number of niche-oriented films to separate subsidiaries. Significantly, a heightened emphasis on niche targeting was evident not only in conglomerates' investment in indie subsidiaries, but also in their acquisition and creation of niche-oriented cable and broadcast networks (e.g., Fox, UPN, IFC, Sundance Channel).

Political economic approaches to Hollywood have skillfully provided broad surveys of industry practices and patterns. One limitation of this approach, however, is that at times it downplays the contributions that individuals—or specific films—can have. Through providing a case study of a single division of one media conglomerate, especially one discussed as frequently in the media as Miramax, we are able to balance the "top-down" concerns of political economy with the "bottom-up" perspective of cultural studies. By focusing primarily on Miramax, it is easier to see the complexity involved in cultural production. The notion circulated in cruder forms of political economy that media conglomerates are monolithic entities in their operations or output quickly gets disproven.[14]

A case study of Miramax also proves valuable because many critics and scholars have viewed its films as important not only economically, but also culturally and creatively. As the analysis of the media coverage offered throughout this book illustrates, the attention paid to the indie film sector was disproportionate to its economic impact. Certainly the growing profitability of indie film contributed to heightened media attention, but this was not the only reason Miramax and its films generated so much press. As it developed, expanded, and diversified, Miramax figured prominently in broader debates and struggles over cultural power. From the time of its purchase by Disney through its release of such films as *Kids* (1995), *Priest* (1995), and *Dogma* (1999), Miramax was central to discussions about authenticity, autonomy, and creative freedom. When convenient, the company exploited such discourses for the purposes of marketing and product differentiation. When inconvenient, Miramax downplayed its involvement with certain films (e.g., genre films such as *The Crow* [1994] and *Hellraiser IV: Bloodline* [1996], released by its Dimension label). Often in response to activities by Miramax, a range of stakeholders—including journalists, critics, festival planners, executives, representatives of award-granting organizations, and filmmakers—engaged in debates about what constituted "independent" or "indie" film. As Michael Newman notes, these discourses were highly ideological in nature.[15] The need to demarcate boundaries over what constituted independent film became connected to particular taste cultures linked by background and education.[16] Those participating in such conversations often had very personal investments in what criteria were—or were not—used to identify a film as independent or indie.

Recent scholarship on contemporary low-budget film has integrated economic, cultural, and aesthetic analyses productively. In fact, a significant body of work has developed on what variably has been labeled independent or indie film. There is no agreed-on definition of what constitutes either; indeed, how each of these terms is used depends on a given writer's focus or objectives. In the last two decades, both the popular press and scholars frequently have used independent and indie interchangeably. Of course, this has only contributed to the confusion about the meaning of each label—a confusion that has often served the desires of media companies in promoting their films to particular groups as "hip," "edgy," and "cool." As Newman observes, "indie" gained increasing cachet from the 1980s onward. The word's appeal expanded as it became more closely linked to a particular subculture of white, male, upper-middle-class tastes in music and fashion.[17]

Despite the lack of agreement and consistency in scholars' and journalists' use of these terms, as I have noted elsewhere,[18] among the most common criteria used to define a film as independent include the following: its source of financing;[19] the industrial affiliations of its distributor;[20] the sites in which it is exhibited;[21] the status of its talent in relation to Hollywood;[22] and the "spirit" of the film (usually interpreted to mean its aesthetic or generic ties to commercial or alternative media traditions).[23] In *American Independent Cinema*, Geoff King surveys a variety of different ways that films can be perceived to be independent, identifying a range of industrial, narrative, formal, genre-based, and ideological-political criteria.[24] Given *Indie, Inc.'s* industrial emphasis, a film or company will be described by me as independent if it is unaffiliated with a major media conglomerate. If a conglomerate has an investment in it, I label it an indie. Thus, following its purchase by Disney, the formerly independent distributor Miramax became an indie division. This book focuses primarily on Miramax during its time under Disney's control. As will be explored in the following pages, though Miramax began as an independent distributor, it *always* operated quite differently from most of its 1980s-era competitors. In fact, it functioned as a de facto indie division even before Disney acquired it. Conglomerate resources simply enabled it to realize its objectives more fully.

Although it is important to make the distinction between "indie" and "independent" to clarify my own analytical framework, a key focus of this book involves following the varied ways that the press, critics, and industry employed these and other labels to discuss niche-oriented films throughout the 1990s. In this manner, I adhere to the approach taken by Yannis Tzioumakis, who examines independent cinema "as a discourse that expands and contracts when socially authorized institutions (filmmakers, industry practitioners, trade publications, academics, film critics, and so on) contribute toward its definition at different periods in the history of American cinema."[25] In *American Independent Cinema: An Introduction*, Tzioumakis traces the different ways that discourses of independence have been activated throughout U.S. film history. He provides a corrective for those who believe that independent film is a relatively recent development. As his book functions largely as a survey of the fluid independent-Hollywood relationship during the twentieth century, Tzioumakis offers only a cursory examination of the evolution and expansion of indie film during the 1990s.

Tzioumakis is one of many individuals writing about American independent cinema who argue that a series of institutional, economic, and cultural shifts begun during the 1970s laid the foundation for the rise of 1990s-era indie divisions.[26] Others, including Geoff King, Emanuel

Levy, John Pierson, and John Berra, similarly see 1990s-era indie films as direct descendants of earlier independents. In particular, each draws a relationship between the releases of art house–oriented independent distributors (e.g., Island/Alive, Skouras, Cinecom) and "classics divisions" (e.g., United Artists Classics, Orion Classics, 20th Century-Fox International Classics) of the late 1970s and early 1980s, and those distributed by specialty divisions such as Miramax, Fox Searchlight, and Focus Features in the 1990s and 2000s. Though there certainly are connections between the films, executives, and practices of independent distributors of these two eras, it is important not to overstate these linkages. (Chapter 4 elaborates on the cultural, aesthetic, and industrial distinctions between 1980s-era independents and 1990s-era indies.) In fact, there is a danger in drawing connections between independents of the 1980s and those of the 1990s. Frequently, the 1980s-era independent films, filmmakers, and distributors are positioned as more "authentic" because they are seen as being more removed from Hollywood industrially, politically, and aesthetically. Such an approach risks minimizing the long and complicated relationship between Hollywood and independents, implying that the two are diametrically opposed in terms of politics, style, and content.[27]

Value judgments are frequently made by those who view the rise of indies as a move away from a particular strand of 1980s-era, art house–oriented independents and toward Hollywood practices and conventions. More specifically, commerce is seen to be overriding art as "outsiders" are incorporated into the system, and the vibrancy and vitality of independent film is seen as being depoliticized and homogenized in the process. Divisions such as Miramax are viewed as exploiting the rhetoric of independence when in practice they serve as little more than marketing arms for media conglomerates. In terminology that often echoes Horkheimer and Adorno, indie divisions are viewed as "brands" that exploit naive or gullible consumers with their vacuous products.[28] Nowhere is this attitude more evident than in the journalist Peter Biskind's *Down and Dirty Pictures: Miramax, Sundance, and the Rise of Independent Film*.[29] In this book, Biskind chronicles the rise of Miramax, the Sundance Film Festival, and, to a lesser extent, the independent distributor October Films. He begins with the 1989 premiere of *sex, lies, and videotape* at Sundance and the film's subsequent acquisition by Miramax, and concludes with the Weinsteins' struggles with Martin Scorsese over the pricey, bloated *Gangs of New York* (2002).

Down and Dirty Pictures was designed as a follow-up to Biskind's earlier best seller, *Easy Riders, Raging Bulls*, which chronicles the rise of the Hollywood Renaissance in the late 1960s and tracks the careers of the film school–educated "movie brat" generation (Scorsese, Coppola, Cimino, Spielberg, etc.).[30] The reverential tone that Biskind uses toward baby boomer filmmakers in *Easy Riders, Raging Bulls* is replaced with a sense of disdain in *Down and Dirty Pictures* toward what I discuss in chapter 4 as the "cinema of cool"—a group of mostly self-educated Gen Xers that includes Kevin Smith, Quentin Tarantino, and Robert Rodriguez.[31] In addition, in the latter book, Biskind focuses far less on the textual characteristics of the films, thereby implying that most of these films are scarcely worthy of serious consideration. Inasmuch as he discusses the films themselves, they are often seen as empty exercises in style over substance, paling in comparison to both the Hollywood Renaissance films and the "truly" independent films of the 1980s. Such independents, directed by filmmakers like Jim Jarmusch, John Sayles, Wayne Wang, Susan Seidelman, and Spike Lee, are discussed in chapter 4 as part of a "cinema of quality" that can be contrasted to the later "cinema of cool." In a statement that reflects the attitude he takes throughout the book, Biskind declares that "the triumph of *sex, lies* over *Do the Right Thing* ratified the turn away from the angry, topical strain of the indie movement that had its roots in the 1960s and 1970s toward the milder aesthetic of the slacker era."[32]

Whereas in *Easy Riders, Raging Bulls* Biskind depicted art and commerce combining for a brief moment to yield politically charged, creatively inspired films worthy of respect, in *Down and Dirty Pictures* he suggests that commerce trumped art before a truly great American cinema on par with that of the 1970s could be realized. He places most of the "blame" for the missed opportunities squarely on the shoulders of Miramax, and in particular on Harvey Weinstein. Rather than supporting auteurs with strong social realist visions (e.g., James Mangold, James Gray) or avant-garde tendencies (e.g., Bernardo Bertolucci, Todd Haynes), Biskind suggests that Weinstein intervened in a manner that harmed these individuals' films and careers.[33] Concurrently, he argues, Miramax became ever more focused on releasing a combination of amoral, Tarantino-esque product (which he portrays as the triumph of the "tastes of the barbarians"),[34] lowbrow genre fare in the vein of *Scary Movie* (2000) (at one point, he describes Miramax's Dimension genre division as a "roach motel"),[35] and sentimental, middlebrow Euro-American "kitsch" like *Chocolat* (2000).[36] From Biskind's perspective, Weinstein's desire to be a modern-day David O. Selznick—a creative producer who took an active role in shaping projects from inception to final cut—combined with his obsession with market research, not only hurt filmmakers and their films but also influenced the direction that indie film took from the mid-1990s onward.

Perhaps because he is so dismissive of the films released by Miramax following its purchase by Disney, Biskind expends little effort analyzing them. Instead, he focuses almost exclusively on the ways that select individuals in the indie world—in particular Harvey Weinstein—screwed over everyone and anyone. The book strings together a series of ugly anecdotes about the backroom machinations of the Weinsteins and Robert Redford. Biskind culled such tales from the dozens of interviews he conducted with countless disgruntled filmmakers, former employees, and direct competitors of Miramax and Sundance. Through this "cult of personality" approach, *Down and Dirty Pictures* certainly offers plenty of juicy gossip about the conflicts and confrontations that transpired between Miramax executives and others in the indie film business. For that reason, the book is an enjoyable read for those wanting to understand the key figures behind many of the indie films of the 1990s.

Yet, in a variety of ways, his book falls short. Though Biskind constructs *Down and Dirty Pictures* as an exposé of the shady goings-on in the indie film world, he frequently reinforces a number of unproductive misperceptions about the companies and their films. For example, he provides a highly selective approach to Miramax's releases and activities. In supporting his position that Miramax helped drain art house–oriented American independent film of substance as it evolved under Disney's control, he overlooks the company's long-standing investment in a diverse slate of niche films from around the world. Further, though Miramax did place a greater emphasis on emotionally charged films such as *Sling Blade, Good Will Hunting*, and *The Cider House Rules* (1999) as the 1990s wore on, the company had *always* invested heavily in such material. Just because these films did not realize the particular vision of quality cinema he preferred is no reason to reject them out of hand.

Biskind's value judgments—as well as his view of what independent film *should have* become—lead him to present an incomplete snapshot of the indie film business in the 1990s. As another example of the partial perspective provided, his nearly 550-page tome offers only about twenty substantive pages of discussion of Miramax's genre division, Dimension. This limited coverage reflects his (un-interrogated) view that this division's films were disposable cultural products and had little to do with the broader indie film business beyond generating revenue. While he may not be fond of the *Scream, Spy Kids*, and *Scary Movie* franchises, their economic and cultural impact should not be dismissed. Meanwhile, Biskind is so busy identifying the indie film movement of the 1990s as a distinctly

American phenomenon that he fails to explore those films that do not fit within this narrative. Even as the culturally hybrid nature of films such as *The English Patient* and *Shakespeare in Love* is dismissed, the ties of films such as *The Crying Game* to the UK and *The Piano* (1993) to Australia–New Zealand are scarcely remarked on. Biskind downplays such connections in the interest of constructing a tale of the co-optation of authentically independent American cinema by the evil brute Miramax. This one company—along with the lone festival, Sundance—is presented in near isolation throughout the book. There is little sense of a larger industrial or cultural context, either at the independent or conglomerate level. He mentions Disney on only a handful of pages; the prominent 1990s-era indie competitors Gramercy and Sony Pictures Classics are brought up even less often. By failing to discuss such major films and companies at any length, *Down and Dirty Pictures* provides a distorted depiction of this defining moment for low-budget film.

While Biskind should be praised for providing the first (and thus far only) book-length exploration of Miramax's practices during the 1990s,[37] his approach needs to be expanded and modified in significant ways. *Indie, Inc.* provides a corrective to many of the misleading assumptions and arguments that Biskind makes about both Miramax and indie film during the 1990s. Through case studies of key releases such as *sex, lies, and videotape, The Crying Game, The Piano, Pulp Fiction, Kids, Scream, The English Patient, Life is Beautiful,* and *Shakespeare in Love,* I reconsider many of the ideas that have come to be taken for granted by Biskind as well as many others writing about the Hollywood-independent relationship. Cumulatively, my book challenges the notion forwarded by Biskind that Miramax's greatest accomplishment came from helping to make American independent film mainstream. Instead, we need to see Miramax as part of a much larger process: the restructuring of global Hollywood.[38] Rather than focusing predominantly on those so-called quality films that appealed to a particular white, male, upper-middle-class demographic and were most extensively celebrated by the press and critics, this study surveys a much broader range of English-language product, genre films, mid-range transnational prestige pictures, and foreign-language imports released by Miramax. In addition, it explores how, on a smaller scale, Miramax exploited Disney's resources to transform a diverse set of films into multimedia franchises. To undertake this analysis, I turn to a wide range of documents, including feature articles and reviews in trade publications, newspapers, and magazines; marketing materials such as press releases, press kits, print advertisements, and trailers; and a broad sample of Miramax feature films. These sources are used to construct a revisionist history of the rise and fall of Miramax that integrates a discussion of shifts in the film industry, in discourses about independence, and in film aesthetics.

The 1990s as the "Age of Miramax"

Enough time has now passed since the ascendance—and complete collapse—of Miramax that the company's story can be told *as a history*. Previous analyses of Miramax and indie film, including Biskind's, were written while the company remained a vibrant part of the larger film industry. This is no longer the case. Many of the indie film companies in operation during the 1990s and 2000s—Miramax included—have been closed or substantially downsized. Media analysts do not agree exactly when the decline began, but most point to the Weinsteins' departure from Miramax in 2005 and the closure of the indie distributors Picturehouse, Warner Independent, and Paramount Vantage in 2008 as key turning points. The only scholar to have written extensively about indie film in the 2000s thus far is Geoff King in *Indiewood, USA*. In this book, King identifies Indiewood as a hybrid form that synthesizes Hollywood and independent film aesthetics. Most of the films he analyzes are pricey mid-range releases that appealed primarily to those with greater cultural capital. According to King, though specialty divisions have distributed Indiewood-style films (e.g., *Traffic*, 2000; *Eternal Sunshine of the Spotless Mind*, 2004), the majors have traded in them as well (e.g., *Three Kings*, 1999; *Being John Malkovich*, 1999). Though he does note this in his book in passing, it is worth underscoring that all the films for which he offers detailed case studies were released within a rather narrow time frame: December 1998—April 2004. Rather than historically situating Indiewood within a particular industrial moment, King is mainly interested in exploring the distinct textual strategies and taste cultures connected to a particular set of films. Had he contextualized these films industrially, he might have seen the extent to which Indiewood can be viewed as marking the *end* of the indie film phenomenon.[39] As I discuss in the conclusion, his use of the label Indiewood to describe both the films released by the majors' distribution arms and those released by indie specialty divisions works counter to most contemporary usages. Interestingly, the earliest film for which King offers a case study is *Shakespeare in Love* (1998). In contrast, I use this film as my final case study; with it, I argue, Miramax and the indie film business entered into their "mature" phase.

By identifying the 1989–1999 period as the focus of my book, I am countering the ways that many others—including producer's representative John Pierson (1984–1994), as well as King (1998–2004) and Biskind (1989–2002)[40]—have structured their respective studies of commercially oriented low-budget cinema. Pierson's autobiographical book, *Spike, Mike, Slackers, and Dykes*, chronicles the ten-year period *before* the explosion of indie film. At that time, it was easier for many first-time filmmakers—including Spike Lee (*She's Gotta Have It*, 1986), Michael Moore (*Roger & Me*, 1989), Richard Linklater (*Slacker*, 1991), and Rose Troche (*Go Fish*, 1994)—to produce ultra-low-budget films, generate attention on the festival circuit, receive critical acclaim, and attain modest box office successes (i.e., in the $1 million to $10 million range). Pierson's emphasis is almost exclusively on a particular strand of critically acclaimed, art house—oriented American independent films. Though focusing on a different time span, he expresses attitudes toward independent film strikingly similar to those on display in Biskind's book. Significantly, the moment for these types of films was passing at precisely the time that Pierson published his book, something he acknowledges with some melancholy in the second edition, *Spike Mike Reloaded*.[41]

Meanwhile, as noted above, King homes in on the tail end of the indie moment, when independent and studio aesthetics fused within a relatively small subset of films. Both of these writers, along with Biskind, have authored books about independent film in which Miramax figures prominently. And Miramax, as we shall see below, did affect the independent film world in substantive and dramatic ways. But this book is not about the rise and fall of independent film. Rather, it is about the rise and fall of Miramax. The stories are not the same, though I illustrate how they intersected at times. One of the most common mistakes made by those writing about independent film is to equate the two. In doing so, Miramax has been made into something other than what it was. Miramax was *not* the preeminent *independent* distributor throughout the 1980s and 1990s; rather, it occupied this position only briefly, in tandem with New Line, from 1989 through early 1993. As chapter 2 demonstrates, many other companies figured far more prominently in the independent landscape prior to 1989. Further, following Miramax's purchase by Disney in 1993—the same year Turner acquired New Line—the Weinstein-led company began to transform into something altogether different. Most notably, Miramax emerged as the most high-profile and well-respected brand name for a wide range of niche films. In addition, throughout the 1990s, it had the most substantive and consistent impact on the *indie* film business of any company. It is for these reasons that the 1990s was the decade of Miramax. Beginning with *My Left Foot*, *Cinema Paradiso*, and, *sex, lies, and videotape* in 1989–1990, Miramax demonstrated the economic and creative possibilities for a diverse set of low-budget films. It continued to earn a larger market share and higher profile for such films for the next several years. Only when it deviated from its original business of releasing low-cost, high-quality films—which it began to do during the late 1990s—did its demise ensue. But this demise occurred not only because Miramax busted its business model, but also because it tarnished its reputation and adversely affected its relationships with talent and executives both at Disney and throughout the industry. Unfortunately, when Miramax went down, it brought much of the broader indie film business down along with it.

In charting the rise and fall of Miramax, *Indie, Inc.* focuses on the *process* by which a three-tier structure of independents, indie divisions, and big-budget studio distribution arms developed and then subsequently declined. Significantly, this book is not about individual personalities à la Biskind, nor is it a behind-the-scenes story of on-set dramas and boardroom battles. Rather, what is offered here is a historical analysis of shifting industrial practices and cultural discourses about independence, indie, Indiewood, and Hollywood during the 1990s. As discussed in chapter 8, by the time Miramax released *Shakespeare in Love*, the seeds of its destruction—and, in turn, the destruction of the conglomerates' specialty divisions—had been sown. This is not to suggest that the collapse of the "Miramax model" was inevitable. Indeed, as the following pages detail, the path taken by Miramax and its competitors in production, acquisitions, distribution, and marketing was a consequence of particular business and creative decisions made by individuals within a specific set of industrial, technological, and cultural circumstances that began to crystallize in 1989.

The Rise of Miramax and the Quality Indie Blockbuster

(1979–Fall 1992)

The film that put the capper on one decade and jump-started the next one, Steven Soderbergh's *sex, lies, and videotape* [1989].

John Pierson, Spike, Mike, Slackers, and Dykes, *1997*

The release of *sex, lies, and videotape* marked a turning point for both Miramax and the independent scene. This film wielded an impact that resonated throughout the coming decade as Miramax released such later "indie blockbusters"[1] as *The Crying Game* (1992), *Pulp Fiction* (1994), *The English Patient* (1996), and *Good Will Hunting* (1997). Indeed, with *sex, lies, and videotape*, Miramax carved out its early brand identity, helped establish the aesthetic parameters for low-budget independent films, and began to define the contours of the niche-oriented landscape of the 1990s. By "indie blockbuster," I mean a film that, on a smaller scale, replicates the marketing and box office performance of the major studio event pictures. The box office performance of *sex, lies, and videotape* was certainly stunning for the time: with a budget of only about $1.2 million, the film generated more than $24 million at the North American box office.[2] Such figures suggest how this one film set the initial standard for specialty film distribution in the 1990s. In fact, *sex, lies, and video-tape* helped lay the groundwork for a larger transformation within the entertainment industry during the decade. This industrial environment was one in which the studios focused predominantly on the distribution of big-budget event spectacles, while studio-based subsidiaries (which, as discussed in the next chapter, Miramax became upon its purchase by Disney) focused mainly on low-budget, niche-targeted films.

With the screening of Steven Soderbergh's film at Sundance in January 1989, festivals became increasingly important as industry gathering spots and marketing sites. In addition, *sex, lies, and videotape* reinforced the potential for "quality" films to cross over to a broader audience. Quality, as employed below, is seen as an ideological term deployed by marketers to suggest sophisticated material geared toward a more educated and discriminating audience.[3] Even as *sex, lies, and videotape* hinted at the beginning of a quality American indie aesthetic, it represented an altered means of marketing for low-budget features. What's more, in Miramax's hands, the film contributed to the redefinition of the label of independence by the press and entertainment industry. During the next several years, a number of films would replicate the financial success and media attention garnered by *sex, lies, and videotape*; the vast majority of these (e.g., *Clerks* [1994], *Pulp Fiction, Sling Blade* [1996], *Good Will Hunting*) would be theatrically distributed in the United States by Miramax. Given the crucial role that *sex, lies, and videotape* played in the development of Miramax and the evolution of the low-budget film scene, it is necessary to trace the film's aesthetics, theatrical distribution, and critical reception. But before doing so, it is important to outline the turbulent industrial environment from which Miramax emerged. Rather than immediately becoming a major player in the independent film business, Miramax was in fact a marginal operation throughout the 1980s. As chronicled below, the industrial environment of the 1980s favored a different type of independent distributor—those such as Cinecom, Island, and Vestron, which depended heavily on the nascent video business for their financial success. As we shall see, Miramax did not begin its ascent until the late 1980s, when most other major independent distributors went into decline due to a range of factors, including overproduction, mismanagement, and broader industry consolidation.

A number of scholars and journalists have traced the beginnings of the "age of Miramax" to the "independent shakedown" of 1989 in general and the release of *sex, lies, and videotape* in particular.[4] But despite the frequent observations about the influence of *sex, lies, and videotape* on low-budget filmmaking and aesthetics in the 1990s, there has not yet been a methodical exploration of the ways that this film's distribution, marketing, and critical reception affected the landscape of contemporary Hollywood. Similarly, there has been little in-depth analysis of the means by which *sex, lies, and videotape* started to pave the way for the studio-subsidiary environment of the 1990s—an environment in which nearly every studio purchased or created one or more quality, specialty, or classics film divisions. This chapter examines all these matters, as well as the symbiotic relationship that developed between *sex, lies, and videotape* and Miramax in shaping the discourse of independence, affecting the marketing of low-budget films, and defining the stylistic and thematic concerns of niche films in the 1990s. What follows is a survey of the pre-Disney years of Miramax, beginning with the company's slow start in the late 1970s and concluding with an account of its vicissitudes following the success of *sex, lies, and videotape*. During this fourteen-year period, the roots of an independent film business and culture were established—roots that Miramax would later variably exploit and modify.

Miramax, Independents, and Hollywood in the 1980s

We're David . . . and they're Goliath. So I'm bringing my slingshot.

Harvey Weinstein, 1988

When the Weinsteins created Miramax in 1979, the Hollywood majors were in the process of refining their marketing and production practices in favor of high-concept films. By this time, American New Wave filmmakers had either shifted toward the mainstream (George Lucas) or become increasingly marginalized (Robert Altman).[5] *Saturday Night Fever* (1977), *Grease* (1978), and *Superman* (1978) dominated the box office charts and multiplex screens. The status of low-budget independents at this point remained much more uncertain. Though genre films such as *The Kentucky Fried Movie* (1977) and *Halloween* (1978) became surprising box office successes, more art house–oriented films such as *Northern Lights* (1978) and *Gal Young 'Un* (1979) struggled to find an audience.

Independent operations faced several challenges in the mid-to-late 1970s, including the lack of a clear market and the absence of a cohesive community for support. A large-scale infrastructure did not yet exist for those interested in producing and distributing low-budget films. Though downtown art houses remained key sites for viewing independently released films, they struggled as many urban areas continued to go into decline, as new suburban multiplexes emerged, and as home video's popularity increased. In addition, with the exception of more genre-based material, the majors began to lose interest in lower-budget projects; high-concept event films attracted more of the majors' attention and resources. Meanwhile, festivals remained relatively small in number and in attendance. Outside the trade publications, the press offered minimal coverage of festivals. Though there were a handful of high-profile

European film festivals (i.e., Venice, Cannes), until the Toronto and Seattle Film Festivals launched in 1975, the main North American festivals were only those in San Francisco and New York.

Despite these difficulties, by the late 1970s there were several promising signs for independent producers and distributors. First, existing sources of funding, such as the National Endowment for the Arts and the Corporation for Public Broadcasting, were complemented by new foundations. The Association of Independent Video and Filmmakers, the Independent Feature Project, and the Sundance Institute were among the organizations founded in the late 1970s and early 1980s to encourage both narrative and documentary filmmakers hoping to develop their projects outside the Hollywood system. Second, a number of developing technologies such as video and cable promised alternate means of gaining financing and distribution.[6] Further, recently founded mom-and-pop video stores seemed more open to offering independent projects than the local theaters. Third, as ancillary markets continued to develop, it became increasingly common and accepted for low-budget filmmakers to presell distribution rights to their films in order to finance production. Often cable, video, domestic theatrical, and television distribution as well as select foreign distribution rights would be sold off as needed to help fund a project.[7] Preselling served as a means of protecting initial investors' interests.[8] Fourth, baby boomers offered the possibility of a market for films targeted to different, older constituencies than were currently being favored by the Hollywood studios and their predominantly youth-oriented films.

Into this complicated climate emerged a number of distribution companies, formed in myriad ways and with varying amounts of capital. Some of the companies began their operations independently of the studios; others marked the earliest formulations of studio-based "classics" divisions. These included the Samuel Goldwyn Company (1978), United Artists Classics (1980), Universal Classics (1980), Cinecom (1980), 20th Century-Fox International Classics (1980), Triumph (1980), and Orion Classics (1982). Cumulatively, these low-budget-oriented distributors tended to focus on a combination of documentaries, foreign-language imports (which still were considered to have a dedicated, albeit dwindling, audience), and narratively and stylistically experimental character studies.

These new companies released many films from beginning filmmakers—for the most part, a new generation of directors who were distinct from the American New Wave by virtue of their particular regional-, class-, race-, and gender-based concerns. Among the directors getting their start at this time were John Sayles (*Return of the Secaucus 7*, 1980), Susan Seidelman (*Smithereens*, 1982), Jim Jarmusch (*Permanent Vacation*, 1982), and Joel and Ethan Coen (*Blood Simple*, 1984). The budgets of these films tended to range from $2 million to at most $5 million—as compared with the budgets of studio films, which were heading upward of $17 million by the mid-1980s.[9] The majority of these independent distributors acquired all or some of the rights once the film was finished or close to completion (labeled a "negative pickup"). This helped to limit the financial risk of young companies, which often lacked sufficient capital. For the typical independent release, the marketing approach usually consisted of pushing the film's specific content (story line, style, etc.) and then relying on word of mouth and solid critical response to help it take off. These films usually were released on an extremely limited number of screens, often located in only the largest urban centers (e.g., Chicago, Los Angeles, New York).[10]

It was in this environment that Miramax developed. Looking at its evolution during the 1980s helps demonstrate the range of options available to independent distributors at the time, just as it provides a context for understanding the genesis of this specific company. Discussing Miramax's prehistory and early years proves challenging, as there is limited press coverage about the company available and the Weinsteins have labored to build an elaborate narrative—some might say mythology—about their early years. Nonetheless, certain details can be gleaned. Notably, Harvey Weinstein had ventured into the entertainment business in a variety of ways before cofounding Miramax in 1979. The story goes that Harvey Weinstein's first entertainment-related negotiation took place while he was at the University of Buffalo, when he was trying to book a Stephen Stills concert for the campus. When "school funding suddenly came up short," he joined with Bob to borrow a friend's wedding gift of $2,500 and some money from a local pizza restaurant. The brothers proceeded to produce the concert on their own.[11] Over the course of the next few years, Harvey dabbled in music booking and concert promotion as the cofounder of the Harvey and Corky Corporation (with Corky Burger).[12]

By the late 1970s, this venture was a multimillion-dollar operation, employing more than fifty people (including Harvey's younger brother, Bob) and producing and promoting approximately 125 concerts a year. The Harvey and Corky Corporation ran the fifty-year-old, 2,600-seat Century Theater in Buffalo until it became too costly to maintain. They restored the theater and began booking national tours with artists such as Genesis, Billy Joel, and the Grateful Dead. In spite of these big names, the Weinsteins struggled to stay in business. According to Bob Weinstein, "To pay for the heating bills, we needed another source of income. . . . I went downstairs and found some broken-down, unused film projectors. We refurbished the projectors and started to run film festivals on Friday and Saturday nights. Two thousand kids would show up and live at the theater on weekends."[13]

Along with exhibiting films, the Weinsteins soon began making movies themselves. In 1977, Harvey Weinstein earned his first producer credit with *White Rock* (1977), a documentary covering the Innsbruck Winter Olympics that prominently featured music composed and performed by the Yes keyboardist Rick Wakeman. Two years later, amid their successes running weekend screenings and booking bands, the Weinsteins made their first major foray into distribution under the name of Miramax. They began the operation on an ad hoc basis, booking city-to-city campaigns for concert movies. Among their earliest ventures were *Rockshow* (1980) with Paul McCartney, *The Genesis Concert Movie* (1977), and *The Concert for Kampuchea* (1980).[14] It was not long before they made their first "official" attempts at distributing feature films. In the summer of 1980, Miramax moved out of concert films with its release on five screens in the Buffalo area of *Goodbye Emmanuelle* (1977), the third in the *Emmanuelle* series of erotic films.[15] *Goodbye Emmanuelle* earned an R rating, which permitted those under seventeen years of age to view a film in theaters if accompanied by an adult. The previous two *Emmanuelle* films (which Miramax did not distribute) had received X ratings, thereby limiting the potential audience only to those over age seventeen. The days when an X rating promised greater box office returns were long gone. Certainly an X had served as an effective means of attracting "adult" audiences with more explicit sexual situations in the late 1960s and early 1970s (e.g., *Midnight Cowboy*, 1969; *Last Tango in Paris*, 1973). By the early 1980s, however, an R proved likelier to generate larger returns than an X because the former rating enabled the film to be advertised in more newspapers and screened at more theaters. In the ensuing years, the Weinsteins would make a habit of testing the limits of the R rating and call attention to the "borderline X" status of films in their marketing materials.

With the company's expansion beyond exhibition and concert film distribution, the Weinsteins set up their first "office" in a one-bedroom apartment on 57th Street in New York City, which doubled as Harvey's living quarters.[16] Throughout the early and mid-1980s, Miramax focused on releasing films for home video, television, and theatrical markets that "target[ed] three audiences: rock music fans, children, and mainstream."[17]

The typical Miramax film of this time was a negative pickup, acquired at as low a cost as possible, with the company usually holding North American theatrical rights. Miramax would then operate through a network of twenty to thirty sub-distributors.[18] The company generated additional revenue by acting as an overseas sales representative for a number of movies. The Paul McCartney-produced *The Real Buddy Holly Story* (1985), distributed domestically via HBO, was just one of the films for which Miramax negotiated foreign distribution. Throughout the early and mid-1980s, the company kept overhead at a minimum, employing about a dozen people who focused on distributing up to five or six films a year.[19] Miramax developed more slowly than many of its independent and classics counterparts, such as Circle, Island, and Cinecom.[20] The types of films it focused on releasing differed as well.

Early watersheds in the company's history included the releases of *The Secret Policeman's Other Ball* (1982) and *Eréndira* (1983). In the case of the former film, the brothers purchased a recording of a live benefit concert for Amnesty International that featured Monty Python comedy sketches and performances by musicians such as Phil Collins, Eric Clapton, and Sting.[21] They subsequently bought a second film of the concert tour and edited the two together for release as *The Secret Policeman's Other Ball*. They put together a television trailer for the film that featured the Monty Python comedian Graham Chapman satirizing the Moral Majority. As would often be the case in the future, controversy ensued, with NBC refusing to run the commercial. This no doubt fueled the film's box office of more than $6 million, realized on an investment of only $180,000.[22]

With the release of *Eréndira*, the Weinsteins again used the low-cost method of nurturing a film's more controversial elements. Once more, this tactic garnered them high returns at the domestic box office—nearly $3 million.[23] While the film's story line focused on the fifty-something star Irene Papas, the baby boomer Weinsteins saw her as appealing to a less lucrative "older audience."[24] Thus they chose to focus the marketing campaign around the young Brazilian supporting actress Claudia Ohana. They convinced Ohana to do a publicity tour in the United States and to pose for a *Playboy* layout.

The promotional tactics employed with *Eréndira* point to a major factor in Miramax's rise in the independent distribution world: the Weinsteins' use of "exploitation" marketing tactics to make art house–oriented foreign-language and American independent films more appealing to a wide range of demographic groups. At this point, they began a dual strategy of selling films as "quality" products beloved by critics at the same time that they called attention to the films' more "low-culture" elements. In essence, the Weinsteins took the marketing strategies developed by pioneering 1950s- and 1960s-era independents such as American International Pictures and New World Pictures in promoting sex, drugs, and rock-and-roll films, and pushed them to their limits with Miramax—promoting the sexiest elements of high-culture products. These tactics played a major role in expanding the appeal of many Miramax films from the mid-1980s onward, enabling them to begin to move beyond the narrow art house audience.

During this time, the Weinsteins and their small staff continued to refine the marketing tactics that would become the company's trademark in the next decade. By 1986, Miramax executives had developed a number of sales philosophies, as indicated by Bob Weinstein's comments in relation to the Lizzie Borden–directed drama *Working Girls*. Declaring that "our strength is marketing," the younger Weinstein continued, "We feel [marketing] is an essential ingredient of all our pictures—you can't just put them out. With *Working Girls*, we were able to change its documentary taint by bringing it uptown, giving the ads a classy look, and saying this is something that can crossover and make an issue out of middle-class prostitution. The package changed. It became accessible to everyone, and with the great marketing came great reviews."[25] Such a perspective set Miramax apart both at this time and in the years that followed. Yet while this emphasis on marketing in shaping the perception of and response toward niche films was distinctive in the mid-1980s, it would become a crucial aspect in helping such films carve out a larger place in the market during the 1990s. What the Weinsteins recognized before most other independent distributors was the value of selling low-budget films via a combination of exploitation marketing tactics and an emphasis on quality and difference.

Among Miramax's most popular and critically acclaimed titles during the mid-1980s were *Edith and Marcel* (1984), *Twist and Shout* (1986), *Crossover Dreams* (1985), *The Dog Who Stopped the War* (1985), *The Quest* (1986), *I've Heard the Mermaids Singing* (1987), *Pelle the Conqueror* (1987), and *The Thin Blue Line* (1988). *Pelle the Conqueror* earned Miramax its first Oscar, for Best Foreign Film. In addition to these Miramax-released negative pickups, the Weinsteins also branched out during the 1980s by experimenting with writing, directing, and producing projects for other companies. These forays into the production process were made with genre fare of the type that would become standard for the company's Dimension division in the 1990s. In most cases, these 1980s genre films met with lukewarm critical and box office responses. One of the earliest efforts came in 1981, when Bob took a stab at the horror genre in cowriting *The Burning* (Harvey took a coproducer credit). This $1.5 million imitation of *Friday the 13th* (1980), which featured a camp custodian seeking revenge, was distributed domestically by Filmways and Orion. Although the film met with only modest success in the United States, it was a hit abroad, especially in Japan.[26] Another project (notable mainly for its box office failure) was *Playing for Keeps* (1986), a teen rock-and-roll movie. This $2.6 million production was cowritten and codirected by the brothers and distributed by Universal. While neither film ended up establishing the Weinsteins as bankable filmmakers or expert storytellers, the brothers nonetheless learned an important lesson from these ventures: they should focus their energies on the intricacies of acquiring, marketing, and placing films in theaters.[27] Neither Weinstein would venture into directing or writing again after 1987 (when Harvey made one last directorial attempt with the animated children's film *The Gnomes' Great Adventure*).

Although the Weinsteins may have lacked the golden touch with films they made themselves, they had several hits with their acquisitions. Moreover, during most of the 1980s they steered clear of the in-house production bug that afflicted so many of the independents. Instead of expanding into production themselves, they branched out in other ways, which dramatically improved their economic position relative to their competitors. The Weinsteins took a cue from the majors early on by pushing to retain merchandising, publishing, and music rights for their films.[28] In addition, the company sought to increase its bank account by pursuing additional investors and financing partners whenever possible. For example, in 1987, the Weinsteins struck a twelve-picture, multimillion-dollar deal with Embassy Home Entertainment.[29] By providing a two-year license of home video rights to Embassy, Miramax was able to pursue more actively acquisitions and coproduction deals.

As Miramax engaed in a slow-growth strategy throughout the mid-1980s, a number of other independents and classics divisions expanded far more rapidly. In fact, most 1980s-era independent distributors peaked between 1984 and 1987. Among the domestic box office success stories were Island Alive's *El Norte* (1983, $5.5 million domestic gross), the Samuel Goldwyn Company's *Stranger Than Paradise* (1984, $2.4 million), Island Alive's *Kiss of the Spider Woman* (1985, $6.3 million), Island's *The Trip to Bountiful* (1985, $7.2 million), Island's *She's Gotta Have It* (1986, $7.1 million), and Cinecom's *A Room with a View* (1986, $12 million).[30] Grosses of $2 million to $12 million were remarkable for independently distributed, art house–oriented films. Many industry observers were

Though skillful executives, the Weinsteins proved less talented as screenwriters and directors. The teen musical-comedy *Playing for Keeps* (1986), released by Universal, was a box office disappointment.

surprised to see these releases find a place in the market against such high-concept offerings as *Back to the Future* (1985), *Rambo: First Blood Part II* (1985), and *Aliens* (1986).

Although companies such as Island Alive, Cinecom, MCEG, Circle, and Vestron had a run of good luck for a couple of years, they made a number of missteps that, combined with a changing industrial climate, proved fatal to their future development. Most significantly, while these distributors had achieved most of their box office successes from negative pickups, they began to shift away from acquisitions and transitioned to in-house productions. In one respect, this shift seemed a logical and wise business decision: while acquisitions were safer in spreading risk and lessening a distributor's investment, they also diminished the amount that could be taken in by any one company. This was due to the increasingly common practice of preselling rights. The splitting of rights became particularly troubling for the distributors who had the domestic theatrical rights but nothing else; these companies would expend most of the effort in marketing the films but then receive none of the benefits from ancillary markets.

Despite their drawbacks, negative pickups were much safer than in-house productions—a fact that became clear to many distributors in the mid-to-late 1980s. Whereas companies relying on a negative pickup strategy made their distribution decisions based on nearly finished or finished films, relying on in-house productions meant that companies had to decide on the potential of a project based solely on the quality of the script and the talent attached. In other words, producing in-house was clearly a much less reliable method. It was also, for the most part, a much more expensive strategy. Whereas costs were capped with acquisitions, in-house production budgets could rapidly spiral out of control. This was a dangerous truism since returns for independents tended to be relatively small to begin with: $5 million was the largest sum that most independents brought in at the North American box office during this period.[31]

In fact, most of the independent distributors who chose to shift to in-house productions met with disaster. As just one example, Vestron followed the unexpected box office hit *Dirty Dancing* (1987) with several in-house productions, including *Parents* (1989), *Dream a Little Dream* (1989), and *Earth Girls Are Easy* (1989). Each film failed at the box office, leaving Vestron's distribution schedule "in limbo" by September 1989.[32] Such was the case for dozens of companies that blossomed during the 1980s, including Island, Cinecom, and MCEG. Just a few of the independent films to bomb at the box office in 1988 were *Patty Hearst* (Atlantic), *Pascali's Island* (Avenue), *The Lighthorsemen* (Cinecom), *Miles from Home* (Cinecom), *The Wizard of Loneliness* (Skouras), *Far North* (Alive), and *Tokyo Pop* (Spectrafilm). Not only were many of these companies brought down by overextending themselves with in-house productions, many were also mismanaged or undercapitalized. Cumulatively, several of the same independent distributors that had predicted a new and glorious chapter in independent production and distribution during the early 1980s were declaring Chapter 11 bankruptcy by 1989.

Meanwhile, the classics divisions had their own problems, due in part to the aforementioned factors, but also due to their place within their larger parent companies. Classics divisions of the 1980s tended to be closely affiliated with their parents, meaning that the studios regularly tinkered with the divisions rather than allowing them to operate as relatively autonomous entities. The interference of too many executives from too many levels of the studio hierarchy blurred the distinctions between independent and mainstream content. In addition, the ambitions of the 1980s-era classics divisions were much more modest, in both the kinds of films chosen and the ways they were distributed and marketed. This limited the box office potential for these films from the outset.

Thus, by the late 1980s, both independent distributors and classics divisions were quickly disappearing from the industry landscape. Their rapid demise—after an equally rapid rise—was due to external industrial factors as much as it was due to such internal problems as overextension, over-production and over-expenditure. Among the broader challenges these companies faced in the late 1980s were the following: a Wall Street crash in late 1987, which led to greater financial conservatism on the part of many investors; changing tax laws that reduced much of the private financing that had fueled independent production; and the consolidation of the video market.[33] The changing shape of the video market proved the most detrimental factor. While a select number of 1980s independents released specialty films targeted to the traditional art house market, the vast majority focused on producing low-grade "B" fare—inexpensive action, science fiction, and horror films that featured lesser talent.[34] A large number of these films were knockoffs of such slasher films as *Halloween* and *Friday the 13th*.[35] Most of these movies were made quickly and cheaply, and were intended to serve as filler on video store shelves (e.g., *The Toxic Avenger Part III*, 1989; *Prom Night III*, 1990). It is worth underscoring that the bulk of the 1980s B product was standard genre fare with poor production values—in other words, it had little in common with the indies that would become the focal point of specialty operations of the 1990s.

One genre-oriented company that stayed vibrant amid the transformation of the marketplace throughout the 1980s was New Line. Even as many of its competitors faded from the scene, New Line continued to prosper. The company remained among the most prominent independent distributors primarily due to its success with a handful of genre franchises, including *A Nightmare on Elm Street* (seven films from 1984 to 1994), *Teenage Mutant Ninja Turtles* (three films from 1990 to 1993), and *House Party* (three films from 1990 to 1994).[36] Because the company played such a crucial role in defining the contours of the genre business of the 1980s and 1990s, it is worth outlining New Line's development. It is also important to survey the company's development because it influenced the strategies Miramax employed as it, too, entered the genre business.

By the early 1990s, New Line was one of the oldest independent distributors still in operation. Started by Robert Shaye in 1967, New Line began by catering to college campuses through a combination of film screenings and lecture presentations.[37] The company met with early success by releasing such films as a restored version of the 1930s exploitation film *Reefer Madness* and the Jean-Luc Godard Rolling Stones documentary *Sympathy for the Devil* (1970). Relatively early on, Shaye cultivated a relationship with the director John Waters and over the years released the lion's share of his films, including *Multiple Maniacs* (1970), *Pink Flamingos* (1972), and *Female Trouble* (1974). As Waters became more mainstream in both style and content, so did New Line. *Hairspray* (1988) was one of New Line's (and Waters's) biggest successes, earning in excess of $6 million at the box office. New Line traded on far more than just John Waters films during the 1970s and 1980s, however; as Justin Wyatt notes, the company's "distribution slate mixed foreign, sexploitation, gay cinema, rock documentaries, and 'midnight specials' reserved exclusively for midnight exhibition."[38]

As this list indicates, throughout its first two decades in business New Line focused on genres that appealed to relatively narrow niches. In general, it went where the major studios did not. During this time, the company predominantly focused on distribution, making only the occasional foray into production.[39] The turning point for New Line came with its release of the $1.8 million *A Nightmare on Elm Street* in 1984. By this time, the latest horror cycle was relatively far along—for example, the third *Halloween* (1982) and *Friday the 13th* (1982) films had completed their theatrical runs and fourth installments of both series were being developed. Nonetheless, *Nightmare* was a stunning success, earning more than $25 million in theaters and making Freddy Krueger an icon. From then on, New Line would be seen as the company built by Freddy Krueger.[40] The regular infusion of cash from the *Nightmare* films sustained New Line through the highs and (mainly) lows encountered by all independents when the video market consolidated.

And consolidate it did: as Blockbuster franchises replaced mom-and-pop video stores, studio hits were increasingly given priority in the chain stores' inventories.[41] In 1988 alone, video dealer purchases of B titles dropped 23 percent from the previous year, validating gloom-and-doom predictions by many industry analysts about the fate of independents.[42] An additional problem that independent distributors faced was a growing dominance by the studios within the international marketplace. European theaters and television stations—which had earlier purchased independent projects to fill their continuous demand for product—began to become more selective, rejecting what became perceived as "inferior" product.[43] Further, independents increasingly struggled to find screens in the North American market. As the studios refined their wide release strategies, they opened films on more and more screens, leaving less room for alternative fare. High-concept films dominated multiplexes, and urban art houses continued to disappear.

By late 1989, it remained unclear to most observers whether independents were experiencing a cyclical "shakedown" or if big-budget event films would dominate conglomerate Hollywood, leaving fewer and fewer commercial opportunities for alternative viewpoints and styles. At the time, independent distributors and their low-budget films certainly seemed to be pushed ever farther to the margins of the industry. Yet, as would become more evident by early 1990, the market was just in the process of realigning. Executives were learning from the mistakes made in recent years. Soon new marketing strategies, and fresh voices, began to emerge once again.

Many of these new strategies and voices would come from Miramax during the 1990s—although this certainly was not apparent even during the late 1980s. Miramax remained a marginal company until 1988. Only after many other independent operations began to struggle did the Weinsteins and their company come into their own. Through a series of low-cost deals, Miramax increased the number of films it released each year. To help increase their annual output to eight to ten films, Miramax contracted with the Canadian company S. C. Entertainment. By way of this arrangement, Miramax gained domestic distribution to seven features with an estimated total production cost of $20 million; S. C. Entertainment retained worldwide and Canadian rights.[44] Among the films produced as part of the deal were the thrillers *Eric* (1988) and *Blood*

Relations (1989), the comedy *Dixie Lanes* (1988), and the drama *Murder One* (1988). Cumulatively, the films made under the S. C. Entertainment deal were representative of the B product churned out by the independents in the mid-to-late 1980s. On the heels of the S. C. Entertainment deal, Miramax agreed to represent Almi as the exclusive sales agent for its three hundred–plus films. Miramax announced its plans to incorporate the films into its library, ideally packaging them along with its own films for TV sales to network, syndication, and basic and pay cable users.[45]

These moves coincided with Miramax's relocation to new offices on Madison Avenue and an increase in its staff size to twenty, which further indicated that the company wanted to be a much bigger player in the film business. Harvey Weinstein also began to publicly declare his interest in "watching for 'original visions' rather than 'exploitation pics,'" acquiring films like *Aria* (1987, a compilation of short films directed by such prominent filmmakers as Robert Altman, Ken Russell, Jean-Luc Godard, and Nicolas Roeg), a Kiefer Sutherland coming-of-age film called *Crazy Moon* (1987), and a Dennis Hopper–Michael J. Pollard comedy called *The American Way* (1986).[46] By 1988, the company had done well enough in the marketplace to pique the interest of the British bank Midland Montague, which became a partner in Miramax, investing $5 million and extending the company a $25 million line of credit.[47] Though this level of money could not even cover the production costs of one Hollywood event film, it marked a crucial step in this small company's development. With the financial backing of Montague, Miramax was able to further increase its staff size and its expenditures in acquisitions, expanding at a time when most independents were retrenching.

With a $25 million debt/equity package, the brothers began to shift from acquiring and distributing films to also producing them through Miramax.[48] Their first production through this arrangement, in cooperation with the British company Palace Pictures, was the aptly titled *Scandal* (1989), a film about the sexual affair between the British defense minister John Profumo (played by Ian McKellen) and Christine Keeler (Joanne Whalley-Kilmer). The controversy may have contributed to the fall of the Conservative government in 1963, but it helped Miramax produce a hit. Costing $7 million, the film grossed $30 million worldwide, in part due to a poster that featured a nude Joanne Whalley-Kilmer provocatively straddling a chair, and in part due to a promotional/talk-show tour by Keeler herself.[49]

With the Montague money and the success of *Scandal*, Miramax had the means to move beyond its standard range of products. In what turned out to be a prescient comment regarding Miramax's role in the future, Harvey in 1987 declared that the company would have a "new emphasis toward mainstream American pictures, and that includes the American independents."[50] Little did he know that the company would have more than just a "new emphasis." Rather, Miramax would lead the way in redefining the financial, critical, and aesthetic value of niche-oriented films—and the meaning of independence—with its 1989 release of *sex, lies, and videotape*.

The Beginning of the Boom

In exploring the history of *sex, lies, and videotape*, it is instructive to note that Miramax played no role in the initial development of the project. In fact, the company was not involved with the movie until after it premiered in January 1989 at the U.S. Film Festival (later renamed the Sundance Film Festival). The project was cofinanced by RCA/Columbia Home Video and Virgin; RCA/Columbia obtained domestic video rights while Virgin retained foreign video. The producers were free to seek a theatrical distributor if RCA/Columbia rejected it upon first look. This expectation of earning the investment back by video sales and rentals was a holdover from the early 1980s, before the consolidation of the video rental industry.

Although the financiers expected to make back their money through VHS rentals, they were concerned about the word "videotape" in the film's title. Even before viewing it, according to Soderbergh, the marketing people at RCA/Columbia asked for a change in the film's name, believing that "the vendors would *say* that the buying public would *think* that the film was shot on videotape."[51] Such a statement implies a perception on the part of the film's marketers—even before Miramax—that an independent movie carried connotations bearing specific "qualities." These qualities may have included the more controversial (and hence saleable) elements of sex and lies, but did not include the suggested "low-quality" appearance of videotape.

Ultimately, the very word "videotape" in the title was probably a boon. As John Pierson explains, the word resonated symbolically: "By using videotape both in the title . . . and in the film itself, Soderbergh almost literally ushered in the new era of the video-educated filmmaker."[52] Thus the stylistic nature of the film—in which a series of women confess their sexual histories and anxieties on videotape to help the protagonist satisfy himself sexually—marked it as both timely and distinct for technological as well as social reasons. The themes of impotence and sexual paranoia further rang true at a time when AIDS panics were headlining the news of the late 1980s.

The film gained in popularity during the festival, which at this time sold approximately thirty thousand tickets and was a much more low-profile event than in later years.[53] By the end of the U.S. Film Festival, the film had received rave reviews from numerous critics and been screened in front of sold-out audiences. *sex, lies, and videotape* left the festival with the Dramatic Competition Audience Award and theatrical distribution offers from several independent distributors as well as one major studio.[54] That the film was a phenomenon from its earliest screenings is apparent from comments made by a number of attendees at the festival. Then program director Tony Safford saw the film as an "unheralded" treat that was "fresh to the professional community as well to the filmgoers."[55] Soderbergh, however, simply noted that the praise was "getting out of hand."[56]

Although the press lavished extensive acclaim on the film, North American theatrical rights for *sex, lies, and videotape* were not sold until a few weeks later, when Miramax purchased them at the American Film Market in Los Angeles. According to Soderbergh, Harvey Weinstein said that he would not go back to New York until he had the movie. By 1989, Miramax had already established a reputation for outbidding the other independent distributors. As crucial as the money they bid, however, was their distribution strategy; indeed, when later reflecting on how they "won" the rights to *sex, lies, and videotape*, "the Weinsteins maintain[ed] that their marketing plan was as crucial as their cash advance."[57]

Despite the company's minimal role in shaping the film's actual development, Miramax was crucial in establishing *sex, lies, and videotape*'s box office success and its status as a quality independent blockbuster. The company's marketing of the film was as significant as the content itself. Ultimately, the interest created in the film because of Miramax's skillful distribution cannot be distinguished from the interest created by virtue of the film's subject matter and story line. The company played up *sex, lies, and videotape* to the press in ways that helped the film move out of the "art-house ghetto."[58] By the late 1980s, art houses were disappearing rapidly. The name alone seemed guaranteed to keep many moviegoers away from theaters.

In the process of marketing *sex, lies, and videotape* as a quality independent as opposed to an art house film, Miramax also played itself up to the press. The company's marketers often constructed Miramax as the primary force in the film's development and financial success. Miramax thus altered the independent landscape through its distribution strategies *and* created the perception that it was altering this landscape. A study of Miramax's release strategy provides a template for the techniques employed by almost any 1990s niche- or specialty-oriented distributor. It also shows why Miramax was the most prominent of these distributors during that decade.

The marketing of *sex, lies, and videotape* began months before its August opening. According to Bob Weinstein, Miramax began to develop the prerelease buzz for the film at the Cannes Film Festival in May 1989.[59] Initially the film was screened for the main competition but rejected and placed in the Director's Fortnight, the venue for new films from up-and-coming directors. A last-minute cancellation from another American film, however, placed *sex, lies, and videotape* in the main competition. Soderbergh worried about the movie being lost in the shuffle, particularly as it was competing against Spike Lee's high-profile *Do the Right Thing* (1989). Yet *sex, lies, and videotape* ended up playing to standing ovations and shutting out Lee's film for awards. *sex, lies, and videotape* went on to win the prestigious Palme d'Or, provided Soderbergh and Miramax with much publicity, and added to the cachet of festivals as valuable sites for building word of mouth.

Cannes marked just the beginning of the summer marketing blitz initiated by Miramax. The press kit for *sex, lies, and videotape* hints at the image of itself that the company tried to craft for the press and public: "The Weinstein brothers built their company with an aggressive marketing and distribution strategy, individually tailoring each film's release to suit its particular strengths."[60] This implies that Miramax gave each film special care and designed its advertisements and trailers accordingly; indeed, the very notion of "tailoring" a film based on its strengths reveals the company's focus on niche marketing. "Marketing is not a dirty word," Harvey Weinstein told the *Los Angeles Times* in May 1989.[61] In what may be seen as a shorthand manifesto for Miramax, and a more emphatic articulation of previous conceptions of quality independents, Weinstein explained, "Although we market artistic films, we don't use the starving-artist mentality in our releases. Other distributors slap out a movie, put an ad in the newspaper—usually not a very good one—and hope that the audience will find it by miracle. And most often they don't. It's the distributor's responsibility to find the audience."[62]

For *sex, lies, and videotape*, this amounted to an attempt to give the film the specialized attention that Soderbergh wanted, packaged in a way that the major studios might do if they were distributing an event film. Just one of Miramax's tactics was to tap into the most commercial elements—the "high-concept" components—in even the lowest budget film.[63] Thus Miramax rejected Soderbergh's own trailer for *sex, lies, and videotape*, telling him it was "art-house death."[64] Although Soderbergh saw his trailer as expressing "a mood perfectly emulat[ing] the mood of the film . . . [and] not like any other trailer [he'd] seen," Miramax demurred.[65] Soderbergh finally reached a compromise with Miramax, in which the company used its own trailer but also filled in some additional footage shot by Soderbergh as a transitional device.[66]

This example suggests that although Miramax may have sold each film on its merits, the company also had certain ideas about what worked in promoting niche films—and artsy trailers were not part of the company's conception of good marketing. Indeed, by the late 1980s, any link to the art house was seen as limiting a film's box office potential. An analysis of the print advertisement for *sex, lies, and videotape* shows several characteristics of Miramax marketing. As the one-sheet for the domestic theatrical distribution of the film suggests, Miramax tried to appeal to several distinct niches through one advertisement. First, by declaring the film's status as a festival award winner, Miramax targeted the traditional art house audience, presumed to be familiar with these festivals for their role in highlighting the best of global cinema. Second, below the list of awards, Miramax took advantage of the positive press response. Quotations from critics representing major publications—the *New York Times*, the *Chicago Sun-Times*, and *Time*—gave the film additional credibility and created an appeal beyond the narrow festival route. Reviewers whom any filmgoer might trust explained why the movie was worth seeing. Yet even advertising the remarks from individual critics appealed to a particular, relatively limited constituency. So, third, the content of the quotations attempted to further broaden the appeal.

The largest print in the ad, aside from the title, came from two critics' statements: "One of the Best of 1989!" and "An Edgy, Intense Comedy." These remarks showed two different visions of the film: The first associated the movie with the kinds of films that usually receive kudos, such as dramas, while the second suggested a lighter movie well suited for the August release date. Thus the movie was differentiated as being more serious than its August blockbuster counterparts, even as it was drawn closer to studio product by its associations with comedy. The images depicted in the advertisement, meanwhile, contributed to the "edgy" mystique of the film; the pictures of the main characters embracing and kissing—taken with the film's title—conveyed raciness, excitement, something more adult. As one reporter observed of Miramax's effective print ads, the company readily hinted at sexual themes and situations that were not necessarily apparent within the films themselves.[67] More

A Miramax Films Release © 1989. Photo credit: Greg Gorman.

A Miramax Films Release © 1989. Consistent with Miramax's overall marketing strategy for the film, sexual attraction was foregrounded in the press photos of the cast of *sex, lies, and videotape* (1989).

than depict the content of the movie, such ads constructed images of what the movie could be.

Such constructions appealed to a variety of audience segments, including traditional art house crowds and Gen Xers. As a result, they facilitated a number of different readings of the film, depending on the viewer's background and the particular aspects of the advertisements that caught his or her attention. Ultimately, the diverse niches targeted by Miramax were united by the film's status as a quality independent—an identity that, in later years, would evolve into a subgenre of its own. The film's generic connections to drama and comedy were refreshed with this newer identity. Miramax tried to make the movie whatever viewers wanted it to be—thus offering the chance for greater crossover appeal. Nonetheless, the company continued to maintain a specific-enough identity that the potential audience member would not be confused or disinterested.

To many within the industry, Miramax's attempts to find the most commercial elements in low-budget films, while still targeting specific niches in the market, was a welcome approach to a then struggling independent film scene. As one public relations executive stated, in a manner that summed up the sentiments of many, "the marketers of quality independent films really aren't doing as effective a job as they might be doing."[68] Miramax certainly proved itself on this occasion, thereby differentiating both the company and its films. The company's marketing tactics were so successful that exhibitors honored the Weinsteins as "independent distributors of the year" at their annual ShowEast conference in the fall of 1989.

Although the Weinsteins may have penetrated multiplexes in 1989, they remained acutely aware of their position relative to the studios. Specifically, they recognized that their films had to complement, rather than compete with, the studios' product. They had no illusions that they could match the studios in terms of either financial investment or marketing scale. Thus they relied heavily on free publicity, word of mouth, and counterprogramming strategies. While they eventually released *sex, lies, and videotape* on about 350 screens, they initially opened it only on a few. They expanded the film slowly, letting it build an audience based on positive reviews, responses, and awards. They scheduled a platform release, opening it in early August only in Los Angeles and New York, and then later moving it into nationwide release by the end of the month. As a result, *sex, lies, and videotape* had its broadest opening in the period when the studio blockbusters were fading and "quality" product was in short supply.[69]

Press and Industry Discourse on *sex, lies, and videotape*

To Steven Soderbergh, the overall impact of his film was disconcerting. In 1990, he returned to Sundance to find a far different scene, one to which he responded negatively. "I'm a little concerned by what *sex, lies* might have wrought here," Soderbergh told the Associated Press, adding, "This can become more of a film market than a film festival."[70] Soderbergh's opinion seemed to be in the minority, however. Many more of those working for independents, and those writing about them, looked favorably at the mutually beneficial relationship developing between independents and festivals. Few could have anticipated that this relationship would evolve to the point where the pervasive attitude at Sundance a decade later would be "Buy low, but *buy, dammit.* Fail to snap up a certain movie and you might miss out on the next $140 million dollar cash cow. Turn up your nose at a trend and the future might pass you by."[71]

What was not apparent in 1989 was that the "small is beautiful" mentality on display at festivals and reported in press coverage of independents such as *sex, lies, and videotape* was part of a more expansive industrial shift. The same summer that witnessed the successful release of *sex, lies, and videotape* also witnessed the stunning box office performance of such blockbusters as *Batman, Ghostbusters II,* and *Indiana Jones and the Last Crusade. Batman,* in particular, became a "milestone in entertainment licensing and merchandising."[72] According to Schatz, the financial potential that the *Batman* franchise demonstrated with its merchandising and product licensing may have been the single most significant development in the New Hollywood.[73]

At the same time that *Batman* was ushering in this newest phase of New Hollywood, *sex, lies, and videotape* was having a similar effect at the niche level. As the studios were reviving the same formulas with such 1990 releases as *Rocky V, Predator 2,* and *Back to the Future Part III,* the independents seemed comparatively fresh and cutting-edge with such films as *Longtime Companion, Pump Up the Volume, Metropolitan,* and *The Grifters.* The dichotomy between these two groups of films indicates the emerging split in the types of projects being produced. The movies that were starting to return the most profits with the smallest risks were either high-budget, high-concept franchises that had broad international appeal, or low-budget films that could be targeted to a number of audiences and promoted inexpensively through festivals, word of mouth, and positive critical response.

Though the studios were placing an increasing emphasis on event films, these were far from their sole emphasis in the late 1980s and early

1990s. On many occasions, the conglomerates released films that could just as easily have found a home with an independent distributor. For example, the Spike Lee–directed *Do the Right Thing* returned more than $27 million to Universal–on a budget of $6.5 million. Similarly, Michael Moore's nonfiction exposé of General Motors, *Roger & Me* (1989), played widely on the festival circuit and was pursued by a range of companies, including Roxie Releasing, Miramax, Universal, and Warner Bros. Ultimately Warner Bros. acquired worldwide rights for what was then a sizable sum: $3 million.[74] The film's domestic theatrical gross exceeded $5 million.

The box office returns of such films as *Roger & Me*, *Do the Right Thing*, and *sex, lies and videotape* helped to counter the claims of those industry analysts predicting the inevitable demise of all but the high-concept blockbuster. Then Cinecom president Amir Malin further illustrated why niche films, in particular, would remain attractive both culturally and economically: "Just because someone sees *Indiana Jones* doesn't mean they won't want to see a sophisticated film like *sex, lies, and videotape* or *Scenes from the Class Struggle* [*in Beverly Hills*, 1989]. The fallout will occur with the standard studio fare that cannot compete with the *Raiders*, *Ghostbusters* and *Batmans*."[75]

Malin's comments were prescient for two reasons. First, on the level of industrial structure, he suggests why standard studio fare (the "mid-level" or "middle-class" film) would be the least cost-effective. These mid-level movies, which at the time of *sex, lies, and videotape* included thrillers such as *Pacific Heights* (1990) and romances such as *Joe Versus the Volcano* (1990), based their appeal primarily on their stories or their stars. The studios' event films, conversely, based their appeal on action, special effects, superstars, and simple marketing hooks.[76] Event pictures drove up the marketing, production, and distribution costs of all studio films. From the mid-1970s onward, however, the studios increasingly viewed them as worthwhile because of their broader international appeal and possibilities for synergy.

To a growing number of industry executives, mid-level films did not offer the same global opportunities as event films. If event films failed at home, they could still make money abroad; a Stallone film (typically an event due to his superstar presence) could easily be translated in every country, guaranteeing international box office success even if its fate was uncertain in the United States. If mid-level films failed at home, they were not likely to perform any better abroad, since they had neither the effects and action nor the simple marketing hooks that were the foundations of the global appeal–oriented Hollywood films. In 1989 there were still a fair number of solid performers in the mid-range category, including *When Harry Met Sally . . .* , *Parenthood*, and *Dead Poets Society*. Yet, in general, mid-level star-genre vehicles—the types of films that were the staple of the Hollywood studio era—were both less predictable in the global box office and less easy to exploit through various ancillary markets.[77]

Malin's comments were also prescient in his exploitation of the rhetoric of quality. In using the label "sophisticated" to describe *sex, lies, and videotape*, Malin employs the same rhetoric as the Weinsteins. In other words, he depicts these movies as special films rather than industry products. More important than the actual industrial circumstances within which a movie such as *sex, lies, and videotape* was produced was how it was constructed by the company and the press. Companies such as Miramax were capable of using terms such as "independent," "quality," "specialty," and "sophisticated" as points of distinction. They could do this because, in the late 1980s, the studios were so frequently portrayed in the media as ever-expanding monoliths cranking out cookie-cutter sequels with excessive action, minimal character development, and undeveloped story lines.

Miramax's rapid growth stemmed mainly from making itself and its films a favorite of the press. The company did this by showing how films such as *sex, lies, and videotape* were different from what Hollywood produced. At the same time, Miramax expanded the appeal of movies like *sex, lies, and videotape* by promoting them as having what Hollywood had to offer and more: sex, violence, and risqué content. This marketing sleight of hand, in which the films were at once similar to and different from Hollywood fare, helped to carve out an often financially lucrative and aesthetically viable space for low-budget cinema from the late 1980s through the 1990s.

Setting the Stage for the 1990s Indie Scene

sex, lies, and videotape served as both an example and a model for the future of the low-budget film scene in several important ways. First, the film's earnings at the box office demonstrated the economic potential for well-marketed, quality product. Whereas previously the independent films that had done well at the box office had been primarily of the genre variety (e.g., New Line's *A Nightmare on Elm Street* films; New World's *Hellraiser* series), the $24 million brought in by Soderbergh's film indicated that an aggressive distributor could find an audience for more mature or highbrow fare. Second, the film's substantial earnings compelled many in the industry to seriously consider the importance of demographic shifts in moviegoing patterns. There emerged a realization that the baby boomer audience was viable and, even more to the point, willing to spend money on movies. A study conducted by the MPAA in 1989 found that the over-forty age group was turning out in record numbers at theaters. Whereas in 1987 this audience accounted for 14 percent of admissions, by 1989 the number had increased to 22.3 percent.[78] Third, the ability of *sex, lies, and videotape* to attract audiences during the summer—historically the time when big-budget event films dominated theaters—proved the effectiveness of counterprogramming niche-targeted films against event film releases. Miramax sought to attract viewers worn out by explosions, effects, and car chases. While Miramax was by no means the first company to use such a tactic, the company's glowing success with the strategy encouraged other distributors to reconsider their own release schedules.[79]

Fourth, the profitability of *sex, lies, and videotape* laid the groundwork for a realignment of the industry away from B-grade genre product and toward American indies. As discussed above, the majority of 1980s-era independents thrived by churning out low-quality genre material, largely for the home video and foreign markets. As these markets matured, however, independents were forced out of business. The few that survived—companies such as New Line, Goldwyn, and Miramax—began to reevaluate their business tactics. With the success of *sex, lies, and videotape,* the seeds were sown for a shift in strategy: a strong script with an "edge" could attract established talent, and this talent, combined with a savvy sales campaign and some good reviews, could bring in solid box office. It is important to note that although this strategy was in the works, it would be a few years before a sizeable number of companies fully exploited this approach. Reporting on the 1989 Independent Feature Film Market in in *Variety*, Richard Gold observed the widespread sentiment by fledgling filmmakers that the gathering still served as "virtually the only event where their work [had] a chance of being noticed."[80] The same would not be the case in but a few short years.

As important as *sex, lies, and videotape* was in defining the quality American indie blockbuster of the 1990s, two other films played a significant role in solidifying Miramax's financial fortunes and critical status in the late 1980s and early 1990s. *Cinema Paradiso* (1990) and *My Left Foot* (1989) together brought Miramax more than $27 million in their North American theatrical releases.[81] In addition, they added to Miramax's rapidly developing reputation as a premier marketer of low-budget films. The company received acclaim from the press and from many

A Miramax Films Release © 1989. Left photo credit: Jonathan Hession. Right photo credit: Alistair Morrison. Promotional materials for *My Left Foot* (1989) featured only brief glimpses of Daniel Day-Lewis in character as Christy Brown. Often such images were accompanied by far more glamorous shots of the performer, out of character.

industry executives for its skillful distribution of these films. In addition, this trio of films brought the company its largest number of Academy Award nominations yet—a total of seven. Soderbergh was nominated for Best Original Screenplay for *sex, lies, and videotape*, and *Cinema Paradiso* took home an Oscar for Best Foreign Language Film. In addition, *My Left Foot* received five nominations (including Best Picture and Best Director) and won two awards, for Best Actor (Daniel Day-Lewis) and Best Supporting Actress (Brenda Fricker).

As with *sex, lies, and videotape*, *My Left Foot's* success can be attributed to Miramax's expert marketing. Once again, Miramax exploited positive reviews and awards with *My Left Foot*, even as it fashioned a distinctive campaign tailored to this very different film. The movie was a challenge to market due to its subject matter. The film was based on the life of Christy Brown, a quadriplegic artist confined to a wheelchair and unable to speak due to cerebral palsy. Though it ultimately presented Brown's triumph in learning to communicate with his family and the world through paint and pen, the material was difficult to convey easily in promotional materials. It was also a tough sell because it was set in mid-twentieth-century Ireland and full of thick accents foreign to American audiences.

In crafting the trailer for the film, Miramax marketers cleverly avoided all these elements. The spot featured photos of a handsome Daniel Day-Lewis as he had recently appeared in *A Room with a View* (1986) and *The Unbearable Lightness of Being* (1988). There was minimal dialogue in the trailer, and there were no moving images of Day-Lewis as Christy Brown (rather, only stills were shown of him, posed triumphant). The initial trailer was later supplemented by "person-on-the-street" ads, featuring interviews with viewers raving about the movie. In addition to targeting the traditional art house crowd, Miramax developed a promotional campaign geared to the forty-three million Americans with physical disabilities.[82] The campaign included direct mail, follow-up phone calls, and lobbying in Washington.[83] The company also enlisted the disabled spokesperson Paul K. Longmore to help sell the film as promoting civil rights for people with special needs.[84]

The momentum for *My Left Foot* grew following its Oscar nominations in February 1990. While it had earned a respectable $2.8 million at North American theaters prior to the announcement of the nominations, the arrival of awards season yielded several millions more.[85] Ultimately, the movie went on to earn in excess of $14 million in the United States—a solid box office performance for an often hard-to-watch film that featured challenging and frequently downbeat material.

Cinema Paradiso was a difficult sell as well, although for very different reasons. During the heyday of international art cinema in the 1950s and 1960s, foreign-language films regularly played at art houses and generated respectable returns. During the 1970s and 1980s, however, grosses for foreign-language films declined. After 1982, foreign imports repeatedly brought in less than 1 percent of ticket sales annually.[86] The market became increasingly hit-driven, with a limited number of titles earning a few million dollars at the box office and most others barely scraping by. The last foreign-language import to reach the level of grosses of *Cinema Paradiso* was the 1982 German film *Das Boot*, which brought in $11.8 million in North America.

By the late 1980s, most companies that distributed foreign-language films had either moved away from that market or declared bankruptcy. Miramax and Orion Classics were two of only a handful of distributors to continue to focus their energies on foreign-language product. In 1991, Orion Classics, along with its parent company, Orion, ceased operations altogether.[87] Orion Classics' top executives swiftly moved to Sony and launched Sony Pictures Classics. Reasons for the post-1970s decline of foreign-language films were numerous. One of the primary factors was the incorporation of these films' modernist aesthetics into numerous American films from the late 1960s onward (e.g., *Bonnie and Clyde*, 1967; *The Graduate*, 1967; *Nashville*, 1975).

Although selling subtitled movies had never been easy, with the release of *Cinema Paradiso* Miramax began to discover the type of foreign-language film most likely to bring in North American viewers in the 1990s.[88] What Miramax tried to do in marketing the film was to point out its "universal" qualities. The film was depicted as both a sentimental homage to the history of cinema and a tribute to love lost and friendship found. Whereas the trailer for *sex, lies, and videotape* used a combination of New Wave music, images of sexual acts (and flirtations), and voice-over discussions of the meaning of sex in relationships to depict a hip, contemporary film, the trailer for *Cinema Paradiso* used a widely divergent set of sales strategies. The *Cinema Paradiso* trailer blended a powerful, emotionally affecting score with sepia-toned images of a quaint Italian village and its inhabitants. With its images of youth kissing in meadows and running through fields, the spot harked back to classical Hollywood melodramas of the 1930s and 1940s. Whereas foreign-language films of previous decades were sold predominantly on their difference from Hollywood product, *Cinema Paradiso*, along with many other Miramax films to follow, were promoted based on their accessibility and their similarity to vintage Hollywood story lines.

The sales strategy for *Cinema Paradiso* worked wonders. The movie went on to earn more than $12 million during its North American run — the most taken in by a foreign-language import since *La cage aux folles* earned $13 million for United Artists in 1979. *Cinema Paradiso* began Miramax's ascendance to the position of top foreign-language distributor, which it held throughout the 1990s. And Italian films in particular would play an important role in Miramax's box office and critical ascendance. Following the success of *Cinema Paradiso*, Miramax yielded high returns on a number of other Italian imports, including *Mediterraneo* (1992), *Il Postino* (1995), and *Life Is Beautiful* (1998). *Cinema Paradiso* also marked the start of Miramax's long-standing relationship with the director Giuseppe Tornatore. The company would work with him repeatedly, from the 1993 release *Especially on Sunday* through to the 2000 release of *Malèna*.

Tornatore's first union with Miramax carried symbolic weight for the Weinsteins and their company. The brothers often made connections in interviews between *Cinema Paradiso* and Truffaut's *The 400 Blows* (1959). They frequently told how their love for films began with their youthful viewing of *The 400 Blows*, which they claimed to have seen under the mistaken impression it would be an "adult" film. They made no secret of the importance of *Cinema Paradiso* to the developing identity of Miramax. They were attracted to *Cinema Paradiso*'s unabashed nostalgia and its tribute to cinema past and present. They considered these characteristics representative of why they went into the film business and what they looked for in their hunt for new films and fresh talent.[89]

Cinema Paradiso was not the only film to elicit a passionate response from the Weinsteins. They were just as enthusiastic about a handful of controversial films in their distribution pipeline, including the 1990 releases *The Cook, the Thief, His Wife, and Her Lover* and *Tie Me Up! Tie Me Down!* During the late 1980s and early 1990s, the Weinsteins regularly engaged in highly public legal battles with the MPAA. In most cases, the conflicts involved decisions to give X ratings to Miramax films. The X was created in 1968 to identify a film that contained adult material unsuitable for children. The rapid adoption of the X as a marketing tool by the adult film industry, however, led the rating to become associated with pornography. By the 1980s, many newspapers refused to accept ads for X-rated films and most television stations refused to air their promotional spots. In addition, numerous theaters refused to exhibit X-rated films. Consequently, from a studio perspective, a film that received an X-rating was considered tainted.[90] But Miramax turned the meaning of X on its head, and, in the process, played a major role in leading to the rating's demise.

When a Miramax film was slapped with an X rating, the company cried foul to the press then used it as a means to gain inexpensive publicity.[91] The company simultaneously exploited the rating by drawing attention to the film's racy content at the same time that it declared the X inappropriate and unfair given the "artsy" nature of the film. For example, when the Peter Greenaway–directed *The Cook, the Thief, His Wife, and Her Lover* received an X rating, Miramax marketers attacked the MPAA while at the same time using the rating to publicize the film, foregrounding a quote by the *Time* critic Richard Corliss declaring, "X as in excellent, exciting, exemplary and extraordinary."[92]

One of the most extensive battles between Miramax and the MPAA occurred when the X rating was assigned to the Pedro Almodóvar film *Tie Me Up! Tie Me Down!* Upon receiving the X, the Weinsteins, along with their vice president of marketing, Russell Schwartz, hired the civil rights lawyer William Kunstler to sue the MPAA.[93] In their suit, they challenged the legality of the rating system, citing economic prejudice and discrimination as side effects of attaining the X rating.[94] The case went all the way to the New York Supreme Court, which ultimately upheld the X. Although the court ruled in favor of the MPAA's decision, the judge also used the case to attack the means by which the ratings board classified films.[95]

The decision came at a time when discontent toward the rating system was growing. In 1989–1990, a number of heated battles with the MPAA had already occurred over ratings; among the films caught in the crossfire were *Henry: Portrait of a Serial Killer* (Greycat), *Life Is Cheap . . . but Toilet Paper Is Expensive* (Silverlight), *Hardware* (Miramax), and *Wild at Heart* (Samuel Goldwyn). But the court's reprimand in the *Tie Me Up! Tie Me Down!* decision served as the final blow. Within two months of the decision, the MPAA jettisoned the X and created the NC-17 rating to replace it.

Miramax's challenges to the X may have contributed to what many in the industry had long viewed as a problematic rating. But the courts did not see the company's lawsuit as driven primarily by altruistic goals. Rather, the judge recognized the case for the marketing ploy that it was. In the process of issuing his verdict, the judge questioned the good faith of Miramax in pursuing the case, observing that the company continued to exploit the X in its advertisements while it questioned the legitimacy of the ratings system.[96] The judge also saw Miramax's motivations as suspect due to the company's unwillingness to cooperate in the review process until after they had received the X certificate.[97]

The court's suspicions certainly seem warranted, as Miramax continued to engage in heated battles with the MPAA long after the X had been retired from use. For example, when the MPAA required Miramax to place a restricted label in front of its trailers for *Madonna: Truth or Dare* (1991) and *A Rage in Harlem* (1991), the company loudly protested, thereby garnering coverage from such media outlets as *Entertainment Tonight*. Similarly, Miramax contested the MPAA's demand for revisions to the company's newspaper ad for *Drowning by Numbers* (1991); the organization objected to the silhouetted picture of a naked couple embracing.[98] Meanwhile, Miramax immediately began to exploit the new NC-17, as *The Cook, the Thief, His Wife, and Her Lover* became the first home video to carry the rating.[99]

The MPAA was not the only organization that Miramax took to court. In 1991, the company filed suit when the television networks refused to air commercials for its film *The Pope Must Die*.[100] The Weinsteins hired the high-profile lawyer Alan Dershowitz to help them. Although the company lost the legal battle and had to change the name of the film to *The Pope Must Diet*, Miramax won tons of publicity—as Harvey Weinstein readily acknowledged when he declared that "we looked at those legal expenses as our advertising budget."[101]

The ratings controversies did indeed boost the profile of both Miramax's movies and the company itself. As the 1990s began, Miramax was one of few independent distributors continuing to turn a profit—a fact that did not go unnoticed by the press and industry observers alike. *sex, lies, and videotape, My Left Foot,* and *Cinema Paradiso* cumulatively returned between $18 and $21.2 million in film rentals.[102] The income generated by these movies was more than matched by their impact on the production, marketing, and distribution practices in the low-budget film world. While *My Left Foot* and *Cinema Paradiso* demonstrated the viability of English and foreign-language imports in the American market, *sex, lies, and videotape* shattered the barrier of what quality independents could earn. In the process, the latter film's success encouraged producers and distributors to pay greater attention to the role of festivals, critics, awards, and, of course, a little controversy in the marketing of specialty films.

Fueled by these successes, Miramax began to accelerate its growth plans as the new decade began. This involved developing additional divisions, moving to new offices, hiring more staff, increasing acquisitions, and ramping up in-house productions. Even as the body count of independents seemed to rise almost daily, the Weinsteins expanded their company's reach.

Developing the 1990s-Era Indie

In the early 1990s, Miramax experienced growth of a scale and scope far greater than what had come before. Whereas it had focused most of its energy during the late 1980s on trying to "upscale" its product line through a greater emphasis on quality American independent features, at the beginning of the next decade the company pursued a much wider range of objectives. Riding high from its string of box office hits in 1989–1990, the Weinsteins decided to open a Los Angeles office and hire a head of production, Fred Milstein, indicating the company's intention to increase the number of films it developed and produced in-house.[103] During most of the 1980s, the Weinsteins held back from financing and producing their own films—and consequently survived when most other companies failed. But the company became more willing to take risks as it increased its number of financing partners and received additional income from its wave of box office hits. Unfortunately, many of these risks did not pay off. *The Lemon Sisters* (1990), *Strike It Rich* (1990),

Mr. and Mrs. Bridge (1990), *The Tall Guy* (1990), and *Love Crimes* (1991) were just a few of the many flops the company had as it began developing more projects from the script stage. Even *Rage in Harlem*, which returned its investment, was a disappointment considering that it cost more than $6 million to produce.

In tandem with its heightened emphasis on more ambitious and expensive projects, the company formed a new division, Prestige, in the summer of 1990. The division was created with the specific intention of keeping the company involved in more specialized films even as the Miramax label transitioned to more expensive, star-driven product. Prestige was designed to focus on the kinds of films favored by the 1980s version of Miramax, namely, foreign-language and nonfiction fare. Among the first Prestige releases were *¡Ay, Carmela!* (1991), *Iron and Silk* (1991), *Tatie Danielle* (1991), and *Drowning by Numbers*. In keeping with a traditional art house mode of distribution, Prestige films were generally given a more limited release than films released by Miramax. In acknowledgment of the goals of this new subsidiary—and also indicating an awareness of the slight shift in emphasis occurring at Miramax—Prestige executive Mark Lipsky stated, "There are films out there falling through the cracks because no one has the time and energy to give the hands-on attention needed for these films. Hopefully, nobody can say you can't go to Miramax because the film is too small or too difficult."[104] Of course, the cracks could be exploited all the more easily at this time because there were so few other specialty companies on the scene.

One of the most successful Prestige releases was *Paris Is Burning* (1990), a $500,000 documentary about New York City drag balls that grossed nearly $4 million domestically. In what Lipsky brashly called "unprecedented" and "a first for a documentary put into the theatrical marketplace by an independent," the film opened in twenty major markets beginning in August, then expanded to seventy-five screens by the end of the month.[105] In typical early-1990s Miramax style, much of the success of *Paris Is Burning* was due to protests from a number of groups, the most vocal of which was the Christian Film and Television Commission, which called for a boycott of the film.[106] The Weinsteins responded to the controversy with a declaration of their support for the film and stated their intent to take legal action against anyone interfering with any screenings.[107]

Few Prestige releases met with the kind of media attention or box office returns of *Paris Is Burning*. The division nonetheless served a larger purpose for the company by helping to increase the size of its library. This library, which had more than 120 titles by 1991, became increasingly important to the Weinsteins as they tried to develop relationships with other companies.[108] In 1991 and 1992, Miramax tapped into the library heavily, striking a series of licensing arrangements with a number of distributors.[109] In March 1991, HBO signed on to distribute a minimum of twenty Miramax titles on home video and pay television; in May, Warner Bros. agreed to finance and domestically distribute the U.S. versions of select Miramax foreign-language films.[110] In February 1992, Miramax signed several different deals with Paramount. Included in their various agreements were Paramount's payments for video distribution rights to seventeen Miramax titles as well as cable and broadcast rights for eighteen others.[111] Paramount also took on domestic distribution rights for the Miramax-produced *K2* (1992) and agreed to coproduce *Bob Roberts* (1992). Miramax continued its deal making by signing a licensing, output, and cross-promotion contract with the Bravo cable network. This transaction provided Bravo with the rights to Miramax films after their initial HBO run. In addition, Bravo committed to air promotions of Miramax films currently in theatrical release.[112] The Bravo deal, in particular, signaled how the demand among niche-oriented cable outlets for specialty product would help drive the growth of specialty companies during the 1990s.

Miramax's 1991 efforts at expansion paled in comparison to its diversification efforts the following year. In the course of 1992, Miramax launched a home video division as well as a foreign division to oversee the sale of international rights (dubbed Miramax Int'l).[113] The wave of deal making continued as well, with BMG agreeing to represent Miramax for its existing and future music catalogs, and the UK-based Rank Organization advancing $5 million to Miramax as part of a potentially more wide-ranging relationship between the two companies.[114] These moves enabled Miramax to continue to increase its investment in the production and marketing of select films. In July 1992, Miramax announced its intention of committing $10 million toward the prints and advertising (P&A) costs of the animated children's film *Freddie as F.R.O.7*.[115] This was followed by one of Miramax's biggest production commitments yet, for the Jamie Lee Curtis thriller *Mother's Boys* (1994).[116] The company's overall output increased as well: whereas Miramax released ten films in both 1988 and 1989, the number increased to sixteen in 1990 and twenty-six in 1991.[117] The volume of Miramax releases led one reporter to observe that the company was functioning at the independent level in a manner mirroring the majors.[118]

Much of this heightened output came from yet another division created by Miramax in 1992, Dimension Films. The roots of Dimension were in Millimeter Films, a label developed by Bob Weinstein in the late 1980s to distribute genre pictures and give Miramax access to the exploitation market dominated by New Line. Some considered the genre label euphemistic, instead seeing Millimeter as a Miramax warehouse, a means by which the company could release its more commercial, mass-appeal (and critically reviled) films. In releasing its more disreputable material through Millimeter/Dimension, Miramax could avoid the stigma these films might bring to its image as a distributor of quality independents.[119] This would seem a reasonable conclusion considering that some of the first Millimeter releases were *Return of Swamp Thing* (1989), an Anthony Perkins horror vehicle called *Edge of Sanity* (1989), *Stepfather II* (1989), and *Hardware* (1990). During its short existence, Millimeter released several troubled projects as well. These included the romantic comedy *Animal Behavior* (1989), the period romance *Strike It Rich*, and the erotic thriller *Love Crimes*. All began with the Miramax label attached to them but were eventually shunted off to Millimeter and given perfunctory theatrical releases. In general, Millimeter titles were well suited to the straight-to-video, ultra-low-budget nature of the genre market at that time.

The Weinsteins had long recognized the immense value genre films could have for their company's bottom line. As Harvey Weinstein observed in 1990, "One Millimeter film will do better on tv and cassette than five Miramax films."[120] Even as the company rebranded Millimeter as Dimension, the Weinsteins retained the hope that their genre division could serve as a commercial boon that would help make Miramax more financially stable.[121] Commerce could subsidize art, lowbrow would pay for highbrow.

Though Millimeter/Dimension continued to be viewed as the venue for more low-end product, the Weinsteins always tried to present Dimension as a more "upscale" genre division perfectly in line with the Miramax pedigree. In the process, though, they also attempted to maintain a clear division between the films Dimension released and those handled by its more "sophisticated" sibling, Miramax.[122] An early statement by Bob Weinstein shows this tension at work: "We're not changing our stripes whatsoever," he declared in a 1992 interview. "The films we usually do are our first love. But genre films are also important. They carry a sense of less quality, of stigma, and that shouldn't happen."[123] Despite such statements, early Dimension releases seemed relatively indistinguishable from titles distributed under the Millimeter label. Dimension's initial slate included such films as *Children of the Corn II: The Final Sacrifice* (1992) and *Hellraiser III: Hell on Earth* (1992). As will be discussed in chapter 5, Dimension remained a relatively modest, low-profile operation until after the Disney purchase, at which point the division began to generate a larger number of films and spawn some of Miramax's biggest hits.

These efforts to expand the company drew attention from several journalists and executives. Many publicly queried why Miramax would be trying to branch out at a time when there seemed to be a new independent casualty every week. The independents Island, MCEG, Vestron, and Cinecom had all gone under, and the mini-majors Orion and Carolco were fading fast. As noted above, Miramax had drawn much praise for its slow growth policy in the 1980s—a time when most companies were rapidly diversifying, increasing output, and expanding their in-house productions. Now that the company was one of only a few survivors in the independent landscape, some critics asked why it was taking these kinds of risks. Speculation ran rampant in the trade papers during the early 1990s as to the company's intentions. Some journalists believed that Miramax perceived a gap in the marketplace vacated by the bankrupt independents, while others thought that Miramax was attempting to become a mini-major. As early as 1990, rumors began to circulate that the Weinsteins were attempting to inflate the value of the company in preparation for its sale.[124] If this was their intent, their attempts yielded mixed results. As noted above, most of the in-house productions in the early 1990s failed miserably. Acquisitions did not fare much better. Though *The Grifters* (1990) was a success, the company had several underperformers released at the same time, including *The Krays* (1990), *Strapless* (1990), *The Long Walk Home* (1991), and *Spotswood* (1991). High expenditures, met with (at best) mediocre returns, gave credence to the prediction by one marketing consultant that "like every indie . . . they'll have their three-month window."[125]

With its growing divisions and increased marketing, production, and acquisitions costs, Miramax seemed to be expanding beyond its means. Observing a general climate in which independent distributors paid too much for both productions and acquisitions, then Skouras president Jeff Lipsky observed, "If you're spending seven figures, you're competing with the majors."[126] Even if this comment was an overstatement, it does tap into a perpetual problem faced by Miramax and its few remaining independent distribution brethren, such as Samuel Goldwyn and New Line. As long as Miramax was truly independent—that is, distributing films not financed by a major studio—the company had to function as an independent. In other words, it had to spend wisely on a limited number of in-house productions and carefully monitor its acquisitions, marketing budgets, and general corporate expansion. Yet the success of a few films, combined with the Weinsteins' grander ambitions, seemed to lead to the reckless pursuit of something more. This "something more" took Miramax out of its clearly defined niche setting and into more direct competition with the studios. Despite the credibility gained throughout 1989 and early 1990, the release of eight straight box office failures in 1990 made its position once again tenuous.[127]

Along with the problems the company faced with its new divisions and acquisitions, Miramax also encountered a number of other barriers that threatened to limit its growth. One main problem involved an ever-declining number of art house screens during the 1990s. Miramax tried to combat the problem by forging relationships with large multiplex circuits—the very chains helping to drive the art houses out of business through their rapid expansion and their emphasis on playing the same film on multiple screens. In fact, a key reason that Miramax began releasing more broad-based films was due to its inability to secure screens for its more specialized product. According to *Variety*, the company tried to use its more mainstream product "as a wedge to force in less commercial foreign movies."[128] Such a strategy was crucial in an environment in which Miramax claimed to have postponed the opening of *Ju Dou* (1990) due to an inability to find theaters in which to show the film, despite its Oscar nomination for Best Foreign Language Film.[129]

In addition to Miramax's struggles to procure theater screens for its films, it had difficulty retaining successful talent. According to Pierson, Miramax was well regarded within the industry in terms of its ability to pay advances, delivery costs, and P&A expenses.[130] Nonetheless, as long as it remained an independent, Miramax would never have either the money or power to compete directly with the majors. The studios usually could lure talent with offers of financial security or long-term production deals—especially by the early 1990s, when so many independent distributors had gone out of business. Spike Lee (Universal's *Do the Right Thing*, 1989), Joel and Ethan Coen (Fox's *Miller's Crossing*, 1990), and Wayne Wang (Disney/Hollywood Pictures' *Joy Luck Club*, 1993) were just a few 1980s independent filmmakers who began making movies for the studios during the early 1990s.

Thus Miramax's problem could be easily summed up: money. The case of *Reservoir Dogs* (1992) is instructive in showing the many ways that the company's expansion was hindered by its minimal capitalization relative to the studios. It also reveals that Miramax's marketing prowess could go only so far. While Miramax was able to help several films break out, there were limits to what the company could do. Financed by LIVE Entertainment for $1.2 million in exchange for the video rights, the film premiered at Sundance without a theatrical distributor. After coming out of the festival with strong buzz, this hyper-violent gangster/caper film unsuccessfully made the rounds at a number of studios, including Universal and TriStar.[131] Although its violence proved too much for the studios, Miramax purchased the rights in the spring of 1992. The film had a number of attractive marketing elements, including a hip and flashy style, creative editing, witty dialogue, a catchy soundtrack, and established actors (Harvey Keitel) as well as up-and-coming stars (Steve Buscemi). In addition, it played off a number of different styles (e.g., Hong Kong action, film noir, blaxploitation) and paid tribute to several established directors (e.g., Kubrick, Scorsese).

From Miramax's point of view, *Reservoir Dogs* had the makings of a hit, and consequently the company invested a lot of time and money in the hope that the film would build on the positive reviews and word of mouth it had garnered from Sundance. Unfortunately, although *Reservoir Dogs* later became a cult phenomenon with a long afterlife in video and made its director and writer, Quentin Tarantino, a star, the film did not prove another independent blockbuster on the order of *sex, lies, and videotape. Reservoir Dogs* earned just $2.8 million at the North American box office, not nearly enough to help heal Miramax's rapidly growing financial woes. Meanwhile, Miramax did not benefit at all from the film's strong afterlife, as video rights belonged to LIVE Entertainment. Further, the company's executives could not even be reassured that new "indie auteur" Tarantino would return to work with them again; he had already been advanced $900,000 by TriStar to develop, write, and direct *Pulp Fiction*.[132]

By the fall of 1992, Miramax seemed to be in a precarious position. On the one hand, the company had survived—and for a short time thrived—long after most of its competitors had declared bankruptcy. It had established a reputation as one of the top independent distributors, a company run by two men who were skilled at acquiring and marketing movies. Indeed, Miramax earned a great deal of respect for the unrestrained tactics it employed in buying film rights and then selling those films to the public. What's more, the company played a major role in raising the expectations of what an independent film could earn. Joining *sex, lies, and videotape* in the ranks of its early 1990s independent blockbuster hits were *The Grifters* ($6 million budget, $13 million domestic gross) and *Madonna: Truth or Dare* ($3 million budget, $15 million domestic gross).[133] In the process, the Weinsteins, their films, and the company itself earned repeated praise from critics and journalists alike. The company was singled out by many for being one of the few champions of independent visions and creative voices in a film marketplace dominated by high-concept product such as *Kindergarten Cop* (1990), *Days of Thunder* (1990), and *Hook* (1991).

On the other hand, it seemed Miramax's days were numbered; it would not be long before it became just another casualty of a consolidating marketplace. In an attempt to stave off what appeared to be the inevitable demise that seemed to come to all independents, the Weinsteins sought investment partners, sold video rights to films, and struck exclusive contracts with cable networks. As the 1990s wore on, the Weinsteins were faced with two options: Miramax could take its chances and continue nurturing talent and films on the periphery—and then proceed to lose those filmmakers (and their follow-up films) to the studios. Or it could seek the safety and the deep pockets of a studio. A studio might protect Miramax from the financial difficulties that had already afflicted its many competitors and seemed likely to destroy it as well. The second option would become more viable as Miramax continued to stumble in its attempts to expand. And the second option would become more possible as Miramax helped propel one particular film released late in 1992 to the status of cultural phenomenon and independent mega-blockbuster. The success of *The Crying Game* would make the Weinsteins' decision about the future of their company much easier.

The "Secret" of Miramax's Success

The Crying Game (Winter 1992–Spring 1993)

> Miramax will now be able to get full value for their product,
> which they have not been able to do in the past. . . . To give them
> the financial backing like ours ensures that they will continue to
> be the best independent film company in the world.
>
> *Jeffrey Katzenberg, Walt Disney Co. chair, 1993*

> It will destroy independent filmmaking. . . . Would Disney have
> allowed *The Crying Game*? Take that kind of chance? This drasti-
> cally changes the face of independent film.
>
> *Allen Hughes, 1993*

By 1992, Miramax, New Line, and Samuel Goldwyn were the only major 1980s independents left standing. It was an uncertain time for all three companies, as each struggled to redefine itself and remain afloat in a rapidly changing entertainment industry. Miramax responded to this instability by adding to its staff, acquiring more films, increasing its number of productions, and creating new divisions.[1] Such moves raised the company's profile while at the same time diminishing its profit margins from 9 percent to 5 percent from 1990 to 1992.[2] Amid these changes, the company faced accusations from the press that it was starting to lose "its edge from the early days" due to its acquisition of too many films.[3] In addition, as addressed in the prior chapter, some critics speculated that the Weinsteins were doing nothing more than pumping up the company in the hopes of selling it for a higher price.

Rumors about Miramax's increasingly dire straits regularly circulated in the trade press. The first reports that the company was for sale surfaced in the summer of 1990, when the Weinsteins retained Allen & Co. and Salomon Brothers to look at potential financing options, including a public offering.[4] Upon reporting this news in August 1991, Paul Noglows observed that Allen & Co. had been working on a deal for over a year, "and that in itself indicates a resounding lack of interest on Wall Street's part."[5] Almost every studio was seen as a prospective buyer at some point: in 1989 it was PolyGram, in 1990 Universal, in 1991 Warner Bros., and in 1992 Paramount.[6]

Miramax was not the only company feeling pressure to expand and develop new business strategies. In December 1990, New Line, which had formerly focused largely on genre product, announced plans to get into the quality independent game. Though New Line had previously made forays into the art house side of the business with films such as *Sid and Nancy* (1986), *A Handful of Dust* (1988), and *Metropolitan* (1990), it was mainly with horror, urban, and children's-oriented product that the company generated profits and built a brand identity. Yet, like most of the other independent companies that remained by the early 1990s, New Line made an effort to diversify.[7] Between 1990 and 1992, the company began its own home video and television distribution divisions. In addition, emulating Miramax, it launched an official "art house" division with Fine Line Pictures.[8] It did not take long for Fine Line to build up its own slate of films, many of which attained a remarkable amount of critical acclaim and media attention. *Night on Earth* (1991), *My Own Private Idaho* (1991), *The Player* (1992), and *Hoop Dreams* (1994) were among the many notable early Fine Line releases.

Meanwhile, in the wake of such hits as *Henry V* (1989), *Wild at Heart* (1990), and *Longtime Companion* (1990), Samuel Goldwyn also continued to expand its release slate and the number of films produced in-house.[9] Some new competitors emerged at this time as well: In September 1991, PolyGram and Universal announced plans to venture into low-budget film distribution in North America with a joint project called Gramercy Pictures; a month later, October Films was formed to pursue a similar objective. The following spring, a group of investors launched Savoy Pictures. Run by a couple of former TriStar executives, Savoy was intended to serve as an alternate distribution avenue for independent producers.

As the formation of these new companies indicates, this was a time of considerable churn. The 1980s generation of B-film distributors and mini-majors were on their way out, and a new generation of quality indie distributors focused on releasing "A" product were beginning to emerge.[10] The 1990s independent world already was becoming quite distinct from the 1980s environment. These specialized distributors found themselves in a landscape in which long-term deals were increasingly important; as *Variety* noted at Cannes in 1991, "the buzzword for the indie film business of the 1990s is relationships."[11] Output arrangements, first-look agreements, and various other alliances were replacing one-time deals.[12] Independent distributors had to change their strategies, if for no other reason than the fact that the majors were demonstrating an "increasing clout and appetite."[13] The studios had long since strengthened their position in the videocassette market, pushing out or marginalizing many previously high-flying independent distributors; several studios were now taking their first tentative steps into the theatrically based specialized film business.

There were multiple reasons for the majors' growing interest in the specialized film arena. First, production budgets and marketing costs for studio films continued to rise at a speed far exceeding the rate of inflation. For example, the studios' 1992 holiday films had an average budget of $40 million; P&A costs added another $20 million.[14] Second, the studios had become much more focused on marketing and distributing event films; the machinery of the majors was geared toward wide releases of thousands of prints of high-concept movies. This focus meant that the studios were less and less capable of effectively handling the release of prestige pictures. The disappointing performance in 1992 of such high-profile star-genre vehicles as *Hero, Leap of Faith*, and *Mr. Saturday Night* underscored how ill equipped the studios were to deal with films lacking in special effects and spectacle. The majors needed to come up with an alternate means of distributing films that were not broadly targeted to all moviegoers. An indie subsidiary offered one way to accomplish this goal. Third, the continued rise in popularity of video, combined with the growing number of cable channels, made the afterlife of films more valuable. As a result, the majors were searching for ways to increase the size of their libraries. Once again, specialty divisions seemed a viable way to do this at a relatively low cost. Fourth, statistics continued to indicate the aging of the moviegoing audience. By spring of 1993, "mature folks" (members of the over-forty age group) accounted for 30.4 percent of admissions—twice their attendance just seven years prior.[15] These figures were borne out by the success of several low-budget films released in 1992. *Howard's End, The Player*, and *Enchanted April* all made a tidy profit and did so at a relatively low marketing cost for their respective distributors.

In pondering how to reenter the specialized film business, the studios recognized that they had to proceed differently than they had before. As noted in chapter 2, most of the earlier incarnations of classics divisions had been rather narrow in their focus; they mainly released foreign-language and highly specialized art house product. In addition, the studios often exercised a substantial degree of oversight of such divisions, interfering with their executives' decisions. The next generation of specialized distributors would be conceptualized differently—at least initially. In the spring of 1992, the first of this new breed appeared when Sony recruited former Orion Classics copresidents Michael Barker, Tom Bernard, and Marcie Bloom to be the coheads of Sony Pictures Classics (SPC). This new label expected to release between eight and ten titles annually, most of which would be acquisitions. The operation was rather conservative in strategy; the start-up budget was less than $10 million.[16] Of all the 1990s-era specialty companies, SPC would retain the most similarities to the 1980s-era independents. Even so, the expansive size and scope of Sony led SPC to function differently within its parent company than Orion Classics had within Orion. (SPC will be discussed in more detail in chapter 7.)

Sony was the first of several conglomerates to create a specialty division from scratch. But there was another direction that some conglomerates opted to take: buying a "ready-made" specialty company. Miramax was one of only a handful of such companies available for purchase at this time. Shortly after the 1992 launch of SPC, Disney initiated a series of deals with Miramax. These flirtations culminated in its purchase of Miramax the following spring. The first arrangement between Disney and Miramax came in July 1992, when Disney purchased the domestic rights to *Sarafina!* from Miramax for approximately $7 million.[17] Soon after making this deal, Miramax representatives anticipated the importance Disney would serve in their company's future by telling the press, "The 'Sarafina!' sale could emerge as [a] singular event in company history."[18] The next transaction between the two companies came in October 1992, when Disney paid about $13 million for the video rights to several Miramax films, including *Mediterraneo* and *Strictly Ballroom.*[19]

By no means were these small-scale arrangements between Miramax and Disney seen by the press as portents of things to come. Critics of Miramax remained doubtful as to whether anyone would seriously consider making an offer for the company. As one Fox executive observed just days before the Disney-Miramax deal was announced, the Weinsteins had "shopped themselves all over town."[20] As this executive explained, "They came to us and made their pitch. We looked at it but as far as we were concerned, their library is encumbered, so there's nothing there other than the services of those two guys. We're not paying $80 million for their services. If we want that, we'd hire them. Any major would be crazy to pay that price."[21]

Yet, not much later, Disney did in fact pay "that price." What caused Miramax to go from being an unattractive, "cash-starved" company to a hot prospect?[22] As noted above, Miramax struggled on a number of fronts from 1990 to 1992. Perhaps most significantly, the company had been unable to follow up *sex, lies, and videotape* with another independent blockbuster. While the company had a modest hit with the four-time Oscar nominee *The Grifters* in 1990, the bulk of Miramax's releases for the year proved disappointments. Similarly, in 1991 the Weinsteins thought they had another set of hits with *High Heels*, *The Double Life of Veronique*, and Soderbergh's sophomore effort, *Kafka*. They placed a particular emphasis on the British comedy *Hear My Song*, campaigning heavily for Oscar nominations for the film. Yet all of the company's efforts came up short; Miramax received only one Academy Award nomination for its 1991 slate of films (for the Italian comedy *Mediterraneo*, which ended up taking home the Best Foreign Film award). Box office returns were equally disappointing.

What ultimately marked a turning point for Miramax was a low-budget British acquisition financed by a company in the throes of bankruptcy. This film already had bombed at the UK box office and was not expected to make much of a mark in its North American release either. But through a skillful marketing campaign—which incorporated nearly universally favorable reviews, a score of awards, and a brilliant manipulation of the commercial press—Miramax finally found its next independent blockbuster. This film would go on to earn in excess of $60 million in North America. In other words, it brought in nearly three times more money at the box office than had *sex, lies, and videotape*. Not only did it break box office records for a specialty film, it also revived Miramax and, in the process, helped make the company attractive to Disney. What movie accomplished all this? *The Crying Game* (1992).

Through a case study of *The Crying Game*, it is possible to understand how and why Miramax became a worthwhile investment to Disney. In addition, this analysis shows how Miramax's marketing expertise went far beyond selling low-budget American independents. In fact, English-language imports were an equally important part of Miramax's business. This chapter's examination of Miramax and its handling of *The Crying Game* further challenges widely held ideas about the parameters of the 1990s indie film movement. An exploration of the surprising success of *The Crying Game* complicates the now well-accepted narrative that the rise of a specific strand of edgy American independent films drove the 1990s-era indie movement.

Rethinking 1990s-Era British Cinema

When *The Crying Game* was produced, British cinema was at a transitional point creatively and financially. Several signs suggested that England's film industry was in a continuing slump. British films made up 16 percent of domestic releases in 1991 and less than 6 percent of ticket sales.[23] While the number of studios, production services, and postproduction facilities was growing, film production remained low. Much of the money for the film industry came from television companies; terrestrial services such as BBC Films and Channel Four Films provided some financial support and guaranteed television distribution for numerous motion pictures (e.g., *The Pope Must Die, Hear My Song, Enchanted April*).

Despite the grim state of the British film industry in the early 1990s, journalists began to perceive a growing interest among emerging and established filmmakers in approaching riskier subjects than they had in the past several decades. Along with the continued nurturing of heritage films (e.g., *Howard's End; Enchanted April*) came a number of gritty dramas such as *The Cook, the Thief, His Wife, and Her Lover* (1990), *The Krays* (1990), and *Young Soul Rebels* (1991). Of the latter group, only *The Cook, the Thief, His Wife, and Her Lover* performed well at the box office. The growing presence of British films filled with gunplay, racial, class, and ethnic conflicts, and racy sexual exploits (with different films carrying each component to varying degrees) suggested that the winds of change were upon British cinema.

Interestingly, a number of these British films, including all those mentioned above, were distributed in North America by Miramax. In fact, Miramax was one of the most consistent distributors of UK product in North America during much of the late 1980s and early 1990s. The company established an office in London at this time to keep an eye on both the talent and product coming out of the local film, television, and theater scenes. Among the UK-themed titles released in North America by Miramax in the late 1980s and early 1990s were *My Left Foot* (1989), *Scandal* (1989), *Strapless* (1990), *The Tall Guy* (1990), *Antonia and Jane* (1991), *The Big Man* (1991), *Prospero's Books* (1991), and *Spotswood* (1992). The style, subject matter, and popularity of these films' stars ran the gamut, as did their box office fortunes. Much as the British film industry was struggling to reestablish itself after years of turmoil, so, too, was the creative community laboring to establish a clear identity (or set of identities) for its films.

By the mid-1990s, the British film industry did regain its footing and find its focus. This reorientation was motivated in no small part by a number of creative efforts by the government to infuse money into the business. As Jeongmee Kim discusses, the British film industry benefited from a range of financing experiments throughout the 1990s. Public funding, regional broadcasters, and international investors were combined in ways that enabled the industry's "potential to be seen as a new kind of popular British cinema within [the] globalized market."[24]

One especially prominent international investor was the London-based, Anglo-Dutch company PolyGram Filmed Entertainment (PFE). PFE's investment in the British film industry in the mid-1990s played a significant role in reenergizing both UK production and distribution.[25] From 1994 to the time of its purchase by Seagram in 1998, PFE financed some of the most ambitious and successful British films of the decade, including *Four Weddings and a Funeral* (1994), *Shallow Grave* (1994), *Lock, Stock and Two Smoking Barrels* (1998), and *Elizabeth* (1998).

Robert Murphy synopsizes the three primary strands of British cinema that dominated movie screens both at home and abroad by the mid-to-late 1990s.[26] These include the aforementioned heritage films; "urban fairy-tales" like *Four Weddings and a Funeral* and *Sliding Doors* (1998); and films focusing on the lives of the poor and oppressed, like *Trainspotting* (1996) and *Brassed Off* (1996). While Murphy focuses predominantly on the characteristics of urban fairy-tales, others have written about the growing international presence of films focusing on lower-class British life.[27] Although the means of classifying these films varies, there are some general terms on which critics agree: The main characters are typically male outsiders—people who, by dint of their race, ethnicity, sexuality, class, or politics, find themselves unable to fit in. The setting is usually contemporary, or at least set in a time no earlier than the 1960s. Characters frequently reside outside London—in Wales, Scotland, Ireland, or a more isolated rural area of England. If they do live in London, then they typically inhabit the more impoverished areas of the city. In the course of these films, characters often find themselves in over their heads, frequently by virtue of committing a crime—be it murder, robbery, kidnapping, or some combination thereof. Even though the main characters often spend much of their time trying to dig themselves out of unfortunate circumstances, the narratives frequently consist of a strong blend of irony and dark humor.

These characteristics describe a large number of films, which comprise varying tones and divergent story lines. Other films fitting within this classification scheme are *Shallow Grave, The Full Monty* (1997), *Lock, Stock and Two Smoking Barrels,* and *B. Monkey* (1998). Critics have cited a wide range of cinematic influences for these films, including the British documentary movement of the 1930s, the British New Wave filmmakers of the late 1950s and early 1960s, the American New Wave of the late 1960s and early 1970s, and, for those released after the mid-1990s, Quentin Tarantino. Yet in almost all the discussions of contemporary British cinema of this ilk, one film is rarely cited as either an example of this movement or an influence on it: *The Crying Game.* It is worth spending a moment discussing the possible reasons for this film's exclusion from many discussions of prominent British working-class cinema when it seems to fit clearly within the parameters described here.

There are four main reasons why *The Crying Game* has been overlooked in so much analysis of 1990s British cinema. First, the film came slightly before the boom time in British film and thus does not fit neatly into the "boom and bust" narratives developed about the industry. A common misperception, supported within much academic literature, has been that PolyGram played *the* dominant role in resuscitating the British film industry in the mid-1990s. PolyGram's later demise in 1998 following its purchase by the North American "outsider," Seagram, thus provides a facile explanation for the subsequent struggles encountered by the British film industry at the turn of the century.[28] While PolyGram certainly was responsible for financing several British hits, it was not the only company to help revitalize the British film industry—nor was it by any means the first, as the discussion of Miramax's role in releasing UK films during the late 1980s and early 1990s indicates.

Second, *The Crying Game* was the product of a company that, by 1992, was in the throes of bankruptcy. By the time of the film's release, the British press was regularly attacking *Crying Game* producer Palace Pictures for its business practices. *The Crying Game* thus suffered from the bad will generated toward its producer. A third reason for the neglect of *The Crying Game* stems from the film's greater financial and critical success in the United States than in Britain. Beyond this, the film's national affiliations were complex. Rather than being solely the product of British money and labor, its financing came from diverse international sources, it featured an American in a leading role, and it was directed by Neil Jordan, who was widely perceived to have "sold out" by making *High Spirits* (1988) and *We're No Angels* (1989) for Hollywood. Yet such an explanation only works up to a point, for Jordan was much heralded in the 1980s for his direction of the British crime thriller *Mona Lisa* (1986), and *The Crying Game* was produced out of a London office. Even if the film is judged to be a UK product, it is still difficult to label as "strictly British" due to its Irish setting for the first half of the story—a characteristic that serves as the fourth reason the film might be neglected in many analyses of British cinema. Yet, as noted above, several of the "poor and oppressed" films of the 1990s took place outside London proper, and, in fact, many were set in Ireland and featured non-Brits in prominent roles.

Much as the film itself challenged constructions of race, gender, sexuality, and national identity, this history of its distribution complicates many of the assumptions about what constitutes a "British" film. For the purposes of my study, the case of *The Crying Game* is important not because of what it represented to British cinema per se, but rather because of what it indicated about the popularity of the British films that obtained distribution in the United States. The whole of British cinema produced in the 1990s is distinct from the British cinema seen on North American screens during that same period.[29] Due to the large size of the U.S. market, however, what made it to North American screens had a profound influence on the kinds of British films produced. The success of *The Crying Game* was important because it presaged the popularity of a certain type of British cinema in the American market—one that focused on lower-class criminals, outsiders to their country, and yet, at the same time, characters perceived by some to be more distinctively British than those previously seen on-screen.[30]

In the same way that *The Crying Game* often has been overlooked in discussions of British cinema, it also has been neglected in most analyses of the rise of contemporary independent cinema. In considering why this is the case, we are once again directed to some larger problems in the ways that many scholars and journalists have discussed 1990s independent cinema. The main reason *The Crying Game* has not been mentioned is that, as noted in chapter 1, most formulations of the low-budget film movement of the 1990s have focused almost entirely on a very specific definition of American independent film. Titles such as *Celluloid Mavericks: A History of American Independent Film*, *American Independent Cinema: A Sight and Sound Reader*, *Cinema of Outsiders: The Rise of American Independent Film*, and *American Independent Cinema* reaffirm a staunchly "Amero-centric" focus in their analyses. While such publications rightly note the transformation afoot in the American indie scene, the writers, by cordoning off their discussion almost entirely to the United States, uniformly fail to account for the broader transformation occurring across the cinema—and larger media—landscape. This transformation involved the increasing dependence of Hollywood on niche product that exhibited the potential to cross over from specific demographic groups to broader audiences. And as argued throughout, this transformation included not only American indies but also genre films, English-language imports, and foreign-language imports—each group having its own particular stylistic traits and narrative characteristics.

The Crying Game highlights the vitality of the low-budget English-language film and its prominence in U.S. theaters in the 1990s. It also illustrates the growing complexity of the label of "independent." At the time of the release of *The Crying Game*, independents reached a peak financially, industrially, and aesthetically. Yet the fact that the term "independent" is rarely applied in discussions of this film underscores the diminishing value and accuracy of the word. When *The Crying Game* earned in excess of $62 million at the North American box office, the stakes changed for low-budget filmmaking. It was *because* Miramax attained these heights that the company became attractive to Disney. And it was due to the ability of a low-budget film to earn this sum that other studios began to take notice of the breakout possibilities of niche-oriented films. In other words, it was not an American independent film that ultimately stimulated the studios to form subsidiaries to distribute low-budget films, but rather *The Crying Game*, a UK import.

Selling the Secret

> This Miramax pickup presents one of the toughest marketing challenges in recent memory. Title is unenticing, cast has no certified stars and Irish Republican Army backdrop reps a turn-off for many.
>
> *Todd McCarthy,* Variety, *September 1992*

> Give audiences something they have never seen before, something Hollywood is not doing and something TV can never do. Result? "The Crying Game."
>
> *Simon Perry, chief executive of British Screen Finance, 1993*

No one in the press or the industry anticipated *The Crying Game*'s status as one of the biggest low-budget hits of the 1990s. In fact, its seeming lack of commercial appeal had delayed its production for years. After attaining critical kudos for *The Company of Wolves* (1984) and *Mona Lisa,* the writer-director Neil Jordan had tried his luck with Hollywood—and failed miserably, with both *High Spirits* and *We're No Angels*. Jordan subsequently returned to the United Kingdom and made a low-budget Irish drama, *The Miracle* (1991), which was produced by Palace Pictures and distributed in North America by Miramax. Although the film received some acclaim, it was unable to find an audience. After the release of *The Miracle*, Jordan returned to a screenplay he had been revising for several years called *The Soldier's Wife*. The script, soon to be renamed *The Crying Game*, was part romance, part thriller, part political drama, and entirely a tough sell due to its unusual structure. While the first half of the story focused on the friendship that developed between an IRA terrorist and his captive and took place in Ireland, the second half shifted to London and focused on the terrorist's search for redemption in the hands of his (now-dead) captive's lover.

Jordan's longtime producer, Palace Pictures head Stephen Wooley, shopped the script around to the major studios, which showed little interest in the project. The film seemed particularly unattractive because of its lack of big names. The attached talent consisted almost entirely of British actors unknown to the U.S. market, with the exception of the American Forest Whitaker, who was perceived as an odd choice for the role of the British soldier held hostage by the IRA. Wooley attempted to obtain financing for the project at Cannes in 1991 but was unable to secure the necessary funds.[31] According to Jane Giles, the film's combination of race, sexuality, and political violence made it an unattractive prospect to investors.[32] Financing was eventually patched together with money from Nippon Development and Finance, Channel Four, and Eurotrustees (a consortium of UK, Spanish, French, German, and Italian distributors).[33] Such means of securing financing were becoming increasingly commonplace in the early 1990s, as money from the American video market dried up and U.S. investors became ever more wary about putting money into low-budget films after the demise of so many independent distributors.[34] At this time, European companies began to fill this investment vacuum, putting money into movies as a means of exercising greater control over the content they distributed. Yet *The Crying Game*'s budget still had to be reduced by approximately 25 to 30 percent through deferrals in order to get made.[35]

The Crying Game was completed in time for the 1992 Cannes Film Festival but was twice rejected by the organizers.[36] Festival director Gilles Jacob was dissatisfied with the shift in tone that occurred midway through the film. Although the film did not screen in competition at the festival, Miramax acquired it during the Cannes market.[37] *The Crying Game* marked the continuation of a lengthy relationship between Miramax and Palace Pictures. The two companies, which had first partnered on *Scandal*, went on to strike deals for eight additional films. A number of the Palace-produced films, including *A Rage in Harlem* (1991), *The Grifters* and *The Pope Must Die* (1991), were among Miramax's most ambitious and financially successful projects. But Palace was in the process of declaring bankruptcy at the time *The Crying Game* neared completion, thus marking the end of the relationship between the two companies.[38]

Even as *The Crying Game* put a nail in the coffin of Palace Pictures due to its failure in the United Kingdom, it served as the means by which Miramax was reborn. Yet it was by no means clear that Miramax had a hit on its hands even after the film was finished. Mayfair released *The Crying Game* in Britain on 30 October 1992 to minimal fanfare and mixed reviews.[39] The film suffered from a combination of bad timing, poor marketing, and lukewarm critical response in its UK release.[40] Unfortunately, *The Crying Game* was released during a period in which the IRA had increased its attacks on Britain. The sympathetic depiction of the main character, the IRA terrorist Fergus (Stephen Rea), made the film an easy target for attack by journalists.

Poor marketing was most apparent through the film's one-sheet. The poster's hand-drawn artwork was cartoonish, its tagline ("Desire is a danger zone") vague. Neither the images nor the text of the poster did much to evoke a clear sense of the film's story line or tone. Critics did not help either; according to Giles, UK critics "were bemused by PR company pleas not to reveal the twist [that the lover, played by Jaye Davidson, was not a 'she' but rather a 'he'] and commented on this in their reviews, making it sound as though they were dutifully exposing a con man's cheap gimmick."[41]

Everything that worked as a negative for the film in its UK release was turned into a positive by Miramax for the North American release. The company created strong buzz for the film by screening it at the Telluride, Toronto, and New York festivals in the fall. Audiences at the film festivals were given letters from the director or from Miramax requesting that they keep plot developments secret.[42] Following a traditional art house distribution strategy, Miramax opened the film in a limited number of markets, and slowly increased the screen count as critical support and word of mouth grew. North American critics came out overwhelmingly in favor of the film. Upon the film's initial release on 25 November 1992, *Variety* reported the critical response to the film as thirty-nine "pro," one "con," and six "mixed."[43] U.S. critics not only responded positively to the film, they willingly and enthusiastically endorsed the request to hide the "secret."

While Miramax's promotion of *The Crying Game*'s twist certainly played a major part in enabling the film to cross over from a fairly narrow art house niche to a broader audience, the company made several other subtle yet equally crucial marketing choices. First, Miramax chose to deemphasize the political elements of the film.[44] Certainly *The Crying Game* lacked the political immediacy in its American exhibition that had worked to its detriment in the UK context. But Miramax also worked hard to downplay the IRA components of the narrative in its marketing materials. The company instead drew attention to the film's moments of suspense and passion. This is apparent from the two new taglines generated for the one-sheets and trailer: "Sex. Murder. Betrayal. In Neil Jordan's new thriller, nothing is what it seems to be" and "Play at your own risk."

The trailer similarly highlighted the film's moments of action and drama—in essence making a traditional art house film appear to be a big event film. Miramax pulled seemingly every explosion, act of violence, and chase scene out of the film and assembled them into a rapidly paced trailer, thus effectively transforming a methodical, relatively slow-paced film that had a limited number of such sequences. Guns figured prominently in both the trailer and the poster as well. Particularly effective was the revamped one-sheet, which featured a femme fatale (bearing only a slight resemblance to supporting actress Miranda Richardson) brandishing a smoking gun.

The second key marketing choice made by Miramax involved celebrating the plot's twists and turns in publicity materials. This helped Miramax avoid some the problems that the UK distributor had faced with critics who found the story line unwieldy. In its British advertisements, Mayfair used a quote from a critic paralleling the film to *Psycho* (1960). Miramax extended this connection one step further, encouraging critics to view the film as Hitchcockian in nature, echoing both *Psycho* and *Vertigo* (1958) in style and structure.[45] Thus what had been interpreted within the British release as a weakness became an asset, and the script appeared that much more innovative as a result. Ultimately this reinterpretation of the plot would serve the interests of the film as well as Neil Jordan's career; in the spring of 1993, he was awarded the Oscar for Best Original Screenplay.

The third important marketing decision involved pitching the film to a variety of different demographic groups. This strategy required commissioning the kinds of market research that at the time had been largely the domain of the majors. Miramax conducted extensive press screenings of the film before its release.[46] Once *The Crying Game* opened, National

A Miramax Films Release
© 1992. This publicity still
from *The Crying Game*
(1992) conveyed a sense
of intrigue and mystery.

Research Group was hired to conduct movie-house exit surveys to determine what worked and what did not for audiences.[47] In addition, Miramax conducted telephone research to further fine-tune the marketing of the film.[48] These campaigns reinforced the way that different aspects of the film could be pitched to different groups. While the two initial targets were the traditional art house audience wooed by critics and the forty-five million Irish Americans residing in the United States, additional groups were pursued as the film began to take off.[49] Whereas the UK marketers were unable to separate the film's interwoven elements of sexuality, race, and politics in the film's promotional materials, Miramax called attention to different elements depending on the specific demographic groups being sought.

One overarching goal—and the fourth crucial element of Miramax's marketing of the film—involved concealing the film's "Britishness." At the time of *The Crying Game*'s release, the films that most effectively foregrounded their British roots were the aforementioned heritage films (*A Room with a View*) or adaptations of Shakespeare (*Henry V*). Recognizing that contemporary British productions historically had not been a large draw for American audiences, the trailer featured no conversation. Rather, the soundtrack consisted of a pulsing, suspenseful score that augmented the tension depicted through the rapid-fire display of images.

The Crying Game's North American theatrical run well indicates that Miramax's marketing tactics contributed to the film's success. Following its limited release in New York and Los Angeles in late November, the film expanded to 25 screens in mid-December and then increased again to 120 screens by the end of 1992. During the early weeks of its release, the film capitalized on poor showings by many of the studios' prestige films. A number of the studios' holiday films expected to generate Oscar buzz, including *Toys*, *Malcolm X*, *Hoffa*, and *Chaplin*, garnered lukewarm responses from the press and public. As it became apparent the studios had little to offer that awards season, Miramax heightened its marketing push by running fifteen- and thirty-second commercials on prime-time television and by placing the trailer in front of such studio releases as *A Few Good Men* and *Scent of a Woman*.[50] At the same time that Miramax began escalating its Oscar campaign, the company itself began to draw press for its effective promotion of the film. Thus all things *Crying Game* were saturating both the arts and business sections of newspapers and magazines. As Giles notes, Miramax also profited from news events occurring in the United States; most important, the film began to be alluded to in articles discussing the proposed end to the banning of gays in the military.[51]

In early 1993, Warner Bros. approached Miramax with a proposal to take over distribution of the film, arguing that it could attain better settlements from exhibitors.[52] Miramax refused, forging ahead on its own. By February 1993, Miramax had become the golden child of the media and the industry. The Film Information Council awarded the company an excellence in marketing award in January, and publications ranging from *Newsweek* to the *New York Times* ran features on the company's crafty marketing campaign—all the while not giving away the now-infamous "secret." In January, the film received nine Golden Globe nominations; in February, it earned six Academy Award nominations. Miramax drew further attention to itself by throwing a very public fit about Jaye Davidson's nomination for Best Supporting Actor (a move that revealed the twist of the film to those few souls who did not yet know it). By the time the Oscars rolled around, the film was playing on nearly eight hundred screens and had earned close to $50 million at the box office, thereby shattering *sex, lies, and videotape*'s record for an independent blockbuster and disproving the long-held belief that a relatively traditional art house film had an "absolute ceiling" of $30 million.[53]

By early April 1993, *The Crying Game* had become the most successful independent British import of all time.[54] As Miramax's advertising enthusiastically declared, the film had been featured on more than 130 critics "ten best" lists and more than two dozen critics had called it the "best film of the year." Miramax predicted that it would earn in excess of $10 million in profits from the film—a sum far greater than the company's entire earnings the previous year.[55] At the same time, other Miramax releases were also performing well with critics and audiences. *Passion Fish* and *Enchanted April* brought the company another five Oscar nominations and more than $18 million during their North American theatrical releases. In addition, the Mexican feature *Like Water for Chocolate* opened in February and was slowly building an audience.

With the astounding success of *The Crying Game*, as well as the noteworthy receipts from these other films, the press showered the Weinsteins with renewed praise for their impeccable skill in acquiring and marketing films. The past few lean years for Miramax quickly became a distant memory; the company now seemed ripe for the sale that had previously eluded it. After several failed efforts to find a buyer, *The Crying Game* gave Miramax the momentum it needed. On Friday, 30 April 1993, Harvey and Bob Weinstein joined Disney Studios chair Jeffrey Katzenberg to announce Disney's purchase of Miramax for what at the time was reported to be between $60 and $80 million—an amount roughly equal to the sum earned by *The Crying Game* during its theatrical release.[56]

With this purchase, a new era began for contemporary Hollywood. The relationship forged between the two companies over the next several years would proceed to alter the structure, conduct, and content of the entire entertainment industry.

Miramax Goes to Disneyland

> You see what's happened to independents like Miramax and Merchant Ivory being taken over by Disney. Big dinosaurs like Disney realize that there are holes in the market that haven't been filled by the big outfits. So they take on independents, offering them financing and wider distribution. The studios say they're not going to interfere with these people—well, we'll see. But people get fat and not sassy and they say, "Oh boy we're really doing good, let's protect it." Maybe five years from now we'll be talking about the two big companies and it'll be Miramax and New Line.
>
> *Robert Altman, 1993*

> The word "corporate" is not bad. . . . I think we're getting much more corporate, but still not changing our taste in films.
>
> *Harvey Weinstein, 1993*

In a variety of ways, Disney seemed a logical choice as a buyer for Miramax. At the time of the purchase, Disney was in top form, regularly winning or placing second in the theatrical market with a 20 percent share.[57] Under the management team of CEO Michael Eisner, COO Frank Wells, and Walt Disney Studios chair Jeffrey Katzenberg, the company had rapidly built itself up from its prior status as a second-tier distributor of family films to a diversified, integrated conglomerate with a wide range of media products. From the mid-1980s through the mid-1990s, Disney continued to create new divisions and increase its film output. After a long period of decline, *The Little Mermaid* (1989), *Beauty and the Beast* (1991), and *Aladdin* (1992) initiated a new golden age for Disney's animation division.

A range of hits from Disney's live-action division, Touchstone, complemented the animation division's success. From the mid-1980s onward, Disney had been active in releasing live-action films through Touchstone. This division tended to release broad comedies that featured well-known television actors or stars whose careers had gone into decline (e.g., Bette Midler, Richard Dreyfuss, Shelley Long, Ted Danson, Lily Tomlin). Among the solid performers to come out of Touchstone were *Down and Out in Beverly Hills* (1986), *Stakeout* (1987), *3 Men and a Baby* (1987), *Big Business* (1988), *Pretty Woman* (1990), *What About Bob?* (1991), and *Father of the Bride* (1991). Along with the Disney and Touchstone labels, there was Hollywood Pictures, launched in 1988 to distribute more mature, adult-oriented fare.[58] By 1993, the three labels cumulatively released more than thirty films per year. Given the small size of the company's library relative to the other studios, the company's top executives viewed this output as essential.

Despite this expansion, by the early 1990s Disney was still lacking one key element: prestige. Meanwhile, Hollywood Pictures continued to meet with limited success both critically and financially. Although the division had moderate hits with such films as *Arachnophobia* (1990), *The Hand That Rocks the Cradle* (1992), and *The Distinguished Gentleman* (1992), it had an inordinately large number of disappointments, including *V. I. Warshawski* (1991), *The Marrying Man* (1991), and *Medicine Man* (1992). Further, none of the releases coming from Hollywood Pictures earned critical acclaim. In fact, most generated quite the opposite response.

The purchase of Miramax thus served as a quick fix for Disney, providing the conglomerate with heightened prestige and adult-oriented material at a relatively low cost. For the most part, Miramax product complemented, rather than competed with, the films generated by Disney's other divisions. There were other benefits to the deal for Disney as well. Miramax came with the rights to more than two hundred titles— rights that were transferred to Disney, thereby nearly doubling the size of its library from three hundred to five hundred and fifty films.[59] Disney would handle Miramax product through its Buena Vista label in ancillary markets. In most cases, Miramax films would be bundled with the films from Disney's Hollywood Pictures, Touchstone, and Disney divisions for sale in the home video, pay-per-view, cable, and broadcast markets. Disney also gained the added assurance that the primary sources of Miramax's content and marketing know-how would not be leaving any time soon: at the time of the deal, the Weinstein brothers each signed five-year contracts.[60]

The potential benefits to Miramax were even more extensive. The company's financial woes were solved immediately, with Disney not only paying tens of millions of dollars but also settling Miramax's outstanding debts. The linchpin of the purchase involved Disney's guarantee that Miramax would retain "complete autonomy."[61] According to Harvey Weinstein, this was "the most important issue."[62] This involved keeping the Miramax office in New York, three thousand miles away from Disney's Burbank headquarters. This autonomy was not only a crucial deal point but also a key means by which Miramax's relationship as a subsidiary differed from the way the "classics" divisions of the studios had been conceptualized in the past. Miramax had the authority to produce or acquire any films with budgets below $12.5 million; there was no limit to the number of films Miramax could produce or distribute as long as they remained below this price.[63] The promise of this cash infusion led Miramax to anticipate a greater investment in coproductions and cofinancing arrangements than had previously been the case.

Much as the deal assured Miramax a continued authority over the production process, it assured a similar amount of control over the company's theatrical distribution activities. Miramax would continue to be in control of its domestic theatrical distribution and marketing. In addition, the company planned to handle its own foreign sales; Disney had "first look" on international rights. This meant Miramax could use Disney's distribution channels as needed or desired; distribution decisions would be made on a film-by-film basis. Such an arrangement allowed Miramax to exploit much-sought-after synergies with Disney at times when extra income could be nurtured, while also enabling Miramax to maintain a distinct brand identity in marketing and distributing its films.[64]

Miramax fully intended to exploit Disney's marketing and distribution muscle to increase its profile and profits. The Weinsteins predicted that the backing of a studio would increase the value of each title by $750,000 to $2 million, an estimate that proved conservative.[65] One of the most striking benefits of the arrangement was the extent to which it increased Miramax's clout through every stage of a product's life cycle, from development through exhibition. For example, with Disney's support, Miramax had a better chance of holding on to up-and-coming talent. Not only would the Weinsteins be able to finance a number of production deals, they also would have a larger amount of money to invest in scripts. No longer would Miramax help launch new stars (e.g., Quentin Tarantino) only to see them flee to the studios at the first sign of success. Another expected benefit of the deal involved Miramax's bargaining position with exhibitors.[66] With the backing of a major, Miramax had a better chance of obtaining screens in top markets, receiving higher distribution fees, increasing its ability to collect rentals rapidly, and ensuring a wider distribution of its product.

For the two parties involved, the union seemed to be a match made in heaven. As *Variety* noted following the announcement of the deal, "The marriage melds two companies with the rarest of qualities in Hollywood: brand identity."[67] Disney had long since publicly established itself as the source for media products for all ages; the Disney imprimatur was believed by many media consumers to be synonymous with quality entertainment for the whole family. Miramax, meanwhile, had carefully crafted its image as the source for intelligent, sophisticated films. At the time of its purchase, the Miramax logo was perceived to represent edgy, smart, and sometimes even visionary cinema. At first glance, this matchup seemed to offer infinite possibilities for both sides.

Yet even though journalists, industry executives, independent filmmakers, and low-budget distributors recognized the potential benefits the deal offered the two parties, many found it problematic on several fronts. The announcement of the purchase of Miramax by Disney was an important moment in the history of the media business not only for the impact the deal had on its primary participants, but also because of the extent to which it motivated a high degree of introspection on the part of the industry and its observers. Several individuals recognized the deal for what it was—the beginning of a transformation of the economics and culture of the entertainment world. The potential cultural and creative consequences of this new relationship were foremost on the minds of many.

Assessing the Purchase

The move marks the latest swell of a sea change in Hollywood, as studios and independents increasingly align to battle booming marketing and production costs, capture fragmented audiences and scramble for bigger market shares. . . . The deal melds two of the most powerful marketing and distribution companies in the business.

Variety, *May 1993*

Different stakeholders had diverging opinions about the implications of Disney's latest acquisition. Independent distributors were among the most critical. As noted above, the independent film business was already in a period of consolidation and restructuring. In general, the more specialized the distributor, the harder the times. Most of the survivors—First Look, Skouras, Mad Dog, Cinevista, Arrow, and Triton— were already bare-bones operations with limited cash flow. The general opinion expressed by this group was that the deal would only help to accelerate the divide between the "haves" and "have-nots" in the low-budget film world. As Triton president Jonathan Dana observed, "What's really happening is that our definitions are changing. . . . It's no longer a case of majors versus independents but rather the option of going mainstream or specialized. When you realize that, it becomes clear that the studios could wind up owning everything."[68]

Dana's comments convey many of the fears expressed by independent distributors. One of the most frequently articulated concerns—which soon proved well-founded—was the belief that the Miramax deal was only the first of many such arrangements. There was tremendous anxiety that these newly deep-pocketed subsidiaries would drive up prices for acquisitions and stimulate buying frenzies earlier in the development process. This would cause the "truly independent" distributors to fight for fewer, tinier scraps than usual, ultimately leading to the demise of several smaller companies. Dana's apprehensions seemed justified. Just a few months after Disney acquired Miramax, Turner Broadcasting System purchased New Line—and Dana shut down Triton Pictures.[69] "We realized we couldn't compete with Miramax," he explained. "We didn't want to lower the standard of the product, and we didn't want to work for anyone else."[70] While there were some low-budget distributors who believed that Miramax's stronger financial situation could help "grow" the specialty film market, such views were in the minority.

Filmmakers supplied a wider range of responses. Some believed Miramax would continue to finance and acquire the same kinds of films it had previously, only now it would have greater financial means. Others were more skeptical, arguing that Miramax's larger bank account guaranteed that its projects would become bigger in scale and more commercial in subject matter and style. Speaking only a few months after Miramax was purchased, Steven Soderbergh already perceived a substantive change in the low-budget environment. Echoing the ideas expressed by Dana, Soderbergh noted, "More lately, the independents seem to look for sure-fire films on a smaller-scale, in the same way that the studios do on a bigger scale. . . . It's a lot harder for people to get independent films made now—films that don't fit into any particular category—than it was for me five years ago."[71] In other words, independent distributors now had become more commercially minded, more driven by market imperatives than had previously been the case.

It is true that Miramax's deeper pockets did have a dramatic and immediate impact on the industry—a fact that will be discussed in more detail in the next chapter. But the company often was unfairly held responsible for many of the problems that independent filmmakers and distributors faced. It must be remembered that Miramax so desperately searched for a suitor in part because of the changes already occurring within the industry; its failure to secure a deal could have taken it down the same path as Vestron, Orion, and Cinecom. While a select number of quality independent films had earned unexpected sums at the box office, a significantly larger number had failed—as is apparent from the earlier discussion of Miramax's own release slate during the 1990 to 1992 period. Low-budget distributors often did not have enough cash reserves to survive the drought periods between hits. A studio parent enabled specialty distributors to withstand the rougher weather they were sure to encounter in the specialty business. And Miramax took advantage of this newfound benefactor, fully exploiting Disney's money, influence, and relationships.

American journalists widely covered the transaction, with many recognizing its importance even if they could not be certain of the outcome. In addition to speculating on the impact of the deal and giving various parties a chance to comment, several journalists wondered what effects the purchase might have on Miramax's content. Their concerns primarily involved First Amendment issues. More specifically, several writers asked whether Miramax would continue to acquire films with sex, violence, and challenging subject matter. Some speculated as to whether the company would retain its practice of using controversy as a marketing technique. In the press conference announcing the deal, the Weinsteins insisted that the provision of full autonomy meant just that—they would have "complete freedom to operate as we always have."[72] Jeffrey Katzenberg similarly declared himself "unconcerned" with the potential clash between Disney's wholesome image and the often risqué films released by Miramax.[73]

A key issue that journalists were only starting to assess was the meaning of the label "independent" now that conglomerates such as Disney and Turner were investing in select companies. It was too early to say with any certainty what the effects of the studios' entrance into the independent world would be, although the stakes were clearly changing. "Independent" had only recently started to have some marketing cachet. Yet no sooner had independent films become associated with hipness and edginess than the conglomerates gained interest in the companies that released them. What is particularly notable is the extent to which the increasing incorporation of specialty distributors under studio supervision heightened—rather than diminished—the attention given to the rise of independents. In fact, not *until* the major studios entered into the low-budget film business did many articles about the rise of independents appear in the mainstream press. Significantly, such discourses were only beginning to emerge at this point; they would not reach their peak until 1996, the oft-labeled "year of the independents" (to be discussed in chapter 6).

The dramatic transformation occurring in the industry is apparent by looking at the "Indie Scorecard" published by *Variety* in December 1993. The trade publication provided a series of charts that ranked the top indie distributors on an annual basis from 1988 to 1993 in terms of both domestic box office and market share.[74] On the 1992 chart, the companies listed (in order of market share) included New Line/Fine Line, Miramax, Goldwyn, InterStar, Triton, IRS Media, October, Aries, Kino, and Hemdale. All the distributors lacked studio affiliations. Cumulatively, the companies listed earned $217.7 million from their films' North American theatrical releases. The 1993 chart looked quite different. Once again, in order of market share, the companies listed were New Line, Miramax, Goldwyn, Orion, Gramercy, Savoy, Trimark, Fine Line, October, and First National. Of these, four companies (New Line, Miramax, Fine Line, and Gramercy) were now owned by major media conglomerates; two others were soon to disappear (Goldwyn and Orion). The earnings of these distributors were on the rise as well; domestic box office for the 1993 year totaled $396.1, almost double the amount earned in 1992.

This data not only shows the extent of the changes taking place, but also underscores the problematic nature of the word "independent" after the Disney/Miramax alliance. In order to maintain greater clarity in terms of industrial affiliations, from this point onward the films released by Miramax and other studio subsidiaries will be referred to as "niche," "indie," or "specialty" films. This not only facilitates a more critical assessment of the discursive uses of "indie" and "independence," but also helps to highlight the larger transformations occurring in Hollywood. Further, it points to something that is often neglected by scholars, critics, and journalists in their assessments of the independents of the 1990s, and was made evident through this chapter's case study of *The Crying Game*: namely, that the rise of the indie film was part of a broader, industry-wide reorientation. While the rise of the American independent film made for a sexy and compelling story, it was only one component of a much larger process.

The blockbuster success of post-1993 indies resulted from the intersection of their distributors' substantial financial resources and influence with the increased emphasis placed on targeting a diverse array of demographic groups. A box office hit typically appealed to multiple audience sectors—sectors targeted through the kinds of marketing methods fine-tuned by Miramax in its pre-Disney days. While the content of this new generation of specialty distributors changed incrementally, their resources changed rapidly. The next chapter explores at greater length precisely how Miramax negotiated its early relationship as a studio subsidiary, especially with regard to two major indie blockbuster hits, *The Piano* (1993) and *Pulp Fiction* (1994).

Corsets, Clerks, and Criminals

Miramax in the Age of Disney (Summer 1993 – Spring 1995)

When the deal was announced, independent producers and distributors pointed to the marriage of Jeffrey Katzenberg and Miramax co-chairmen Harvey and Bob Weinstein as the ultimate culture clash, pitting the singularly commercial Disney against mercurial Miramax. But a relationship thought to be one match away from inferno is proving to be a match made in heaven — and worth every penny of its reported $60 million to $90 million acquisition price.

Variety, *November 1993*

I think right now is the most exciting time in Hollywood since 1971. Because Hollywood is never more exciting than when you don't know.

Quentin Tarantino, 1996

No sooner had Disney announced its purchase of Miramax in the spring of 1993 than all eyes seemed to fix on the new subsidiary. The press and industry anxiously tracked Miramax's actions, seeing the Weinsteins' post-acquisition moves as general indications of the status of low-budget cinema and the independent film business at large. While optimists looked for expanding opportunities for filmmakers, pessimists watched for the first signs of co-optation or creative compromise. Both sides could—and did—easily find evidence to support their opinions in the ensuing years. But the consequences of the purchase both on the industry and on motion picture aesthetics were more complicated than either the cheerleaders or naysayers allowed. In the first few years after the deal, most discussion proved speculative at best.

The complex nature of the union can be seen when comparing the distinct trajectories and influences of two of Miramax's most profitable post-Disney "indie blockbusters": *The Piano* in 1993 and *Pulp Fiction* in 1994. The films' production and distribution histories—as well as their styles—could not have been more different. *The Piano* was an international coproduction acquired in nearly completed form by a pre-Disney Miramax; *Pulp Fiction* was picked up in script stage when it was put in turnaround (i.e., shelved) at TriStar and became one of Miramax's first films produced in-house post-Disney. *The Piano* contributed to the reformulation of art cinema for the 1990s; *Pulp Fiction* continued the process of reinventing the quality American indie and helped herald a new generation of filmmakers. *The Piano* was distributed via the traditional independent strategy of a slow-growth, platform release; *Pulp Fiction* was launched much like a traditional studio film, as it opened wide on more than a thousand screens in its first weekend. Meanwhile, in marketing both films, Miramax incorporated promotional practices drawn from both art cinema and the Hollywood studios.

These two films' distinctive industrial histories—and the discourses that circulated about each—indicate how the low-budget film world was being reconstituted at mid-decade. A comparison of *The Piano* and *Pulp Fiction* reveals how and why the low-budget business, largely under the guidance of Miramax, became increasingly associated with a certain type of cinema—what Jeff Dawson aptly calls a "cinema of cool."[1] While at this time such films as *Clerks* (1994), *From Dusk Till Dawn* (1996), *Pulp Fiction*, and *Swingers* (1996) regularly garnered press coverage, they were by no means the only films generating box office dollars or attention from distributors. But this "cinema of cool," under the auspices of Tarantino and fellow Miramax-based directors Robert Rodriguez and Kevin Smith, rapidly became what specialty companies invested most heavily in and what mainstream journalists focused on. A key consequence of this heightened attention on a certain strand of "American indie auteurs" was that critics, journalists, and industry executives began to conceptualize the low-budget film scene within ever-narrower terms. In what started to become a vicious cycle, by focusing on this component of niche-oriented cinema the press further marginalized discussions of other types of filmmakers, such as *The Piano*'s writer-director, Jane Campion, and other writer-directors, like Nicole Holofcener and Allison Anders. As the cinema of cool gained in popularity, the financial support directed toward certain types of American indies diminished. This is not to say that filmmakers outside the cinema of cool were unable to sustain careers, but they certainly found raising money, gaining distribution, attaining publicity, and procuring conglomerate support more challenging. This heightened focus on the cinema of cool, then, contributed to the increased marginalization of films that proved more challenging for specialty divisions to market.

While stories about a new wave of American indie auteurs provided strong press hooks and an easy means by which to differentiate low-budget films from effects-driven event films, such narratives misrepresented what was taking place during the 1990s. This chapter looks at how, from the time when *The Piano* premiered at Cannes in May 1993 to the time that *Pulp Fiction* went to the Oscars in March 1995, the practices and products of the specialty film business shifted. At the same time that *Pulp Fiction* reaffirmed the arrival of a new era of American indies and the dawn of Miramax's "golden age,"[2] *The Piano* more quietly and subtly began the process of reformulating the English-language coproduction. Together, these two films reinforced the financial promise of certain types of studio-based, niche-oriented cinema in the 1990s. A Disney-based Miramax, as one of the earliest, savviest, most aggressive, and wealthiest entrants in indie territory, was able to play a pivotal role in defining this developing terrain. *The Piano* would be the first major success for a post-Disney Miramax, and as such, it is worth starting with an investigation of this film's impact.

A (Marketing) Passion with No Limits: The Case of *The Piano*

The period films of Merchant-Ivory were never like this.

Felicity Coombs and Suzanne Gemmell, Piano Lessons, *1999*

In February 1993, Miramax acquired the North American theatrical rights to *The Piano*. When *Variety* looked back on the acquisition a year and a half later, it labeled the deal "perhaps the sale that most changed the marketplace."[3] From the perspective of the trade publication, this acquisition was so significant because Miramax ignored the scheduled screening time that had been set up for executives. Instead, Harvey Weinstein flew to Paris for a "pre-screening" of the film with Jean-Francois Fonlupt, the head of the company that held the film's rights, CiBy 2000.[4] This pre-emptive purchase only further heightened the competitive atmosphere developing between acquisitions executives at the numerous emerging specialty companies.

At the time that Miramax acquired *The Piano*'s domestic rights, the film had not yet screened publicly. Rather, it was being readied for its premiere at the May 1993 Cannes Film Festival. As it turned out, the film had a stellar showing at Cannes, sharing the festival's top prize, the Palme d'Or, with another Miramax title, Chen Kaige's Chinese epic *Farewell My Concubine*. In addition, *The Piano* star Holly Hunter took home the Best Actress award at the festival. The Cannes awards were just the first of many honors bestowed on *The Piano*. The film became one of the most highly feted films of the year. Jane Campion went on to win Best Original Screenplay honors from the Writers Guild of America, the New York Film Critics, the National Society of Film Critics, and the Los Angeles Film Critics. She also received Best Director honors from both the Los Angeles and New York Film Critics, surprising many who considered Steven Spielberg a lock for *Schindler's List*. In addition to the several awards received by Campion for her screenplay and direction, numerous accolades were also bestowed on actresses Holly Hunter and Anna Paquin, as well as cinematographer Stuart Dryburgh and composer Michael Nyman.

In many respects, *The Piano* conformed to international art-cinema traditions. A lush, visually compelling Victorian costume romance, the film played in part like a revisionist version of *Jane Eyre* and *Wuthering Heights* and in part like a Merchant Ivory–style period piece reformulated for the land down under.[5] Critics praised its "haunting" tone and "dazzling" visuals.[6] Miramax's distribution was fairly standard for an art house film: the company released it on a limited number of screens in November 1993 and then, as it received awards and as word of mouth grew, the company gradually expanded it to hundreds of screens in time for the 1994 Academy Awards.

Though on a superficial level *The Piano*'s content and Miramax's distribution tactics could be likened to such contemporary films as *Howard's End* (1992, Sony Pictures Classics) and *Much Ado About Nothing* (Samuel Goldwyn, 1993), a closer look indicates that the marketing of Campion's film was quite distinctive in a number of ways. It is true that Miramax employed a number of the tried-and-true distribution strategies that specialty companies had been using for years. Such practices helped build an awareness of the film with the core art house audience, perceived as the "upscale" and "mature" (i.e., baby boom–era) viewers.[7] But it is unlikely that this audience alone could have driven *The Piano* to the box office performance it achieved. By the time the film completed its theatrical run, it had grossed nearly $40 million in the United States alone.[8] In other words, millions of American viewers went to see an imported film about the struggle of a mute Englishwoman (Holly Hunter) to come to terms with her sexuality when she is forced via an arranged marriage to move into the wilds of New Zealand. A great deal of interest was shown in a film in which the primary way a lead character communicates is through her piano—a piano that her insensitive husband (Sam Neill) has traded to a neighbor (Harvey Keitel) who, in turn, pressures the woman to exchange sexual favors for the right to play the instrument.

The presence of a handful of name actors in Hunter, Keitel, and Neill did not necessarily ensure the film's salability. Though Hunter had been in some prominent roles in the late 1980s (e.g., *Raising Arizona*, 1987; *Broadcast News*, 1987), by the early 1990s she had been relegated largely to roles in television movies such as NBC's *Roe vs. Wade* (1989) and TNT's *Crazy in Love* (1992). Further, Miramax could not exploit her most notable asset—her "southern belle" persona—for, with the exception of voice-over narration at the beginning and end of the film, Hunter's character, Ada, did not speak a word of dialogue. As for Keitel, though he was amid a career resurrection thanks to supporting roles in films such as *Bugsy* (1991), *Thelma and Louise* (1991), and *Reservoir Dogs* (1992), he was best known for his "tough guy" image. This was a far cry from his part in *The Piano*; here he was playing against type, depicting a sensitive man who has "gone native" after years of living in the wilderness with the Maori. The New Zealander Sam Neill, meanwhile, recently had gained exposure with the summer 1993 box office phenomenon *Jurassic Park*. He hardly stood out in Spielberg's mega-blockbuster, however, especially when matched against its then state-of-the-art digital dinosaurs.

Despite the limited star power and the seeming lack of a "high concept," Miramax did what it did best—the company developed a number of creative marketing strategies that enabled the film to cross over from the art house to the multiplex. The film's theme of sexual discovery was foregrounded in promotional images; images of caressing, fondling, and illicit interactions were prevalent. *The Piano*'s tagline, "Passion has no limits," evoked the raw sexual, physical, and emotional energy on display in the film. Though sex may have been prominent in the promotional imagery, it was not the only lens through which the film was presented. *The Piano* was simultaneously depicted as a traditional Hollywood romance, the latest imported heritage drama, the newest iteration of a modernist art film, the product of a unique (female) cinematic vision, and an erotic romance. Indeed, as Dana Polan points out, all these traits were evident to varying degrees in the film itself: "Combining the uplifting traits of the prestige film (and in particular the sub-genre of the cos-

A Miramax Films Release © 1993. This publicity still helped underscore that *The Piano* (1993) was about far more than a musical instrument.

tume genre) with the enigmatic traits of European art cinema (ambiguous symbolism, unexplained character background, and so on) but balancing these with a mass-market accessibility (through name stars and a forward-moving narrative that ultimately was not all that ambiguous) and sensationalism (explicit sexuality, extreme violence), *The Piano* participates in a refashioning of the art film for the 1990s."[9]

What is particularly interesting about this multipronged marketing strategy—and, by extension, Polan's remarks—is that *The Piano* can be seen as representative of the status of art cinema in the 1990s. Further, the film indicates the transitional status of Miramax—and, by extension, niche-oriented cinema at large—in the pre- and post-Disney eras. On the one hand, its modernist sensibility,[10] sexually suggestive content, and promotion as high art from a visionary female auteur echoes the content and distribution of such late 1960s and early 1970s films as *Belle de Jour* (Allied Artists, 1967), *Last Tango in Paris* (1973, United Artists), and *Swept Away* (1974, Cinema V). On the other hand, the film's linear narrative, relatively upbeat resolution (Keitel and Hunter's characters fall in love and return to Britain), and promotion as "hip" via the circulation of images of sex and violence signal a shift into a new phase for specialty cinema.

The former traits were evident in a highly controversial brochure that Miramax sent out during Oscar season. The company assembled a multipage packet focusing predominantly on the innovative women involved in making the film. Titled "The Voices of the Nominees" (in an amusing play off the lead character's status as a mute), the text referred repeatedly to the groundbreaking nature of *The Piano*. The film should be celebrated, the ad seemed to suggest, because it was largely the product of the "creative achievements of women."[11] Beginning by noting that Campion was only the second woman in the sixty-six-year history of the Academy Awards to be nominated for Best Director, the advertisement proceeded to discuss how Miramax and CiBy 2000 perceived their promotional materials as "breaking with tradition" by offering "insight into the long, challenging journey from original idea."[12] Images of Hunter and Paquin were complemented by quotes from key talent involved, including producer Jan Chapman, editor Veronika Janet, and costume designer Janet Patterson. In addition, comments from such prominent critics as Roger Ebert, Michael Wilmington, Vincent Canby, and Kenneth Turan were included.

The advertisement was anything but subtle. Indeed, some critics attacked Miramax for its heavy-handed sales tactics. One producer labeled the promotion "pretentious."[13] Harvey Weinstein took a defensive posture in the press, claiming that Miramax spent only $250,000 on the campaign—a sum he maintained was far less than that spent by the major studios in their Oscar campaigns.[14] The reasons for such critiques seem twofold. First, to many critics it appeared unseemly and déclassé to be selling "art" in such a fashion. Art cinema, after all, was linked to high culture, the domain of the elite, yet here was Miramax using such discourses as a means of making a movie more popular with wider audiences. A second reason for such critiques can be tied to Miramax's new relationship with Disney. As was discussed in the prior chapter, there already had appeared much anxiety about the degree to which market imperatives and conglomerate mandates would "corrupt" independent cinema. Those looking at this aggressive selling of *The Piano* could find ample evidence to further fuel their fears.

On top of the use of what some perceived to be over-the-top promotional tactics, Miramax, with the help of Disney resources, was turning an art film into a media franchise. Campion's screenplay, released by Disney's Hyperion publishing arm, was the first Miramax product to be placed in print.[15] The initial run of 47,500 copies sold out; by 1995, Hyperion had sold more than 62,000 copies.[16] The success of the film also fueled soundtrack sales; Michael Nyman's score, distributed by Virgin Records, ultimately sold more than 700,000 copies worldwide and reached a number one ranking on both the classical and crossover charts in the United States.[17]

The Piano's tremendous success played a significant role in Miramax's decision to expand its presence in Australia and New Zealand. Previously, the company had invested much more heavily in European imports than Australian ones. Before *The Piano*, Miramax's only notable Australian import was Baz Luhrmann's first film, *Strictly Ballroom* (1992).[18] New Line's art house division, Fine Line, had a much more Australian-heavy slate in the early 1990s, releasing such pictures as *The Last Days of Chez Nous* (1991), *Proof* (1991), and one of Jane Campion's earlier films, *An Angel at My Table* (1991). Shortly after acquiring *The Piano*, however, Miramax made clear its plan to enhance its presence down under. The first post-Disney acquisition to be announced was *Sirens* (1993), another period film starring Sam Neill and dealing with sexual repression.[19] Soon after, Miramax added a second person to its Australia-based staff and signed a first-look deal with *The Piano*'s producer, Jan Chapman.[20]

At the time of this announcement, the company declared itself "to be the first U.S. distrib to start targeting Australia."[21] Miramax did in fact proceed to acquire a disproportionately large number of Australian and New Zealand titles throughout the mid-1990s. *Country Life* (1994),

Muriel's Wedding (1994), *Billy's Holiday* (1995), *Children of the Revolution* (1996), *Love Serenade* (1996), and *Cosi* (1996) were among the Australian-financed films released by Miramax following *The Piano's* success. In addition, the company also handled the New Zealand-financed features *Desperate Remedies* (1993) and *Heavenly Creatures* (1994). Meanwhile, the Gramercy-released *The Adventures of Priscilla, Queen of the Desert* (1994) and the Fine Line–released *Shine* (1996) became box office hits for their respective distributors.[22]

The Australian films distributed by Miramax—as well as those coming from other prominent specialty distributors of the time—generally fell into one of two camps. Either the films were period costume pieces like *The Piano* or they were contemporary comedies, often with a satirical twist and a playful take on traditional gender roles. Across this range of films, a dominant theme involved an exploration of—and challenge to—oppressive social and sexual mores. It is worth underscoring that there was a great deal of generic and thematic continuity between the Australian and UK productions released in the United States during this time. In fact, speaking of these films as specifically "Australian" or "British" in nature proves somewhat problematic, as many of them were international coproductions set in multiple countries, featuring talent from a variety of nations, and supported by grants from several different regions. *The Piano* itself could be seen as a product of either Europe or the English-speaking world as much as it could be identified as originating from either Australia or New Zealand. As indicated in the film's production notes, *The Piano* was a "French-financed, New Zealand–based, Australian production of a New Zealand story."[23] Meanwhile, the New Zealand–born, Australian-educated Campion described the film as ultimately a "European story"—albeit one that dealt in part with a group indigenous to New Zealand, the Maori.[24]

Addressing the complicated lineage of *The Piano*—and, by extension, many of the 1990s films often promoted as Australian—is not merely an academic endeavor. Rather, it calls attention to a number of issues pertinent to the specialty film world at large during the decade. A particular nation may have identified the film as its own based on its connections to key talent or its dominant role in providing funding. But it was in the commercial interest of the film to have identifiable affiliations with a number of different nations or regions. With funding from video companies having dried up substantially, and rights for all media (theatrical, cable, broadcast, video, etc.) increasingly being licensed as a package on a territory-by-territory basis, it was wise for any given low-budget film produced outside the United States to have connections to a number of different parts of the world. These connections came from setting the film in multiple countries, by integrating stylistic traits linked to European art cinema with classical Hollywood narrative and generic conventions, and by casting a combination of internationally established individuals with relatively young, up-and-coming stars from numerous parts of the world.[25]

The impact of these industrial factors on motion picture content could be interpreted as either a promising development, indicating the increasingly fluid and multidirectional nature of cultural flows, or a threat to the "purity" of cultural products, leading to the dilution of art in the interest of commerce. Polan, for one, perceived the development in largely negative terms. He observed that "Miramax, specifically, [became] a key player in a redefinition of the independent art film to one that maintains superficial traits of art cinema, while making it more palatable for wider global distribution and frequently allows crossover into a mass market."[26] He cites such late 1990s and early 2000s Miramax films as *Shakespeare in Love* (1998) and *Chocolat* (2000) as additional examples of this phenomenon.[27] Others have attached the label of "Europudding" to these art film–classical Hollywood–indie hybrids.[28] The perception of such critics was that these films lost their "authenticity" or their "distinction" as art when produced and distributed with larger audiences in mind.

As might be evident from the identification of films such as *Shakespeare in Love* and *Chocolat*, as the 1990s proceeded a shift occurred in both the content and budgets of such films. Miramax, in particular, moved from focusing on visually and thematically darker material to warmer, cheerier fare. As will be explored in greater length in chapter 7, the reasons behind this transition had a great deal to do with Miramax's heightened resources and the shifting status of the specialty film market. But it is worth noting here that the emergence of such films was not just a function of Miramax going soft or becoming less edgy later in the decade; a direct trajectory can be followed from *The Piano* through to films such as *The English Patient* (1996) and *Chocolat*. Regardless of the degree to which one takes Polan's view of these films, it is clear that a significant trend in the specialty film world during the 1990s involved the practice of making international coproductions but then identifying them in marketing discourses as being affiliated with a specific nation. Although scholars have observed this practice concerning big-budget event films, less attention has been paid to the impact of this trend on the low-budget arena.[29] Yet to attend to this occurrence in specialty cinema is important, as it serves to challenge key conceptions about both national product and independent cinema.

Even as art cinema continued to be reinvented, the transformation of American indies persisted as well. During the first half of the 1990s, a new generation of filmmakers such as Quentin Tarantino, Kevin Smith, and Robert Rodriguez generated extensive media coverage. Journalists and scholars typically identified this turn as the rise of the "commercial indie" and perceived it as a specifically American phenomenon, characterized by particular stylistic traits and thematic preoccupations. As both the previous chapter's discussion of *The Crying Game* and this chapter's exploration of *The Piano* indicate, however, it was not just a certain type of American indie film that grew in prominence during 1990s. It may have served the interests of specialty companies to increasingly focus their promotional energies—and, as the decade wore on, their resources—on this singular new phenomenon. And it may have provided a catchy angle for the press. Nonetheless, the rise of the commercial indie was part of a much larger story—the rise of the niche film and the coming of age of a new generation of talent on a *global* scale. Nowhere is this broader pattern more apparent than with the numerous individuals from Australia and New Zealand who emerged out of these mid-1990s specialty films. Among the actors to garner critical and press attention via their performances in films from Australia and New Zealand were Toni Collette (*Spotswood*, 1992; *Muriel's Wedding; Cosi*), Guy Pearce (*Priscilla, Queen of the Desert*), Russell Crowe (*Proof; Spotswood; The Sum of Us*, 1994), Anna Paquin (*The Piano*), Hugo Weaving (*Proof; Priscilla, Queen of the Desert*), Rachel Griffiths (*Muriel's Wedding; Cosi*), Geoffrey Rush (*Shine*), and Kate Winslet (*Heavenly Creatures*). As was the case with the American indie talent that emerged mid-decade, almost all these individuals moved back and forth between Hollywood event films and niche-oriented specialty films in the ensuing years.

There are some specific reasons why specialty distributors released numerous English-language imports into North American theaters during the 1990s. From the beginning of the decade, Australian cinema began its own renaissance of sorts, as increased funding from national and regional bodies was directed toward the arts.[30] Thus there were a growing number of films available for acquisition. In addition, English-language films had obvious linguistic and cultural advantages in the North American market over films from other nations, which played no small part in easing the marketing, distribution, and ultimate box office performance of English-language over non-English-language imports in general. But there were several instances of foreign-language imports that contained similar traits and proved equally viable at the U.S. box office. Not surprisingly, Miramax released many of these films, including *Like Water for Chocolate* (1992, $21.6 million U.S. box office), *Mediterraneo* (1992, $4.5 million), *Ciao, Profesore!* (1994, $1.1 million), *Il Postino* (1995, $20.6 million), and the *Three Colors* trilogy, *Red*, *White*, and *Blue* (1993–1994, cumulative box office $6.7 million).[31]

The presence of so many strong performers at the North American box office reinforces the point that the specialty market was more expansive during the mid-1990s than has been discussed. While the market for foreign-language films had relatively fixed parameters (as will be discussed in chapter 7), there were numerous English- and foreign-language imports launched theatrically in the United States. According to Harvey Weinstein, by consistently releasing films such as *The Piano*, Miramax was in effect "seeding the audience"—in other words, building an appreciation with new viewers for certain styles and a new generation of performers.[32] Jack Foley, executive vice president of distribution at Miramax, elaborated on this concept: "What Miramax has done over the years is to develop an audience, and it's certainly contributed to the mainstay patrons of art theatres. It's also been able to nurture and develop the tastes of audiences, both the graying audience . . . and the young kids coming up over the last decade."[33]

As addressed previously, through the early 1990s, the primary audience for art house films had been the baby boom generation. Specialty companies recognized the value of this demographic, especially since this group was now of an age where their children were growing up and they once again had more time and perhaps more disposable income. As *Variety* noted in 1994, "As the population grows older, developing product for the 50-plus demographic is not folly."[34] One study found that the "over-40 crowd" constituted 36 percent of moviegoers by 1995, an increase of more than 23 percent since 1990.[35] Notably, boomers not only went to see art house films, they also frequently bought the films' merchandise.[36] But the baby boom generation was not the only audience being "seeded," to use Weinstein's parlance. Rather, the audience that was increasingly being cultivated was the emerging Generation X—those individuals born from the mid-1960s to the early 1980s who, by mid-decade, were becoming a prominent consumer force and cultural entity in their own right. This generation, raised on video and cable, was perfectly matched for the ancillary-driven specialty companies. It would be with specialty product created by and for this generation that Miramax would make its next mark on the indie film world. While *The Piano* shows one major direction taken by English-language cinema in the mid-1990s, *Pulp Fiction* reveals the extent to which one film provided Miramax—and the indie scene at large—with a refreshed identity and enhanced audience base.

Reformulating the American Indie at Mid-Decade

> Where are all the hot young filmmakers who are supposed to be taking the business by storm? Why is Hollywood drawing on names from an earlier generation? The answer is rather disturbing: There is no "new wave." Not even a ripple.
>
> Peter Bart, Variety *editor in chief, 1992*

As noted at the end of chapter 2, Miramax's handling of the domestic theatrical release for *Reservoir Dogs* resulted in lukewarm box office returns. Despite the attention it received at festivals and from critics, American audiences were not receptive to the film during its theatrical release. Only once LIVE Entertainment released it on video did the movie begin to build a devoted fan base in the United States. Both Miramax and Tarantino learned a number of lessons from *Reservoir Dogs'* underperformance in U.S. theaters. First, both Miramax executives and Tarantino later said that the film should have been marketed like a commercial product rather than as a piece of art.[37] They recognized after the fact that the film would have been better served by a more aggressive promotional campaign. Second, Miramax acknowledged that the director should have been foregrounded more extensively in the film's marketing.[38] *Reservoir Dogs* did much better overseas than in the United States, and Tarantino believed this was largely due to the substantial number of interviews and touring he did there on behalf of the film.[39] Third, the afterlife of *Reservoir Dogs* in ancillary markets further reinforced the importance of holding on to as many rights as possible for a project. Miramax had done much of the legwork in promoting the film, only to have another company (the video rights holder) reap the financial benefits down the road. This latter point would be less of a problem in the Disney era, when Miramax had the resources to procure more rights to projects earlier in their development.

Something else that proved less of a problem in the post-Disney era was holding on to talent that Miramax had worked hard to develop. Harvey Weinstein observed that before the deal with Disney, "No matter how successful we were, we never could have the situations where we could do an overhead deal with a Jim Sheridan [director of *My Left Foot*, 1989] or have relationships with directors like Jane Campion, whose canvas can get bigger, or Neil Jordan, whose canvas got much bigger after 'The Crying Game.'"[40] Indeed, Sheridan went on to work again with Day-Lewis in Universal's *In the Name of the Father* (1993), and Jordan directed the starstudded *Interview with the Vampire* (1994) for Warner Bros. Meanwhile, Campion was preparing *The Portrait of a Lady* (1996) for the Universal-PolyGram specialty division, Gramercy.

As noted earlier, at first it looked like Miramax had lost Tarantino as well. Before the Weinsteins made their deal with Disney, Sony's TriStar division paid $900,000 for a package that involved Tarantino developing, writing, and directing his follow-up to *Reservoir Dogs, Pulp Fiction.*[41] The project stalled at TriStar, however, and in the summer of 1993 Miramax was able to pick up the rights to the film while it was in turnaround.[42] When Miramax acquired *Pulp Fiction* at the script stage, *Daily Variety* labeled it "one of the most aggressive deals by company co-chairmen Bob and Harvey Weinstein since selling the company to Walt Disney Co. in April."[43] The deal was indicative of a number of changes taking place at Miramax in the post-Disney era. Most notably, it marked Miramax's increasing emphasis on acquiring projects relatively early in their development. By doing so, the company not only would possess more rights to films, but also could have more control over their creative development and exploitation in ancillary markets. By no means did this indicate that Miramax was becoming less aggressive in the acquisitions market—far from it. But considering that acquisitions prices were rapidly escalating and that more specialty companies were investing earlier in the life cycle of projects, such a move could be seen at least partly as a defensive strategy.[44] The deal also suggested Miramax's heightened efforts to retain and develop its own talent, which would become an ever-more important goal of the company in the ensuing years. This talent, in turn, would do much to shape the style and subject matter of low-budget films in the 1990s and influence the journalistic and critical discourses about American indies. Of course, Tarantino was at the forefront of such changes, along with a number of other emerging Miramax-based filmmakers such as Robert Rodriguez and Kevin Smith.

Ultimately, *Pulp Fiction*, like *The Piano*, can be viewed as a significant bridge between the business strategies and content of Miramax in the pre- and post-Disney eras. Much like *sex, lies, and videotape* and *The Crying Game, Pulp Fiction* indicated the potential for niche films to reach "indie blockbuster" status. As with many of the Miramax films of yore, *Pulp Fiction* made its debut at the Cannes festival, where it generated much of its early buzz and took home the Palme d'Or.[45] And like Soderbergh's and Campion's Cannes darlings, Tarantino's film used the attention it gained on the Croisette to begin its publicity campaign, which culminated with the film surpassing the $100 million mark at the North American box office, a first for Miramax. With *Pulp Fiction*, Miramax also explored key relationships that it had forged before Disney entered the picture. Not only had the company worked with Tarantino before, but it had also worked with producer Lawrence Bender (*Reservoir Dogs*; *Fresh*, 1994). Bender would be involved in numerous Miramax and Dimension projects in the years to come, including *Four Rooms* (1995), the *From Dusk Till Dawn* series (1996–2000), *Good Will Hunting* (1997), *A Price Above Rubies* (1998), *Jackie Brown* (1997), and the *Kill Bill* films (2003, 2004).

Pulp Fiction also continued Miramax's long-standing tradition of courting controversy. The film's violence and seemingly amoral world-view became the subject of a great deal of debate, and it garnered much media attention when it was cited by presidential candidate and then-senator Bob Dole as an example of the ways that Hollywood films were "debasing the nation's culture."[46] The fact that *Pulp Fiction* was given as an example of a Hollywood film in Dole's speech is noteworthy in itself, and suggests the continually shifting status of independence by the mid-1990s. Debates about what did and did not constitute independence moved into high gear as many elements of the film—including its multimillion-dollar budget, long list of well-known actors, Disney backing, and Hollywood setting—all seemed to push the meaning of the term to its limit. Yet the film's fresh style and expansive influence on emerging low-budget filmmakers suggested that the label was not without some merit—a factor further reinforced when it received multiple Independent Spirit awards, including Best Feature, Best Director, and Best Screenplay. Meanwhile, *Pulp Fiction* was seen as ushering in a "new era of indie chic" when it received seven Academy Award nominations, including Best Picture, Best Original Screenplay, and Best Director.[47]

The marketing and distribution of the film were similarly "hybrid" in nature.[48] Miramax once again integrated exploitation and art house sales strategies, but this time they were accompanied by a studio-level publicity blitz. The film's sex and violence were targeted toward younger viewers, while its numerous awards and critical plaudits were directed at the traditional art house crowd. A savvy tagline—"You won't know the facts until you see the fiction"—carried echoes of *The Crying Game* and tried to convey to viewers that they had to see the film for themselves before they could pass judgment on it. Meanwhile, Tarantino was sent on tour for months on end to promote the film around the world. Tarantino was no 1960s-era auteur, talking to college students at the local art house. Rather, he was the ultimate 1990s-era pop auteur, giving lectures, appearing on talk shows, and talking to reporters at every turn.[49]

Meanwhile, in the days leading up to its release, advertisements for the film flooded the television airwaves. Miramax used Disney's money to make the kind of television ad buys that previously had been largely the domain of the Hollywood majors.[50] The saturation marketing strategy was accompanied by a wide release in which the film opened on 1,338 screens in October 1994.[51] This high-profile launch led *Pulp Fiction* to come in neck and neck with the other major opening release of the weekend, the Sylvester Stallone–Sharon Stone action film *The Specialist*.[52] Whereas *The Specialist* yielded only about $57 million domestically, *Pulp Fiction* ultimately took in $107 million in the United States.[53] The worldwide box office was equally impressive, with the film earning more than $100 million outside North America.[54] Then there was its stellar video release. Disney's Buena Vista Home Video division benefited from the sustained hype surrounding *Pulp Fiction* when it launched the film on video in the summer of 1995. *Pulp Fiction* set a new sales record for a video priced for the rental market, generating 715,000 retail orders in the United States alone.[55] Buena Vista estimated that its portion of the sales revenue would amount to about $50 million—a sum only slightly less than what Disney had paid for Miramax two years prior.[56]

Both journalists and critics widely agreed that *Pulp Fiction* was nothing less than a cultural and industrial phenomenon. Though the *Los Angeles Times* critic Kenneth Turan was not a big supporter of the film, he acknowledged its import, noting, "From the moment it hit the screen at Cannes, even before it was awarded that festival's celebrated Palme d'Or, 'Pulp Fiction' and its writer-director Quentin Tarantino have been given the big-type, Second Coming treatment, drenching them in the kind of media awe and appreciation reserved for paradigms of cinematic accomplishment."[57] Lawrence Lerman of *Variety*, meanwhile, argued that "Miramax's *Pulp Fiction* [is] leading the latest charge against the art-house confines that once defined the independents—redefining audience demographics and market potential along the way."[58]

The latter quotation suggests why *Pulp Fiction* was ultimately so notable for both low-budget cinema and contemporary Hollywood at large. The film's success signaled a significant aesthetic, industrial, and cultural shift for American indies. It moved specialty cinema further away from the art house as an exhibition site and as an aesthetic. It represented the coming of age of a new generation of both filmmakers and filmgoers. It readily blended high and low culture, classical Hollywood genres and 1950s-era AIP teenpics, Japanese *yakuza* films and blaxploitation cinema, Stanley Kubrick and Sergio Leone.[59] Of course, there had been stylistic and thematic precedents, many of which, including *El mariachi* (1992) and *Laws of Gravity* (1992), were part of the "ultra-low-budget" moment that independent cinema experienced during the 1992–1993 period.[60]

Nonetheless, *Pulp Fiction* marked a new moment for American indies in terms of budget, style, cultural affiliations, and institutional relationships. Tarantino's film was very much the product of a 1990s-era studio subsidiary as opposed to a 1980s-era independent. Even more to the point, it was a marker of where Miramax had been and an indication of where the company was going in terms of the type of talent it cultivated and the styles of film that it prioritized in production and marketing. Tarantino, along with Robert Rodriguez, Kevin Smith, Paul Thomas Anderson, and Bryan Singer, signaled a dramatic shift in American indie film.

From the Cinema of Quality to the Cinema of Cool

In general, the 1980s-era independents could be labeled as part of a "cinema of quality." Films in this vein include *Return of the Secaucus 7* (1980), *Smithereens* (1982), *Chan Is Missing* (1982), *Stranger Than Paradise* (1984), *She's Gotta Have It* (1986), and *Parting Glances* (1987). The budgets for these films typically ranged from approximately $100,000 to $1 million at most. While some of this money came from presales by independents and mini-majors, much of their financial support came from a number of public and private organizations, including the PBS American Playhouse, the Black Filmmakers Foundation, and the Independent Feature Project (all of which were launched in the late 1970s). Many 1980s independents both represented and targeted particular cultural groups that historically had been marginalized in mainstream cinema, such as African Americans, women, and gays and lesbians. The vast majority of these "cinema of quality" filmmakers were based out of New York and, to a lesser extent, San Francisco and Los Angeles. Many of these individuals—including Spike Lee, Susan Seidelman, Jim Jarmusch, and Tom DiCillo—had been students at either NYU or Columbia.[61] Several were on the fringes of the baby boom generation; many went through their teen years toward the end of the U.S. involvement in Vietnam and were college students when punk was moving from the underground into the mainstream. Several had ties to the New York City underground, which itself was becoming increasingly commercial by the early 1980s. They came of age pre-video, when revival movie houses, midnight movies, and art house cinemas still had a strong presence in the United States. Their influences included the avant-garde, punk, the European new waves, and the New American Cinema.

As diverse as the above films and filmmakers are, many of their 1980s-era films had a number of thematic and stylistic similarities. Their movies often followed in the tradition of John Cassavetes in terms of being very "personal"—intimate dramas that focused on a small number of middle-class characters. The films were character driven and episodic in nature. Rarely did they conform to standard generic conventions—in fact, traditional genres seemed largely absent. The emphasis was on presenting "slices of life" rather than moments of conflict or tension. In terms of style, the films were regularly characterized by minimalism, long takes, limited editing, and a gritty look. The humor was typically understated and subtle.

These films benefited from awards at festivals and critical acclaim. They were usually distributed via platform release and rarely played on more than a few hundred screens. The target audience consisted of traditional art house viewers—people of the same generation as the filmmakers. In other words, their films had a clear niche appeal. Such movies might at best earn a few million dollars at the box office. The label of "cinema of quality" is useful, for it reflects the discourses that circulated about most of these films. These releases were often seen by critics as a welcome relief from the wave of action films and broad comedies that dominated multiplexes at the time, such as the *Indiana Jones* trilogy (1981–1989), the *Beverly Hills Cop* series (1984–1994), the *Ghostbusters* films (1984, 1989), and the *Three Men and a Baby* films (1987, 1990).

Notably, films possessing many of these stylistic traits continued to be made after the 1980s. Examples of 1990s-era "cinema of quality" films include *Metropolitan* (1990), *The Wedding Banquet* (1993), *Smoke* (1995), and *Big Night* (1996). *sex, lies, and videotape* is an interesting case in that it has traits linking it to both the "cinema of quality" and the later "cinema of cool." Stylistically its ties to the cinema of quality are stronger; however, as discussed in chapter 2, Miramax marketed it in a manner more akin to later films of the cinema of cool.

Precursors to the cinema of cool include Joel and Ethan Coen's *Blood Simple* (1984) and Gus Van Sant's *Drugstore Cowboy* (1989). In the early 1990s, a couple different strands of American independent cinema showed many of the traits that would come to characterize the cinema of cool. For example, the genre-blending and hyper-stylization of the New Queer Cinema later came to characterize many 1990s-era indies.[62] But the aggressive politics that motivated New Queer Cinema, and were evident in such films as *Poison* (1991) and *The Living End* (1992), had faded by the time studio-based indie divisions became prominent mid-decade.[63] Also, many of the "guerrilla productions" of the early 1990s—projects such as *Laws of Gravity* and *The Living End*, which were produced on budgets of a few thousand dollars—may have been stylistically similar to the emerging cinema of cool, but they lacked its increasingly polished look and name talent. The micro-budget phenomenon was briefly favored by studio divisions and prominent indie companies; indeed, it was with such films that the prominent Miramax-based figures Robert Rodriguez (with *El mariachi*, distributed by Columbia Pictures) and Kevin Smith (with *Clerks*, Miramax) got their start. But its novelty and utility as a marketing angle had worn off by the mid-1990s and the budgets for this strand of American indies rose accordingly, regularly reaching several millions of dollars.

Though presales frequently helped fund 1990s-era indies, typically the rights that were presold were select foreign territories, rather than the domestic video rights that had driven the market in the 1980s. By the 1990s, North American video rights were usually packaged with domestic theatrical distribution rights. Increasingly, studio subsidiaries such as Miramax tried—and had the deep pockets to be able to—retain as many rights as possible. As the rights scenario shifted, the economic model for many 1990s-era indies such as *Pulp Fiction* changed as well. Increasingly these indies operated in a fashion akin to event films, with the theatrical release becoming the means by which to launch the indie brand. Rights holders could thereby benefit more fully from the profits derived from ancillary markets.[64] Meanwhile, less and less money came from foundations and grant-giving organizations as the 1990s continued; such entities became increasingly financially strapped and unable to support the films' rapidly rising budgets.

The sources of funding and types of budgets were not the only things different about the 1990s-era indies. The filmmakers were of a different breed as well. Though many still came out of New York and Los Angeles, several filmmakers had ties to other regions of the United States. For example, Kevin Smith was closely identified with the suburban Red Bank, New Jersey, while Robert Rodriguez was linked to Austin, Texas. Even more important than where they were from was the generation with which they were affiliated. This "new wave" of "hot young filmmakers"—a group that, as the epigraph to this section shows, *Variety* editor in chief Peter Bart did not foresee as late as 1992—consisted largely of Gen Xers.[65] Accordingly, their films often displayed the cynicism and disillusionment generally linked to this generation.

Whereas the 1980s independents learned in the classroom, the

A Miramax Films Release © 1994. Photo credit: Linda R. Chen. Miramax featured the "cinema of cool" director Quentin Tarantino prominently in its promotion of *Pulp Fiction*.

A Miramax Films Release © 1996. Its lead characters, played by Jon Favreau and Vince Vaughn, may have tried a little too hard to be hip; nonetheless, *Swingers* (1996) stands as an exemplar of the "cinema of cool."

1990s indies were the first true "video generation" of filmmakers—a fact many of them enthusiastically publicized. Several key 1990s-era indie filmmakers did not have traditional film school educations; rather, they learned about film history by visiting the local multiplex and renting films at the nearest video store. Tarantino, of course, worked for years as a clerk at a video store alongside his *Pulp Fiction* cowriter Roger Avary.[66] Rodriguez learned to shoot and edit with a home video camera.[67] Many of them bragged that they dropped out of film school; for instance, Smith discussed how he quit two different schools, opting to use the money targeted for his education to make *Clerks* instead.[68]

The media that influenced this generation of filmmakers were quite distinct from those that shaped the 1980s-era independents. Many professed a love for all things pop culture—from comic books and pulp novels to the films of Spielberg and Lucas. Though they may have been knowledgeable about such canonical directors as Kubrick and Welles, their tastes were tied to many low-culture products as well, including studio-era crime films, 1950s-era rock-and-roll teenpics, 1960s drug films, 1970s-era kung fu movies, and so on. Their films readily incorporated these influences, moving from a visual homage to 1970s disco to a verbal allusion to Jayne Mansfield (in the case of *Pulp Fiction*, for instance). The films often were characterized by intertextuality and self-reflexivity as well as a high degree of stylization, replete with frenetic editing and memorable pop soundtracks.

While these 1990s indies were frequently as character/dialogue–driven as their 1980s predecessors, the kinds of characters and conversations found within them were quite different. They routinely featured criminals—or, at least, individuals of questionable morals. The characters liked to shoot people (*Pulp Fiction*), talk about sex (*Clerks*), steal (*The Usual Suspects*, 1995) or go clubbing (*Swingers*). Visions of the underworld and the inner city dominated; one could expect to see many a seedy club, jail cell, run-down bar, and overcrowded apartment in these films. The upwardly mobile middle-class professionals in their thirties of *Return of the Secaucus 7* or even *sex, lies, and videotape* gave way to wannabe gangsters and semi-employed twentysomethings struggling to make ends meet.

Both narrative structure and genre also mutated in 1990s-era indies. With 1980s independents, the movies might cut in and out of key emotional moments in multiple characters' lives, but for the most part the narratives were linear. The 1990s indies, however, were often constructed like games (e.g., *The Usual Suspects*; *Lost Highway*, 1997), and viewers were challenged to assemble coherent story lines for multiple characters out of the various scenes. At the same time, the 1980s films' absence of genre gave way to the reworking of multiple genres, often simultaneously. *From Dusk Till Dawn* shifted abruptly at its midway point from being a criminals-on-the-run film to a vampire tale; *Things to Do in Denver When You're Dead* (1995) reworked the 1950 noir *D.O.A.*

While critics showered many of the 1980s independents with unqualified praise, responses to these 1990s indies were much more mixed. The critical reaction to *Pulp Fiction* is telling: though the film was celebrated in some quarters for its innovative style and engaging dialogue, it was far from universally liked. The journalist Ian Penman echoed the response of many when noting that "the problem with Quentin is that there seems to be no sensible middle-ground: people either rave relentlessly and uncritically on about his gory glory or (like me) just Don't Get It."[69] In describing the frequently extreme responses to *Pulp Fiction*, Polan writes, "The film seems to have served as a rallying point for a heavily emotionally invested taste culture that had to celebrate the emergence of a new cool voice."[70]

The presence of a "distinct taste culture" cannot be emphasized enough. The 1990s-era indies often generated their strongest support from very different groups than did the 1980s-era independents. The movies appealed primarily to an audience of teenage boys and twentysomething men. In other words, just like the 1980s-era films, the audience consisted of people whose sensibilities and cultural referents were similar to the individuals who made them. The films just happened to appeal to a different set of people in many cases. This helps explain the widely divergent responses between critics and audiences to many of these movies. It also explains why the marketing and distribution strategies for these movies differed from those for the 1980s independents. Increasingly these films were launched in multiplexes via wide releases, and thus they were more dependent on opening weekend results and prerelease buzz than on critical accolades and slowly growing word of mouth. Yet just because specialty companies used a wide release strategy did not mean that they replicated the way the major studios prepared for their event film launches. Specialty marketers placed a much greater emphasis on niche-oriented ad buys to get viewers into theaters. The 1990s-era indie companies regularly promoted their films through locally oriented alternative weekly newspapers along with the rapidly growing range of cable channels suited to a specific film's demographic profile.[71]

In addition, excitement for the films was cultivated among the key demographics of teenage boys and twentysomething men by establishing relationships with them over the Internet. Kevin Smith was a crucial figure here, being one of the first filmmakers to develop a strong following on the web. From early in his career, Smith gave regular updates as to his activities on his website, http://www.viewaskew.com/. His web presence intersected nicely with his key followers, a group that consisted largely of fan boys who loved "*Star Wars*, comic books, and raunchy humor."[72] This same group frequented Harry Knowles's website, http://www.aintitcool. com/, which by the mid-1990s had gained a prominent cult following among young men. These demographic groups also became significant consumers of the films' merchandise, which included soundtracks, script reprints, and posters.

While there was a notable core audience for the 1990s-era indies, many of these films crossed over to other demographic groups in a way that the 1980s-era independents never had. While the films may have been sold to Gen Xers based on their "hipness" and "edginess," they frequently appealed to wider audiences as well—ranging from baby boomers to the "urban" (i.e., African American) audience by virtue of such elements as festival exposure, controversy, and critical support.[73] Also a factor in the appeal of these films was their relative newness, especially in contrast to the event films that had long since become the primary focus for the studios. The status of these films—and their filmmakers—as fresh and distinctive helped fuel the media attention they generated.

It is no coincidence that the vast majority of the 1990s indies came from one company: Miramax. In the wake of *Pulp Fiction* came such "cinema of cool" films from Miramax as *Clerks, Things to Do in Denver When You're Dead, Four Rooms, Swingers, Chasing Amy* (1997), *Cop Land* (1997), *The House of Yes* (1997), *Jackie Brown, 54* (1998), and *Rounders* (1998). This is not to say that other companies did not jump on the bandwagon. Among such films coming from other specialty companies were *Killing Zoe* (October, 1994), *The Usual Suspects* (Gramercy), *Feeling Minnesota* (Fine Line, 1996), *Bound* (Gramercy, 1996), *Boogie Nights* (New Line, 1997), and *Clay Pigeons* (Gramercy, 1998). As the years passed, this strand of filmmaking was emulated overseas as well. Nowhere was Tarantino and company's influence more evident than in Britain, where such films as *Trainspotting* (1996), *B. Monkey* (1998), and *Lock, Stock and Two Smoking Barrels* (1998) reconfigured the "cinema of cool" within the British context.

Cumulatively, the prominence of this strand of cinema by mid-decade reinforced that a changing of the guard—in terms of both talent and style—was underway. The stylistic distinctiveness and the rapid emergence of dozens of new faces led many in the press to make comparisons between the late 1960s–early 1970s New American Cinema and the

1990s cinema of cool. But much as there were substantive differences between the 1980s independents and the 1990s indies, so, too, were there major textual and industrial variations between the New American Cinema and the 1990s American indies. Both the influences on the 1990s-era filmmakers and the means by which they learned their craft came out of a specific social and cultural moment. Further, the business the 1990s-era indies entered into—and, in the following years, rose to prominence in—was substantially different from the business out of which filmmakers such as Martin Scorsese, Brian De Palma, and Hal Ashby emerged. Dwelling too much on the variations or distinctions of one strand over the other becomes difficult given the very different conditions within which each group of films was produced and distributed. The next section expands on several of the industrial reasons why Miramax became a primary site for this highly commercial type of indie during the mid-1990s.

A "Golden Age" for Miramax and Indie Film

> The change reflects shifting fortunes in the indie world, with the market for direct-to-video exploitation pix declining and interest in the more upscale, niche films on the rise. In fact, the arthouse crowd has essentially co-opted financing techniques honed by their commercial brethren.

Variety, *February 1994*

Miramax's ability to dominate the specialty scene by the mid-1990s had as much to do with specific business strategies employed by the company vis-à-vis the rest of the industry as it had to do with the kinds of films it released. At first glance, it might appear that the influx of Disney money facilitated these strategies. Yet Miramax took part in—or at least wanted to take part in—many of these activities even before its deal with Disney. Thus it is more accurate to say that Disney money helped Miramax accelerate or heighten certain practices, such as aggressive deal making and marketing, in which it already was engaged. As early as January 1990, Harvey Weinstein declared that such behavior simply reflected his "passion for movies."[74] Similarly, in early 1994 Arnold Rifkin, senior vice president of the talent agency William Morris, noted that "Miramax has always been aggressive to the point where you either yield or change your address and phone number, and I think the injection of Disney has only enhanced this tenacity."[75]

Sony Pictures Classics' copresident Michael Barker commented on

Miramax's practice of purchasing anything that showed the remotest sign of commercial viability by saying that "Miramax has always been a volume buyer."[76] Miramax's tendency to buy up everything in sight was affirmed by *Daily Variety*, which noted in May 1993 that the company was sitting on a "stockpile of upcoming movies accumulated through its voracious appetite."[77] In the ensuing years, Miramax became notorious for acquiring films and keeping them sitting on its shelves for months and months. Yet this, too, was standard practice long before the Disney buyout. The difference in the post-Disney era was that Miramax paid more and bought more movies, thereby helping to drive up prices in the acquisitions business and contributing to the aforementioned product shortage. As Fine Line's Ira Deutchman noted, "(The Disney-era) Miramax has definitely affected the marketplace. . . . People are buying films earlier and earlier, and paying more and more."[78] *Variety* reported that domestic rights for films that might have sold for $1 million in 1993 were selling for closer to $3 million on average by mid-1994.[79] One of the most notorious stories involved the acquisition of North American rights to the British thriller *Shallow Grave* (1995). Gramercy reportedly acquired the rights to the film sight unseen based "solely on the recommendation of an acquisition consultant, because Miramax was circling for the kill and there was no time to arrange a screening."[80]

Should Miramax overpay for rights—as it did, for example, when it advanced nearly $4 million for the period romance *Victory* (1995)—there was no guarantee the movie would ever be taken off the shelf and placed in theaters.[81] Even when the company paid top dollar for a film, it might hold on to the project indefinitely. When and how Miramax chose to distribute a film depended on a number of factors, including how it played at festivals, how audiences responded to it during test screenings, how it fit into the company's release schedule, and the degree to which top executives supported it. Should a film be fortunate enough to find a place on Miramax's schedule, it still might only get a perfunctory release at best. The company became known for engaging in what *Variety* labeled a "spray and pray" strategy.[82] In other words, Miramax placed a movie in the theaters, and if it generated favorable media coverage, support from awards organizations, or immediate audience interest, executives would then continue to work hard on its behalf. If it did not, then they rushed it to video—or buried it. One side effect of these strategies was that Miramax endeared itself to those individuals whose films they were able to launch successfully in the marketplace. At the same time, the company infuriated those whose projects either withered and died on the shelf or received only a cursory (often contractually mandated) theatrical release.

People such as Quentin Tarantino, Robert Rodriguez, and Kevin Smith increasingly benefited as a result; other filmmakers, such as Bernardo Bertolucci (*Little Buddha*, 1994), Allison Anders ("The Missing Ingredient" segment of *Four Rooms*), and Nicole Holofcener (*Walking and Talking*, 1996), did not. This had the effect of further structuring the indie world along certain lines—lines that, as the 1990s wore on, increasingly favored the highly masculine and ultraviolent cinema of cool.[83]

Indeed, cinema of cool filmmakers such as Tarantino, Rodriguez, and Smith quickly became part of Miramax's growing stable of talent. One of the most notable ways that Miramax used Disney's money was in making long-term deals with such individuals. As noted above, Harvey Weinstein cited the inability to hold on to talent as a key reason he pursued a corporate parent. Miramax made good on its promise to build strong talent relations post-Disney by rapidly signing numerous agreements with directors, producers, and actors. One of the first such deals came with the producer Cary Woods, who worked on such Miramax releases as *Things to Do in Denver When You're Dead, Citizen Ruth* (1996), *Beautiful Girls* (1996), *Swingers*, and *Cop Land*, along with the Dimension-released *Scream* (1996).[84] Woods also produced *Kids* (1995), a film that turned out to be highly contentious (as will be discussed in the next chapter).

In 1994, Miramax signed Tarantino to a production deal; Rodriguez followed in 1995.[85] In addition, Tarantino and producing partner Lawrence Bender launched the Rolling Thunder specialty label, whose mission was to acquire films that, as Tarantino put it, were "a kick in the balls."[86] This translated primarily into kung fu and action films from past and present, such as *Chungking Express* (1995) and *Switchblade Sisters* (originally released in 1975, rereleased in 1996). Rolling Thunder was one of several labels initiated by Miramax in the mid-1990s. In addition, the Weinsteins briefly tried out Miramax Family Films. Among the releases from this short-lived venture were the fantasy-adventure *Into the West* (1993), the talking-pig film *Gordy* (1995), and the animated *Arabian Knight* (1995). Citing too much overlap with Disney product, this division was quickly phased out. Similarly, Miramax Zoë was unveiled in 1994, designed to coproduce French films and increase the distribution of such films in the United States.[87] It began operations with the rerelease of Luis Buñuel's *Belle de Jour* (originally released in 1967, rereleased as *Martin Scorsese Presents Belle de Jour* in 1995). Subsequent Zoë titles included *French Twist* (1996) and *Artemisia* (1997). Zoë released films sporadically throughout the 1990s and never reached the levels promised in early press releases.

One division that quickly succeeded far beyond the Weinsteins' expectations was genre label Dimension. As noted in chapter 2, Miramax launched Dimension in 1992, well before Disney appeared on the scene. The impact of Disney money on Dimension could first be seen with its release of the futuristic prison movie *Fortress* (1993). This was the first in a series of efforts by Dimension to turn the actor Christopher Lambert into a superstar. Lambert already had a strong following due to his appearance in the *Highlander* series (which Dimension took over with its third installment in 1994). But the company remained committed to elevating his profile further, and *Fortress* received a 1,200-print release on Labor Day weekend in 1993.[88] Dimension previously had planned to give the film an 800-screen launch, but the new resources provided by Disney enabled it to pursue a much wider theatrical release.[89] The film's box office receipts were modest; it ultimately earned little more than $6 million. This did not stop Dimension from working with Lambert again. Among later Lambert films released by Dimension were *Gunmen* (1994), *The Road Killers* (1994), *Adrenalin: Fear the Rush* (1996), and *Beowulf* (2000). Dimension's involvement with Lambert is notable for two reasons. First, it indicates the extent to which this division, like Miramax proper, attempted to cultivate strong, consistent relationships with key talent from its earliest years in operation. Second, it reinforces the company's repeated efforts to develop viable franchises that could be exploited via sequels and other ancillary revenue streams.[90] Dimension would repeatedly realize both objectives in the ensuing years. As will be explored at length in the next chapter, however, the kinds of films favored by Dimension began to shift from the straight-to-video variety to a more "elevated" brand of genre film.

A notable change for Dimension came in 1994, with its release of the dark action film *The Crow*. Dimension obtained domestic distribution rights for *The Crow* toward the end of the film's production process. Paramount was the film's original distributor. Following star Brandon Lee's on-set death, however, Paramount decided not to distribute the film.[91] For Dimension, the potential financial benefits resulting from the film's increased exposure outweighed any possible fallout from negative publicity. Dimension invested more than $12 million on prints and advertising for *The Crow* and released it on 1,500 screens in May 1994.[92] The risk paid off, as *The Crow's* $16 million opening weekend made it the biggest release yet for Miramax.[93] By the end of its run, the film took in more than $50 million at the North American box office. *The Crow* was significant not only for the revenue it generated but also because, by virtue of its budget and production values, it foreshadowed the direction that genre films would take later in the decade. *The Crow* signaled the arrival of what Miramax's Mark Gill labeled as the "midlevel" genre film.[94] Such films, whose budgets ranged from $10 to $15 million, looked and sounded better than the straight-to-video genre pictures but lacked the extensive special effects or well-known names linked to big-budget studio event films. Such traits made these films appropriate for niche audiences, though there was always the hope that they could cross over to appeal to multiple demographics in a manner akin to *sex, lies, and videotape* and *Pulp Fiction*.

As this discussion indicates, Miramax was expanding in a number of ways from the spring of 1993 to the spring of 1995. From acquisitions to in-house productions, talent deals to the creation of new divisions, the company was becoming the dominant presence in the specialty business. Staff size grew accordingly; by February 1995, the company had gone from a few dozen employees to 160.[95] Miramax began to hire outside the ranks of the independent world as well. Most notable was the hiring of the Columbia Pictures marketing executives Mark Gill and Marcy Granata.[96] As its staff grew, so did the company's reputation for being a hostile work environment, due in no small part to Harvey's notorious outbursts. Again, this reputation had been with Miramax for years; for instance, in March 1993, the *Los Angeles Times* reported the existence of a former Miramax employee support group called "Mir-Anon."[97] In further bad press, by mid-decade a limited number of reports circulated about Miramax's penchant for shelving and reediting films.[98]

Despite the occasional "investigative" report, the vast majority of articles about the company during this time made it look like the savior of cinema and culture. The press almost uniformly wrote glowing pieces about Miramax. In these articles, the great Weinstein men—and particularly Harvey—were the focal points. Indeed, Miramax repeatedly proved itself as skillful at managing the media coverage about itself as it was about its films. Readers were regularly told about Harvey's "passion" and good "instincts"; about how the Weinsteins were contemporary Hollywood's lone "moguls" in the mode of Thalberg and Selznick; and about how Miramax was the last vestige for art and creativity in a world of cookie-cutter products.[99] A piece in *Variety* is representative of the general tenor of the articles about Miramax during this time:

> While Disney and Universal are locking up the services of superstars such as Sean Connery and Sylvester Stallone, Miramax is establishing a stable of cutting-edge contract players that could transform the niche pic purveyor into the arthouse version of a Hollywood Golden

Age studio. By bringing critically acclaimed actors and directors into Miramax—often with non-exclusive, mid-range deals that include an office and a development exec—Miramax co-chairmen Bob and Harvey Weinstein are willing to gamble hundreds of thousands of dollars on the prospect of creating a loyal cadre of talent who will exchange ideas and generate such projects as *Blue in the Face* [1995] through cross-pollination.[100]

This was indeed a "golden age" for Miramax—not only in terms of the kinds of films it was releasing and filmmakers it was striking deals with, but also with regard to the public image it sustained. Miramax was effectively constructing its own mythology—promoting its successes, obscuring its failures, deflecting from its less "artistic" endeavors like Dimension Films. Newspapers and magazines across the country, in turn, repeated this mythology. Though discussions about Disney's impact on the company often arose, they were easily redirected during this time, as the Weinsteins stressed their autonomy from their corporate owner and emphasized how the benefits of the marriage greatly outweighed its costs. Sure, there were the occasional clashes with the MPAA, but these difficulties were easily resolved. The company sold the 1994 Martin Lawrence stand-up concert film *You So Crazy* to Goldwyn when it received the NC-17 rating.[101] In contrast, it released *Clerks* with an R rating after the MPAA reversed its NC-17 upon appeal (with Alan Dershowitz once again providing representation).[102] The potential problems with the Miramax-Disney marriage could be glossed over—at least for now. As for the impact that the September 1994 departure of Jeffrey Katzenberg from Disney would have on Miramax's relationship with its parent company—well, again, it was too soon to say.[103]

This was a golden age for Miramax for another reason: the company's aforementioned business strategies nicely intersected with an industrial climate that gave it a number of short-term advantages over its competitors. As noted above, Miramax was by no means the only company releasing either American indies along the lines of *Pulp Fiction* or specialty films such as *The Piano*. But it was in a unique position in the specialty film world at this moment. October remained underfinanced until Universal Pictures acquired it in 1997; Samuel Goldwyn was in a financial crisis that was forcing it to seek a buyer. Sony Pictures Classics continued to operate like a 1980s-era classics division, focusing on more traditional art house fare than its specialty siblings and adhering to relatively low-cost acquisitions and limited, platform-style release strategies. New Line, meanwhile, was in the process of shifting its emphasis to big-budget event films in the wake of its purchase by Turner Broadcasting in August 1993. If Freddy Krueger and toxic turtles were the symbols of the New Line of days gone by, then Jim Carrey and David Fincher were the symbols for the emerging direction of the company in the 1990s. A key turning point for New Line came in 1994, with the company's release of *The Mask* in July followed by *Dumb and Dumber* in December.[104] The former film generated $119 million in North American theatrical grosses, while the latter yielded $127 million.[105] Then, in late September 1995, only weeks after Time Warner had announced its purchase of Turner Broadcasting System (and with it, New Line), David Fincher's thriller *Se7en* came out and proceeded to earn $101 million at the box office. While none of these films reached the heights of New Line's top earner (the first *Ninja Turtles* film, which grossed $135 million in 1990), they did take the second, third, and fourth positions.[106] At the same time, Fine Line kept shifting strategies due to management turnover. For a time, then, the main competitor to Miramax was Gramercy.

It is easy to forget how prominent Gramercy once was, especially since the company was dismantled so long ago. For a brief moment in the mid-1990s, however, Gramercy's touch seemed every bit as golden as Miramax's. Gramercy was founded in 1992 as a joint venture between Universal and PolyGram. From the start, the company declared that it was "set up to market and distribute films that required specialized marketing but are not art house fare."[107] Russell Schwartz, previously executive vice president of Miramax, assumed leadership at the new company. During his tenure at Miramax, Schwartz had been involved in several of its most prominent marketing campaigns, including *My Left Foot, Cinema Paradiso* (1990), and *The Grifters* (1990).[108] Clearly Gramercy was taking more than one page out of Miramax's playbook in hiring a key Miramax executive to be in charge and declaring that its mission was to cultivate "specialized," as opposed to art house, content. Gramercy planned to distribute about a dozen films per year, each with budgets ranging from $10 million to $12 million.[109] The goal was to release its most promising films on about one thousand screens, all the while limiting marketing expenditures as much as possible.[110] The Brad Pitt–Juliette Lewis crime thriller *Kalifornia* (1993) was cited early on as an example of the type of film that Gramercy wanted to focus on.

Both Universal and PolyGram planned to funnel some of their films through Gramercy; in addition, the subsidiary intended to acquire and produce its own films. Although initially some accused Gramercy of being a "dumping ground" for Universal, it soon became clear that the venture mattered much more to PolyGram.[111] Gramercy represented part of PolyGram's multipronged effort to break into Hollywood. At this time, PolyGram was 75 percent owned by the Dutch company Philips NV and generated 70 percent of its revenues from its music division.[112] However, following its success releasing films to the European market, PolyGram began investing in a number of different motion picture production and distribution entities.[113] Throughout the late 1980s and early 1990s, Poly-Gram built up its media investments; among the companies in which it had an interest were Working Title, Propaganda, and A&M Films.[114] Gramercy represented the next step in PolyGram's pursuit of what CEO Alain Levy envisioned as a "broadly based, multicultural entertainment business."[115]

Thus, despite the occasional allegations that Gramercy was a Universal dumping ground, in fact this new indie division seemed blessed from the outset. The company's first release, *Posse* (1993), a "black Western" directed by and starring Mario Van Peebles, earned $18 million in North American theaters.[116] Other early releases included Steven Soderbergh's first non-Miramax film, *King of the Hill* (1993), Richard Linklater's follow-up to *Slacker* (1991), *Dazed and Confused* (1993), and the crime drama *Romeo Is Bleeding* (1993). Although the box office results for its first full year in operations were mixed, the company's status as a major player was confirmed in its second full year. Among its hits in 1994 were *Shallow Grave*, *Priscilla, Queen of the Desert*, and *Jason's Lyric*. The company also had its first indie blockbuster in 1994 with *Four Weddings and a Funeral*—a $7.5 million romantic comedy produced by Working Title that earned more than $50 million in the United States and $250 million worldwide.[117] By the fall of 1994, Gramercy's steady stream of hits led *Hollywood Reporter* to declare the company "Hollywood's hottest independent distributor."[118] Gramercy did not slow down in 1995 either. In fact, it seemed to be increasingly treading on Miramax's domain in terms of content and awards: among its 1995 releases were Kevin Smith's second film, *Mallrats* (the only film during this period that he would not do with Miramax), *Cold Comfort Farm*, *Dead Man Walking*, and *The Usual Suspects*. While Miramax brought in a then record twenty-two Oscar nominations that year, Gramercy earned four, including a Best Picture nomination for *Four Weddings* and a Best Foreign Film nomination for *Before the Rain* (1994). Considering this was only the company's second full year in business, these figures are particularly impressive.[119] As 1996 approached, Gramercy was preparing to release Joel and Ethan Coen's dark comedy *Fargo* (which would earn seven Oscar nominations) and the Wachowskis' directorial debut, the neo-noir *Bound*.

At mid-decade, Gramercy was giving Miramax a run for its specialty film money—and the company would continue to do so for a couple more years, though its days were numbered. In a move that underscores the instability of the specialty business, Gramercy became a casualty of the wave of corporate consolidation and restructuring taking place at Universal Pictures during the late 1990s and early 2000s. The danger signs began appearing as early as the summer of 1995, when Seagram purchased MCA/Universal. The primary interest of Seagram CEO Edgar Bronfman was in building up Universal's music assets, which is why he allowed PolyGram to buy out Universal's interest in Gramercy.[120] After gaining 100 percent control over Gramercy in January 1996, PolyGram further ramped up its motion picture investments.

The case of Gramercy is a revealing one, as it suggests the extent to which the nature and composition of much of the specialty film business remained perpetually in flux. Although the viability of niche-oriented films—and especially American indies—was increasingly apparent, the precise structure of the companies running them remained less certain. This was one of the key reasons why Miramax had such an advantage at this point and was able to remain the dominant presence throughout the decade. But it also begins to suggest why, by the late 1990s, Miramax's uncontested status as king of the indie world began to diminish. Indeed, the first notable long-term challenger to Miramax's position appeared in 1994 in the form of Fox Searchlight. Searchlight was the first of the post-Miramax studio-based indies. Unlike Gramercy, Fox Searchlight would survive into the next millennium, growing stronger as the years went on. This is not to say that Searchlight did not begin with a splash; in fact, the division was aggressive from the outset, attending its first Sundance in 1995 and walking away with the festival favorite, *The Brothers McMullen* (1995), a film pursued by several prominent companies, including Miramax, New Line, and Samuel Goldwyn.[121] Searchlight's first and only 1995 release, *McMullen* started the company off strongly, earning more than $10 million domestically.[122]

As the examples of Gramercy and Fox Searchlight show, more and more companies wanted to be in the indie business by the mid-1990s. This was hardly surprising considering that in 1993 alone domestic theatrical earnings for indies exceeded $400 million—more than 9 percent of the total box office.[123] This represented a 4.7 percent increase from 1992.[124] By the time *Pulp Fiction* had left theaters in the spring of 1995, several key components of the developing indie infrastructure were falling into place. Increased cable channel capacity and the rising public awareness of indie cinema enabled the launch of two new channels dedicated solely to specialty films. Bravo/Rainbow Programming Holdings spun off the Independent Film Channel in 1994, and Robert Redford and Showtime/Viacom launched the Sundance Channel in 1995.[125]

Several prominent talent agencies allocated more resources and attention to indie cinema as well. Up through the early 1990s, CAA dominated the agency business. As a result, ICM, UTA, and William Morris "started building up their independent film rosters as a way to lure material-hungry actors back into the fold."[126] Agents increasingly viewed indie films as a way for fading talent to reinvent themselves or for fresh faces to distinguish themselves.[127] A key moment came in 1994, when the producer Cassian Elwes replaced the agent (and *sex, lies, and videotape* producer) Morgan Mason as head of William Morris's independent division. Elwes's mandate was to "put together movies that to a large extent will include William Morris clients and then raise financing for those pictures."[128] Considering that the agency's clients at the time included Robert Altman, Stephen Frears, Steven Soderbergh, Quentin Tarantino, Alan Rudolph, Gus Van Sant, Richard Linklater, Roger Avary, and Wayne Wang, the newly christened William Morris Independent was well situated to dominate the specialty sector of the representation business.[129]

Given the changes occurring in the realms of financing, production, and distribution, it is no surprise that exhibitors also expressed greater interest in the indie business. A growing number of multiplexes announced plans to dedicate screens year-round to "what used to be considered art-house movies."[130] This quotation from the *Hollywood Reporter* is instructive, as it suggests the ongoing struggles by both the press and the industry to assess precisely what was taking place. The "art house" label continued to be applied, yet it was increasingly inappropriate and insufficient in capturing what was going on. Of course, the same was the case with the term "independent." As demonstrated with the case studies of both *The Piano* and *Pulp Fiction* provided above, the fact is that neither film was an art house movie in the traditional sense—in other words, a film connected first and foremost to the avant-garde and various international art-cinema traditions. As discussed above, *The Piano* arguably had stronger ties to these conventions, but its sex, violence, classical resolution, Hollywood stars, and, most of all, marketing by Miramax cumulatively represented a substantive break from the art house.

Pulp Fiction, meanwhile, represented something altogether different. The immense financial, critical, and popular success of this film signaled the ascent of the age of indie cinema. Stylistically, indie cinema was more closely linked to the grind house than the art house. Its primary appeal was with Generation X, not the baby boomers. It was viewed in the sixteen-screen Cineplex Odeon in the suburbs, not the single-screen Paris Theater in the heart of New York City. It was heavily advertised on niche-oriented channels such as MTV, BET, and IFC, not NBC, CBS, and ABC. And it was marketed and distributed by Miramax (and increasingly Gramercy, Fox Searchlight, and October), not Island, Cinecom, and Orion Classics. As different as *The Piano* and *Pulp Fiction* are from each other, they are nonetheless linked because they represent the two dominant strands of movies favored by Miramax in the post-Disney era. *The Piano* showed the financial viability and crossover potential of a particular type of international coproduction. Though a significant transformation would occur on the road to such films as *The English Patient, Chocolat,* and *Cold Mountain* (2003), the roots of such films can be traced back to *The Piano*. Miramax would remain fond of these English-language prestige dramas as the 1990s continued, placing key figures from its growing stable of talent into these projects and putting its support behind such films each Oscar season. *Pulp Fiction,* meanwhile, represented another prominent type of specialty movie— the "edgy indie." In the discourses that circulated about *Pulp Fiction,* one can find many of the rising tensions and anxieties about the shifting nature of low-budget cinema of the 1990s.

It is telling that the year that Tarantino took home his Independent Spirit Award for *Pulp Fiction* was also the year that the Independent Feature Project adjusted its eligibility rules to allow films that received studio support.[131] In fact, by the time Tarantino won this award, "indie" had transformed into a convenient catchphrase—a term that could be used to refer to an industrial and aesthetic transformation difficult to assess yet very much in progress. On the eve of its second anniversary as part of the Disney empire, Miramax also was in the midst of a transformation. For the first half of the 1990s, Miramax had played the central role in shaping the structure and content of the specialty world. In the process, the press had widely praised both the company and its chief executives. Due in large part to its immense success, an entire infrastructure had begun to develop, replete with new specialty companies, indie cable networks, agents specializing in representing indie talent, and a cutthroat acquisitions scene. In the second half of the decade, Miramax increasingly labored to stay one step ahead of its competitors. This involved expanding the Miramax brand by producing different types of films, continuing to increase its staff size, branching out further into publishing and television, and raising the size and scope of its productions. Two significant developments helped influence the direction the company took. As will be explored in the next chapter, these developments involved the negative publicity that emerged for both Disney and Miramax following the Weinsteins' 1995 acquisition of *Kids* and Dimension's increasing importance to Miramax's bottom line following a string of box office hits that culminated with the December 1996 release of *Scream*.

CHAPTER FIVE

Another Dimension to the Miramax Brand

Kids, Scream, and the Teen Audience
(Spring 1995 – Spring 1997)

> The joke going around . . . is that when Disney first heard Miramax bought a movie about kids, they must have thought, Great, Miramax is finally on board. We see theme park rides.
>
> *A "Gotham indie insider," as per* Variety, *February 1995*

> When Miramax hit the horror-mania jackpot last December with Wes Craven's *Scream* [1996], it sent a shlockwave through the rest of the industry. Suddenly everyone wanted to get their hands on hip, in-your-face fright pics that could be made on the cheap and would gross $100 million from teens dying to see teens dying.
>
> Variety, *July 1997*

In early 1995, Miramax was at a high point. The company had its first $100 million hit with *Pulp Fiction* (1994), continued to sign fresh talent and develop new divisions, and enjoyed a positive relationship with the press. The name Miramax had become a potent brand, synonymous with marketing acuity and high-quality, stylistically innovative, risk-taking content. It seemed the Weinsteins and their company could do no wrong. As the months passed, however, problems began to develop for both Miramax and the indie world at large. Smaller independent distributors continued to close their doors, thereby stimulating a heightened panic by the press and industry about the state of the business. Deep-pocketed competitors like Gramercy and Fox Searchlight were emerging and bidding against Miramax for scripts and finished projects. Miramax's key supporter at Disney, Jeffrey Katzenberg, had departed from the conglomerate and promptly announced he was joining with Steven Spielberg and David Geffen in the creation of a new independent producer-distributor, DreamWorks SKG. All the while, Miramax plowed ahead, acquiring and producing what it wanted while giving little consideration to how these films might impact its parent company's public image.

The departure of Katzenberg and the appearance of new competitors were not major problems in the short term. But the company's continued pursuit of controversial content was about to become a significant concern. *Kids* (1995), a drama about a group of drinking, smoking, drug-taking, sexually active teenagers in New York City, quickly emerged as a hot-button issue. *Kids* spurred the most widely reported public conflict between Miramax and its parent company to date. The controversy over *Kids*, as it played out in the press, represented more than just a struggle over who had final decision-making power within an individual conglomerate. Rather, the clash over this film, occurring in tandem with the mounting financial woes of a number of low-budget distributors, drew attention to the growing incorporation of low-budget niche-market cinema into the conglomerate system. The *Kids* controversy provoked the press and industry to raise questions about the ways that the incorporation of small companies into publicly held global media conglomerates posed a threat to artistic expression, individual autonomy, and the exercise of free speech. On a more mundane level, the controversy raised concerns about the extent to which Miramax's brand identity was related to its image as a distributor of controversial films. If this brand identity was called into question, would Miramax's means of differentiating itself in the marketplace be affected?

The press brought up these types of issues repeatedly as Miramax dealt with the media frenzy surrounding *Kids*. Of course, such matters also could have been discussed in relation to other practices Miramax employed throughout the second half of the 1990s. For example, the press might have noted the degree to which Miramax, via its Dimension division, favored commerce over art, or the extent to which the profit-oriented imperatives of its conglomerate parent encouraged a shift in the kinds of films Miramax produced and distributed. Yet generally these topics were not noted in daily newspapers or weekly magazines at this time.

During the mid-1990s, Miramax was able to limit discussions of some issues (e.g., its relationship to Dimension) while it was less able to contain other conversations (e.g., its distribution of certain controversial films). Case studies of Miramax's handling of *Kids* and Dimension's handling of *Scream*, along with analyses of the press discourses generated in relation to each of these films, illustrate how the company managed its brand image at mid-decade. Further, these case studies reveal some of the ways that Miramax's content, as well as its relationship to the press, shifted from 1995 to 1997. At first glance, discussing *Kids* and *Scream* in the same chapter might seem like an odd choice. But the manner in which the press dealt with each film, and the particular branches of Miramax that released them, exposes a great deal about cultural hierarchies, critical distinctions, and assumptions operating about the media sphere during this time. Further, it suggests the ways that Miramax/Dimension were and were not able to exploit dominant assumptions in nurturing and sustaining distinctive brand identities for their respective divisions.

With both *Kids* and *Scream*, Miramax had to walk a tightrope: it simultaneously presented an image of itself as a specialty company that supported small, artistic films produced by iconoclastic auteurs while, at the same time, it increased the size and scope of a commercially oriented genre division geared toward films widely perceived as trashy or lowbrow. The company's solution, which proved workable during this brief historical moment, was to promote Dimension as a quality genre company that deviated substantially from the B-grade genre companies of years gone by. *Scream* helped Miramax construct Dimension as both a distinctive name in its own right, and as a respectable entity focused on developing superior genre films with links to 1990s-era American indies. These genre films, in turn, not only attracted a new generation of teenagers, but also crossed over to appeal to other niches, including Gen Xers, African Americans, and even, on occasion, the traditional art house crowd. Interestingly, only months before many in the press celebrated Dimension's discovery of a new generation of teen moviegoers (and teen dollars) with *Scream*, they excoriated Miramax for its negative depiction of this same group of individuals on-screen in *Kids*.

Causing Trouble with Kids

> This is a family film. I would like parents and kids to see it together.
>
> *Larry Clark*, Kids *director, 1995*

From the moment the Disney-Miramax union was announced, one of the biggest questions circulating about the marriage was whether the two companies' distinctive brand identities would mesh. This question pertained to Disney's status as the leader in producing and distributing global family entertainment and Miramax's seemingly incompatible status as the leader in marketing films based on their most controversial elements. As noted in previous chapters, one of the primary means by which both Miramax and its films gained a public profile was through campaigning against the MPAA's ratings decisions on *Scandal* (1989), *Tie Me Up! Tie Me Down!* (1990), and *The Cook, the Thief, His Wife, and Her Lover* (1990). In addition to publicizing its conflicts with the MPAA to generate low-cost publicity, another strategy Miramax regularly used involved selling sex in films that were anything but sexually explicit; *sex, lies, and videotape* (1989) and *The Crying Game* (1992) were two of the prime examples of this practice. On rare occasions, violence would become a selling point, as was the case with *Pulp Fiction*, but typically it was a film's sexuality that was exploited. Given many Americans' insecurities about sexual matters, this tactic makes sense. Miramax marketing executive Mark Gill found himself in a bit of hot water at the Toronto Film Festival in 1995 for acknowledging his company's habit of using sexual imagery to sell films that contained minimal amounts of such content.[1] Gill defended this practice, stating that "people want to see things that are provocative. . . . You'll see a lot of women with no clothes on their backs in our ads. You can scorn me for this but it works."[2]

There were two different marketing strategies at work here. The controversies that emerged out of the battles with the MPAA were based on conflicts over the acceptability of the content itself. The controversies that emerged over movies such as *sex, lies, and videotape* and *The Crying Game* were entirely manufactured by Miramax and a consenting press. Notably, Miramax used the latter strategy much more consistently both *before and after* its purchase by Disney. While there were several MPAA conflicts in 1989–1990, for the most part these had become much less frequent even before Disney entered the picture. Yet in most discussions of Miramax's exploitation of controversy, both strategies are lumped together as evidence of the company's inherent mismatch with Disney. Nonetheless, publicizing content battles and publicizing uncontroversial content as controversial are two very different things. All this is to say that many of the scholarly and press discussions of Miramax's rise to prominence have greatly overstated its role in distributing controversial content. This is significant because it suggests that the public debate that developed around *Kids* is not so much about a wholesale shift in the kinds of content the company chose to produce and acquire, as it is about personal issues of ego and increasing anxieties by the creative and journalistic communities about the ongoing structural changes in the media industries.

As noted earlier, there were a handful of films released between 1993 and 1995 that, by virtue of their content, proved problematic for Miramax. The Martin Lawrence concert film *You So Crazy* has the distinction of being the first to cause difficulty for Miramax after its purchase by Disney. In February 1994, the MPAA awarded the film an NC-17 rating due to its explicit language.[3] Miramax protested, but not too much and not for long. By late March 1994, the Weinsteins sold the rights for the film to Samuel Goldwyn.[4] Exploiting the controversy, Goldwyn released *You So Crazy* less than a month later and it took in a solid $10 million in North American theaters.[5] All this transpired quickly and with only a limited amount of controversy. The same held true for a couple of other films Miramax handled during 1994. Both Kevin Smith's *Clerks* and the British historical drama *The Advocate* initially received NC-17 ratings from the MPAA—the former for sexually explicit language, the latter for sexually explicit images. Miramax made minor trims to *The Advocate* to receive an R rating; meanwhile, *Clerks* required no cuts to earn an R, as the MPAA reversed its initial ratings decision upon appeal.[6] Once again, there was only a limited amount of press coverage surrounding these ratings conflicts. What coverage there was largely addressed the MPAA's double standards and unpredictability. This press angle was motivated primarily by the fact that Oliver Stone's *Natural Born Killers* (Warner Bros., 1994)—a studio-based project filled with graphic violence and explicit sexuality—was assigned an R rating at approximately the same time that the "independently produced" *Clerks* and *The Advocate* were initially granted NC-17 ratings.[7] This variation in ratings elicited discussion as to the hypocrisies and inconsistencies of the MPAA rating system as well as the board's tendency to be more lenient in rating big-budget, studio-based projects than in rating lower-budget, specialty fare.

With the exception of these isolated ratings skirmishes, all of which were quickly resolved, few reports of conflicts over Miramax content surfaced in the press through early 1995.[8] The turning point came in the spring of 1995 with the one-two punch of *Priest* and *Kids*. At the same moment that *Pulp Fiction* was clearing $100 million in North American theaters and Miramax was preparing to celebrate its two-year anniversary with Disney, these two films attracted increased attention from the press and drew protests from certain interest groups. Much of the attention was because they dealt with subjects that were highly troublesome for Disney's brand identity: homosexuality within the church (*Priest*) and sexually active, drug-using teenagers (*Kids*). With the release of these films occurring so close together, journalists had a ready-made story handed to them.

Priest, which appeared in theaters first, was a British film about a man of the cloth who secretly carried on a relationship with another man. Despite this story line, the film might well have fallen under the radar were it not for Miramax's decision to release the movie on three hundred screens on Good Friday. The combination of the film's subject matter and its release date drew the attention and ire of a number of conservative religious groups, including the Catholic League and the American Life League.[9] Miramax eventually caved in to the pressure from these groups and pushed the release date back five days. The company claimed that the decision to change the film's release was "out of respect" for those expressing concerns and not the result of pressure from Disney.[10] Regardless, protests directed toward the film continued even after its release. The groups issued calls not only for a boycott of *Priest* and Miramax-released movies, but also for a boycott of all Disney products.[11] After nearly two years together, this was the first real indication of the potential incompatibility of the Disney and Miramax brands and the possible financial repercussions of this incompatibility. Though *Priest* ultimately brought in more than $4 million at the North American box office, such a sum was insignificant when matched against the possible damage to multibillion-dollar conglomerate Disney's bottom line and public image.

The controversy over *Kids* far eclipsed that which occurred over *Priest*. Miramax had the option to acquire *Kids* at the script stage back in 1993 but chose not to.[12] Nonetheless, the company followed the film's development from script stage through postproduction. Only after *Kids* was accepted for the January 1995 Sundance Film Festival and rumors began to circulate that other distributors, including October, were also interested did Miramax actively pursue the film, advancing $3.5 million for worldwide rights.[13] Certainly the company knew from the start that *Kids* was going to be highly controversial. In fact, this was a key factor in why Miramax held off on getting involved while it was in development.[14] As *Variety* observed shortly after Miramax acquired the rights, "*Kids*, which is poised to become one of the most controversial American films ever made, is so sexually frank that some feel it is practically the film for which the adult rating was invented."[15] The film does not hold back in its depiction of illegal and illicit activities among teens. The focus of the story is an amoral boy named Telly (Leo Fitzpatrick), who tries to sleep with as many virgins as possible, despite the fact that he is HIV positive. The story also follows one of the women (Chloe Sevigny), who, upon learning she got the virus from him, tries to track him down. The film, shot in a cinéma verité style, is intended to "realistically" present life in New York City. Whether it was in fact realistic and authentic or simply sensationalistic and exploitative became a matter of much debate among critics and journalists.

From the time of Kids' premiere in rough cut form at Sundance, the critical and audience responses were mixed. Yet the number of positive or negative reviews from critics was the least of Miramax's concerns. The bigger issue for both Miramax and Disney was trying to manage the media coverage that started to appear in late March and grew throughout the spring. The various media reports focused on how a global media monolith might exert pressure on an iconoclastic upstart. Journalists posed the potential implications of Miramax moving forward in its release of Kids as both cultural and creative in nature. The general narrative held that the Weinsteins and their little company were anticorporate, irreverent, and fiercely independent—an obvious clash with Disney's way of doing business. The controversy surrounding Kids seemed to reinforce that the Weinsteins could never toe the corporate line. Within this framework, Disney was constructed as the villain and oppressor, while Miramax, and especially Harvey Weinstein, remained the scrappy, strong-willed supporter of true independence. The indie world might be changing, but Harvey would take every step to ensure that he remained at the center of it, championing visionary filmmakers at all costs. The big question mark was how much control he and his company really had over the films they chose. What topics were off-limits?

There was a sense of inevitability to many of the press reports that followed. Of course these two cultures would clash, of course art and individual expression would be suppressed in the interests of commerce. Suddenly a relationship that thus far had been presented as relatively harmonious and placid was perceived to be on the brink of collapse. The *Wall Street Journal* speculated that the Weinsteins were using the conflict over Kids as a way to "force their exit" from Disney in order to start a new company.[16] Jeffrey Katzenberg, this journalist added, had maintained whatever peace had existed between Miramax and Disney; with him gone, it was only a matter of time before the Weinsteins also left.[17]

The Weinsteins did not end up parting ways with Disney at this time. Publicly, at least, the rift was resolved. Because Disney had a policy to not release NC-17 films, Miramax did not have the option of holding on to Kids. As Roger Ebert observed, "Try to trim it for an R rating and you'd have about 20 minutes left."[18] Thus the Weinsteins devised an innovative solution: they bought back the film's rights themselves and released it via a newly created company not affiliated with Disney. The Weinsteins' view of their role in this endeavor might best be summarized by considering the name they gave the distribution company created to release the film: Shining Excalibur.[19] They acted swiftly in creating this entity, forming Excalibur in June 1995, about a month after *Kids* screened at Cannes. Eamonn Bowles, who recently had left the struggling Samuel Goldwyn Co. to become a vice president at Miramax, was appointed to run the operation.[20] Excalibur employed a small distribution staff, and the bulk of the advertising and publicity work was subcontracted out. The enterprise occupied office space at the Tribeca Film Center, which also housed the Miramax headquarters.[21]

While Disney made no comment publicly about the venture, the Weinsteins (especially Harvey) issued a string of statements. In a press release announcing the formation of Excalibur, they declared that this "financially and structurally independent company" would release *Kids* in order to "remove the speculation about the rating that would otherwise overshadow this important motion picture."[22] The hollowness of such proclamations became clear within weeks, when, after *Kids* received the expected NC-17 rating, the Weinsteins mounted their by-then-standard campaign against the MPAA. As if on cue, Alan Dershowitz came forth to protest the decision. In addition, Jane Pratt, editor of the teen magazine *Sassy*, argued against the NC-17 rating on the grounds that *Kids* was precisely the kind of film that parents should see and discuss together with their children.[23] When the MPAA rejected Excalibur's appeal, the company announced its plan to release the film unrated.

Excalibur wasted no time exploiting the media coverage directed at *Kids*. Using the summer counterprogramming strategy that had worked so well with *sex, lies, and videotape* a few years earlier, the company opened the film on New York and Los Angeles screens in late July. *Kids'* release was gradually expanded over the next couple of months; by September it was playing in nearly two hundred theaters across the country. Upon completion of its theatrical run, it had earned more than $7.4 million in North America. In terms of its cost-to-revenue ratio, *Kids* was among the most profitable films of 1995.[24]

Harvey Weinstein may have believed he was placed at "tremendous risk" by "losing Buena Vista's clout in the home video market and pay TV markets," but in the end, the Weinsteins came out ahead financially by striking a number of deals at the height of the film's notoriety.[25] Within days of its theatrical release, Excalibur licensed *Kids'* video and cable rights for impressive sums: the independent distributor Trimark acquired domestic home video rights for more than $5 million, while

HBO acquired pay cable rights for somewhere between $500,000 and $1 million.[26] Though *Kids* was estimated to cost the Weinsteins between $6.5 and $7 million, by October 1995 Bowles declared that the "brothers' ledgers [were] in the black" and they had already made a small profit.[27] Excalibur, meanwhile, had served its purpose. Upon the conclusion of *Kids'* theatrical release, the division was retired and Bowles resumed work at Miramax.[28]

The Stakes of the *Kids* Controversy

> The mantra at Disney is to keep the ratings "R" and I'm happy to do so. . . . I don't want to cause Disney any problems. Why ruin a perfect relationship?
>
> *Harvey Weinstein, 1996*

The *Kids* controversy came at a pivotal moment for both the indie world at large and Miramax in particular. Miramax's budgets were on the rise, its acquisitions were diminishing relative to in-house productions, its films seemed to be ever-more star-laden, and there was an increasing dependence on large-scale ad buys to support the launch of wide releases. *Pulp Fiction* was only one of the most recent example of these shifts. Within this context, getting behind a movie like *Kids* helped indicate that the Weinsteins had not changed, that they were not being constrained by Disney. By responding as they did to the controversy, the Weinsteins could not only assuage their own egos, but they could also make a strong statement to both the creative community and the press. Further, it was important to get behind a film like *Kids* because a number of prominent indie figures were involved in its creation. Among the notable individuals attached to it were producers Christine Vachon (*Go Fish*, 1994; *Safe*, 1995), Cary Woods and Cathy Konrad (partners on *Things to Do in Denver When You're Dead*, 1995; and *Citizen Ruth*, 1996), and executive producer Gus Van Sant (*My Own Private Idaho*, 1991; *To Die For*, 1995). In the tightly knit world of indie film, to abandon *Kids* might lead to devastating consequences in terms of the company's relationships with talent.

The subject matter also could have factored into the Weinsteins decision to rally behind the film. To abandon a crude concert film like *You So Crazy* was one thing. To fail to get behind a highly provocative drama was quite another. Martin Lawrence's stand-up routine could be dismissed as exploitative junk, and thus to part with it was no big loss. Conversely, to part with *Kids* without a fight would reaffirm what many feared or suspected—that the low-budget landscape was changing, that from now, on institutional forces would overwhelm individual efforts at creative expression. In other words, they had to counteract the growing sense that the indie business was becoming like the studio business.

Both the timing of the controversy and the convenient press angle it offered also help explain why this story exploded like it did. What could be more captivating and provocative than a clash between the quintessential name in children's entertainment and a scrappy little company over an explicit film featuring adolescents out of control? Further fueling the fire was the fact that the *Kids* controversy came at a fortuitous time for specialty companies. On the same day *Variety* reported Miramax's impending sneak preview of *Kids* at Sundance, the publication also ran a story titled "Where Have All the Independents Gone?"[29] A sense of foreboding was present in the piece, as the journalist Leonard Klady observed:

> There's a strong argument that there's virtually no independent scene left in the U.S., considering that New Line has been absorbed into Turner Entertainment and Miramax was acquired by Walt Disney. Gramercy, a new kid on the block, is a joint venture of PolyGram and Universal and the other new entry, Savoy, doesn't quite fit into the same niche as such specialized boutiques as October and First Look Pictures. Indeed, mergers, buyouts and other industry developments over the past two years have radically redefined the indie landscape. Scruffy street fighters have gone respectable, studios have re-established classics divisions and a glutted marketplace has muted many new voices.[30]

The piece articulated the "crisis of classification" facing those trying to describe or work within the low-budget film world. As more than one journalist noted, many of the films of specialty companies like New Line and Miramax looked and sounded a lot like the films they released before being acquired by conglomerates. So should only those films be factored into the market share for independent films? Or were all the films that came from these companies still independent? In the end, how much of a difference did the heightened resources available to companies like New Line and Miramax make? And what were the implications for low-budget filmmakers?

Journalists discussing the *Kids* controversy raised all these points. As of early 1995, Miramax and New Line together accounted for approximately 10 percent of all box office returns.[31] But without accounting for these companies, the independent sector had a market share of less than

3.5 percent.[32] What was particularly alarming for Klady was that "there hasn't really been a company that has stepped into the breach that New Line and Miramax left behind."[33] As another journalist added, the "class system" of the indie world was being "shattered," as "upwardly mobile companies [such] as Miramax [are] transforming from scrappy to dominant, and with the boutiques shut down for good."[34] The independents that remained behind—companies like Roxie Releasing, Zeitgeist, and Caledonia—were seen as negligible in terms of market share, distribution power, and financial resources. Many released only a couple of films per year. Meanwhile, the list of casualties in the low-budget sector continued to grow, as many "once-significant distributors" such as Hemdale, Skouras, and Concorde were "now on life-support systems."[35]

The sense of gloom and doom pervasive in these reports would be sustained throughout the year, as still more low-budget distributors encountered financial difficulties. Particularly notable was the rapid decline of the Samuel Goldwyn Co. Only a few years before, Goldwyn's future had looked quite promising. Driven by such box office hits as *Mystic Pizza* (1988), *Henry V* (1989), and *La Femme Nikita* (1990), Goldwyn had been one of the few companies to survive the tumultuous late 1980s period. The company's situation seemed so positive in the early 1990s that it began to vertically integrate, acquiring the art house chain Landmark Theaters in 1991.[36] Goldwyn went public soon after the Landmark acquisition. Conditions for Samuel Goldwyn continued to improve, with the company having a banner year in 1993 due to the strong performances of *Much Ado About Nothing* and *The Wedding Banquet*. Unfortunately, its fortunes soon took a turn for the worse. Like Miramax and New Line, Goldwyn increasingly focused on in-house productions. Unlike Miramax and New Line, it did not have a corporate parent to protect it. Thus a string of failures, culminating with the expensive box office disappointment *The Perez Family* (1995), which cost more than $11 million and grossed only $2.5 million theatrically, placed the company in dire straits.[37]

In the summer of 1995—on the same day, in fact, that Excalibur appealed *Kids'* NC-17 rating—Goldwyn was reported to be for sale.[38] *Variety* editor in chief Peter Bart declared that "the dilemma of the Samuel Goldwyn Co. may mark the end of an era in indie filmmaking."[39] He went on to ask, "Is there really room any longer for a true 'independent' in today's turbulent film business?"[40] This observation came on the heels of another report only a few weeks prior in which the *Los Angeles Times* noted the extent to which "dependent independence" was the new way of doing business in Hollywood.[41] Miramax was identified as the prime example of this phenomenon; others listed included the newly purchased Turner entities New Line and Castle Rock.[42] Significantly, industry consolidation became only more severe in the ensuing months. Most notable was Disney's purchase of ABC in August 1995, followed a few weeks later by Time Warner's purchase of Turner Entertainment (including New Line and Castle Rock).

Given this context, it is easy to see how circumstances could seem so grim: true independents were fading and there was little evidence of new competitors on the rise. Further, if the controversy and resolution to the *Kids* saga were any indication, dependent independents were showing greater fiscal and topical conservatism. Within this framework, the lengths the Weinsteins went to with *Kids* make more sense. Through the formation of Shining Excalibur, they could assert themselves, show their continued support for filmmakers' visions, and reinforce their respect for the creative community. If there was a battle to be fought, they could come out looking like victors—or, at the very least, like they had reached a stalemate, which was better than nothing.

During the whole *Kids* uproar, one topic rarely discussed was what *kinds* of films were placed at risk due to the ascendance of studio subsidiaries. Much more frequently, the press—along with the executives and filmmakers interviewed in their articles—expressed a generalized fear that certain stories might be silenced, that certain people might be far less able to realize their distinctive visions. Miramax's disowning of *Kids* was viewed with a high degree of foreboding because the company had been such a prominent advocate for some difficult films only a few years prior. Although Miramax had generated a lot of publicity for its distribution of such contentious films as *Tie Me Up! Tie Me Down!* and *The Cook, the Thief, His Wife, and Her Lover*, these movies were exceptions to the kinds of films the company typically acquired and distributed even at that time. By and large, Miramax did not trade in such movies. As noted above, Miramax built up its profile by exploiting controversial content and by creating artificial controversies through its marketing practices. Both before and after Disney entered the picture, the former type of controversy occurred much less frequently than the latter. When Miramax actually did handle films with controversial content, it did everything in its power to draw media attention to this fact. In other words, the company worked to generate controversy over its films in the interest of cultivating additional publicity (and, by extension, box office dollars). The Weinsteins and Miramax were less interested in pushing the limits of free speech, expressing strong political perspectives, and testing the limits of the system for the sake of empowering and enabling outsiders. The number of times the company engaged in battles over content was far eclipsed by the number of times that films were *sold* as being controversial. Further, the myriad films marketed as being controversial were typically anything but. As one former Miramax executive put it, "While everyone thought we were battling the MPAA and doing all these transgressive films, the truth was, we were doing *My Left Foot* [1989]. We were doing *Hear My Song* [1991], we were doing *Mediterraneo* [1991]."[43]

Miramax did support the growth of a number of different types of films and filmmakers during the 1980s and 1990s. But, in the end, the company was far less interested in supporting films that either tested the boundaries of sex and violence or pushed the margins politically or culturally. Rather, it was interested in *suggesting* sex and violence for the purposes of getting people into theaters. At its height, Miramax's greatest innovations were in marketing, in skillfully using the press to call attention to its films, in finding films that appealed to certain underserved niches and, on occasion, helping these films cross over to become mainstream hits. To hold Miramax accountable for the decline or marginalization of independent film is to fail to understand the company— the kinds of filmmakers it hired, the kinds of films it distributed. The anxieties about the degree to which corporate consolidation was pushing aside some voices might have been legitimate, but they should not have been directed toward Miramax. Amazingly, amid all the uproar over *Kids*, the press seemed oblivious to the fact that Miramax's genre subsidiary, Dimension, was increasingly producing and distributing a spate of films featuring graphic violence, sexually explicit situations, foul language, and misbehaving teens.

Genre Films Struggle at Mid-Decade

> The whole idea of Dimension is to go after these kinds of upscale, mass-appeal genre films. We acquired *Hellraiser 3* and *Children of the Corn 2*, which Dimension will release this summer in the U.S.
>
> Bob Weinstein, 1992

A case study of Dimension provides further evidence of Miramax's effective management of its brand identity and its skill in dealing with the press. In addition, it reinforces that Miramax was focused on far more than just a narrow strand of art house–oriented quality indies throughout the 1990s. The diverse slate of films released by Miramax and its Dimension subsidiary indicates the large-scale expansion in niche-oriented companies targeting a wide range of demographic groups. Throughout the first half of the decade, Miramax helped "redis-cover" baby boomers and Gen Xers. Now, via Dimension, it was about to become one of the first film companies to tap into a new generation of teenagers. As with English-language imports and quality American indies previously, Miramax led the way in distributing and marketing crossover genre hits. Dimension's most successful genre films, including *Scream, From Dusk Till Dawn* (1996), and *Scary Movie* (2000), expanded well beyond teenagers, appealing to a variety of additional demographic groups. Within only a couple of years, Dimension rose from being a marginal player in the genre business to becoming the preeminent genre division in Hollywood. This opportunity for Dimension arose in part due to New Line's aforementioned shift away from releasing the lower-budgeted genre product that had long been its forte. Yet Dimension did not merely assume New Line's prior position as the industry's dominant low-budget genre division. Rather, it also reinvigorated the marketplace with fresh approaches to producing and marketing genre films. What's more, Dimension's profits quickly began to surpass those of its parent, Miramax. This achievement is even more striking considering that, up through the late 1990s, Miramax was able to retain its identity as the site for a specific type of quality indie. The Miramax name remained unaf-fected by the potential taint from the less respectable practice of traffick-ing in genre films.

While much has been written about the art house strand of recent indie films, critics and scholars alike have largely neglected the contem-porary genre strand. Though there has been work on both the textual dimensions of specific types of low-budget genre films and their recep-tion by different fan communities, there has been little discussion of their industrial significance.[44] At best, such films—and the divisions that have released them—have received passing mention in surveys of the indie film scene. Typically their revenue-generating attributes are acknowl-edged while their potential cultural or artistic import is dismissed. As noted in chapter 1, Peter Biskind's discussion of Dimension in *Down and Dirty Pictures* is typical. In the couple dozen pages he grudgingly devotes to the topic, he conveys the attitude that when Dimension started to grow in size and scope in the mid-1990s, the quality of Miramax's releases began to deteriorate. The general neglect in discussing Dimension and other commercially minded genre divisions can be attributed in part to their status as low culture. Their content is often visceral, including a great deal of sex, violence, highly stylized action, explicit language, and crude humor. Like their distant antecedent the exploitation film, genre films often have been viewed as artistically bankrupt, produced mainly in the interest of making a quick buck. As with so many cultural prod-ucts that are popular (e.g., reality television shows, comic books), genre films are frequently seen as brainless fodder consumed by indiscrimi-nate audiences. Yet, ironically, their very popularity and widespread com-mercial appeal has rendered them *unappealing* sites of analyses for those who study "paracinema"[45] or "cult movies."[46]

One of Miramax's most impressive accomplishments came from its ability to rebrand and revive genre films through its Dimension division. During the mid-to-late 1990s, the company strove to alter the cultural attitudes toward genre pictures. Concurrently, Dimension continued to elevate their box office performance by targeting a range of underserved demographic groups, including African Americans, teenage girls, and children. Genre films proved desperately in need of a makeover, given the sad state in which they found themselves by the mid-1990s. Indeed, New Line moved away from distributing these types of films in part due to changing business strategies in the wake of its purchase by Time War-ner, but also due to these movies' diminishing profitability.

The declining fortunes of many types of genre films occurred for a variety of reasons. For one, the young adult and teen audience that grew up with the films in the 1980s and 1990s had moved on. Further, over-exploitation of existing franchises such as *Friday the 13th, House Party*, and *Teenage Mutant Ninja Turtles* had eroded their appeal.[47] Several genre cycles, including the most recent wave of horror and teenpic films, were played out. The quality of the stories and the production values went into decline as the producers and distributors of the films rushed out one sequel after another. The increased emphasis in the video business on "A" titles was also a factor. On top of this, the studios themselves were increasingly producing genre-type films, albeit with larger budgets and bigger stars.[48] Significantly, in April 1994 *Variety* rang the death knell for the genre film, and in particular the teen horror film. The article began with the declaration that the "once popular genre looks into the face of b.o. death."[49] Later in the article, Leonard Klady added that "the most damning accusation is that the economics of fright, particularly for mod-est and low-budget chillers, don't work anymore."[50] Indeed, they did not work anymore, at least in the forms they took by the mid-1990s. New Line itself made a valiant effort to resuscitate one of its most lucrative franchises, *A Nightmare on Elm Street*, but to no avail.

This attempt to "upscale" the *Elm Street* series is worth discussing briefly, as it both underscores the status of genre films in the market-place at the time and suggests precisely how significant Miramax's role was in revitalizing their content and public image. In 1994, New Line resurrected Freddy Krueger once more in a seventh installment of the series; with *Wes Craven's New Nightmare*, New Line tried to completely overhaul the franchise. The film also served as a move by Craven to revitalize his career, which had been in a turbulent state since he directed the first *Nightmare*. While Craven had attained a few moderate box office successes with such films as *The Serpent and the Rainbow* (1988) and *Shocker* (1989), several years had passed since he had directed a feature film (*The People Under the Stairs*, 1991). *New Nightmare* was an ambitious movie, one that foreshadowed the direction that Craven would take with the Dimension/Miramax *Scream* franchise a few years later. The premise of this highly self-reflexive film is that Wes Craven (playing himself) is writing a new installment of *A Nightmare on Elm Street* for New Line. He returns to the star of the original, Heather Langenkamp, and asks her to reprise her role as Nancy. She is hesitant to do so, as she has moved on with her life, but then her husband is killed and her son starts to have nightmares of his own. Others who had been involved with previous *Nightmare* films also have restless nights. The film meshes "real life" and "reel life," with several characters from the series making appearances. In addition, a number of people affiliated with New Line and Craven have cameos, including the studio's founder and CEO, Robert Shaye, and Craven's longtime producer, Marianne Maddalena.

Many critics assessed the film favorably and took it more seriously than they had either previous *Nightmare* installments or most recent horror movies. Roger Ebert wrote, "This is the first horror movie that is actually about the question, 'Don't you people ever think about the effect your movies have on the people who watch them?'"[51] He continued, "I haven't been exactly a fan of the *Nightmare* series, but I found this movie, with its unsettling questions about the effect of horror on those who create it, strangely intriguing."[52] Similarly, Janet Maslin of the *New York Times* noted that Craven, with "equal debts to Pirandello and P. T. Barnum," has crafted "an ingenious, cathartic exercise in illusion and fear. [It embraces] horror as a creative outlet for the imagination."[53] Despite several favorable reviews from prominent critics, the film's box office receipts were mediocre. Ultimately it ended up earning about $18 million domestically on a budget of $8 million.[54] These returns were smaller than any prior *Nightmare* film or most of Craven's other directorial efforts. A couple of weeks after its release, *Variety* attacked both the film and the marketing campaign attached to it, stating, "*Wes Craven's New Nightmare* campaign received poor grades for attempting to hide the obvious (*Elm Street No. 7*) to take a stab at drawing in a tonier audience before it had snagged its regulars. There was also general curiosity about trying to put the weight of the film on its director's shoulders—not quite a household name on the level of horrormeister Stephen King."[55]

What is particularly interesting about these comments is that the same things New Line was attacked for in 1994 are what Dimension would be celebrated for a few years later. Moreover, Craven's effort to "elevate" the horror film was dismissed at the time. Yet following *Scream's* release in 1996, Craven ended up being elevated to the very "level of horrormeister Stephen King" noted above, becoming a brand name and gaining a level of clout held by few in the genre business. Craven's rise, *Scream*, and Dimension—along with *Scream* screenwriter Kevin Williamson— are all intricately interconnected. Miramax, with its Dimension label, ended up being able to accomplish the very feat that New Line could not: to "snag" regular horror moviegoers while also drawing in a "tonier" audience.

Yet as late as 1995, Dimension remained a small-scale genre division overseen by Bob Weinstein and employing only a handful of development executives.[56] Throughout that year, it mainly released lower-end genre product that had limited theatrical ambitions. The films handled by Dimension in 1995 were not unlike those distributed in the years prior. Among the company's releases were the martial arts film *Best of the Best 3*, *Halloween: The Curse of Michael Myers* (the sixth in the series), and the Dolph Lundgren features *Hidden Assassin* and *Men of War*. One year later, much had changed, as Dimension released a series of films that initiated a new age for both the division and the genre film.

Miramax, Dimension, and the "Upscale" Genre Film

> "Genre" has a bad connotation, and we want to bring Miramax's reputation for quality to science-fiction and horror films. . . .
> Alfred Hitchcock and Brian De Palma are just some of the great ones who made genre films.
>
> *Bob Weinstein, 1995*

If 1989 was the year that Miramax began to establish its presence with its own brand of quality independents, then 1996 was the year that Dimension did the same with genre films. Much as *sex, lies, and videotape*, *My Left Foot*, and *Cinema Paradiso* helped Miramax solidify its identity, so, too, did *From Dusk Till Dawn* and *Scream* accomplish a similar task for

Dimension a few years later. These two Dimension releases cemented relationships with talent that would be sustained for several years to come. In addition, together they indicated the types of content that Dimension increasingly would become known for in the ensuing years.

From Dusk Till Dawn was the first of the two films to appear in theaters. Opening in January 1996, the film marked the second teaming of Robert Rodriguez and Quentin Tarantino. The two had worked together once before to direct segments of Miramax's troubled anthology film *Four Rooms* (1995). *From Dusk Till Dawn* was their first joint effort for the Dimension label. Rodriguez directed, while Tarantino wrote the script and costarred as one half of the villainous Gecko brothers (with the other brother played by rising star George Clooney). Conceived as an homage to 1960s- and 1970s-era exploitation pictures, *From Dusk Till Dawn* starts as a film about criminals on the lam before abruptly turning into a vampire-cum-war film at its halfway mark.

The film proved quite successful at the box office, earning in excess of $25 million in North America.[57] This made *From Dusk Till Dawn* Dimension's highest-earning film for the 1996 calendar year.[58] Even more significant than its box office performance was the extent to which the film helped crystallize both a house style and distinct talent base for Dimension. With *From Dusk Till Dawn*, Rodriguez and Tarantino increasingly became affiliated with Dimension rather than Miramax. This change in affiliation enabled them to embrace more explicitly their lowbrow sensibilities than might have been possible had they remained linked directly to Miramax. While *Pulp Fiction* stretched the boundaries of what a Miramax film could be, in the end, both the film and the discourses that circulated about it were bound to ideas of art and quality that were the stock-in-trade of the Miramax brand. Dimension could—and did— much more readily and frequently embrace lowbrow and trash culture.

Thus, under the Dimension umbrella, Tarantino and Rodriguez were able to produce a new kind of genre film in *From Dusk Till Dawn*. Such a film was promoted as a product of B movies, exploitation cinema, and popular culture, but it was also widely perceived as something more than these influences. Because it was paying homage to these predecessors, it was of higher quality—in other words, it was an upscale genre film. At least this was the spin that Bob Weinstein and Dimension executives tried to put on the subsidiary's products. As Weinstein observed in a revealing statement, "The idea is that Dimension, like Miramax, will have its own brand name in terms of cool, hip genre movies—horror and sci-fi—like *Scream* and *From Dusk Till Dawn*. The directors and writers we have under contract at Miramax are also working for the genre

© Dimension Films. George Clooney took a break from his role on *ER* to play against type as one half of the criminal Gecko brothers in *From Dusk Till Dawn* (1996).

label. So Quentin does a movie for Miramax, then a movie for Dimension. Same with Robert Rodriguez."[59]

Even as Weinstein's declaration of talent "under contract" harks back to the Hollywood studio era, he suggests the forward-thinking tendencies of his young, iconoclastic filmmakers. As he suggests here, Weinstein and his staff were performing a balancing act, at once linking Dimension's product to the quality reputation of Miramax, while at the same time struggling to keep an arm's-length distance, so that Dimension's lowbrow fare would not adversely affect the image of Miramax and its films. It was a delicate negotiation between wanting to use the parent company's identity to benefit Dimension while not corrupting the Miramax brand. *From Dusk Till Dawn* was noteworthy not only because it kept Dimension's momentum going and furthered the careers of Tarantino and Rodriguez, but also because it provided Dimension with a lucrative franchise. The company went on to produce a straight-to-video prequel and sequel (*Texas Blood Money*, 1999; *The Hangman's Daughter*, 2000), both of which were executive-produced by Tarantino and Rodriguez.[60] The practice of launching straight-to-video counterparts from established film franchises would become common industry-wide in the new millennium.[61]

As significant as *From Dusk Till Dawn* was, the *Scream* franchise would prove even more lucrative. With *Scream's* financial success, the relationship between Miramax and Dimension shifted. The latter division rapidly began to increase its output and generate a greater percentage of the overall market share for the company. This development did not go unobserved by the rest of the industry; other studios rushed to emulate Dimension's success with genre films in general and horror films in particular. *Scream* fundamentally revitalized and reinvented the horror film, resuscitated Wes Craven's career, and launched screenwriter Kevin Williamson's multimedia trajectory. Moreover, *Scream* led the way in the industry's "rediscovery" of the teen audience, this time in the form of Generation Y.

Certainly none of this could have been anticipated when *Scream* began its theatrical run in December 1996. Budgeted at a relatively modest $15 million, *Scream* featured mainly television stars (e.g., Courteney Cox of *Friends*, Neve Campbell of *Party of Five*) and B-level talent (e.g., Matthew Lillard, Rose McGowan, Skeet Ulrich).[62] The most high-profile actor was Drew Barrymore, whose role was notable mainly because she was killed off within the first few minutes of the film. This fact did not stop Dimension from prominently featuring her in *Scream's* promotional materials. Dimension executives suspected they had a potential hit on their hands, and thus provided sneak previews at a number of college campuses in November and December.[63] The company decided to take the then unusual step of opening the film in late December. The belief was that *Scream* would serve as effective counterprogramming against the onslaught of family-friendly holiday films and prestige pictures opening in time for Oscar consideration.[64] Such a tactic in itself generated some early press coverage for the film.

The initial reviews for *Scream* were quite mixed.[65] In fact, *Wes Craven's New Nightmare* generated more favorable responses from mainstream publications. While critics acknowledged *Scream's* incorporation and parody of horror conventions, this did not mean such traits were viewed as assets. For example, *Variety's* Leonard Klady wrote that Craven "may have gone to the trough once too often, employing an uneven balance here of genre convention and sophisticated parody."[66] He went on to predict "no more than modest commercial returns and fast theatrical playoff."[67] Janet Maslin of the *New York Times* considered the film "exploitative" and found its humor to be "one-note and thin."[68] Richard Corliss of *Time* called *Scream* an "idiot-savant movie, knowing but not smart."[69] Meanwhile, Jay Carr of the *Boston Globe* labeled it a "tirelessly self-reflexive splatterfest."[70] Not all critics were quite as harsh. David Ansen of *Newsweek* predicted the film would be a "sleeper," while Kevin Thomas of the *Los Angeles Times* declared it to be "sensational in both senses of the word: a bravura, provocative sendup of horror pictures that's also scary and gruesome yet too swift-moving to lapse into morbidity."[71]

The reviews were perhaps of little concern to *Scream's* producers and distributors, since a key virtue of genre films is their relatively "critic-proof" nature. Typically such films generate the bulk of their box office income in their first weeks in release, before poor word of mouth and negative reviews have had an impact. Further, genre pictures tend to attract younger viewers, who are perceived to be less concerned with critical reaction than older moviegoers. *Scream's* theatrical run, however, was quite distinct from the vast majority of genre films that came both before and after it. While it launched widely, premiering on approximately 1,400 screens, its opening weekend box office totaled a lukewarm $6 million.[72] Yet, despite its relatively slow start at the box office, growing word of mouth compelled Dimension to overlook the mixed critical reaction and continue its promotional push well into January 1997.[73] By mid-January, it became clear that Dimension had a major hit on its hands. At that time, Miramax marketing head Mark Gill remarked, "The only person who really believed 'Scream' could do $25 million at Christ-

A Dimension Films Release © 1998. Photo: Joyce Podell. Dimension darlings Tarantino and Rodriguez teamed up for the second time on *From Dusk Till Dawn*. Miramax promotional materials placed the filmmakers front and center once again. This photograph was distributed in conjunction with the release of *Full-Tilt Boogie* (1998), a documentary about the making of *From Dusk Till Dawn*.

mas was Bob Weinstein."[74] He continued, "No one dreamed of the kind of business it's doing or that it would cross over to an older audience. It's unprecedented."[75] The film was not only attracting a new generation of teenagers, but it was also bringing in twenty- and thirtysomething viewers eager for a fresh horror rush or a self-conscious retread through horror history. By late January, Miramax's $20 million–plus in P&A expenditures had yielded nearly $70 million at the North American box office.[76] *Scream*'s grosses continued to rise steadily over the ensuing months. In a pattern highly unusual for a horror film, *Scream* continued its theatrical run into the summer, ultimately generating $103 million during its more than thirty weeks in U.S. theaters.[77] It also earned in excess of $70 million overseas.[78] These returns placed *Scream* among an elite group of horror films. Accounting for adjusted gross at the box office, it earned more than any horror film had in American theaters in more than fifteen years. Its income exceeded that of *Friday the 13th* (1980), *Halloween* (1978), and Craven's own *A Nightmare on Elm Street* (1984).[79] Only a handful of films from the 1970s—including such big-budget classics as *The Exorcist* (1973), *The Omen* (1976), and *The Amityville Horror* (1979)—had earned more during their theatrical releases.[80]

Such facts did not go unnoticed by the press. A mere two months after the film's release, *Daily Variety* trumpeted *Scream* as reviving the horror genre and leading to the reemergence of the teen audience.[81] Meanwhile, the *Dallas Morning News* journalist Chris Vognar observed, "*Scream's* wicked blend of self-reflexive humor and good old-fashioned fear has scared the horror genre out of a lengthy creative and financial slump."[82] An October 1997 *Variety* headline declared, "'Scream' Catalyst for New Horror Era."[83] The article went on to note how *Scream's* generic revisionism was perfectly matched for 1990s sensibilities: "Call it 'hip horror' or 'Generation Next slashers,' the wave of interest in this fresh redefinition of the genre follows the historical pattern of how horror and other genres go through cycles of reinventing themselves."[84] Dimension's executives, and in particular the Weinsteins, called attention to the film's impact and the value of the techniques they employed in marketing it. Bob, Harvey, and the marketing team celebrated Dimension's accomplishments in launching the 1990s-era horror film and discovering a new audience

A Dimension Films Release © 1996. Photo: David M. Moir. With *Scream* (1996), Miramax began to build its stable of teen talent—and launched its first major teen franchise.

in the process. Bob called *Scream* an example of the kind of "intelligent genre movies" that were to be Dimension's stock-in-trade from now on.[85] He declared that Dimension would try to make genre films the equal of Hitchcock's *The Birds* (1963) or Ridley Scott's *Alien* (1979). He added, "Just because it's genre doesn't mean it has to be downscale."[86]

While Bob led the way in showing the press how *Scream* represented the Dimension brand of genre film, he and the rest of the Miramax/Dimension team maintained the delicate discursive distinction between Miramax-as-quality-cinema and Dimension-as-genre-product. Harvey Weinstein often took on the role of high-culture guru and representative of Miramax proper. As such, he repeatedly noted how Dimension's success served to benefit Miramax (and, by extension, high culture) as a whole. For instance, he told the *Los Angeles Times* that he made "no apologies" for *Scream*. He continued, since genre movies are potentially so profitable, "I'll be happy to be the Robin Hood of film distributors, robbing from the rich—my brother—and giving to the poor—foreign language movies."[87]

Harvey's use of the Robin Hood metaphor appeared in print on multiple occasions and served as a particularly effective means by which to keep Miramax's brand identity intact.[88] The repeated implication was that while genre films might be disreputable, their financial success ultimately enabled Miramax to promote art cinema in ways it otherwise could not. Never mind that Miramax had never been heavily invested in producing and distributing "art cinema." Through such statements, Miramax was rewriting its own history, erasing the presence of Disney money and downplaying the substantial sums generated by movies such as *sex, lies, and videotape* and *The Crying Game*. Such comments also minimized the strong connections that Miramax-based films such as *Pulp Fiction* and *Clerks* had to genre traditions.

As Harvey worked to show that the quality of Miramax's product had not eroded while Dimension's profile and income rose, Bob shrewdly suggested how Miramax's sensibility and high standards influenced Dimension's product. In fact, from Bob's perspective, Dimension was *better* than Miramax because its name was connected to very specific types of films: edgy, hip genre films. As he noted in one interview, "With Dimension, you know what kind of movie you're doing. . . . It ain't going to be *Wings of the Dove* [1997] or *Good Will Hunting* [1997]. Our label means something."[89] Its films were presented as the creations of artists who could skillfully balance the traditions of genre films and art cinema. Dimension executives effectively used the extensive fanfare following

Scream's release as a means by which to reinforce the whole company's brand identity. Dimension employees, and especially the Weinsteins, cited Scream as evidence of far more than just the resurgence of the horror film. Rather, it was used as an example of how a superior company had the ability to cultivate an exceptional brand of genre film. As the statements above illustrate, the Dimension brand was implied to be smarter, hipper, edgier, and more sophisticated; this message operated on multiple levels, appealing not only to the ordinary teenager but also to the media-savvy Gen Xer or nostalgic baby boomer.

In the months immediately after the release of Scream, such rhetoric was useful in a variety of ways. It differentiated Miramax from Dimension while reinforcing a specific image for Dimension—both as a company and for its individual films. These statements were equally useful for what they obscured. For instance, they helped downplay the pre-Scream history of Dimension—one, as noted above, dominated largely by B-grade straight-to-video product. They also concealed Dimension's continuing dependence on such product. Though Scream may have aided Dimension in revising its public image, the company still released a number of less "respectable" titles both theatrically and direct to video. But drawing attention to such Dimension-affiliated titles as Best of the Best 4: Without Warning (1998), The Prophecy II (1998), and Tale of the Mummy (1998) would do little to enhance the Dimension (or Miramax) brand name.

The contrast between how the press treated Miramax with Kids and Dimension with Scream is striking. In the case of Kids, every move Miramax made generated anxiety-laden headlines about the future prospects for companies that supported authentic artistic expression. Conversely, during this time, most journalists and critics bought Dimension's public relations push without question. Scream's box office longevity helped spur a wave of articles in trade and mainstream publications throughout 1997 trying to understand it as an emerging popular culture phenomenon. Dimension, and by extension Miramax, was seen as having a substantial influence on the film's appeal. For instance, in early 1997, Variety ran a profile on Dimension in which writer Monica Roman discussed how Dimension lacked "the resources to compete against the major studios in securing high-priced talent and creating costly special effects."[90] The company's solution, argued Roman, was to draw from "sister company Miramax's indie sensibility to deliver genre pics with a hip, arthouse flavor."[91] Similarly, later that year, USA Today's Susan Wloszczyna argued that "Scream's impact as a Dimension production, not a film acquired from an outside source, equaled the effect that Quentin Tarantino's groundbreaker *Pulp Fiction* had in lifting Miramax a notch in 1994. *Scream* shouted that Dimension is an artistic as well as a money-making entity."[92] Miramax poster boy Tarantino also chimed in with his own opinion on *Scream*'s far-reaching influence, stating, "Williamson did with *Scream* what I did with gangster films. Horror was pretty much fucking dead when he did that. Not only did he revitalize it and give some respect to the slasher genre, but he even commented on why all these other horror films have been so crappy. . . . *Scream* kind of made invalid that horror has a [box office] ceiling and science fiction doesn't."[93]

While many journalists attributed the film's box office success at least in part to its appeal to multiple demographic groups, the film's core audience was perceived to be teenagers. *Scream* was often seen as playing a crucial role in uncovering the next generation of moviegoers.[94] Though this group had been accessed to some extent through television outlets such as Fox and MTV, theatrically oriented motion picture divisions had not yet been substantially exploited it. *Scream*—and by extension, Dimension—was at the forefront of the late 1990s teen boom, which included an explosion in media featuring and targeting junior high and high schoolers. According to Bob Weinstein, such an audience had been underserved for years. In recalling his decision to green-light *Scream*, he stated, "There were no movies being made for teenagers anymore. It had become an adult-oriented business. I knew there was an audience that was not being satiated."[95]

Launching the 1990s-Era Teen Franchise

The teen audience was doubly satiated on the week of *Scream*'s release. On the precise date that *Scream* launched, another teen-oriented film, Paramount's *Beavis and Butt-Head Do America*, also opened. The latter film, based on the cult MTV series *Beavis and Butt-Head* (1993–1997), also proved a surprise hit at the box office, earning more than $63 million in its North American release.[96] The substantial earnings of both films helped draw attention from both the industry and journalists alike to a "neglected" audience. As one journalist noted in mid-January 1997, "The two films' success has spurred new consideration of the teen audience—a segment that's largely been ignored by the majors for the past five years."[97] *Beavis and Butt-Head*'s rapid decline at the box office helps explain why it did not receive the same kind of prolonged attention and analysis from the press that was directed toward *Scream*. Nonetheless, both films provided useful lessons to industry executives: teenagers once again promised millions (and even billions) of dollars. Box office returns were not the only factor spurring an increased emphasis on developing more teen-oriented media; demographic shifts also came into play. Members of "Generation Y" were born during the 1982 to 1995 period.[98] This meant that at the time of the release of *Scream* and *Beavis and Butt-Head*, the oldest members of this demographic bulge of approximately eighty million Americans were becoming teenagers.[99] More to the point, they were becoming teenagers with a high degree of expendable cash.

Box office returns from *Scream* and *Beavis and Butt-Head* reinforced what census reports long had promised. Namely, as the *San Diego Herald-Tribune* declared in late December 1997, "Teens Hold Ticket to Movie Success."[100] Money was also to be made through the sale of CDs (Britney Spears, Backstreet Boys, Christina Aguilera), television (especially on such WB/UPN programs as *Buffy the Vampire Slayer*, 1997–2003; and *The Gilmore Girls*, 2000–2007), and associated merchandise. Suddenly executives throughout the various media industries rushed to green-light projects geared toward a teenage audience. As one of the first projects to "find" this audience, *Scream* provided a template not only for the film industry but also for the media industries at large. The film's tongue-in-cheek tone, strikingly articulate characters, high degree of self-reflexivity, and hyper-stylization all served as common traits in the teen media explosion that followed. Dimension was at the vanguard of this teen proliferation *across* media.[101] Among the many reasons *Scream* was significant for Dimension was that it marked the company's first bona fide multimedia franchise to be produced in-house. As successful as Miramax had been in developing tie-ins and ancillary merchandise for a handful of its films, Dimension reached a completely different level in terms of sequels and synergies. As Bob Weinstein noted wryly, "Hollywood is built on franchises. . . . Miramax never had that ability. You couldn't have a *Piano 2* or *My Right Foot*. With Dimension, the opportunity to have a franchise is there."[102]

Scream was well on its way to being a full-fledged franchise within a year of its 20 December 1996 theatrical premiere. In an attempt to capitalize on *Scream*'s widespread popularity, Dimension quickly signed screenwriter Kevin Williamson to write two sequels.[103] The company rushed *Scream 2* into production and opened it on 12 December 1997—a week after the first installment was released on home video. The first sequel earned a stunning $33 million in its opening weekend, and went on to pass the $100 million mark in North American box office grosses.[104] It earned another $71 million overseas.[105] Throughout 1997, a wide array of *Scream*-related merchandise began to appear in the marketplace, including a *Scream* screenplay via Miramax Books, multiple music soundtracks (one with the film's score, one with rock music), two different VHS versions (a standard pan-and-scan version and a "deluxe" edition), and extensive licensed merchandise.[106] The killer's mask, meanwhile, remained a popular Halloween costume for years to come.

Exploiting his newfound success, Williamson signed on to write a treatment for a new installment of the *Halloween* series for Dimension.[107] This film, later titled *Halloween H2O*, ultimately would be released in celebration of the twentieth anniversary of the original. Concurrently, Williamson became involved with a number of other teen-oriented projects for both film and television. He wrote the screenplay version of the classic Lois Duncan book *I Know What You Did Last Summer* for Sony. This film, which starred a number of B-grade actors and television stars (including *Party of Five*'s Jennifer Love Hewitt and the newly minted Buffy, Sarah Michelle Gellar), emerged as another surprise hit. *I Know What You Did* had a $15 million opening weekend in October 1997 and ended up generating more than $72 million in North America.[108] Its high returns on the heels of *Scream*'s release further confirmed the arrival of the late 1990s teen media boom.

Williamson milked this moment as much as possible. Within two years of *Scream*'s premiere, he had created *Dawson's Creek* (1998–2003) for the WB network. In addition, he became one of the go-to writers for the Weinsteins. In addition to all the *Scream* films, he also wrote the screenplay for the Robert Rodriguez–helmed high school science-fiction thriller *The Faculty* (1998), and wrote and directed the teen suspense film *Teaching Mrs. Tingle* (1999). Further, he created the short-lived Miramax-produced, ABC-distributed television drama *Wasteland* (1999). By 1999, one journalist described Williamson as possessing "more name recognition with young moviegoers than any filmmaker since John Hughes."[109]

In much the same way that Miramax brought key talent such as Rodriguez, Smith, and Tarantino into its fold a few years earlier, Dimension was now making long-term deals with *Scream* talent. One month after Williamson's deal was announced in the trade publications, director Wes Craven signed a three-picture contract with Miramax. *Scream 2* was the first film produced under this agreement; the second would be the drama *Music of the Heart*, released under the Miramax label in 1999.[110] Craven and Williamson were among the many filmmakers who, depending on the nature of the product, would move back and forth between the Dimension and Miramax labels. As the 1990s wore on, Tarantino,

Smith, and Rodriguez would do the same. Even Steven Soderbergh had his Dimension moment in 1997, as cowriter of the thriller *Nightwatch*, a remake of the Danish film *Nattevagten* (1994). Meanwhile, Keenen Ivory, Shawn, and Marlon Wayans, who had worked with Miramax on the hit parody of early 1990s "hood films," *Don't Be a Menace to South Central While Drinking Your Juice in the Hood* (1996), prepared to work with Dimension. Their project this time was a parody of the latest wave of self-reflexive genre films spawned by *Scream*.[111] The title of this new film, *Scary Movie*, had been the working title for *Scream*.[112]

As these many talent deals indicate, Dimension shifted into high gear following the release of *Scream*. The year 1997 was truly a high point for the division, beginning with surprising returns for the first installment of *Scream* and ending with the phenomenal opening weekend for the second installment. Dimension's market share continued to grow, as did its box office returns relative to Miramax. As a means of comparison, back in 1993, when its biggest hits were *Children of the Corn II* and *Fortress*, Dimension yielded $14 million and constituted only 9 percent of Miramax's total income.[113] For the 1996 calendar year, Dimension's grosses tallied $93.4 million, thereby accounting for approximately 37 percent of Miramax's total box office revenues of $250 million.[114] Meanwhile, with only a few exceptions, production budgets for Dimension releases remained within the moderately priced $12 million–$20 million range.[115] Dimension's fortunes looked even rosier in 1997, as *Scream*, *Mimic*, *Operation Condor*, and *Scream 2* helped the division earn more than $190 million.[116] As will be discussed in the next chapter, Miramax-label releases also performed well that year, yielding $229 million in North American theaters.[117] Proportionally, in 1997, Dimension's films accounted for about 45 percent of parent operation Miramax's total income of $419 million.[118] These figures are particularly noteworthy because only about a half dozen Dimension films contributed to that $190 million. In contrast, it took more than two dozen Miramax division releases to earn $229 million.[119]

Though horror may have been the most prominent type of film in terms of box office returns and publicity for Dimension early on, *Scream*'s influence was evident in a wide range of other genres that the company was involved in throughout the late 1990s. Dimension dabbled in science fiction (*The Faculty*), comedy (*Jay and Silent Bob Strike Back*, 2001) and children's fare (the *Spy Kids* trilogy, 2001, 2002, 2003) with mixed success. Certainly the extent to which Dimension's releases replicated the style and sensibility of *Scream* varied from film to film. What remained consistent, however, was that most of the films were *sold* as being superior in content and production values to earlier genre films. The disparity between content and marketing was apparent to some. For example, as one critic noted in his review of *Halloween H2o*, "Aside from the *Scream* pics that kickstarted it, the latest horror wave is starting to look no less routine—if glossier—than all those '80s teen slash-'em-ups that had previously run this genre aground."[120] Similarly, upon attending the American Film Market following the release of *Scream*, one journalist found acquisitions executives complaining that "outright genre pics with weak scripts are being gussied up as arthouse fare with cult casting choices."[121]

Such responses would become even more prevalent as the millennium neared and the number of genre companies grew. The range of entities devoted to releasing genre films skyrocketed in the late 1990s and early 2000s. Much as Miramax's good fortune with such films as *sex, lies, and videotape*, *The Crying Game*, and *Pulp Fiction* helped motivate other studios to start developing their own specialty divisions a few years prior, Dimension's rapid and remarkable rise similarly spurred a widespread move to create more genre films and develop studio-based genre divisions. The first such divisions were announced in 1998. In April, October Films created Rogue Pictures to release genre films.[122] In December of the same year, Sony rebranded its Screen Gems label to serve a similar purpose.[123] At the same time, rising independent distributors Artisan and Lions Gate also began to trade more heavily in genre films.

The release of *Scream* marked a turning point for Dimension and for genre films. At this moment, the company managed to have it both ways: Miramax extended its "aura of quality" to the Dimension label *at the same time* that it presented its content as distinctive from that of Dimension. Miramax proper sustained its status as the champion of true art. For the most part, its involvement with Dimension was presented as elevating the quality of genre films, or as an example of the "necessary evils" that enabled the company to attain heightened resources. These resources, in turn, would allow it to venture more frequently into the production and distribution of art and foreign-language films. The divergent nature of the discourses about Miramax and Dimension suggests a great deal about ongoing attitudes toward film and popular culture at large. Both critics and scholars have remained unsure of how to categorize genre films, and thus (if discussing them at all) have placed them in a separate box—one that is almost always perceived to contain inferior product to that found in the Miramax/specialty film box. This tendency to compartmentalize genre films, if not dismiss them outright, is a miscalculation. Both industrially and textually, there is a great deal of overlap between the films released by the Miramax and Dimension divisions. *Scream*'s generic revisionism, postmodern aesthetic, witty banter, and self-awareness all made it a perfect companion to the Miramax-branded films directed by Kevin Smith, Quentin Tarantino, David O. Russell, Alexander Payne, and Doug Liman. The lines between Miramax and Dimension, genre and art, are not nearly as discrete as the companies and the mainstream press would have us believe. Yet, as the next chapter shows, such discourses became particularly prominent in early 1997.

Majors, Indies, Independents

The Rise of a Three-Tier System (Winter 1996 – Spring 1997)

No one could argue with the contention that 1996 was the year of the independent film. But what is up for debate is how the major studios will respond, if at all, to being overwhelmed by the independents in the Oscar race this year.

Los Angeles Times, *February 1997*

Wouldn't it be the ultimate Hollywood irony if a so-called independent ended up owning the Hollywood spectacle?

Peter Bart, Variety *editor in chief, 1997*

A handful of journalists declared nearly every year during the early-to-mid-1990s as the "year of the independents."[1] Yet this appellation failed to gain much traction until the announcement of the Best Picture nominees for 1996. Then, suddenly, this headline appeared on seemingly every newspaper and magazine in the United States. In the spring of 1997, one publication after another discussed how independents had pummeled the Hollywood majors in Academy Award nominations—and, soon after, award wins. Many in the press saw the praise directed toward indies as reaffirming that the Hollywood studios were no longer capable of—or cared to—produce and distribute quality films. While the majors released such action-oriented, effects-driven fare as *The Rock, Star Trek: First Contact, Twister,* and *Independence Day,* indies offered a bounty of critically lauded, character-driven movies such as *Sling Blade, Breaking the Waves, Emma, Kolya, Secrets & Lies, Lone Star,* and *Fargo.* Several of the latter films were not only highly praised but were also strong performers at the box office.

Journalists may have often uncritically attached the label "year of the independents" to their articles, yet something far more complex was taking place. As has been noted in previous chapters, the rise of independents actually occurred several years prior. What in the mid-1990s was usually being described as the coming-of-age of independents actually involved the widespread institutionalization of studio-based specialty divisions. The mainstream press was certainly correct in noting the changes in Hollywood by early 1997; their main mistake came in how they defined these changes. The press typically presented a dramatic conflict between small, intimate works of art crafted by outsiders magically triumphing over big, brash pieces of commerce churned out by corporate oppressors. As we shall see, what in fact was happening was far more fluid, cooperative, and strategic.

This chapter provides a broad examination of the state of the industry during this "year of the independents." Yet rather than blindly adhering to such prior designations, I illustrate how in fact this was the "year of the indies." In tweaking the phrase in such a manner, it is possible to call attention to the extent to which a new industrial structure was taking shape. The pages that follow indicate precisely *how* a new, three-tier industry structure, consisting of the majors, studio-based indies, and true independents, developed. Included is a survey of the rapid transformation of the structure and content of Hollywood at both the big-budget and indie levels. In addition, what follows is an examination of how companies unaffiliated with major conglomerates continued to be marginalized. This defining period began with the Sundance Film Festival in January 1996, continued through the Academy Awards ceremony in March 1997, and culminated with the acquisition of the most high-profile independent company, October Films, by Universal Pictures in May 1997. During this time frame, activity in the festival scene became much more pronounced, battles for the rights to potential indie blockbusters heightened, in-house productions escalated, new talent both in front of and behind the camera continued to rise to the fore, and indie films increasingly were conceptualized as a genre in their own right.

Even as this new structure began to solidify, Miramax plowed ahead with little regard for larger industrial conditions. The Weinsteins responded to the new market entrants and heightened competition in the specialty film business by expanding in size and scope. The company bought more films, spent more on production and distribution, hired more executives, signed more deals with talent, created more divisions, and wooed the press more aggressively. In the short term, these moves proved stunningly successful, as the company's market share rose and its films attained additional awards and honors. Further, Miramax garnered a great deal of acclaim for the part it played in this landmark year. Along with winning half of the twenty-four Academy Award nominations it received in the spring of 1997, Miramax received its first Best Picture win with *The English Patient* (1996). If this was the year of the indies, then Miramax was the preeminent such producer and distributor of the time. The Weinsteins were widely feted as well. Not only did the Independent Feature Project honor them with the Gotham Lifetime Achievement award in the spring of 1997, but *Time* magazine also declared "movie mogul" Harvey Weinstein one of its most influential people of the year.[2]

Miramax was scaling new heights and the Weinsteins (especially Harvey) readily took credit for the many accomplishments achieved by the employees under their command. The Miramax brand retained a strong cultural cachet, and its influence was felt far beyond the realm of motion picture production and distribution. At the time, *The English Patient* represented a peak moment for Miramax with regard to earnings, prestige, and narrative experimentation. In the longer term, however, it signaled something far more perilous. Up to this period, Miramax had unquestionably played a central role in defining the economic and aesthetic parameters of the 1990s-era low-budget film world. In the process, it had retained a favorable relationship between itself and its parent company. But *The English Patient*, though immensely successful for Miramax in terms of its balance sheet and image, represented a move in a dangerous direction for the company. The film's massive critical and commercial success encouraged Miramax to venture into developing more "mid-range" prestige pictures. These projects—which were becoming increasingly challenging to produce, market, and profit from in the emergent industrial environment—were precisely the types of films the rest of the industry was rapidly moving away from.

Fighting for a Deal: Sundance Comes of Age

> It was a good year and a pivotal one. If "sex, lies, and videotape" [1989] marked Sundance's puberty, '96 brings it to majority.
>
> Variety, *January 1996*

"Circuslike environment" was the description applied by *Variety*'s Todd McCarthy to the January 1996 Sundance Film Festival.[3] This was a far cry from the relatively sedate affair the festival had been in the early 1990s. Every year during the 1990s, Sundance attracted more film submissions as well as a greater numbers of journalists, acquisitions executives, public relations agents, talent agents, and moviegoers. The trend showed little sign of abating at mid-decade. Some figures give a sense of how Sundance had been transformed in just the few years since *El mariachi* took home the Audience Award in 1993. At that time, attendance was increasing roughly 30 percent per year.[4] With total attendance reaching five thousand, one observer declared that Sundance had reached its "saturation point."[5] By 1996, festival planners likely wished for such mellow days, as attendance now exceeded nine thousand.[6] Meanwhile, film submissions increased from two hundred fifty for the 1993 festival[7] to eight hundred for the 1997 event.[8] This increase was all the more striking since most of the features submitted were still shot on film (shooting on digital video had not yet become widespread). A shift was also apparent in the types of films submitted; increasingly, features veered away from avant-garde and experimental traditions and toward more politically conservative and commercially oriented fare.[9] The ultra-low-budget moment of the early 1990s, which had been characterized by 16mm films proudly displaying their meager resources, gave way to larger numbers of million-dollar-plus budgets and higher production values.

The arrival of more journalists on the scene suggested the festival's broadening appeal (or, at least, its perceived popular appeal). Press accreditations rose more than 20 percent per year. The 106 journalists attending in 1991 were far eclipsed by the 261 attending in 1995.[10] Roughly 400 journalists descended on the streets of Park City, Utah, just one year later.[11] The most dramatic shift was in the festival's emergence as a site for brokering deals. Though Sundance lacked an official market where films were bought and sold, by the mid-1990s it had attained the unofficial status of an indie film marketplace. As *Variety* noted at the festival in 1996, "It now appears that Sundance at least equals Cannes as a place where new filmmakers are discovered and U.S. distribution deals are made."[12] With the deep-pocketed buyers now including not only Miramax but also Fine Line/New Line, Fox Searchlight, Sony Pictures Classics, and Gramercy, intense bidding wars became commonplace.[13] One widely reported incident involved a "verbal altercation" between Harvey Weinstein and a sales representative for *Shine* (1996). The event took place at a restaurant when Weinstein discovered that Fine Line had acquired North American rights for the film.[14]

It might seem odd that, with the glut of product, executives literally fought over the distribution rights to one picture. With more than one hundred films screening at the festival, and North American theatrical distribution rights for the vast majority of them still available, what could be the explanation for such behavior?[15] In short, few of these films were perceived to have the potential of becoming the next indie blockbusters à la *sex, lies, and videotape* and *Pulp Fiction* (1994). Specialty divisions were on the hunt for the next big thing that could be funneled into the various distribution pipelines of their conglomerate parents. Such films had to be able to generate the kind of critical accolades, word of mouth, and awards attention that could make the expenditures on them worthwhile. If they were not easy to promote as high-culture products extraordinaire, hyper-stylized genre-bending exercises, or displays of powerful performances by stars playing against type, then these companies rarely looked twice at them. Studio-based specialty divisions were investing in these films for the long term; they wanted the distribution dollars spent for theatrical distribution to pay off in ancillary markets such as videocassette and cable. Grossing a few hundred thousand dollars at the box office was no longer enough; the films had to have the potential to earn *tens of millions* of dollars.

The competition for potential breakout films was further accentuated because there were so few actually available for purchase. Though trade publications regularly reported on deals struck during Sundance, these arrangements were more often brokered far in advance of the event.[16] Issuing press releases about deals during the festival simply served as an easy way to create early publicity.[17] Similarly, many specialty companies started to come to festivals such as Sundance with films that they long had been involved with in order to conduct low-cost "test screenings" with real audiences. If a film played well, early press coverage and word of mouth might be stimulated.

Contrary to the widely circulated coverage about a select number of ultra-low-budget films (e.g., *Go Fish*, 1994; *Clerks*, 1994; *What Happened Was . . .*, 1994; *Clean, Shaven*, 1995), Sundance films with budgets far exceeding $100,000 were quickly becoming the norm. Of course, films at these budget levels were usually *not* self-financed by the filmmakers, their friends, and their family.[18] Rather, money came from a diverse array of sources. These included private investors attracted by the well-publicized tales of "little films" that hit the box office jackpot, along with regional television stations (particularly those affiliated with PBS), emerging cable services such as the Sundance Channel and IFC, and the old standby, videocassette distributors.[19] A greater influx of cash also came from overseas.[20] Deregulation and privatization in many countries around the world fueled the growth of new film and television companies. These new companies needed to feed their content-hungry distribution systems, and thus they advanced growing sums up front. In exchange for these monies, financiers often retained distribution rights for markets in which these companies were based or had affiliations.

Despite increasingly complicated rights situations, some films reached the festival with key rights still available. Occasionally a picture would play surprisingly well with festival audiences, thereby piquing the interest of select distributors. Sometimes producers would avoid pre-screening a film for acquisitions executives in the hope that it would play well with the festival audience and thus provoke a bidding war. This was always a risky proposition, for films could just as easily disappoint an audience and executives as they could please them. While *Shine* exceeded expectations, the same could not be said for the well-received drama *The Spitfire Grill* (1996). Time Warner's recently acquired Castle Rock division attracted coverage for the unprecedented $10 million it spent to acquire the film.[21] No competitor came close to matching the company's bid; reportedly the second-highest offer was from Trimark for approximately $1 million.[22] Even *Shine* was acquired for a far more reasonable price of $2.5 million.[23] Advancing lots of money guaranteed both the company and the film widespread media coverage; though much of this coverage was of the "what were they thinking?" variety, it nonetheless meant free publicity for the film and demonstrated Castle Rock's desire to become a major player in the indie business. Unfortunately, *The Spitfire Grill* did not become the next big indie blockbuster. Though it earned a respectable $12.6 million domestically, given the amount spent to acquire it, *The Spitfire Grill* was widely viewed as a disappointment. Except in the rare instances where it was cited as a cautionary tale about an increasingly out-of-control acquisitions business, the film quickly faded from the public memory. Castle Rock made no other such dramatic statements about its buying power in subsequent years.

The Spitfire Grill is an instructive example of the extent to which widely circulated discourses about the indie boom of 1996–1997 did not match market realities. Nonetheless, in terms of sheer numbers, this period was a high point for indies. Included among the specialty films released in North American theaters to much fanfare and numerous awards nominations during 1996 alone were those listed in table 6.1.[24] Several of these played at Sundance in 1996, including *Shine, Welcome to the Dollhouse, Big Night, Citizen Ruth, I Shot Andy Warhol, When We Were Kings, Walking and Talking, Flirt,* and *Bound.*

To be sure, indies generated an immense amount of critical praise and press coverage during 1996. Yet most of these films were lucky if they cleared $10 million in North American box office—and these were the successes. Much more numerous were the films that barely regis-

High-profile 1996 Indie and Independent Releases

Miramax	*The English Patient, Marvin's Room, Sling Blade, Flirting with Disaster, Basquiat, Walking and Talking, Dead Man, Emma, Trainspotting, Citizen Ruth*
Gramercy	*Fargo, Bound, When We Were Kings*
Sony Pictures Classics (SPC)	*Lone Star, Welcome to the Dollhouse, Manny & Lo*
Fine Line	*Shine*
October	*Secrets & Lies, Breaking the Waves*
Cinepix Film Properties (CFP)	*Flirt*
Samuel Goldwyn	*Big Night, I Shot Andy Warhol*

tered a blip on the radar of the press, critics, or audiences. At the same time that *Shine* and *The Spitfire Grill* secured much ballyhooed distribution deals, *The Darien Gap, Eden, Follow Me Home, Bandwagon, God's Lonely Man, The Keeper,* and *Late Bloomers* also played in competition at Sundance in 1996. If these films did go on to obtain some type of distribution, it was with a small-scale, true independent—companies such as Strand or Kino, which had limited financial resources and no affiliation with a major media conglomerate. At best, these films achieved modest theatrical releases on a handful of screens. In other words, most of the "Sundance films" lacking name talent, edgy content, an identifiable marketing angle, or explicit links to Hollywood narrative and generic conventions experienced the same fate that met most independently distributed features throughout history: marginalization. Further, the failure of many of the titles identified above to perform according to distributors' expectations affected what was funded, produced, and acquired in future years.[25] This contributed to a further solidification of the narrative and aesthetic traits of indie films that received support from specialty divisions.

The launch of specialty cable channels tailored to indie fare—namely, IFC (launched in 1994) and the Sundance Channel (launched in February 1996, soon after that year's festival)—also delimited what companies deemed financially viable. Certainly these new outlets were a boon to the indie film business, as they provided another distribution outlet and an additional revenue stream for select specialty films. But as these outlets typically pursued the most high-profile product in order to be attractive to multiple system operators, they benefited only a limited number of filmmakers and companies. Since these new cable outlets were trying to cultivate brand identities in an increasingly crowded media landscape, they pursued well-known films that conformed to particular discourses of independence. The films selected were generally those that fit with the channels' desire to attract the much sought-after demographic of upscale urban professionals.[26]

From the perspective of these new cable program services, as well as many video stores and media publications, indie films increasingly were being conceptualized as one coherent and identifiable body of films. Some went so far as to call them a genre. For example, as Sundance Channel president Nora Ryan noted soon after the launch of the service, cable systems were enthusiastic about carrying the channel because "the genre is in the spotlight."[27] Similarly, Blockbuster stores began to carve out a place for specialty films in much the same way that comedies and dramas had their own shelf space: approximately one hundred independent films could be found on a shelf labeled "Sundance Channel Recommends."[28]

The Sundance Channel's launch was but one of many signs of the festival's expansive and dramatic growth. As part of programmers' efforts to accommodate more festival submissions, an American Spectrum sidebar was added in 1996, designed to feature "20 first or second U.S. indie efforts that, for one reason or another, didn't make it into the competition but were deemed worthy of presentation."[29] Sundance's central place in the indie cinema infrastructure could also be seen from its prominence in John Pierson's influential book *Spike, Mike, Slacker, and Dykes*, released shortly before the January 1996 festival.[30] Though an intensely personal and highly anecdotal narrative, the book was one of the first attempts to situate historically the contemporary indie film moment. Interestingly, the newly formed Miramax Books published Pierson's tome. The publisher also held one of Pierson's early book signings at Sundance in 1996.[31]

Perhaps the strongest evidence that Sundance had become a sizable institution in its own right can be seen from the ascendance of its first local emulator, the Slamdance Film Festival. Begun in 1995 by "dissident filmmakers" who claimed they were dissatisfied with Sundance's move away from its roots, Slamdance ran concurrently with Sundance.[32]

Significantly, these individuals launched Slamdance not because they wanted a venue for more experimental works, but simply because Sundance rejected their own films. In its first year, Slamdance took place in Salt Lake City and screened eight features and a selection of shorts. In 1996, however, Slamdance took on Sundance directly, moving to Park City and featuring a dozen films in competition as well as several out-of-competition screenings. Emerging indie talents such as James LeGros, Greg Mottola, and Marc Forster screened films, and nearly five thousand people attended the event.[33] There was even a high-profile acquisition, Mottola's *The Daytrippers*, which Steven Soderbergh executive-produced.[34] Cinepix Film Properties acquired the dramedy, starring Stanley Tucci, Hope Davis, Parker Posey, Liev Schreiber, and Campbell Scott, and released it nationwide in March 1997. The $700,000 film earned a respectable $2 million at the box office.[35]

As Slamdance rapidly grew, Sundance programmers continued rethinking the mission of their festival and reassessing their objectives in choosing films. Did they want to support unknown talents? Regional productions? Those marginalized by virtue of their race, class, gender, politics, or sexuality? Or did they merely want to support the "best" of filmmaking—the strongest voices and visions—however those might be defined? Did sources of funding matter? Should films that had already secured distribution from studio subsidiaries be given prominent placement at the festival? Responses by the Sundance staff varied from year to year.[36] Yet given the speed and degree that the entire industry was being restructured, it hardly seems fair to take Sundance programmers to task for their ambivalence. The challenges faced by Sundance were a microcosm of those faced by all involved in the production and distribution of low-budget films in 1996–1997. People throughout the industry—along with those covering it—were trying to come to terms with precisely what was happening and what the implications of these changes were.

The Structure Takes Shape

> The focus of our efforts has got to be on the mainstream. The size of these companies, the amounts of money you spend to make and market a film, our agenda of distributing these films all over the world—with the size of the staff we have—puts the bulk of our attention on making movies that will be accessible to as many people as possible.
>
> *Joe Roth, Walt Disney Studios chair, 1997*

This statement by Disney executive Joe Roth reflects an industry-wide reassessment being made at this time by the heads of film divisions at the media conglomerates. A combination of factors, including rising production and distribution costs, a series of failures at the mid-budget level, and continuing evidence that indie subsidiaries could better handle niche-oriented product led the studios to increasingly refine the types of films that they chose to develop, produce, and release. At the same time that the majors began to identify their preferred budget levels, target audiences, genres, and content, so, too, did the growing number of studio-based indie companies. Specialty divisions formulated theories about what worked best in terms of producing greater box office returns, press coverage, and awards. The actions of these indie subsidiaries, in turn, adversely affected the companies that remained unaffiliated with major conglomerates.

In general, journalists and critics conceptualized this emerging industrial structure as consisting of two expansive tiers (nicknamed the "two Hollywoods" by the *New York Times*):[37] the Hollywood majors and an imprecisely defined group of independents. What entities and films qualified as these so-called independents depended greatly on the writer's beat and individual tastes. The term might refer to a broad array of films of diverse budgets, genres, talent, and industrial affiliations. Regardless of the particular angle taken by an individual writer, the relationship depicted was usually an *oppositional* one.[38] Journalists tended to portray these two sectors of the industry as diametrically opposed, perhaps even in mortal combat for audience attention, rather than as interactive and codependent.

Such discourses grew more pronounced as 1996 continued and a growing number of specialty films eclipsed the Hollywood majors' product in terms of critical acclaim and awards. It was not long before the "year of the independents" angle took on a life of its own, at which point few paused to complicate this developing narrative. Several newspaper and magazine headlines run during Oscar season reflect the relatively uniform position taken in the articles: "Independents' Day . . . Anthony Minghella's Triumph over Hollywood" (*Washington Post*); "Indies Spiking Oscar's Punch: Studios Fear Losing Party to Crashers" (*Variety*); "Independents Day for Oscars" (*Los Angeles Times*); "Independents' Day" (*Time*).[39] Besides suggesting a lack of creativity on the part of the press, the headlines also indicate the extent to which journalists miscalculated the changes taking place. "Independent" became a blanket term for many writers.

One of the rare exceptions to such industry assessments appeared

Main Tiers of Theatrically Released Films, 1996–1997

	Category	Key financials	Target audience	Types of films
Tier 1: Majors	Disney-Touchstone, Warner Bros., Paramount, etc.	Budgets of $60 million and up; desired box office of $100 million–plus	"Most mass," aim for at least two of four quadrants: men over/under 25; women over/under 25	Action; science fiction; fantasy; family; animation; broad comedy; often based on presold properties
Tier 2: Studio-based indies	Miramax, Gramercy, Fox Searchlight, etc.	Budgets from $3 million to 20 million; avg. acquisition cost of $4 million; increasingly reliant on in-house productions; "dream" box office of $100 million	Initially target specific niches (teens, African Americans, Gen Xers, etc.); hope films will cross over to other demographics	American indies ("cinema of cool," "cinema of quality"); genre films (horror, teen comedy, etc.); English-language imports; limited number of foreign-language imports
Tier 3: True independents	Strand, CFP, Trimark, etc.	Minuscule budgets; mainly acquisitions, bought for well below $1 million; "good" box office ranges from $200,000 to $1 million	Primarily traditional art house moviegoers (college students, boomers) based in major cities or college towns	Wide variety, but especially foreign-language; auteur-driven; LGBT; nonfiction films
Danger zone: "Mid-range" films or "tweeners"**	Studios cutting output; Miramax begins to do more as of The English Patient	Negative cost** of $25 million to $60 million; box office consistently disappoints	Target audience often hard to identify; must appeal beyond one niche, which often proves challenging in practice	Ties to classical Hollywood fare (period films, romantic comedies, musicals, serious dramas, biopics, literary adaptations); often seen as "safely middlebrow"

Data compiled from various reports in *Variety* and *Hollywood Reporter*.

* The label "tweeners" is used by Peter Biskind in *Down and Dirty Pictures* (New York: Simon & Schuster, 2004), 323, 416.

** "Negative cost" refers to the actual production cost of the film. Figures typically reflect expenses from the development phase to final cut.

in a brief February 1997 *Observer* article. In this piece, the journalist Edward Helmore identified an emerging industry structure: a *three-tier system* consisting of the Hollywood studios, "semi-independents," and "true low-budget independents."[40] Though he did not delve into the characteristics of any tier in detail, this article is nonetheless useful in providing a launching point from which to begin to reassess—and, in the process, challenge—dominant representations of the industry during this period. This section expands on the characteristics of the developing three-tier structure identified in Helmore's article. Since the goal here is to offer a snapshot of the industry, at times it will be necessary to briefly shift away from explicitly discussing Miramax and indie divisions. It should be clear, however, that what occurred at one tier often affected the others. As the chart above shows, three main tiers took shape by 1996: the majors (tier 1), the studio-based indies (tier 2), and the true independents (tier 3, referred to from this point onward simply as independents). Whether by choice (at the major level) or by virtue of limited resources (at the independent level), each tier increasingly focused on particular types of films with specific budgetary ranges; employed distinctive production, distribution, and marketing strategies; and was covered—and valued—differently by journalists. By outlining the characteristics of these tiers, and indicating where they overlapped or deviated from one another, it is possible to move past the oversimplifications that have been and continue to be widely used to describe the companies and the films they released during this period.

The roots of this three-tier structure can be found in the late 1980s and early 1990s. One key turning point in the solidification of tier 1 took place in 1995, however, when a wave of major mergers and acquisitions, along with substantial turnover in the executive ranks, set the scene for the substantive changes that would take place in many conglomerates' motion picture divisions the following year. Over the course of this one event-filled year, the beverage distillery Seagram purchased MCA/Universal from Matsushita, Disney acquired Capital Cities/ABC, and Time Warner bought Turner Entertainment (whose holdings included not only New Line and Castle Rock, but also the Atlanta Braves baseball team, CNN, TBS, TNT, and a host of other media entities). In addition, huge management shake-ups took place at both Sony and Disney. At Disney, for instance, CEO Michael Eisner hired CAA talent agency head Michael Ovitz to become second in command, filling the gap left by the death of Walt Disney Co. president and chief operating officer Frank Wells and the recent departure of Disney Studios chairman Jeffrey Katzenberg to DreamWorks.[41]

If 1995 was a dramatic year at the conglomerate level, 1996 was equally dramatic for both tiers 1 and 2. Even as new owners and fresh management rethought their business practices, reports of high levels of excess at the major studios proliferated. Rising costs throughout the industry far exceeded the level of inflation. For example, in 1995, average negative costs (actual costs of production of a film) were $36.4 million. P&A costs accounted for an additional $17.7 million, leading to an average of $54.1 million spent on tier 1 studio projects.[42] Just one year later, total costs had risen to $59.6 million.[43] As the media world continued to fragment, marketing costs surged. A growing number of cable and broadcast outlets fractured the mass audience further, forcing studio marketers to allocate more marketing dollars to a wider range of venues.

Given these circumstances, the studios refocused their energies on certain types of event films, including high-concept action adventures, science fiction, and fantasy (e.g., *Eraser*; *Mission: Impossible*; *Ransom*; *Star Trek: First Contact*, all 1996). The strong aftermarket performance of family films led many companies to emphasize these further as well (e.g., the live-action *101 Dalmatians*; *Harriet the Spy*, both 1996). With $191 million taken in at the North American box office alone, Disney/Pixar's first fully computer-animated feature-length film, *Toy Story* (1995), marked a significant turning point for the industry. Cumulatively, all these films were considered "four-quadrant" films, thus labeled for their appeal to what the industry defined as the four major audience sectors: men over twenty-five, men under twenty-five, women over twenty-five, and women under twenty-five.[44] Due to their lower production costs, the studios also continued to green-light broad comedies. Often these films were seen as having two-quadrant appeal, though the particular quadrants varied depending on the film. Yet, on occasion, such films exceeded expectations, as was the case with *The Birdcage*, *The Nutty Professor*, *A Very Brady Sequel*, and *Happy Gilmore* (all 1996).

Proving much less dependable were the aforementioned "mid-range" studio-level films, which fell between tiers 1 and 2 in terms of budget. These films consisted of period pieces, traditional romantic comedies, musicals, "serious" dramas, biopics, and literary adaptations. Though many of these pictures may have cost less to produce than event films, their box office fortunes were often far more mixed. Not only were they harder to market, but they also were more sensitive to both critical response and word of mouth. During the course of 1996, such films struggled to find audiences. Among the pictures viewed as critical and box office disappointments during the year were *Evita*, *The Evening Star*, *The Juror*, *The People vs. Larry Flynt*, *Mary Reilly*, *The Crucible*, *Up Close* and *Personal, In Love and War,* and *The Mirror Has Two Faces.* The studios did not necessarily prioritize making many of these movies in the first place, at least at the budget levels they eventually reached. Either these films were designed to be the studios' Oscar-worthy "prestige pictures," or else executives signed off on them because they wished to attract or keep top-level talent.[45] Nonetheless, the underperformance of such a large number of "mid-range" movies over the course of the year, in tandem with the box office success of so many indie films, further reinforced the problematic nature of producing and distributing them.

During late 1996 and early 1997, the press came to identify these as "middle-range," "middle-class," or "mid-budgeted" movies.[46] In November 1996, *Variety* published the findings of a study it commissioned on the studios that foreshadowed what would become even clearer by the spring of 1997: namely, that the least and most expensive films to make were the ones that typically earned the most.[47] According to Leonard Klady, films with budgets in excess of $60 million were actually more likely to generate profits than those produced for less than that amount. Based on a survey of 164 studio films released the previous year, the study found that half the films costing between $25 and $60 million were commercial failures. Klady went on to add, "Given the tremendous costs in making and marketing pictures, the obvious conclusion from recent experience would be for the studios to either produce pricey event pictures or low-budget (by their standards) genre actioners and comedies. Quirky yarns, social dramas, and the like could be consigned to indies, specialized arms of the majors—or TV movies."[48]

What is striking is that these mid-range films—which in terms of content were the primary emphasis of the majors during the heyday of the studio system—were increasingly viewed as "pariahs."[49] Executives eagerly placed the blame on such films (and their budgets) for the shortcomings on their balance sheets; dozens of journalists, in turn, picked up these stories and ran with them. In reporting on a generally impressive year for movies in terms of earnings, for instance, Klady declared that "the major reason the global picture wasn't even brighter boils down to mid-range successes."[50] Bill Mechanic, chairman of 20th Century Fox, observed on another occasion that "we basically got out of the 'middle-class' picture. . . . The movie that costs twenty-five to forty million dollars to produce, that has a middle-range star and a middle-range idea—that is the most difficult to make work."[51]

If, according to Mechanic, mid-range films such as *City Hall, The Juror, The Fan,* and *Chain Reaction* (all 1996) were challenging to "make work," then the majors viewed low-budget productions as virtually impossible in the current industry climate. According to the same study described above, union rates and labor costs being what they were, a major studio simply could not produce a film for less than $8 million.[52] Cumulatively, these realizations contributed to a further refinement of the types of movies that the majors willingly supported. Those ventures that did not fit within these parameters began to be shunted off to the conglomerates' specialty divisions—which, by early 1997, included Miramax, New Line/Fine Line, Sony Pictures Classics, Fox Searchlight, and Gramercy.

Breaking up the audience into four quadrants suggests much about the current state of the industry and thus is worth commenting on further here. The use of this practice reinforces the extent to which the studios produced and marketed films for a presumed "mass" audience. Though it may have been decades since film was truly a mass medium in the sense meant during the Hollywood studio era, the majors were still pursuing the largest possible audience and the greatest number of box office dollars. Thus, in assessing whether to make a tier 1 film—and how to market it—the audience need only be constructed as four main segments. In the process of doing so, the films were often attacked for being "made by committee." Echoing the attacks wielded against television programming in the classic network era of the 1960s and 1970s, tier 1 films were typically perceived as mindless or homogenous drivel, geared to the widest audience. Such discourses enabled tier 2 films such as *Sling Blade, Welcome to the Dollhouse, Dead Man, Breaking the Waves*, and *Trainspotting* to be viewed as "true" cinema, "real" movies, the site of individualized artistic expression. As has been underscored throughout this book, despite the tendency by Miramax and other indie subsidiaries to play up their role in releasing quality fare, a far broader range of niche-oriented films came from these entities. Nonetheless, journalists reproduced the public relations jargon put out by indie companies, reinforcing a major/indie polarization in terms of content and quality that simply does not hold up on greater scrutiny.[53]

Regardless of whether it was a genre picture, English-language import, foreign-language film, or quality American indie, specialty companies had entirely different sets of expectations for their releases. Though they might have hoped their films would cross over to become indie blockbusters, the budgets and acquisition prices for specialty films were developed with the expectation that they would have a much more limited appeal. In 1996, acquisitions prices for tier 2 films, at least for Miramax, averaged $4 million; marketing expenditures were in the $5 million range.[54] Budgets for films varied tremendously, but at a minimum, indie divisions could expect to spend $3 million to make a film. In addition, it was generally agreed on that if a film exceeded a $20 million negative cost, it was moving into the danger zone of the "mid-range" film alluded to above.[55] A budget in excess of $20 million meant that profits would be much more difficult to recoup through a traditional theatrical release of a few hundred screens, international presales, and assorted ancillary markets. It also posed additional marketing challenges, as mid-range films tended to be seen as "softer" and more difficult to sell as distinctive media products in existing advertising venues.

It was at this time that producers and distributors began to reconceptualize the studios' mid-range films as indies. This involved lowering films' budgets by employing nonunion labor or asking well-known talent to work for less—something individuals might do if they "believed" in the project or wanted to stretch their acting chops. Sometimes this meant employing television or theater talent who wanted the opportunity to branch out into feature-length films.[56] It might also demand enhancing the potential appeal of the project to an identifiable niche audience such as teenagers (e.g., by casting stars from the brand-new WB network). To reinvent projects as tier 2 films, often the material had to be streamlined or reworked in some fashion; this might involve heightening the "edginess" by increasing the explicit language, sexuality, and violence, or it might involve shooting in less-expensive locales.

Significantly, during this period, tier 2 companies such as Miramax, Sony Pictures Classics, Gramercy, and New Line/Fine Line were still in the process of identifying precisely what kinds of films they wanted to release, how much they expected to spend, what their exact relationship with their parent company was, and what distribution strategies they wished to employ. Miramax may have already done much to establish the broad parameters of tier 2 companies, but by no means were the boundaries rigidly set. For example, though Sony had its own indie division with Sony Pictures Classics, it was the tier 1 division Columbia that released Wes Anderson's first feature, *Bottle Rocket* (1996). Similarly, it was this same division, rather than SPC, that released *El mariachi* (1993) a few years prior. Relationships between talent, producers, and conglomerate divisions, as well as the tastes of individual executives, factored into which branch of a company released what film. *Bottle Rocket*, for example, was produced by James L. Brooks and Polly Platt's production company, Gracie Films, which had a relationship with Columbia. This connection helps explain why Anderson's first feature, starring unproved talent in the lead roles, came out of that division. Nonetheless, it is quite possible that a generally well-reviewed movie budgeted at $7 million would have earned far more than the $1 million it took in at the box office had it been released by a specialty division more skilled at niche marketing, platform releasing, and exploiting critical acclaim. Yet such expertise was less and less important to a tier 1 division geared toward wide-releasing films on thousands of screens and pursuing global mass audiences.

In the same way that there was some degree of fluidity between tier 1 and tier 2 entities, there also remained some murkiness between tier 2 and tier 3 entities. Indeed, it was largely due to the existence of this gray area that the use of the term "independence" continued to be so imprecise and contradictory during this time. If distinctions between indie and major studio films were at times uncertain, then those between indies and independents could be downright perplexing. Without a doubt, the purchase of companies such as Miramax and New Line by major conglomerates played a large part in creating this confusion. But there were several other factors also at play. For instance, with film financing coming from a wider range of sources than ever before, the web of institutional allegiances of any given movie became even more complex.[57] Further, as with film festivals, film markets that used to be largely the domain of independents now became sites where studio-based indies did much of their business as well. As one example, tier 2 companies now dominated the massive American Film Market, an annual Los Angeles–based site for buyers and sellers to congregate every spring. According to one journalist at the 1996 gathering, "The bedrock of the current AFM membership, and the most solvent outfits, number only a few vertically integrated and diversified companies such as Turner-owned New Line and Castle Rock and Disney-owned Miramax, plus A-product companies such as Summit and Largo."[58] Meanwhile, the newly launched online trade publication *indieWIRE* (started in 1996) covered films released by both indies and independents. Though the lines between indies and independents often remained fuzzy, in May 1997 a little clarity appeared with Seagram/Universal's acquisition of the independent distributor October Films.[59]

The Next Miramax? The Case of October Films

In terms of size, scope, business strategies, and range of releases, the October Films of 1996 strongly resembled the Miramax of the late 1980s. This resemblance did not go unnoticed by the press; indeed, on myriad occasions, October was positioned as the "next Miramax."[60] Yet though such analogies appeared for only a brief time, October's ascendance from independent to studio-based indie occurred at a far accelerated pace. Launched in April 1991, October was the product of several individuals affiliated with 1980s-era independent companies. Creators Jeff Lipsky and Bingham Ray were joined early on by Amir Malin and John Schmidt.[61] In its first year, October lived a "hand-to-mouth existence"; money from private investors funded its initial acquisitions.[62] October's very first release, Mike Leigh's *Life Is Sweet* (1991), was a minor hit on the art house circuit, earning more than $1.5 million.[63] As was the case with most independents by the 1990s, October cobbled together money through various ad hoc arrangements with investors as well as output deals with video and international distribution companies.[64] For example, in May 1992, October struck an agreement worth at least $5 million with Cineplex Odeon to release its films in Canada.[65] The company also made "service deals" with select genre film producers; production companies in effect paid October to distribute their films theatrically.[66] The company's initial successes, along with its experienced management, kept it afloat until significant money came in from large investment groups. In October 1992, the financial firm Siegler, Collery & Co. and the investment-banking firm of Allen & Co. advanced about $15 million in debt and equity in exchange for a stake in the company.[67]

The money was intended to help October rise to the "top tier of independent distributors"[68] at precisely the moment when most other independent distributors were either fading fast (as was the case with Cinecom and Samuel Goldwyn) or becoming studio subsidiaries. With Miramax and New Line now tier 2 companies, there appeared to be a niche that October could occupy in the low-budget-film distribution business, which would be well above other tier 3 companies such as LIVE, Cinepix, Strand, Northern Arts, Trimark, Fox Lorber, Cabin Fever, and Unapix.[69] As would become apparent by 1996, however, this space between tiers 2 and 3 was as untenable as was the space between tiers 1 and 2. Nonetheless, from 1992 to 1996, October rose to become by far the most successful independent distributor. Its practices from 1992 to 1996 show the upper limits possible for independents during this time. Most companies never came close to attaining these heights before going out of business and being replaced by the next wave of similarly shoestring operations. Outlining these conditions reveals precisely how difficult circumstances were for companies unaffiliated with the majors, and it also underscores why October took the first opportunity available to escape this existence.

As was typical for independents in the mid-1990s, October remained purely acquisitions-driven, avoiding financing productions altogether.[70]

October paid less than $1 million on average for the North American rights of films it acquired, whose budgets were well below $5 million. Release patterns adhered to the practices of 1980s-era independents: films opened on anywhere from a couple of screens in New York and Los Angeles to a few hundred screens. A film could be considered a success if it took in between $500,000 and $1 million at the box office.[71] Annually, the company released anywhere from a half dozen to a dozen films at most—a far cry from the twenty to thirty releases now coming out of Miramax each year. The types of films October distributed were consistent with 1980s-era independents as well. It favored films that played well on the festival circuit but which indie divisions did not see as having crossover potential. For the relatively well-financed October, this meant a mix of foreign-language films (Pedro Almodóvar's *Kika*, 1994; Abbas Kiarostami's *The White Balloon*, 1995), genre films from both the United States and abroad (Guillermo del Toro's *Cronos*, 1994; Abel Ferrara's *The Addiction*, 1995), quality American independents (Victor Nuñez's *Ruby in Paradise*, 1993; Roger Avary's *Killing Zoe*, 1994), and a handful of high-profile nonfiction films (Chris Hegedus and D. A. Pennebaker's *The War Room*, 1994; Michael Apted's *Moving the Mountain*, 1995). As these examples indicate, October focused heavily on pursuing movies made by filmmakers celebrated as auteurs by festivals and critics.

An early breakthrough moment came for October in 1994, when the company released the John Dahl–directed noir *The Last Seduction*. Oscar buzz surrounded actress Linda Fiorentino's performance. October campaigned for her to be nominated, but the Academy ruled her ineligible because the film had been shown on HBO prior to its theatrical release. Nonetheless, *The Last Seduction* grossed approximately $6 million at the box office. After this success, October chugged along, releasing more than twenty-five films by 1996.

Though 1996 was a stellar year for October, the conditions for most other tier 3 companies were worsening quickly. As Kino executive Don Krim observed in late 1995, "There's much more competition and a more hostile environment today than I've ever seen before."[72] After the intense bidding wars of Sundance 1996, another executive opined, "It's a feral environment where the strongest and smartest survive."[73] Multiple factors contributed to the declining conditions for independents. These companies had neither the deep pockets nor the press attention of the studio indies. As the number of indies grew, so did acquisition prices. This meant that independents might have to spend more for acquisitions than they had three years earlier. As Fox Searchlight executive Lindsay Law remarked, "The type of movies which once cost $200,000 to acquire now cost $3 million to acquire by the time they have reached a festival. Also, the movies that are available for acquisition these days are smaller in scale and more personal." In addition, he noted, "the bigger independent films like *The Piano* [1993] seldom appear out of nowhere anymore."[74] Yet even as prices rose, box office returns for independents continued to decline. This was partly because the films from specialty divisions took up more screens at theaters historically devoted to showing traditional art house product. It was also because, with a growing number of low-budget films from both independents and indies, exhibitors swiftly pulled films off screens if they did not show indie blockbuster potential.

In sum, press reports to the contrary, in most cases independents eked out the modest living they always had. The total box office for independently distributed films remained remarkably consistent from year to year, typically making up anywhere from 3 to 5 percent of total box office annually.[75] As Phoenix Pictures executive Rick Hess put it, "There is a big dichotomy between the media attention received by independent films and their financial performance."[76] In other words, in the same year declared to be one of the best ever for independent films by publications ranging from *Time* to the *Los Angeles Times*, little had changed for most of those unaffiliated with the major Hollywood system and large conglomerates. The mythology of the "little film that could" grew, but their box office returns did not. In fact, the situation could be seen as *more* dire: production and distribution costs were mounting, potential crossover product was harder to find, competition for screens continued to grow, a glut of ultra-low-budget films flooded festivals and film markets, and the press provided less attention to and coverage of this sector of the business than it had in the late 1980s and early 1990s.[77] The combination of unrelenting media hype and lower-cost digital technologies promised to make conditions even more challenging for both outsiders looking to break in to the business or investors hoping to make a profit.

By mid-1996, October recognized the warning signs. Unlike most other independent distributors of the time, it had enough momentum to respond to the worsening market conditions for tier 3 companies. The company's executives realized that they either had to substantially expand the company's ambitions (i.e., become more like Miramax) or risk experiencing the same fate of other independents such as Orion and Samuel Goldwyn.[78] The latter two companies were in the midst of being purchased and restructured by Metromedia; what their final form would be remained in doubt. October subsequently took several major steps to indicate that it wanted to operate at the level of a tier 2 company.

After procuring another $15 million in equity and credit, in May 1996 October announced plans to develop a foreign sales division and begin financing and developing its own projects. The first fully financed film was standard "cinema of cool" fare: *The Funeral*, a gangster film directed by Abel Ferrara and starring Chris Penn, Christopher Walken, Annabella Sciorra, Isabella Rossellini, and Benicio Del Toro.[79] Concurrently, October beat out Warner Bros. by paying a reported $10 million to acquire David Lynch's latest film, the noir *Lost Highway* (1997).[80]

The same month, May 1996, that October Films took these dramatic steps, a couple of the company's acquisitions performed remarkably well at Cannes. Mike Leigh's *Secrets & Lies* won the Palme d'Or while Lars von Trier's *Breaking the Waves* was awarded the Grand Jury Prize. With these high-profile films being prepared for a fall 1996 release, October started to position itself more explicitly as "the next Miramax."[81] Much as the Weinsteins used press coverage and industry buzz surrounding *The Crying Game* to make Miramax more attractive to buyers in 1993, so did October executives exploit the critical attention and honors bestowed on it for *Secrets & Lies* and *Breaking the Waves* to prepare it for a sale. By January 1997, reports of interest from both Paramount and Universal circulated in trade publications.[82] This coverage, however, was far eclipsed by the media fury accompanying the critical and box office response to a wave of indie films released in the summer and fall of 1996. One film in particular led the pack: Miramax's *The English Patient*.

An "Emotional Event": Miramax Wins Best Picture

> There are huge audiences for pieces like Independence Day, but there are also audiences for small films. There's a hunger for works that have emotional depth and that are about something.
>
> *Anthony Minghella,* English Patient *director, 1996*

As of 1997, *The English Patient* was Miramax's most prominent mid-range film. But it was not the first such film produced by the company: Miramax had ventured into the realm of historical dramas the previous year with *Restoration*. With an impressive cast featuring Robert Downey Jr., Hugh Grant, Meg Ryan, Sam Neill, and Ian McKellen, *Restoration* was an ambitious, $18.5 million romance set in the seventeenth century.[83] Miramax expected the film to be a front-runner for the 1996 Academy Awards.[84] Yet the critics' responses were lukewarm, and the only Oscar nominations the film received were for Costume Design and Art Direction (both of which it won). Audiences were equally disinterested.

A Miramax Films Release © 1995. Photo: David Appleby. Audiences expressed little interest in seeing Robert Downey Jr. in this particular period piece. The $18.5 million *Restoration* (1995) earned only $4 million at the North American box office.

A Miramax Films Release © 1996. Photo: Phil Bray. *The English Patient*'s World War II–era setting attracted far more interest and critical attention than *Restoration* had a year earlier. Miramax aggressively pitched the film's romantic elements to female moviegoers through promotional images such as this.

This film, along with *The Crossing Guard* (1995) and *Four Rooms* (1995), each ended up taking in less than $1 million in rentals in the United States.[85] Miramax claimed that foreign presales arranged in collaboration with Disney kept the company from realizing too large a loss on any of these projects.[86]

Despite the setback with *Restoration*, Miramax proceeded with a remarkably similar strategy for *The English Patient* the following year. Further, Disney not only permitted Miramax to continue with such a grandiose production despite its earlier missteps, but in fact endorsed the strategy by further loosening its purse strings. Previously, the Weinsteins had to seek green-light approval from Disney executives before moving forward with productions budgeted at over $12.5 million. In late 1995, however, Disney executive Joe Roth revised the arrangement. Miramax subsequently only had to have its budgets *average* out to $12.5 million. Productions with budgets in excess of $12.5 million no longer needed to be sanctioned in advance by Disney executives, so long as the average remained at or below $12.5 million.[87] So, according to *Variety*, "the Weinsteins can OK a *Marvin's Room* [1996] ($17 million) or *The English Patient* ($27 million) without Disney's pre-approval, just so long as they make enough low-budgeters to achieve the $12.5 million average."[88] The expectation was that lower-budget projects would balance out bigger-budget films, thereby ensuring that Miramax released a diverse slate of pictures.[89] In fact, Miramax simply produced more low-budget *and* high-budget films to maintain the $12.5 million average.

With Disney's blessing, Miramax moved ahead with the roughly $30 million *English Patient*.[90] In terms of both critical plaudits and box office receipts, Miramax's success with *The English Patient* marked one of its crowning achievements of the 1990s. The press, public, and Academy once more bought into the hype generated by the company's marketers. In a year of tremendous competition for specialty films, *The English Patient* earned in excess of $75 million in the United States alone. By the time of the Oscars in March 1997, *Variety* predicted that the film would take in approximately $250 million in theaters worldwide.[91] Along with these impressive figures, *The English Patient* became Miramax's first Best Picture winner. The Weinsteins were widely praised for their support for the film; further, journalists repeatedly likened them to Old Hollywood studio moguls such as Irving Thalberg, Harry Cohn, and Louis B. Mayer.[92] At the same time, the company's top executives were heralded for making the kind of David Lean–style epic production the Hollywood majors no longer dared attempt.[93]

With *The English Patient*, Miramax moved into producing and distributing mid-range fare, albeit tentatively, cautiously straddling the line between tier 2 and mid-range material in terms of budget, content, and marketing strategies. Indeed, the media discourses that circulated around the film reflected the varied impressions of what it represented. Was it a solid example of the diversity of independent films on offer at the time? An indication of how the New Hollywood could make Old Hollywood–style films? Proof that mid-range films could still work, if tightly managed by studio-based indies? On different occasions, the press covered *The English Patient* in all these ways.

Executives crafted a compelling story about the difficulties involved in producing *The English Patient* in the contemporary industrial climate, and the press eagerly snapped it up. The widely circulated narrative about *The English Patient* went something like this: Were it not for Miramax, an unconventional film such as this would never have been made. As it had done with *Pulp Fiction* previously, Miramax executives seized *The English Patient* from turnaround at a major studio. In this case, it was Fox, whose Fox Searchlight and Fox 2000 divisions had been jointly producing the film. Fox soon balked at certain casting decisions and the rising budget.[94] The project's viability improved somewhat following an infusion of cash from producer Saul Zaentz and the willingness of several crew members to defer or reduce their salaries.[95] While recognizing the inherent difficulties involved in marketing a historical epic lacking both a linear narrative and well-known talent, Miramax believed in the project and moved ahead. Though at the time it was a pricey film for Miramax—or any other indie company—it would have cost a major far more to make.

There is no question that Miramax executives did a tremendous job in promoting what was widely seen as a "hard-to-sell" film. As had long been the company's practice, Miramax released several prospective Oscar nominees during the year, including *Emma, Marvin's Room, Sling Blade,* and *Trainspotting.* With *The English Patient* yielding the most favorable critical reaction overall and substantial pre–awards season attention, the company quickly reallocated its resources to make this its primary candidate for the Academy Awards, especially Best Picture. According to Miramax marketing executive Marcy Granata, the company's strategy involved positioning *The English Patient* as an "event film—not like *Independence Day* or *Twister*, but an emotional event."[96] Rather than selling it as a "small, precious film"—a practice that had become commonplace with indies by this time—Miramax's promotional materials emphasized "big emotions, sweeping environments and a story of intrigue, romance and betrayal."[97] Paradoxically, *The English Patient* could be considered an epic indie. Its status as a mid-range film from the most high-profile and ambitious specialty company of the time rendered it a distinctive media product, unlike most contemporary Hollywood films or recent indie projects.

From limited release in mid-November 1996 through mid-February, when it received an impressive twelve Oscar nominations, Miramax spent a reported $12 million on the film's promotion to the press, public, and Academy.[98] After receiving the Oscar nominations, executives stated plans to spend another $5 million on advertisements for print and television.[99] Spending increased gradually as the film slowly expanded to more screens until, by the time of the Oscars, the *Los Angeles Times* reported that Miramax had spent an amount nearly equal to the film's budget on marketing costs.[100] Miramax marketers developed distinct marketing materials for different media and different audiences. On television, for example, ads consisted of "romantic spots, segmented for women and ads with images of tanks and parachutes and driving music aimed at men."[101] When research revealed that only about 40 percent of the audience was male, the war aspects of the film were further emphasized. Subsequently, the audience segmented 53 percent female, 47 percent male.[102] Another prominent strategy involved broadcasting half-hour infomercials "on local and cable television in the top 20 media markets."[103] Academy members were targeted even more aggressively and consistently than was the general public. According to Claudia Eller, *The English Patient'*s Oscar campaign was "one of the year's most extensive and expensive" for any company, whether major studio or indie subsidiary.[104] While print and advertising costs reached approximately $20 million, materials targeted to Academy members exceeded $650,000.[105] The *New York Times* estimated that Miramax's Oscar-season trade ads (the majority of which promoted *The English Patient*) accounted for about 40 percent of the two hundred pages devoted to award-season promotions—no small sum, considering that each single-page advertisement cost $9,200.[106]

The effort paid off: Domestic box office for *The English Patient* grew by 50 percent following the announcement of the Oscar nominations.[107] After winning nine of the twelve awards for which it was nominated, the film's box office rose by 175 percent, which marked the second-best post-Oscar increase in the past decade (trailing only *Braveheart*, 1995).[108] It defeated *Fargo, Jerry Maguire, Secrets & Lies,* and *Shine* to win Best Picture. Other award-winning Miramax films that year included *Sling Blade* (Best Adapted Screenplay), *Emma* (Best Original Score), and *Kolya* (Best Foreign Language Film).

Several factors facilitated Miramax's Oscar wins. First, as one journalist observed, the majors in 1996 "delivered perhaps the weakest lineup of Oscar prospects since the awards began in 1927."[109] One after another, films viewed as possible "Oscar bait" disappointed in terms of critical reaction and box office dollars. Many of these were the studio-released mid-range films discussed above—movies such as *The Crucible, The Evening Star*, and *Mary Reilly*. Second, Miramax benefited from the fact that both the company itself and the films it released were still being lumped by the press into the independent category. Though by this point Miramax's releases ran the gamut—from a very limited number of mid-range projects (*The English Patient; Marvin's Room*) to solidly tier 2 indie films (*Citizen Ruth; Beautiful Girls*) to the occasional ultra-low-budget, tier 3–style films (*Swingers; Walking and Talking*)—categories and definitions still remained just amorphous enough that the company could promote all its product as independent and get away with it.

Miramax was also aided by the larger narrative being promulgated by the mainstream press at this time—namely, that Hollywood was out of touch and that "outsiders" now made the quality films. The cover of *Entertainment Weekly* aptly illustrates this. Both here and elsewhere, Miramax and *The English Patient* were placed front and center, (misleadingly) presented as symbolizing this new age of low-budget films. Appearing over a photograph of the movie's stars, Ralph Fiennes and Kristin Scott-Thomas, appeared the words "Hollywood vs. the Oscars: The Indie Hit 'The English Patient' Could Sweep the Academy Awards. What Are the Studios Doing Wrong?" "Has Hollywood Lost It?" blared the headline to the article. It continued: "Intent on squeezing every last nickel out of their budget-busting 'event' movies, the big studios have forfeited character, plot—and the Oscars—to the indies."[110] Similar declarations appeared across countless publications in the United States and beyond.[111] Writers did occasionally get around to noting that the boundaries between independent and studio were by no means rigid.[112]

These kinds of nuances were invariably buried deep within the articles, long after deceptive headlines trumpeted a new age in *American* independent cinema. Much as many journalists failed to differentiate between indie and independent, so, too, did they rarely consider that labeling these films as American might be problematic. In fact, these films were the products of complex international relationships. Of the nominees for Best Picture, for instance, one was set in Australia (*Shine*), another in England (*Secrets & Lies*). The distributor releasing *Fargo*, Gramercy, was based out of London and had financial ties to the Netherlands. *The English Patient*, with its production team drawn from eight different countries, continued the trend in international coproductions initiated earlier in the decade with such Miramax releases as *The Piano*, *The House of the Spirits* (1993), *Little Buddha* (1993), and *Restoration*.[113]

The third reason Miramax gained the most from the Oscar buzz in this particular year was that most members of the mainstream press and industry still held the company's practices and accomplishments in relatively high regard. One writer labeled Miramax a "maverick" whose "marketing prowess [helped] turn an esoteric work of art into commerce."[114] Another argued that while the Weinsteins may not always be "nice guys," they could be forgiven because, like studio-era moguls, they "cared passionately about film."[115] A few perceived Miramax as the lone entity offering artistically oriented films that were accessible to the masses. For instance, *Daily Variety* stated that with *The English Patient*, Miramax had found "the movie that could cross the gulf between the Sundance and commercial crowds."[116]

The success Miramax found with *The English Patient* certainly endorsed the company's shift to mid-range material. Yet Miramax was not simply allocating more money for development and production. The company was also a key force in driving up acquisitions prices and marketing expenditures. These practices, of course, would only serve to diminish the company's bottom line. For example, though *Sling Blade* ended up being one of Miramax's biggest success stories in 1996, its profitability remains unclear. Miramax reportedly purchased the rights to this roughly $1 million drama for approximately $10 million.[117] Though it earned a respectable $24 million at the North American box office, the marketing costs involved in getting it to this point were substantial. Further, a small, intimate American drama such as *Sling Blade* lacked the viability overseas that *The English Patient* had. Whereas Buena Vista International Television could (and did) benefit by placing *The English Patient* in a package of films it licensed overseas—a package that also included such prominent 1996 titles as *Ransom, Evita, The Rock,* and *Phenomenon*—a movie like *Sling Blade* added little value to this sixty-three-film deal.[118]

Cumulatively, more productions and more acquisitions translated into more releases overall. From the mid-1990s onward, Miramax released far more movies annually than did any of its indie competitors.[119] In 1994, the company released twenty-eight films; in 1995, the number increased to forty-two.[120] The number declined slightly to thirty-seven in 1996.[121] Several additional projects remained in limbo.[122] Meanwhile, reports surfaced that Disney executives had requested that Miramax reduce its output. A few months before *The English Patient* opened, unidentified "rival distributors" circulated rumors that "top Disney executives advised Miramax brass to go easy on financing big-budget specialized fare and return to the co-production/acquisition strategy that has served them well over the company's 12–year [*sic*] history."[123]

Miramax might have cut back on this "big-budget specialized fare" if *The English Patient* had failed, but given its success, the company continued to stray further from its original mandate. Meanwhile, Disney was not thrilled that its subsidiary was going far afield of what it was purchased to do. As discussed above, industrial conditions favored tier 2 projects, *not* the types of mid-range projects that Miramax was beginning to emphasize and prioritize. While the Weinsteins occasionally told the press that Miramax was responding to Disney's requests and cutting back on the number of acquisitions and productions—as well as the amount spent on them—there was little evidence this was true.[124] Among the more ambitious and pricey projects that would soon come from Miramax were a Sylvester Stallone–Robert De Niro crime film, *Cop Land*; an adaptation of Henry James's *The Wings of the Dove*; a John Travolta–Sean Penn–Robin Wright Penn drama, *She's So Lovely*; and Quentin Tarantino's follow-up to *Pulp Fiction*, *Jackie Brown* (all 1997). Meanwhile, numerous acquisitions gathered dust, waiting for a theatrical release that never came (or came many years after the film was completed). There were any number of reasons a Miramax-owned film did not get released: it might have tested poorly, the filmmakers could have been "punished" for refusing to agree to changes demanded by the Weinsteins, or Miramax might never have planned to release it at all (instead purchasing it solely to reduce competition in the marketplace).[125]

That such information can be reported here indicates that, as of early 1997, a handful of journalists began to present Miramax in less-than-flattering terms. Previously Miramax and the Weinsteins had been able to stay relatively unscathed despite their aggressive and anticompetitive practices. Much had been justified or rationalized in the name of art. And, for the most part, this remained the case; for instance, the film critic Kenneth Turan declared that "the Miramax team has perfected the technique of putting just enough pressure on Academy voters to get results but not so much as to appear unseemly."[126] Yet certain journalists began to break ranks and expose a different side to the Weinsteins and Miramax. Perhaps in the interest of providing "balance" to their stories, some writers mixed praise with criticism. For example, the *Los Angeles Times* journalists Elaine Dutka and John Clark observed that "Hollywood is of two minds about Miramax. . . . No one denies that the brothers have revolutionized independent film, expanding the market and paving the way for others outside the mainstream. But some have come to view the company as the indie film world equivalent of Microsoft—an unapologetic giant capable of smothering the competition."[127] Harvey Weinstein's acuity at exploiting the media to serve his own ends was noted in this article, as was the company's tendency to buy up everything in the marketplace.[128] This was not the only article to expose a dark side to the Weinsteins (and especially Harvey). The nickname "Harvey Scissorhands"—referring to his proclivity for cutting and recutting films—began to appear in print with growing frequency.[129] *Rolling Stone* even went so far as to title its article "The Big Bad Wolves of Miramax." Though the piece proceeded to celebrate the parallels between the Weinsteins and studio moguls of Old Hollywood, the headline reflects the early signs of a shift in how the press was discussing the company and its top executives.

The shift in tone came in tandem with the departure of a number of top-ranking Miramax executives. No longer bound to the company, and indeed, often working at competing companies, some individuals spoke to the press more candidly than they had before.[130] The tonal shift in coverage might also be attributed to Miramax's over-aggressiveness in marketing itself, the growing antipathy of the press and industry toward Miramax's business practices, and "the Miramax story" finally starting to lose some of its luster. Nonetheless, despite the occasional criticism, for the most part Miramax continued to be widely respected and highly praised by critics, journalists, and the industry. It was only as the company began to make more expensive films—and expand more extensively across other sectors of the entertainment business—that it became less able to sell itself as an upstart operation focused on championing small, artistic, cinematic gems.

Building a Studio Within a Studio

> *The English Patient* was a milestone. . . . We all killed ourselves to get here. Now some of our people want to pursue other opportunities or their personal lives.
>
> *Harvey Weinstein, 1997*

The English Patient's Oscar win, combined with the emergence of *Scream* (1996) as Dimension's most successful genre film yet, reaffirmed Miramax's position as the premier specialty film company in Hollywood. Yet the Weinsteins repeatedly indicated they wanted their company to be far more than this. Miramax may have dominated the niche business

A Miramax Films Release © 1996. Photo: Michael Yarish. Miramax worked hard to establish the character actor Billy Bob Thornton as a prominent auteur with its Oscar campaign for *Sling Blade* (1996). Thornton proceeded to win an Academy Award for Best Adapted Screenplay and become part of Miramax's stable of talent.

in movies, but now the company was starting to make far more ambitious movements into a range of other media. In short, with increasingly aggressive moves into music, publishing, and television, Miramax tried to set itself up to be a diversified media company within the diversified media company that was Disney. The Weinsteins freely used Disney's money to hire staff, launch new divisions, and sign talent to production deals. By early 1997, Miramax's staff numbered three hundred.[131] This staff was involved not only in motion picture production and acquisitions, but also in television production as well as magazine and book publishing. After three years in operation, Miramax Books had published about two dozen books. Screenplays published by this division included *The English Patient, Smoke/Blue in the Face,* and *Swingers.* There were also "movie-related books" that were not direct adaptations, such as *Love: Ten Poems,* a compilation of poems by Pablo Neruda (of *Il Postino*), and a reissue of Alexandre Dumas's *Queen Margot* timed to the movie's release.[132] Meanwhile, reports began to circulate about a potential "upscale feature magazine" as well as several television series in development.[133]

The greater ambitions on display by the Weinsteins as of early 1997 might have been fueled by the vote of confidence they had recently received from Disney. In May 1996, following nearly a year of negotiations (and after only three years at Disney), the Weinsteins renewed their contracts. Their prior five-year contract was replaced by a seven-year agreement.[134] This new contract helped to quash speculation as to how the brothers "would fare in Disney's new Joe Roth–Mike Ovitz era."[135] The contract, negotiated primarily by Chris McGurk, president of Disney's Motion Pictures Group, was signed after what was reported to be a year of "difficult negotiations."[136] According to *Variety,* "Economic compensation apparently was not the chief stumbling block in the negotiations. Sources said the Weinsteins would not sign until they were granted a significant degree of control over the growing Miramax film library. Specifically, sources said, the Weinsteins wanted considerable say in how the library, its impressive arthouse titles and even the Miramax brand name could be used and marketed."[137] It was believed that Disney had been motivated to renegotiate quickly due to concerns that the Weinsteins might be wooed away by another company. There was particular anxiety that Jeffrey Katzenberg would lure the Weinsteins over to DreamWorks, which had not yet started production on its first film, the George Clooney–Nicole Kidman thriller *The Peacemaker* (released September 1997).[138] By no means was DreamWorks the only place the Weinsteins could have gone; with numerous other studios launching or preparing to launch indie divisions, there were ample opportunities for them to head elsewhere.

Disney executives' enthusiasm to re-sign the brothers indicates that, though the parent company may have been frustrated at times, the arrangement thus far had proved largely favorable. At the time the new agreement was announced, it was already widely believed that Disney had earned back what it had invested in Miramax and then some.[139] And this was *before* Dimension had truly broken through or the "year of the independents" had kicked in. Less than one year later, and only four years after Disney acquired Miramax for approximately $60 million, *Time* reported that Miramax was estimated to be worth more than $1 billion.[140] At this moment, the headaches Miramax wrought were still outweighed by the benefits the company brought to Disney. Still, it was clear to some who closely followed the company that one chapter in Miramax's story had ended and another was about to begin. As noted above, several top executives had left Miramax in recent months, often heading to other specialty companies.[141] With the purchase of October by Universal in May 1997, competition was about to intensify. In an attempt to stay ahead of Fox Searchlight, New Line/Fine Line, Sony Pictures Classics, October, and Gramercy, Miramax signed a growing number of talent agreements and offered up more of the back end to key individuals.[142] *English Patient* director Anthony Minghella, *Emma* star Gwyneth Paltrow, and *Sling Blade* writer-director Billy Bob Thornton were some of the latest additions to Miramax's expanding stable of talent.

The Weinsteins dreamed of reproducing Old Hollywood in both their business practices and their grand historical productions. With *The English Patient*, they had been able to simultaneously hark back to the studio era and test the limits of the contemporary conglomerate system. Yet the New Hollywood was something altogether different from the Old. The Weinsteins would soon learn that despite their best efforts or desires, the system constrained people far more than it enabled them. In the past, they had been able to solve any challenges that had come their way. Running out of money? Seek new investors. Create a controversy out of thin air for free press coverage. Promote themselves as the champions of art. Yet these tactics could work for only so long. What's more, Disney would not be the only party holding them back; there were larger industrial, technological, and cultural forces at work. The Weinsteins may have tried to deny that there existed specific economic and aesthetic parameters for specialty films. Up to 1997, they had little reason to doubt that if they pushed hard enough, they could attain their goals. In the ensuing years, they would test the industry's limits—and the limits of the press's goodwill.

CHAPTER SEVEN

Who Says Life Is Beautiful?

(Summer 1997–Spring 1999)

> The pie is the same size but it's being cut into smaller pieces.
>
> *Mark Gill, Miramax marketing executive, 1998*

By the summer of 1997, the hype about "the year of the indies" had begun to fade from the headlines. So, too, it seemed to many industry observers, did audience interest in indie films, as one release after another yielded disappointing results at the box office. Despite these modest returns, the major studios continued their steady march into the specialty business. Along with Universal's recent purchase of October, Paramount proceeded with staffing its own classics division. The Canadian company Lions Gate also accelerated its shift into motion picture distribution through the acquisition of the independent distributor Cinepix Film Properties.[1] These new market entrants only further pushed up acquisition prices, talent costs, and distribution expenses.[2] In 1998, Fox Searchlight president Lindsay Law estimated that heightened competition had contributed to a rise in marketing costs in excess of 250 percent in a three-year period.[3] More companies releasing more films meant that additional marketing dollars were needed to help a film stand out. In 1997 alone, 271 films were released on a limited basis (i.e., 600 screens or fewer).[4] A growing number of titles coming from a bigger field of competitors translated into films having less time to find an audience. Increasingly, an indie film that failed to draw substantial box office income in its first week of release would be pushed out of theaters. In other words, the "fast burn" that had become commonplace with the tier 1 sector of the business by the 1990s was now becoming more widespread with tier 2 releases as well.

From spring 1997 to spring 1999, the specialty business experienced growing pains. Executives and filmmakers alike were coming to terms with a shifting industrial environment and their place within it. Miramax was not exempt from the challenges being faced by the rest of this sector of the industry. For every success story such as *Good Will Hunting* (1997) or *Chasing Amy* (1997), there were numerous box office failures. During this period, Miramax released a slew of heavily hyped but underperforming films, including *The House of Yes* (1997), *Welcome to Sarajevo* (1997), *54* (1998), *The Mighty* (1998), and *Next Stop Wonderland* (1998).[5] Yet the company continued to plow ahead, ignoring broader market conditions as it increased the budgets of its films, heightened its marketing expenditures, and further diversified into other media.

A defining moment for Miramax came on Oscar night, 21 March 1999. It is only fitting that Miramax dominated the last Academy Awards of the century. Coming into the night with twenty-three nominations — the most it had ever received for a single year — the company ultimately won ten awards. In the period dating from 1989 to 1999, Miramax's films had received 40 awards from 133 nominations.[6] In addition, seven Miramax films had been nominated for Best Picture. Indeed, many of the company's films continued to perform well with critics as well as at the box office. At the time of the 1999 Academy Awards ceremony, reports indicated that Miramax had earned $125 million in pretax profits for Disney in 1998 alone. This was an eighteenfold increase from five years earlier.[7] Yet the tide was about to turn.

Two Miramax films shared the spotlight that evening: *Shakespeare in Love* and *Life Is Beautiful*. Among the awards received by *Shakespeare in Love* were Best Actress (Gwyneth Paltrow), Best Supporting Actress (Judi Dench), Best Original Screenplay (Marc Norman and Tom Stoppard), and, most notably, Best Picture. *Life Is Beautiful* received awards for Best Actor (Roberto Benigni), Best Original Score (Nicola Piovani), and Best Foreign Language Film. Both films generated their fair share of headlines both before and after the awards, due in no small part to Miramax's aggressive campaigning. *Shakespeare's* coverage focused on its "underdog" status relative to *Saving Private Ryan;* many journalists and critics viewed its victory over Spielberg's film as a shocking upset. *Life Is Beautiful's* coverage, meanwhile, was fueled by Benigni's dynamic personality and eccentric behavior, as well as by its status as the highest-grossing foreign-language import ever. By the conclusion of its theatrical run, *Life Is Beautiful* had earned more than $57 million domestically.

In industrial, creative, and cultural terms, this was a crucial turning point in Miramax's history. As the century was ending, Miramax was the dominant niche film company in an industry increasingly overrun with well-funded indie divisions. It had cultivated a clear brand identity that remained distinct from its parent company. It had altered the way that low-budget films were acquired, produced, distributed, and marketed. And it had built a stable of talent and assembled a diverse slate of American indies, English-language imports, genre films, and foreign-language pictures. Yet if, from one angle, *Shakespeare in Love* and *Life Is Beautiful* can be seen in retrospect as signaling a high point for Miramax, from another they might be perceived as initiating the company's downward trajectory—in terms of its status with the press and its broader impact on the specialty business. Though Miramax's many Oscar nominations (and subsequent wins) may have boosted the films' profiles and helped elevate their profits, the awards had the unintended effect of drawing additional scrutiny to the company and its marketing practices. Previously, the press might have celebrated Miramax for its aggressive promotion of art to the masses. Yet now it was being depicted with growing frequency as a belligerent brute that used money, relationships, and fear tactics to dominate the marketplace. A company that for so long could do no wrong swiftly seemed to make misstep after misstep, both with journalists as well as with its acquisitions, production, and marketing decisions.

This chapter examines the 1997 to 1999 period, focusing in particular on Miramax's distribution and marketing of *Life Is Beautiful*. The film's impressive box office returns were seen at the time of its theatrical release as evidence of Miramax's marketing prowess. More recently, Paul McDonald has illustrated how Miramax's distribution of this film marked the effective "Indiewoodization" of the foreign-language film in North America.[8] That Miramax adapted its well-cultivated methods of marketing indie films to *Life Is Beautiful* cannot be disputed. But rather than viewing *Life Is Beautiful*'s $57 million in returns as still one more example of Miramax's accomplishments, instead I argue that this film's distribution trajectory should be looked at through a more bittersweet lens. *Life Is Beautiful* serves as the exception that proved the rule—an indication of the structural constraints that Miramax and other specialty companies continued to face. Though *Life Is Beautiful* represented a peak moment for Benigni, Italian film exports, and the theatrical distribution of foreign-language films in the United States, it also signaled several less desirable trends emerging in the distribution of foreign-language films in particular and niche films more generally.

Cultivating indie blockbusters—whether foreign-language imports, English-language imports, or homebred American indies—remained a challenge. For foreign-language films, the challenges remained the greatest of all. Nonetheless, two companies—Miramax and Sony Pictures Classics—continued to regularly acquire such films and attempt to build interest in subtitled product. The business strategies that each company employed, as well as the types of foreign-language films each acquired, differed markedly. In fact, the ways that Miramax and SPC each handled foreign-language films largely paralleled their wider acquisition and distribution strategies at the time. Therefore, a survey of these two companies' practices with foreign-language films reveals a great deal about the opportunities, and the constraints, met with by those handling specialty films in the latter part of the decade.

This chapter is first and foremost about boundaries—boundaries reached by specialty distributors operating in an ever-more competitive industrial landscape in the late 1990s, and boundaries encountered by those companies that tried to release foreign-language films in the United States throughout the decade. As we shall see, at times Miramax managed to overcome various obstacles with films like *Life Is Beautiful*. Yet rather than interpreting the company's success with *Life Is Beautiful* as a sign of the possibilities for foreign-language films in the United States, it should be seen as a vivid example of the overwhelming and ongoing hurdles faced by those seeking to introduce subtitled fare to American audiences. Very rarely did a foreign-language film cross over from the art house niche to become a widespread success. Even when it did, the returns paled in comparison to even the most modestly performing event film. In most cases, the foreign-language films that were able to become crossover hits in the 1990s were more classical in style and more conservative in politics than much homegrown indie fare. But this is not to suggest that American indies or English-language imports had an easier time. By the end of the decade, even those films produced within American borders—or, more generally, in the English language—found themselves in increasingly crowded, often inhospitable terrain.

Not Every Year Can Be a Year of the Indies

The 1996 "year of the indies" may have fueled a tremendous amount of hype and some impressive box office returns, yet by mid-1997 the picture for indie films no longer seemed so rosy. In general, box office returns between mid-1997 and early 1999 offered mostly grim news. Despite much fanfare, specialty films playing in limited release accounted for roughly 5 percent of total ticket sales.[9] For every indie blockbuster success story, there was a growing number of indies that failed miserably. In 1997, of the aforementioned 271 films placed in limited release, only *The Full Monty* (Fox Searchlight), *Chasing Amy* (Miramax), *The Wings of the Dove* (Miramax), and *Deconstructing Harry* (Fine Line) earned more than $10 million domestically.[10] The situation was not much better for films released on more than six hundred screens: *Eve's Bayou* (Trimark), *Love Jones* (New Line), and *Def Jam's How to Be a Player* (Gramercy) were among the few members of the $10 million–plus club for 1997.[11] Notably, all three of these films were initially targeted to an African American audience; the latter two treaded into genre film territory.

Given these figures, it comes as little surprise that the enthusiasm that had accompanied the year of the indies through the 1997 Oscar season had turned into dejection a mere eighteen months later. Journalists broadcast this distress via bold headlines in the trade papers. "Wave of Fiscal Woes Beaches Mart" read the headline of one article following slow sales at the American Film Market in March 1998; "Arthouses Face Empty Seats—Crowded Sked, High Costs Kill B.O." blared the text of another in July of the same year.[12] By the end of summer 1998, talk turned to whom or what should be held responsible for the emerging slump taking place in indie cinema. A headline in the *Hollywood Reporter* from September 1998 captures the prevailing mood: "Indies Melt Down: Press and Product to Blame."[13] This article is notable for acknowledging that the press might have played a part in fueling unrealistic expectations for specialty films.

In this article, as with so many others published at the time, most of the "blame" went to indie companies for releasing too many films, many of questionable quality.[14] Although this downturn was often framed using the panicked hyperbole common in trade discourse, the underlying logic driving the industry toward the creation of indie subsidiaries was never called into question. The particular business practices employed may very well have been seen as problematic. Nonetheless, the overarching assumption seemed to be that if the "right" films were released—and by "right," what was meant was films that caught on with critics, received prominent awards, and built on word of mouth—then more breakout hits would appear. Even as the industry and press continued to await an upswing, confidence in the long-term viability of the emerging industrial structure remained intact. Indie divisions were still seen as one of the most effective means by which conglomerates could increase overall output, cultivate new talent, and build libraries, especially since the cost of producing and releasing event films continued to skyrocket.[15] As an unidentified executive told *Variety*, "If your average all-in investment in a pic is $5 million, and you make around ten a year, then you only need one or two $20 million hits to justify the [existence of the specialty] division."[16]

The doomsayers' voices may have grown louder, but nonetheless a couple of large-scale hits emerged, which helped reinforce the value of building and sustaining indie divisions. The most prominent such film was Miramax's 1997 indie blockbuster *Good Will Hunting*. Produced for a relatively modest $19 million, this picture seemed to come out of nowhere. It ultimately became Miramax's biggest success story yet, earning close to $140 million in North American theaters and another $87 million in the international marketplace.[17] As the *New York Daily News* noted, the film was significant not just "for its plot" (about a math-genius janitor at MIT who, with the help of a psychologist, comes to terms with both his intellect and his emotions), but also "for its behind-the-scenes story."[18]

The press portrayed the film's genesis as the quintessential Hollywood tale. Here the American Dream was being realized once more: Two buddies from Boston struggle for years in bit parts in movies. They write a script together and shop it around, eventually attracting the interest of Kevin Smith, who brings it to Miramax. Not only is the film made, but it receives nine Academy Award nominations. The young men even take home the Best Original Screenplay Oscar in 1998.[19] In addition, Robin Williams receives a Best Supporting Actor Oscar for his dramatic turn as the psychologist. These young men, of course, were Matt Damon and Ben Affleck, and the awards and publicity surrounding *Good Will Hunting* propelled them to superstar status. In the next few years, when they were not appearing in such big-budget event films as *Armageddon* (1998), *The Sum of All Fears* (2002), and *The Bourne Identity* (2002) for the major studios, they worked regularly with Miramax. Between the two of them, they appeared in more than a dozen different Miramax and Dimension films in less than ten years, including *Shakespeare in Love*, *Rounders* (1998), *The Talented Mr. Ripley* (1999), *All the Pretty Horses* (2000), *Bounce* (2000), *Reindeer Games* (2000), *Jay and Silent Bob Strike Back* (2001), *Jersey Girl* (2004), and *The Brothers Grimm* (2005).

Affleck and Damon's numerous collaborations with Kevin Smith are noteworthy for several reasons. In *Jay and Silent Bob Strike Back* (2001), they parodied their own rapid rise to fame, along with the *Good Will Hunting* story line (through a sequence called *Good Will 2: Hunting Season*). They also spoofed Miramax's emergence as an industry powerhouse. In addition, their production company, LivePlanet, produced the reality TV series *Project Greenlight* (2001–2005) in association with Miramax for

HBO. Their own speedy ascent to the top of the industry via *Good Will Hunting* provided the premise behind the show's "discover a filmmaker and help him (and it usually was him) make a film" story line.[20] Meanwhile, with the religiously themed Smith project *Dogma* (1999), Affleck and Damon were caught up in the controversy surrounding that film's release (which is discussed in the next chapter).

Concurrently, Fox Searchlight had its most successful film to date with the British working-class comedy *The Full Monty*, which earned several Oscar nominations, including Best Picture. This small picture about unemployed steel workers stripping to make a living brought in an impressive $45 million in North American theatrical grosses. As *The Full Monty* and *Good Will Hunting* indicate, if earlier declarations of the financial viability of American and English-language specialty films were heavily exaggerated, the current pronouncements of their decline were equally overstated. Going into the fall of 1998, however, the fate of foreign-language imports was much less certain. Whereas with English-language indies at least a handful of films had earned eight figures annually, the same could not be said of subtitled product. Since 1990, only fourteen films grossed more than $5 million at theaters in North America; most had taken several months in release to accomplish this minor feat.[21] It was apparent that this sector of the business desperately needed to be reenergized. The formula for success with foreign-language films, however, remained unclear. Indeed, as the next section shows, at a time when global expansion was a key industrial mandate, even the precise definition of what constituted a foreign-language film itself was quite uncertain.

What Are Foreign Language Films . . . and Who Watches Them?

The reason there's been a major downturn in the foreign language film business is three-fold. One is, the ancillary values on foreign language films, subtitled films, can never begin to approach the ancillary values on an English-language film that does the same amount of business, it just doesn't happen.
. . . The second thing that has greatly effected this downturn in foreign language films over the decade is the American independent film movement. Ever since *sex, lies, and videotape* [1989] and the Sundance Festival made big noise, the press have spent a lot of the energy that they used to spend on foreign language films as far as profile to the public, they've diverted it to American independent pictures. . . . But (third) it's still a business that you

have to pick and choose, you know. If you look at *Premiere* magazine, we're thankful for any coverage we get for foreign language
film.

Michael Barker, Sony Pictures Classics copresident, 1999

As challenging as the specialty business may have been for most
English-language and American indies in the late 1990s, the situation
for foreign-language films was far more dire. Of course, the box office
returns for these films had been bleak for quite some time. From 1982
to 1992, not even 1 percent of box office dollars went to foreign-language
films annually.[22] This 1 percent represented all subtitled films shown in
U.S. theaters. In 1994, the year that *Belle Époque* (SPC) and *Eat Drink
Man Woman* (SPC) each earned $5 million (considered to be the "break-
through" number for foreign-language films at the time), a total of fifty-
two foreign-language titles opened in the United States, accounting for
$39.36 million, or 0.75 percent of the box office.[23] These figures were
relatively standard. Between 1990 and 1995, the total box office for *all*
foreign-language films in any given year ranged from $30 million to $50
million.[24] Most of this money came from a very limited number of art
house theaters located in four major North American cities: New York,
Los Angeles, Montreal, and Toronto. As one journalist added, factor in
Boston, Chicago, Seattle, San Francisco, and Minneapolis and "the picture is virtually complete."[25] The numbers had gone down even further
by the time Miramax released *Life Is Beautiful* in the fall of 1998. At
that point, roughly 0.5 percent of the annual box office went to foreign-
language fare.[26]

Before proceeding, it is important to address precisely what films
were categorized under the heading of "foreign-language film." Labeling a film as "foreign" is both incredibly simple and extremely challenging. The simple way is merely to identify any film as foreign that has
been produced in a country outside the United States and that predominantly employs subtitles. This is the approach typically taken by most
journalists, box office trackers, and industry organizations that hand out
awards. Though this method of categorizing films is useful up to a point,
it is also incredibly reductive. The biggest complication with this classification scheme is that it assumes most films are primarily created by and
within specific nation-states. Chapter 3 discussed how problematic this
method of labeling films can be when discussing even English-language
films, and it is no less troubling when looking at motion pictures stem-
ming from non-English-speaking countries.

Identifying a film as a "foreign-language" product if it originates from a single nation outside the United States may have been somewhat effective at a time when movies more regularly issued from one particular country. By the 1970s, however, this means of conceptualizing motion picture production and distribution practices had become increasingly fraught. Significantly, one does not even need to leave the borders of the United States before the label of foreign-language film becomes untenable. According to the criteria outlined above, a film would be considered as "foreign" simply if it was produced outside the United States. This position presumes not only that all other nations finance and produce films exclusively within their own national borders, but also that "Hollywood" and the United States are one and the same. Yet in the case of Hollywood, by the 1980s multinational media conglomerates owned most of the major studios. In addition, it had long since grown commonplace for executives to factor in a Hollywood film's global box office in determining whether to green-light it in the first place.[27] While "Hollywood" films may have featured a number of American stars and were spoken primarily in English, their material or ideological connections to "America" had grown tenuous decades before the new millennium.

Frederick Wasser sees the globalization of Hollywood as accelerating since the 1970s because of a growing emphasis by production companies on procuring outside financing through presales.[28] Investors from around the world increasingly developed motion pictures with the international marketplace in mind from the outset. Within a decade of the arrival of the New Hollywood, everything from the owners of a media conglomerate's stock to the locations in which a film was shot to the labor working on a particular project frequently derived from sites far away from the United States. These points are apparent by considering the transnational lineage of the highest-grossing blockbuster through the 1990s, *Titanic* (1997). One of the film's distributors, News Corp., was originally based out of Australia. The writer-director of the film, James Cameron, grew up in Canada. The female lead, Kate Winslet, was from England, as was the production designer and several members of the supporting cast. Much of the film was shot on location in Mexico (on an expensive sound stage built specifically for the project) and in Canada. Even the film's story can be seen as truly transnational—or perhaps transatlantic. Certainly *Titanic*'s global scope was nothing new; one of Hollywood's strengths has always been to incorporate the world's labor, resources, and locations to construct particularly "American" tales of aspiration and success. Nonetheless, with the rise of media conglomerates and the ascendance of global capital in the last decades of the twentieth century, these tales took on an increasingly transnational tenor. As

Michael Curtin notes, Hollywood grew to be one of several sites around the world where talent congregated; other prominent "media capitals" include London, Vancouver, Sydney, and Shanghai.[29]

Labeling a film as either "American" or "foreign" usually does not get any easier with smaller-budget projects. For instance, the Miramax release *Il Postino* (1995) was ruled ineligible for a Best Foreign Film nomination because, according to the Academy's criteria, it was not considered "Italian" since an Englishman, Michael Radford, directed it.[30] This was the case despite the fact that the Italian-language film was shot on location in Italy, relied primarily on Italian talent, and was produced by one of the largest Italian film companies, Cecchi Gori. For *Il Postino*, this ruling did little harm in the end; rather, Miramax used the Academy's ruling to generate extra publicity for the film. The company's campaign was so effective, in fact, that *Il Postino* earned a Best Picture nomination. Nonetheless, as the case of *Il Postino*, as well as the aforementioned example of *Titanic*, indicates, the label of "foreign-language film" is not nearly as clear as it might initially seem to be.

Il Postino's disqualification for a Best Foreign Language Film Oscar due to Radford's English citizenship has significant ramifications in terms of a broader discussion about foreign-language imports. That the director's country of origin was so important to how the film was classified suggests the extent to which foreign-language films are seen as products of distinct auteurs' visions. (This point is further reinforced by the fact that it is the director who accepts the Oscar for Best Foreign Language Film, whereas a film's producer accepts the Best Picture award.) This conception of foreign-language films as deriving from specific authorial voices, in turn, stems from the emergence of this category within a particular historical context.

The foreign-language Oscar classification was created in the post–World War II period. From 1947 to 1955, foreign-language films were sporadically presented with "Honorary Awards." The first official Foreign Language Film Oscar was not handed out until 1957, for Fellini's *La Strada* (1956). Significantly, the emergence of the foreign-language Oscar occurred at the same moment that a select number of national cinemas were being revitalized and the European-based, modernist-tinged international art cinema was gaining momentum. It took the rebuilding of several different nations' film scenes, as well as the emergence of art theaters in the United States and the coming-of-age of a new generation of moviegoers for foreign-language films, for these films to gain traction in the American marketplace. Even with these various forces falling into place, the films that established a foothold tended to do so as much for their explicit content as for their modernist aesthetic (e.g., *And God Created Woman*, 1957; *I Am Curious [Yellow]*, 1969).

In general, the films that received Best Foreign Language Film honors paralleled the types of foreign-language films released theatrically in the United States. This remained the case during the 1990s, as the vast majority of winners came from Europe. Acknowledgment of films from African and Latin American countries was minimal. Only a limited number of nominated films came from Asia; none of those received awards. In fact, with the occasional exception of action films (e.g., those of John Woo and Jackie Chan), East Asian films did not have a strong presence in North American theaters until the beginning of the 2000s.[31] Released in December 2000, Ang Lee's *Crouching Tiger, Hidden Dragon* marked the breakthrough moment for East Asian cinema in North American theaters.[32]

Regardless of their nation of origin, into the 1990s both journalistic and industry discourses framed most foreign-language films primarily as high-culture products, created by and for a discerning group of viewers. This construction of foreign-language films as the domain of the "elite" helps explain why Academy Awards often served as a crucial tool for promoting foreign-language imports.[33] By the late 1990s, a Best Foreign Language Film Oscar had become one of the most significant means of marketing subtitled films. As noted in the discussion of box office above, American indies and English-language imports so dominated the specialty film market by this time that an Oscar nomination—or, even better, an award—became one of the few means by which these films could obtain any publicity. According to *Variety*, from 1983 to 1993, the winner of this award received anywhere from a modest 54 percent to a stunning 2,000 percent bump in box office returns following the Oscars.[34] (Of course, as the table below shows, even the post-awards box office ultimately remained minuscule compared to most English-language releases.) These numbers reinforce both the importance of the honor as well as the degree to which subtitled films struggled in the American market.

Varied reasons have been offered as to why foreign-language films experienced such a decline in U.S. theaters from the early 1980s onward. As noted above, one oft-cited claim was that the "distinctiveness" of foreign films had disappeared as American indies took on the subject matter, style, and explicit content that had previously been the domain of European art cinema.[35] As Michael Barker observes in the remarks that begin this section, recent American indie films also took the lion's share of the media attention that previously had been directed toward foreign-language films. The rise of international coproductions produced in English (the "Europudding" ventures) was also cited as a reason for the decline of foreign-language films in the United States.[36] In other words, those producers (or stars) who hoped to attain significant box office returns opted to cross national boundaries as needed and produce their films in the English language. There were many other explanations for the seeming apathy on the part of both American distributors and audiences for foreign-language fare. The consolidation of the video market was cited as one key factor; less-commercial titles found it harder to gain theatrical distribution deals by the early 1990s.[37] One media observer held the American population responsible, citing the "collapse in cultural sophistication" of the domestic moviegoing audience as a primary reason for the declining market share of foreign films.[38] The flip side of the "blame the audience" approach was to blame the industry. This position was common among many political economists, who held that the Hollywood studios (which, according to this argument, were often conflated with American industry) strove to keep the U.S. marketplace relatively closed to outsiders.[39]

There is a measure of truth to many of these arguments. There is also a fundamental problem, however, in that they all remain bound to highly circumscribed notions of what constitutes a "foreign" film. Foreign films, according to this logic, are art films, created by and for a very specific white, middle-class, college-educated audience of urban, liberal elites. There is little room for the "popular" in this vision of foreign-language films. Regardless of whether the film was a large-scale commercial success in its country of origin, in order to make the journey across the Atlantic (or, less frequently, the Pacific) and into the art house, the foreign film had to be positioned discursively as a high-culture product. Thus, by the 1990s, the potential audience for foreign-language films was already seen as very limited. Those specialty companies choosing to release foreign films in the United States then chased after this small group. A situation had emerged in which industry practices and journalistic perceptions helped breed habitual behavior. Most companies made little effort to modify either their ideas or their business practices about these films over the years.

By the 1990s, most distributors of foreign-language films tended to employ a well-established "art cinema model." Depending on the particular company's available resources, acquisitions choices, distribution decisions, and good (or bad) fortune, this traditional approach met with only modest returns in most circumstances. As the following section shows, during this period Sony Pictures Classics most successfully employed these highly conservative business practices. Miramax, however, operated quite differently. In contrast to SPC, Miramax strived to reenvision the audience for—and reframe the perception of—foreign-language films in the United States. In doing so, the company met with mixed success. In comparing Miramax's strategies with SPC's, it is possible to see both the potential as well as the considerable challenges involved in getting foreign-language films to cross over and attract broader audiences. Unlike the other types of niche films discussed in previous chapters, increasing the appeal of subtitled fare in the United States remained a struggle, regardless of the companies involved and the tactics they employed.

Celebrate the Foreign—or Make the Foreign Familiar?

> The agenda in the independent world that used to never be there, is [all about] things like market share, which is to us crazy. But now you have independent film companies concerned about their market share in the independent world.
>
> *Tom Bernard, Sony Pictures Classics copresident, 1999*

> A foreign-language film hit does $3 million [in domestic box office]; a big hit is $6 million and a blockbuster is $10 million. I can count on these two hands how many foreign films ever have grossed $10 million. And a lot of them, thankfully, have been ours.
>
> *Mark Gill, Miramax marketing executive, 1998*

Throughout the 1990s, Miramax and Sony Pictures Classics were by far the most prominent distributors of foreign-language films in the United States. The vast majority of awards, box office returns, and publicity went to the films released by these two entities.[40] Yet the companies were quite distinctive both in their business strategies and in the kinds of films they chose to release. The way each acquired, produced, and distributed foreign-language films, in turn, reflected their broader practices in the indie film business throughout the decade. Like Miramax, SPC had a deep-pocketed parent in the Sony Corporation. But that is where the similarities ended. During the 1990s, as Miramax moved into development, SPC retained its emphasis on acquisitions. While Miramax diversified into a range of different media forms, SPC's biggest "risk taking" came in the form of its limited involvement as an occasional coproducer and cofinancier (e.g., *The Celluloid Closet*, 1995; *Waiting for Guffman*, 1996).

Best Foreign-Language Film Oscar Winners in the 1990s

Award year	Title	Distributor	Box Office (m)
1988	*Babette's Feast*	Orion Classics	$5.3
1989	*Pelle the Conquerer*	Miramax	$2.5
1990	*Cinema Paradiso*	Miramax	$12.0
1991	*Journey of Hope*	Miramax	$0.2
1992	*Mediterraneo*	Miramax	$4.5
1992	*Indochine*	SPC	$5.6
1994	*Belle Époque*	SPC	$5.4
1995	*Burnt by the Sun*	SPC	$2.3
1996	*Antonia's Line*	First Look	$4.2
1997	*Kolya*	Miramax	$5.8
1998	*Character*	SPC	$0.6
1999	*Life is Beautiful*	Miramax	$57.6
2000	*All About My Mother*	SPC	$8.3

Top Grossing Foreign-Language Films of the 1990s

Release date (U.S)	Title	Distributor	Box office (m)
1998	*Life Is Beautiful*	Miramax	$57.6
1995	*Il Postino*	Miramax	$21.8
1993	*Like Water for Chocolate*	Miramax	$21.7
1990	*Cinema Paradiso*	Miramax	$12.0
1997	*Shall We Dance?*	Miramax	$9.5
1999	*All About My Mother*	SPC	$8.3
1994	*Eat Drink Man Woman*	Goldwyn	$7.3
1999	*Run Lola Run*	SPC	$7.3
1993	*The Wedding Banquet*	Goldwyn	$6.9
1990	*Cyrano de Bergerac*	Orion Classics	$5.8

Miramax's spending on acquisitions and in-house productions contributed to its stratospheric rise; SPC refused to pay exorbitant prices. Miramax employed close to three hundred people; SPC remained a shoestring operation, with a handful of executives making most major decisions. As Miramax began to prioritize more commercially oriented fare with name talent, SPC remained dedicated to a more traditional definition of art house and foreign-language cinema. But this does not mean that SPC released a narrow range of films in either style or content. Rather, throughout the decade, SPC typically distributed films from around

Select List of Sony Pictures Classics Releases

Release Date	Title	Director
1993	*Orlando*	Sally Potter
1993	*The Story of Qiu Jiu*	Yimou Zhang
1993	*Faraway, So Close!*	Wim Wenders
1994	*Vanya on 42nd Street*	Louis Malle
1995	*Crumb*	Terry Zwigoff
1995	*Amateur*	Hal Hartley
1995	*Ashes of Time*	Wong Kar-wai
1995	*The City of Lost Children*	Marc Caro and Jean-Pierre Jeunet
1995	*Safe*	Todd Haynes
1996	*Welcome to the Dollhouse*	Todd Solondz
1996	*Thieves*	André Téchiné
1996	*Lone Star*	John Sayles
1997	*In the Company of Men*	Neil LaBute
1997	*My Life in Pink*	Alain Berliner
1998	*Spanish Prisoner*	David Mamet
1998	*Central Station*	Walter Salles
1998	*The Emperor and the Assassin*	Chen Kaige
1999	*Sweet and Lowdown*	Woody Allen
1999	*Run Lola Run*	Tom Tykwer

the world that were much more formally experimental and politically charged than those released by any other indie company.

In short, SPC continued to operate in the 1990s much like a 1980s-era independent film company.[41] The company's top executives remained aware of—but relatively unaffected by—the changing industry around them. At times, SPC came under attack for retaining its slow rollout strategy as its competitors opened films more widely than ever.[42] A film released by SPC might stay in theaters for longer than specialty releases from other companies, but it was much less likely to become an indie blockbuster that earned in excess of $20 million (or, in most cases, even $5 million). Due to their lack of "break out" hits on par with Miramax, Michael Barker and Tom Bernard sometimes seemed defensive in interviews. Yet they refused to succumb to the Miramax model of niche film distribution. As Bernard observed, "One of the things that has been the curse of this new 'sex, lies, and videotape' generation is that they have become mirror images of the studios. They are controlled by the studio distribution system, they are controlled by the studio creative system."[43]

SPC, he added, would not submit so easily to the growing obsession with box office returns and market share: "It's a sort of a hit mentality [that drives most indie companies. The attitude that] we're going to release 20 and if one hits, it pays for the 20. Whereas our philosophy has always been every movie should be bought and worked to try to succeed, and be a financial success. And so it's a focus and it's a mandate."[44]

SPC's emphasis on "profits over revenues" may have turned away filmmakers seeking a $100 million hit, but its philosophy appealed to many others, notably Neil LaBute, Todd Solondz, Todd Haynes, Yimou Zhang, Sally Potter, Pedro Almodóvar, and Wim Wenders.[45] Certainly in some cases, this attraction may have been because Sony was the only large-scale company expressing interest in these directors' films. Yet other filmmakers proved willing to sacrifice their chance for bigger box office returns in exchange for less direct involvement by studio executives in the creative process.[46] Harvey Weinstein's meddling was well-known throughout the industry, and this certainly provided a useful means of differentiating SPC's relationship with filmmakers. As Bernard observed in discussing his company's arrangement with Pedro Almodóvar on *All About My Mother*, "We don't interfere. We follow the same theory that the old United Artists, Arthur Krim and Eric Pleskow and Bill Bernstein and Mike Medavoy did when we had our first jobs and we were at Orion. Once the script and the director are set, and the movie can be made for the budget that they wanted, then we step aside and let the artist do their work."[47] The statement is revealing: whereas Harvey Weinstein was busy promoting his image as an Old Hollywood mogul to the press, the heads of SPC actually behaved more like many of these moguls. Significantly, SPC executives, like their films, elicited much less media coverage than did Miramax. This may have been partly because the executives themselves did not pursue the kind of press coverage (nor pay the kind of marketing money) that Miramax did. But it also likely stemmed from the fact that there just was not much of a story in a company that simply plugged along, releasing highly praised but narrowly targeted art house films that yielded steady, stable box office returns.[48]

In contrast, Miramax's executives were not satisfied with steady, stable box office returns for their foreign-language releases. Much as was the case with the other types of films it released, Miramax wanted its films to move beyond a specific demographic group and appeal to multiple niches. In other words, Miramax wanted its foreign-language films to be popular. Harvey Weinstein often underscored his belief that subpar marketing on an industry-wide level played a major part in why foreign-language films performed so poorly in the United States.[49] For well over a decade, Weinstein and company repeatedly sought to demonstrate that imported films did not have to be consigned to art house theaters and meager box office returns. The North American box office grosses of $57 million brought in by *Life Is Beautiful* in 1999 marked the culmination of a strategy previously undertaken with such films as *Cinema Paradiso, Like Water for Chocolate, Il Postino, Kolya,* and *Shall We Dance?*

But the company did not merely market films differently; its success came as much from the types of foreign-language films it chose to release. Whereas Sony Pictures Classics often opted for stylistically ambitious and narratively complex foreign-language films, Miramax preferred much safer material. In fact, of all the types of films Miramax released, its foreign-language imports often were the most classical in style, unambitious in structure, and conservative in politics. Thus, if with its American and English-language material Miramax was regularly negotiating precisely how edgy a film could be while still crossing over to broader audiences, with its foreign-language material Miramax seemed to pursue the most inoffensive and heartwarming of material—material that, were it produced in the United States with Hollywood stars, would likely never have made its way to the big screen.

Surveying Miramax's foreign-language releases reveals a number of industrial and stylistic commonalities, particularly with the company's biggest box office successes. Films such as *Cinema Paradiso, Like Water for Chocolate, Il Postino,* and *Shall We Dance?* all received substantial promotional support from Miramax; they also generated significant media coverage and awards attention. Typically these films came from a major film-producing country such as Italy, France, China, Spain, Germany, or Japan. In many cases, these were not only countries that had a high profile in the film business, but also ones with which Miramax wanted to build or maintain relationships.[50] Thus acquiring these films was not purely an act of goodwill on the part of Miramax executives or evidence of their recognition of the best of cinema from around the world. Rather, these acquisitions were part of broader efforts by the company, often through its Miramax International division, to expand its profile in particularly lucrative markets.[51] In most cases, Miramax did not seek to cultivate relationships with a specific country per se (China being the key exception), but rather to expand its association with powerful companies (e.g., Japan's Shochiku with *Shall We Dance?*; Italy's Cecchi Gori with *Il Postino*) or further develop its talent roster (e.g., *Cinema Paradiso's* Giuseppe Tornatore). Further, the films produced by these companies or filmmakers were not "minor" releases in their native countries; rather, they tended to be among the biggest box office hits.[52]

A Miramax Films Release © 1998. Photo: Sergio Strizzi.

A Miramax Films Release © 1998. Photo: Sergio Strizzi. These stills, distributed with the film's press kit, illustrate how Miramax tried to conceal the more disturbing aspects of *Life Is Beautiful*. The promotional materials foregrounded elements of comedy, romance, and familial love.

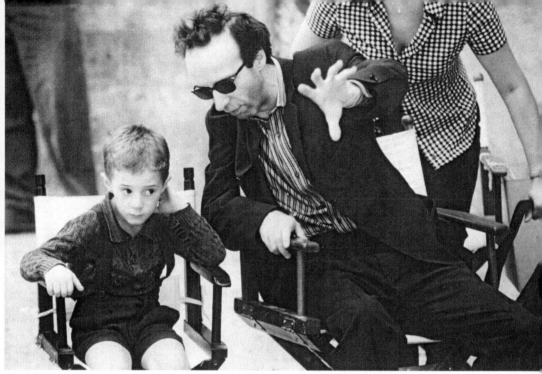

A Miramax Films Release © 1996. Photo: Sergio Strizzi. This image simultaneously calls attention to Benigni's directorial role and his role in the film as a loving father.

As McDonald notes, in releasing these films in the United States Miramax sought to deemphasize the films' "foreignness."[53] Anything that might be perceived as culturally specific was minimized or removed from the promotional materials (and sometimes the films themselves).[54] If, historically, foreign-language films had been sold to American viewers based on their aesthetic or narrative differences from Hollywood product, the goal for Miramax was to underscore how similar these movies were to English-language fare. As will be discussed below through the case study of *Life Is Beautiful*, this was accomplished in part by highlighting the ways that the film broached "universal" subjects and addressed themes that transcended national boundaries. Miramax's by now well-worn marketing tactics also played a part—tactics that included exploiting press and critical discourses about the project, as well as campaigning heavily for awards.

With *Life Is Beautiful*, we can see how all these elements came together in a way that marked a singular moment both for Miramax and for the cultural and financial status of foreign-language imports in the United States. Financed for approximately $7 million by Cecchi Gori and produced by Melampo Cinematografica, Benigni's film remained one of the top three releases at the Italian box office throughout the winter of 1997–1998.[55] The film grossed more than $35 million in its first nine weeks of release in Italy—an outstanding figure, causing one exhibitor to label it the "*Titanic* of foreign language films."[56] Miramax acquired *Life Is Beautiful* in February 1998, at the height of the film's popularity in Italy. The company paid more than $7 million for worldwide rights (excluding Italy).[57] From early on, Miramax intended Roberto Benigni to play a pivotal role in the marketing process. Long established as one of the most popular performers throughout Europe, Benigni had a devoted international fan base from which Miramax could build its publicity. His performances in such Italian-language films as *Nothing Left to Do but Cry* (1984, codirected and costarring *Il Postino* star Massimo Troisi) and *Johnny Stecchino* (1991) had earned him comparisons to such silent comedians as Buster Keaton and Charlie Chaplin. In addition, Benigni had already built awareness with some American viewers through his performances in the Jim Jarmusch films *Down by Law* (1986) and *Night on Earth* (1991). Hollywood had previously attempted to make Benigni a star. For example, in 1993 MGM unsuccessfully tried to revitalize its *Pink Panther* series by featuring Benigni as the son of Peter Sellers's famed Inspector Clouseau in *Son of the Pink Panther.*

But it was not just Benigni that made *Life Is Beautiful* attractive to Miramax. In a suggestive statement made at the time of the film's acquisition, Harvey Weinstein declared, "Roberto Benigni continues to prove himself as a filmmaking and performing genius. . . . *La Vita è Bella* has that rare humanity that will have *universal appeal* among audiences throughout the world. Miramax is very proud to be handling this film, and we are delighted to be partnered once again with our friends at Cecchi Gori, with whom we set the world on fire with *Il Postino.*"[58] Miramax marketers highlighted the film's universal themes and the star's dynamic personality. Rather than call attention to the film's horrific aspects—specifically, a father struggling to shield his son from the horrors of a Nazi death camp during World War II—Miramax instead emphasized its heartwarming and comedic components. Miramax's decision to emphasize sentiment and humor distinguishes its marketing of foreign-language films from the other types of films it released. Whereas with its English-language material Miramax often chose to call attention to controversial aspects of relatively uncontroversial films, the company frequently sought to downplay any potentially unsettling elements in its foreign-language films. *Life Is Beautiful*'s main theatrical trailer is a perfect example of this strategy. The trailer begins by informing the audience that here they will find a story of a "real life Prince Charming . . . [who has] just met the woman of his dreams. There's just one small problem: she's getting married in seven months." This narration is accompanied by images of several amusing physical stunts performed by Benigni. The trailer goes on to proclaim that this a film "written, directed by, and starring Italy's national treasure." In sum, *Life Is Beautiful* offers "a story that proves love, family and imagination conquers all."

And as for the film's depiction of the Holocaust? Images of soldiers pointing guns at Benigni's character, as well as shots of him and his son holding each other tightly as they travel on a train, only obliquely suggest their fate. The voice-over, meanwhile, declares indistinctly that "five years later, his fairy-tale life takes a serious turn," as Benigni's character is forced to "turn the hard truth into a simple game." Thus the film's central focus on the Holocaust becomes ambiguous. What ultimately stands out in the trailer are more general characteristics of the film—a tone of humor mixed with sentiment, a story of the strong bonds of father and son, images of the powerful force of romantic love, impressions of how individuals in a seemingly distant past triumphed over adversity. On many of these counts, *Life Is Beautiful* comes across as remarkably similar to many of Miramax's other high-profile foreign language films in the 1990s.

In an interview published at the time that *Life Is Beautiful* was beginning to build momentum in theaters, Paramount Classics copresident and former Miramax executive David Dinerstein outlined what he perceived to be the "formula" for box office success with foreign-language films. From his perspective, what worked best were upbeat films that "leave the audience with a smile."[59] October Films' copresident Bingham Ray offered a similar view. According to Ray, the biggest foreign-language hits during the 1990s were "emotional stories, usually with lush, romantic vistas, or sentimental stories told on a delicate or precious scale, not films that are trying to accomplish something challenging or edgy."[60] Harvey Weinstein himself reinforced that Miramax explicitly pursued this "softer" fare as a means of product differentiation. As he noted, "There used to be a time when American movies were tame in comparison to foreign films. . . . [But now] the allure of the sexy Italian movie and the French farce has disappeared—we can now see that kind of thing on TV."[61] By extension, Miramax pursued what could not be seen either on TV or in the most widely distributed American independent films at the time. This does not necessarily mean that viewers were always offered happy endings per se, but even more downbeat resolutions tended to be bittersweet and inspiring. For the most part, the company's foreign-language releases offered classically told stories replete with images of quirky foreigners who, despite their eccentricities, were an awful lot "like us." Miramax went to great lengths to make "them" seem more "like us," demanding reediting and rescoring to make the films accessible to a broad-based U.S. audience.[62]

In terms of building prerelease buzz for *Life Is Beautiful*, Miramax employed many of its tried-and-true tactics. For example, as with *sex, lies, and videotape* (and on many subsequent occasions), Harvey Weinstein fought to get *Life Is Beautiful* accepted into the May 1998 Cannes Film Festival. The festival's director, Gilles Jacob, initially hesitated to place the film in competition, believing that it exploited the Holocaust.[63] Weinstein sought to disprove Jacob's opinion by screening it to Jewish leaders and prominent French figures.[64] The strategy worked, as the film not only found a place in the festival competition but also went on to win the Grand Prize (the runner-up award; first place, the Palme d'Or, went to the Greek film *Eternity and a Day*).[65] The audience response at Cannes, and many festivals thereafter, was often highly favorable. The film received audience awards from a range of festivals, including those in Toronto, Los Angeles, Vancouver, and Athens. A particularly significant honor came at the 1998 Jerusalem International Film Festival, where *Life Is Beautiful* earned the Best Jewish Experience Award. This became an important validation for the film, especially in light of the accusations by a number of critics that it trivialized the Holocaust.[66]

While many high-profile critics, including the *Los Angeles Times'* Kenneth Turan, the *New York Times'* Janet Maslin, and the *Chicago Sun-Times'* Roger Ebert, praised the film, a substantial number levied powerful attacks against it. David Sterritt of the *Christian Science Monitor* felt the film "obscures the human and historical events it sets out to illuminate," while J. Hoberman of the *Village Voice* opined that "Benigni's movie is above all reassuring—indeed, that is its greatest absurdity." *Entertainment Weekly's* Owen Gleiberman declared *Life Is Beautiful* to be "some sort of feat—the first feel-good Holocaust weepie." He found the film suspect not only for the degree to which it "stylize[d] reality," but also because it had "the audacity—or is it insensitivity?—to place its lovable clownish hero in a death camp that looks like something out of a '50s musical. You'll laugh! You'll cry! You'll smile through the evils of genocide!"[67]

Miramax executives anticipated such responses and employed several strategies to counteract them. Special care had to be taken, especially because Benigni was not Jewish. Thus feature articles at the time of the film's release dutifully reported that Benigni's own father had been imprisoned in an Italian concentration camp during the war, and that Benigni had carefully researched and written the script in consultation with the Center for Jewish Documentation in Milan.[68] Miramax also arranged several advance screenings targeted to Jewish groups as a means of both framing the film appropriately and helping to build early word of mouth with a vital constituency.[69]

Though Harvey Weinstein may have held huge hopes that the film would be the company's next indie blockbuster, Miramax's release strategy was initially cautious. Significantly, though Miramax and Sony Pictures Classics may have differed greatly in their acquisitions and promotional practices, the two companies' employed similar strategies in opening foreign-language films. The differences in approach only became more apparent once their films had been in theaters for several weeks. Whereas SPC typically kept its foreign-language films in limited release (reaching a few hundred screens at most), Miramax executives were more willing to increase both their advertising expenditures and screen count if the opportunity arose. Such opportunity certainly arose with *Life Is Beautiful*. The film first opened in limited release on 22 October 1998 on screens in New York and Los Angeles; by the end of November, the film had expanded to about 125 screens.[70] Only after months in release—and following an aggressive publicity blitz directed at both the public and the awards organizations (an effort that included an appearance by Benigni on *60 Minutes*)—did the film play on more than 1,100 screens across the United States.[71]

North American audiences were not the only ones drawn to *Life Is Beautiful*. By the end of its worldwide theatrical run, it had grossed more than $171 million.[72] As Miramax International chair Rick Sands presciently observed at the time of its acquisition, "This film's box office career will know no international boundaries."[73] In fact, in diverse ways that went far beyond box office returns, *Life Is Beautiful* played a part in Miramax's ongoing global expansion efforts. For example, the film helped Miramax enter into the Chinese market. As was the case with so many multinational media conglomerates at this time, Miramax (and, by extension, Disney) had repeatedly tried to enter China, only to meet with mixed results. Yet with Benigni's film, Miramax succeeded, striking an agreement with the state-run China Film that included theatrical, video, and television rights.[74] This would be but the first of several such steps Miramax would take in building a relationship with the Chinese film industry.[75] In other words, Miramax gained entrée into a relatively closed market in Asia due to its involvement with a foreign-language film. As this example suggests, for Miramax acquiring foreign films was about much more than merely expanding Americans' exposure to creative works from around the world. It was also about more than simply building up the libraries of Miramax and Disney, or about generating income from a range of ancillary revenue streams. Rather, acquiring and releasing imported films was also about building—or strengthening—relationships with some of the world's most prominent talent, companies, and nations.[76] The love affair among Benigni, Cecchi Gori, and Miramax was but one more example of relationship building. In 2002, these parties reunited for their disastrous take on *Pinocchio*; on Oscar night, 1999, however, their romance was peaking.

A Foreign-Language Fairy Tale Without a Happy Ending

> It's one of the toughest things in the world to make money with foreign-language films.
>
> *Harvey Weinstein, 1992*

One of the most memorable moments in Oscar history took place on 21 March 1999, when Roberto Benigni, the star, cowriter, and director of *Life Is Beautiful*, won the Best Foreign Language Film Oscar. The award's presenter, Sophia Loren, only needed to say "Roberto" and the audience exploded. Benigni enthusiastically made his way to the stage, jumping over multiple chairs in the Dorothy Chandler Pavilion, using Steven Spielberg to prop him up as he waved to the auditorium's audience from the top of a chair, then leapfrogging up the steps to the podium. A standing ovation and an emotional three-minute acceptance speech followed.

Benigni certainly had much to celebrate. With seven nominations, including Best Original Screenplay, Best Film Editing, Best Director, and Best Picture, *Life Is Beautiful* was the most nominated foreign-language film in Oscar history.[77] His nominations as director, actor, and cowriter put him in the company of Orson Welles, Warren Beatty, and Woody Allen.[78] As of Oscar night, the film had already earned an impressive $35 million. By the time it completed its theatrical run in June, it would earn an additional $22 million, thereby making it the highest-grossing foreign-language import in history.[79] *Life Is Beautiful* certainly had earned more money and awards in the United States than many had believed possible for a foreign-language film. This unlikely "Holocaust tragicomedy"[80] followed previous indie blockbusters *sex, lies, and videotape* and *Pulp Fiction* (1994) to become both a box office hit and a cultural phenomenon. *Life Is Beautiful* represented the culmination of a lengthy process in which Miramax sought to expand interest in foreign-language films. Though several earlier Miramax releases, including *Cinema Paradiso*, *Like Water for Chocolate*, and *Il Postino*, had broken domestic box office records, *Life Is Beautiful* more than doubled the amount earned by any previous foreign-language film. As such, Harvey Weinstein seemed to have succeeded in reaching one of his long-standing goals: finding "a sexier way of presenting foreign movies."[81]

As discussed above, this evening was an important one for Miramax not only because of *Life Is Beautiful*, but also due to *Shakespeare in Love*'s surprise victory over *Saving Private Ryan* for Best Picture. Though Miramax had much to be happy about that night, the ensuing weeks did not prove nearly as pleasant. The myriad honors, all aggressively pursued with a high-profile marketing campaign, helped undermine the company's carefully cultivated upstart image. The memorable scene of Benigni's Oscar win might then be read symbolically—not simply as a turning point for the Italian comedian or for foreign-language films, but also, more broadly, for Miramax's industry status and public reputation. The company had reached tremendous financial and critical heights largely through sheer marketing force of will. That evening, however, the ramifications of these activities had not yet been felt. Miramax's success with *Life Is Beautiful* needs to be read against the broader context of the ongoing challenges that it and other distributors faced in introducing foreign-language films to American audiences. In addition, *Life Is Beautiful* needs to be discussed in terms of how it connects to the larger narrative of Miramax and its development.

With regard to foreign-language films specifically, *Life Is Beautiful* did not lead to a wave of foreign-language indie blockbusters, neither for Miramax nor for any other specialty company. The market for foreign-language imports remained negligible at best. The occasional film would break out (e.g., SPC's *Crouching Tiger, Hidden Dragon*, 2000; Miramax's *Amélie*, 2001, and *Hero*, 2004), but these were rare exceptions. Failure remained even more likely for foreign-language films than for English-language material. Unfortunately, the vast majority of the time, imported product came and went on a few screens, earning but a few hundred thousand dollars at most. And these, of course, were the films that were acquired in the first place. As Andrew Gumbel of *The Independent* sagely observed at the time of *Life Is Beautiful*'s release, "If you think its success heralds an explosion of Iranian or Malian or even mainstream European cinema on American screens, don't hold your breath."[82]

Even though, as noted above, acquiring foreign-language films might have served other purposes for major media companies—such as helping to build relationships and increasing their library holdings—in most cases these investments did not benefit a company's bottom line in any tangible way. Nurturing one of these films to $10 million in box office also demanded far more time and labor than it did for the genre or American indie films they released. Miramax may have been able to "find" a market for *Life Is Beautiful* in the United States, but at what cost? Did the money and labor spent on selling the film pay off, considering that its total box office returns were smaller than two weeks of returns for the 1997 teen slasher *Scream 2*? Considering the limited emphasis that Miramax placed on releasing foreign-language films in the ensuing years, it appears that the company decided that the investment was simply not worth it. Significantly, even in the immediate aftermath of its success with *Life Is Beautiful*, Miramax distributed only a handful of foreign-language films. These included a rerelease of Jackie Chan's *Twin Dragons* (1999, via Dimension), designed to capitalize on his growing popularity; the animated Hayao Miyazaki film *Princess Mononoke* (1999), redubbed with the voices of such Hollywood stars as Gillian Anderson, Claire Danes, and Minnie Driver; and the Giuseppe Tornatore–directed *Malèna* (2000), a World War II–era story about a young boy enamored with a beautiful widow, played by Monica Bellucci. With $8.3 million in grosses, the Jackie Chan film was the highest earner by far.

Life Is Beautiful and other occasional hits might have led some in the press and industry to believe that foreign-language films could become more popular in the United States. Yet in the end, no such dramatic transformation in industry practices or American moviegoing occurred. As much as Miramax may have attempted to broaden the interest in foreign-language films in the U.S. market, larger structural conditions constrained the company. Despite Miramax's best efforts, foreign-language imports attracted a small slice of an already modest art house business. Paul McDonald suggests that since the appeal of foreign-language films was based in part on their "difference" and "inaccessibility," U.S.-based distributors were placed in a no-win situation.[83] Dubbing these films to make them more popular (as Miramax tried to do on multiple occasions, with movies ranging from *Life Is Beautiful* to *Princess Mononoke* to Benigni's follow-up, *Pinocchio*), ended up merely diminishing their cachet with the viewers most likely to see them. As he explains, "Dubbing reveals an interesting paradox at work in foreign-language distribution: language differences limit the market for imported films but the preservation of those differences remains essential to the market."[84] This situation destined foreign films to remain a "micro-niche" and "merely a sideline" for specialty companies.[85]

Shakespeare in Love, meanwhile, was anything but a "sideline" for Miramax. Rather, this $26 million film represented the type of content the company increasingly prioritized: a star-laden, multinational,

English-language production, the quintessential mid-level film. *Shakespeare in Love* eclipsed *Life Is Beautiful* in both media attention and box office returns. In terms of grosses, *Shakespeare in Love* generated more than $100 million in North American theaters and $179 million overseas.[86] It similarly overshadowed *Life Is Beautiful* at the Oscars. As notable as *Life Is Beautiful*'s awards may have been in raising the profile of foreign-language film, the honors received by *Shakespeare in Love* were even more significant in terms of what they represented for Miramax both economically and culturally. Indeed, *Shakespeare in Love*'s Best Picture win over *Saving Private Ryan* surprised many journalists and critics. Though Spielberg's World War II drama had been widely expected to win the top award, it was Harvey Weinstein who, as a producer of *Shakespeare in Love*, ultimately ascended the stage to give the final acceptance speech of the night.[87] And while Harvey's Oscar may have been a high point in his career—and the ultimate achievement for his marketing team—it also fed into the growing hostility directed toward Miramax at the end of the 1990s.

The Beginning of the Backlash

Only a few months earlier, not many people would have foreseen *Shakespeare in Love* dominating the Academy Awards. In fact, DreamWorks' *Saving Private Ryan* was considered a likely Best Picture candidate from the time it was released back in July 1998, almost eight months before nominations were announced.[88] Meanwhile, throughout late 1998 Miramax continued to come up short in terms of potential Oscar candidates. Initially the Peter Chelsom–directed drama *The Mighty* had seemed a likely contender. Yet upon its release in October 1998, the film generated only a lukewarm critical response.[89] In January 1999, *Variety*'s Peter Bart reported rumors circulating that Harvey had "taken his eye off the ball."[90] But, as Bart went on to note, the "tide seems to have turned" due to the surprisingly favorable critical reaction to the December limited release *Shakespeare in Love*. The film gained further momentum with the 24 January Golden Globes ceremony, when *Saving Private Ryan* received the Globe for Best Drama and *Shakespeare in Love* won Best Comedy/Musical.[91]

At the same time that *Shakespeare in Love* emerged as a surprise hit at the box office, a number of individuals began to very publicly revise their opinions of *Saving Private Ryan* and reevaluate its presumed lock on the major Oscars.[92] As one journalist observed about the status of the Oscar competition, "Wide open. That seems to be the consensus on this year's

Oscar race, quite a change from last year's Acad 11-award salute to the *Titanic* phenomenon. Aside from DreamWorks' *Saving Private Ryan*, no film has a guaranteed reservation at the best pic table."[93] The prominent Oscar narrative for 1999 began to crystallize as soon as the nominations were announced in early February. Along with *Saving Private Ryan* and *Shakespeare in Love*, the other nominees were *Elizabeth, Life Is Beautiful*, and *The Thin Red Line*. Immediately, stories of "World War II vs. Elizabethan England" ran rampant, with *Shakespeare in Love* and *Saving Private Ryan* gathering the lion's share of attention from the press. The major themes evoked in subsequent media coverage are readily apparent in this introduction to an article in *Time*: "It's a foreign battle fought in Hollywood: Spielberg's France 1944 v. Miramax's olde England. Who'll win the battle—and the award?" The article continued, "Prepare, then, for the final battle: of making war vs. making love, of 1944 v. 1593, of Spielberg's Hollywood vs. Weinstein's Manhattan, of the most successful director in history vs. the round mound of the movie underground. In one word, from another 1998 blockbuster: Armageddon!"[94]

The "matchup" between the two films made for a good story not only because of the films themselves, but also because of the behind-the-scenes drama that began to emerge around them. As suggested by the above comment, there were a number of reasons that the *Shakespeare in Love* versus *Saving Private Ryan* narrative made for a particularly provocative tale. First, Jeffrey Katzenberg figured prominently in both Miramax's past and DreamWorks' present. In addition, Katzenberg was engaged in a high-profile lawsuit against Michael Eisner and Disney. Katzenberg sought additional compensation for the contributions he made to Disney's bottom line—contributions that included his crucial role in bringing Miramax into the Disney fold.[95]

Second, there were the larger-than-life figures involved with both Miramax and DreamWorks. Katzenberg and Harvey Weinstein seemed to take pleasure in playing up the Best Picture "feud" in the press. This contest included debates about not only the relative merits of the two films, but also how much each company spent in campaigning for their awards. Third, along with the drama cultivated by matching various individuals from the two companies against each other, there also was the drama that came out of reporting about the distinctive cultural and industrial positions of the two companies. Many journalists wondered whether DreamWorks might function as a haven for creative, independent-minded talent in much the way that United Artists had, off and on, from its founding by Charlie Chaplin, Douglas Fairbanks, D. W. Griffith, and Mary Pickford in 1919 through its time under the leadership of

Arthur Krim and Robert Benjamin in the 1950s to the 1970s.[96] Despite these analogies, it remained relatively unproved in the marketplace, as it had been distributing films for only about two years. Before *Saving Private Ryan*, DreamWorks had released a mere six films: *The Peacemaker*, *Amistad*, and *Mousehunt* in 1997; and *Paulie*, *Deep Impact*, and *Small Soldiers* in 1998. None of these releases suggested that DreamWorks' fare would differ substantively from those on offer by the other major media companies. Nonetheless, in an industry that was continuing to consolidate and conglomerate, the promise offered by a new upstart run by hybrid entrepreneur-artists elicited a great deal of enthusiasm and support. Meanwhile, Miramax, which had earned its own share of United Artists comparisons over the years, was well on its way to becoming the old guard of the indie scene. As a member of this old guard, Miramax had the deep pockets of a studio parent and an increasingly well-known reputation for abusing its own employees and talent.

Fourth, there were the significant distinctions between *Saving Private Ryan* and *Shakespeare in Love* in both style and tone. One was intense, somber, and dramatic, the other comparatively light, merry, and comedic. One was "obvious" Oscar fare while the other seemed a modest diversion. There were also the notable differences between *Shakespeare in Love* and many of the most high-profile Miramax releases of the past decade— dark, edgy films like *sex, lies, and videotape*, *The Crying Game* (1992), and *Pulp Fiction*. As Sundance Channel executive Liz Manne observed, *Shakespeare in Love* was an example of "nice cinema"—pretty, safe, innocuous costume dramas that played to middlebrow sensibilities.[97]

The oppositions between the films, along with the companies and people involved with each, were repeatedly noted in articles throughout awards season. Up to the time of the Oscars, a degree of ambivalence remained about Miramax and its marketing tactics. Some writers marveled once more at Weinstein and company's salesmanship, while others objected to what were seen as increasingly over-the-top promotional practices. *Time*'s Richard Corliss observed, "The fact that movie people even think there's a horse race is mostly a tribute to Weinstein's entrepreneurial savvy."[98] The *Los Angeles Times* ran a piece arguing that critics can still "help" or "hurt" certain films, with *Shakespeare in Love* given as a prime example. Miramax marketing executive Marcy Granata concurred, stating that "*Shakespeare in Love* was born of the critics. They explained that it was sexy and funny, not a dry biography of Shakespeare." The article continued, "Critics say that no studio and no other independent calls them as often as Miramax to try to arrange convenient screening times for them. Miramax is also the best, they say, at inducing the media

A Miramax Films Release © 1998. Photo: Laurie Sparham. *Shakespeare in Love* (1998) may have secured seven Oscars, including awards for Best Picture and Best Actress, but in the process Miramax came under attack by many in the press for its over-the-top campaigning.

to write and broadcast feature stories that help create a climate of anticipation and excitement before a movie is released—and then providing story ideas that will keep the momentum building once the movie is in theaters."[99]

On the one hand, this passage reflects the fact that some still admired Miramax's effective marketing practices. On the other hand, it indicates the growing tendency of journalists to peek "behind the Miramax curtain." In the weeks leading up to the awards, many articles remained respectful, but not quite celebratory, of Miramax's promotion of *Shakespeare in Love*. But several more critical pieces also began to appear.[100] Especially noteworthy was a column by Nikki Finke in *New York* magazine. If one piece was particularly central in shifting the tone taken toward Miramax, this was it. Titled "Much Ado About Oscars," the subtitle quickly made the article's tone clear in referring to "Miramax's blitzkrieg campaign." Finke used Miramax as a prime example of how campaigning for Oscars had gotten out of control, thereby detracting from the ceremony's ability to truly honor the best in cinema. She reported the lengths to which Miramax was willing to go to get awards, including hosting a "welcome to America" party for *Shakespeare in Love* director John Madden attended by Academy members, hiring prominent publicists to "generate press coverage" and "schmooze their prominent Academy colleagues," and fueling the wave of revisionist criticism of *Saving Private Ryan*.[101] From Finke's perspective, Miramax was not only pushing the limits of the Academy's rules regarding what constituted appropriate Oscar campaigning, but also threatening the good name of the awards. In the process of attacking Miramax's Oscar campaign, Finke also placed the company's broader activities in her crosshairs. She called into question Miramax's status as a true independent, based on both its content and its marketing expenditures. She also turned to anonymous industry sources, who eagerly hurled attacks at the company. For example, one source declared that "Miramax for some reason thinks that because they are media darlings they're above scrutiny. . . . We wouldn't get away with this stuff for two minutes." Of course, the fact that such a statement was published at all suggests that Miramax was not getting away with "this stuff" as easily as it had in the past.

Indeed, Miramax's days as a "media darling" were numbered, due in no small part to what transpired in the ensuing weeks. Many other media outlets picked up Finke's report. For example, the *Los Angeles Times* ran an article citing her piece and then extended the attack.[102] The writer Richard Natale reported that Miramax's "ad blitz" amounted to about $15 million spent in "the trades and other publications." Natale added that "Industry insiders have characterized the media saturation by [DreamWorks and Miramax] as 'highly unusual.' Says one studio executive: 'I would think at some point there's going to be a backlash on the amount of money being spent.'" In an effort to stem the rush of negative press, Miramax executives Gill and Granata wrote a letter to the editor rebutting Natale's piece.[103] In it, they took issue with the figures Natale cited, stating that "the story says Miramax spent $15 million 'to bolster its chances for an Academy Award.' While this sensational number makes for a splashy headline, it is off by a factor of 500%." They continued:

> To be clear, our Oscar campaign (including trade ads, publicity, talent, travel, videocassettes and screenings) came in for slightly less than $2 million. In addition, we bought consumer newspaper and spot television advertisements in New York and Los Angeles for another $1 million. (This spending served the dual purpose of cre-

ating academy awareness and selling tickets in the more than 100 theaters in these two markets.) All of this must be distinguished from the national ad buy that is running concurrently, which is solely designed to sell tickets to moviegoers nationwide for the only best picture nominee that continues to accumulate a significant box office.

Had *Saving Private Ryan* won the Oscar, Miramax's defensive posture might have worked and a full-fledged backlash might have been avoided. But taking home the Best Picture award seemed to intensify the wave of negative attacks. In the weeks following the awards ceremony, *Variety*'s Peter Bart was one of the few journalists to defend Miramax against widespread claims that it had deployed a "marketing juggernaut" to win awards.[104] For the most part, Miramax was left to fend off the attacks on its own. Yet such defenses proved too little, too late. After more than a decade of being treated with kid gloves by the press, suddenly Miramax executives struggled to shield the company from seemingly endless assaults. Miramax might have hoped that the *Shakespeare in Love* brouhaha would be an isolated controversy—an irritation, perhaps, but ultimately containable. Instead, as the next chapter outlines, this was only one of many such high-profile attacks that Miramax suffered in 1999. Subsequently, everything from the company's acquisition strategies to its production decisions, its marketing practices to its diversification activities, came under criticism. A company that for so long could do no wrong swiftly seemed to make one misstep after another.

CHAPTER EIGHT

Maxed Out

Miramax and Indiewood in the New Millennium

You have to tip your hat to Miramax through the 90's. And I would even say that the studios would have to tip their hat to Miramax. Because they have been by far the most consistent film company of this decade in what they've achieved. And I salute them. But at the same time, they are still trying to convince you and me and every journalist in the country that they are still a little indie, upstart, underdog company, and that is so incredibly insane that anyone allows them that in any piece on anything, it just boggles my mind. . . . Miramax is a major studio. They give Disney a run for their money. And there are people who for whatever reason, whether it's the past not being caught up to the present, that still think of Miramax as an underdog, I mean, please, let's get past that as we get into the new millennium. They're a major studio and their philosophy has changed. Their philosophy is now the philosophy of a major studio. But then, so is every other independent company.

Bingham Ray, October Films cofounder, 1999

The creative community will say the Weinsteins give Disney cachet. But what's the point of cachet if it doesn't make money?

David Miller, media equity analyst, 2004

The Weinsteins did not leave Miramax until 2005. Disney did not shut down Miramax until 2010. By late 1999, however, cracks in the Disney-Miramax relationship, and challenges to the indie subsidiary's business model, had already begun to appear. Though media analysts might not have declared "the age of Miramax" over until several years later—and even then, the precise moment of the end was debated—the company's singular cultural status and industrial position had started to diminish before the new millennium began.[1] There were a variety of different reasons for this. First, structurally, the indie sector had expanded substantially since the early 1990s. Miramax now faced several new deep-pocketed competitors willing to spend excessive amounts to secure product. The company lost the significant advantage it had maintained in the marketplace for much of the decade. Second, the relationship between Disney and Miramax took a turn for the worse in ways that affected Miramax's staff, its practices, and its product. Many of these internal struggles between Disney and Miramax regularly played out in the pages of newspapers, magazines, and trade publications. Shifts in the executive ranks at both Disney and Miramax further contributed to modifications in the relationship between the two entities, in ways that significantly diminished Miramax's influence. Third, the Weinsteins themselves became victims of their own hubris. Coming off numerous box office and critical successes, and having recently received votes of confidence from Disney in the form of renewed contracts, the brothers began to overreach to an astounding degree. Not content to merely run the most high-profile and well-respected specialty film division, they attempted to turn Miramax into a mini-conglomerate, involved in a range of publishing, film, theater, music, and television projects. In addition, any prior restraint they may have exercised in terms of budgets or marketing costs disappeared as they spent profligately, without any attention to larger structural conditions or the requests of their own parent company. Fourth, a growing number of journalists started portraying the company in a negative light, thereby further harming its image and the strength of its brand identity.

On the most basic level, Miramax's ability to effectively sell itself as independent or as a young upstart became less and less tenable. Throughout 1999, one harmful report after another appeared in the press. Miramax's acquisitions, production, marketing, distribution, employment, and diversification practices were all extensively dissected and criticized. In addition, a growing number of executives and filmmakers suddenly seemed willing to speak on the record (albeit often anonymously), reciting war stories about their dealings with the company and regaling journalists with tales of the Weinstein brothers' bad behavior. No longer could Miramax sustain the myth that it was the "little guy" facing off against big bad media corporations. No longer could it fight back against the occasional slam piece. Now Miramax's undeniable status as a major media company put it on the defensive. Miramax executives tried to reestablish the terms of how the company was portrayed, but they often flailed in the process. Further, numerous competitors—many of whom Miramax had previously employed—refused to sit idly by as the company strong-armed its way through festivals, markets, screenings, and awards ceremonies. Instead, they fought back, often very publicly.

Attracting the Wrong Type of Media Attention

> Disney's reaction to the ambitious strides of its subsidiary isn't known, but Miramax hasn't behaved like a low-budget, special-ized film division for years. With interests spawning production, distribution, television and publishing, it threatens in some ways to overshadow its corporate parent.
>
> Variety, July 1999

Nearly every month of 1999, some new event took place that threatened Miramax's image. Even before the onslaught of unfavorable publicity on *Shakespeare in Love* (1998) started, reports circulated about Miramax throwing its weight around in the specialty business. In January 1999, for example, several journalists focused on Miramax's recent acquisition of the William H. Macy–Jeremy Northam comedy *Happy, Texas* at Sundance. After the film screened to favorable reaction at the festival, a bidding war took place between Miramax, Fox Searchlight, Paramount Classics, and Cary Woods's Independent Pictures (which had an output deal with New Line).[2] The controversy that emerged related to precisely how much Miramax paid for the rights to the film. Miramax maintained that it offered a $2.5 million minimum guarantee along with first-dollar gross for the filmmakers. Others disagreed vehemently with this figure, arguing that the purchase price exceeded the $10 million previously paid for *The Spitfire Grill* (1996). At Sundance, Amy Wallace of the *Los Angeles Times* asserted that "the way the final deal was brokered—and particu-larly the manner in which Miramax has publicized it—is so galling to some executives here that two [Fox's Tony Safford, a former Miramax employee, and producer Cary Woods, who had regularly worked with the company in the past] have taken the unusual step of complaining publicly."[3]

Though media companies often fudge their numbers, this case was unusual because of *the way* the numbers were fudged. In the past, Mira-max had prided itself on paying more than other companies for acquisi-tions; now it downplayed precisely how much it spent. As *Variety* writers

A Miramax Films Release © 1999. Photo: Claudette Barius. Whereas Miramax had distributed earlier teen films such as *Scream* (1996) and *The Faculty* (1998) under its Dimension label, the company opted to release the teen comedy *She's All That* (1999) via its Miramax arm. In the process, Miramax further deviated from its edgy indie brand identity.

Andrew Hindes and Chris Petrikin astutely observed, "Recently the company has been criticized in the press for some of [its] costly purchases, including two $6 million pickups from last year's Sundance fest: *Next Stop, Wonderland* [1998], which grossed just $3 million domestically, and *The Castle* [1999], which has yet to be released. The minimajor's insistence on publicizing a relatively low purchase price for *Happy* seems to indicate it no longer relishes its image as the indie world's biggest spender."[4] In the coverage surrounding *Happy, Texas*, Miramax came under fire not only for overspending on its acquisitions, but also for either shelving many of these films or releasing them on a limited basis with minimal promotional support. A report in *Newsweek* in late February suggested that, far from having stellar taste in films, Harvey Weinstein "discovered" his hits through an elaborate process of buying up the marketplace, extensively test-screening his acquisitions, and then supporting only those that tested well. Such charges had surfaced periodically in the past, yet the attack seemed more pointed this time. In what amounted to a growing list of indictments against Miramax, *Newsweek* noted, "Weinstein grabs promising flicks (1998 Sundance fave *Jerry and*

Tom), but if they test poorly they get shelved or go straight to video. Thus Weinstein backs only hits, crafting the rep of a Midas touch while playing to broad audiences."[5]

While some condemned Miramax for (over)buying films only to then bury them, others chastised the company for developing a growing proportion of its slate internally. The precise ratio of acquisitions to productions varied annually, but there could be little doubt that Miramax had become much more invested in the product it oversaw from the script stage. In 1993, approximately 10 percent of the films it released were developed in-house. By the late 1990s, half to two-thirds of its total output was developed internally.[6] Of course, when a company releases roughly three dozen films a year, it is possible to maintain a high profile in the acquisitions business even as internally developed productions are emphasized.

In some quarters, these in-house productions began to be viewed as problematic in terms of both content and cost. If some attacked *Shakespeare in Love* as taking Miramax far afield from its edgy indie roots, then the teen romantic comedy *She's All That* left others completely flummoxed. In the past, genre fare in general, and teen films more specifically, were released primarily under the Dimension label. Yet, in what could be seen as a threat to Miramax's well-developed brand identity, this modest Freddie Prinze Jr.–Rachael Leigh Cook film opened on 29 January 1999 with the Miramax logo attached. *She's All That* capitalized on the teen media boom that was now in full force, and in which Prinze figured prominently (*I Know What You Did Last Summer*, 1997; *I Still Know What You Did Last Summer*, 1998). As one critic observed, the film felt like it "could have been made by a team of septuagenarians from the glory days of American Intl. Pictures."[7] Nonetheless, *She's All That* was an immediate hit. The $16.8 million it earned at the box office in its first week in release marked the largest opening yet for Miramax.[8] The $10 million film ultimately grossed an impressive $63 million at the North American box office, making it a boon to Miramax's bottom line. But the effect the film had on Miramax's brand identity is less easy to determine. Following *She's All That*, Miramax seemed less and less concerned with keeping the Miramax and Dimension brands separate. The types of films released by the two divisions blurred further in the ensuing years, in part because Miramax itself continued to release select genre films (e.g., *Down to You*, 2000; *Duplex*, 2003), and in part because the press no longer let the company elide the differences as it had in the past.

As Miramax itself increasingly blurred the distinctions between its genre and quality indie brands, a series of public events directed unfa-

The involvement of Miramax regulars Ben Affleck and Matt Damon—along with director Kevin Smith—led the company to invest in the religious satire *Dogma* (1999). Under Disney pressure, however, the Weinsteins sold off the film's North American theatrical rights to the up-and-coming independent distributor Lions Gate.

vorable attention toward the company's involvement with teen fare. In particular, the 20 April 1999 Columbine high school massacre led to heightened scrutiny of what media companies marketed to teenagers. In the search for whom or what was to blame for the killers' violent acts, the media once again became a target. The press and politicians all discussed violent video games (*Halo*), goth music (Marilyn Manson), and graphic motion pictures (*The Basketball Diaries*, 1995) as potentially contributing to the killers' mental states. Within weeks of Columbine—and mere months before the 2000 presidential primaries—a series of hearings were held in Washington to ascertain the factors contributing to youth violence. As the distributor of the teen-friendly *Scream* franchise, as well as a subsidiary of kid-friendly Disney, Miramax had a featured role at these hearings. At an early gathering of the Senate Committee on

Commerce, for example, "culture warrior" William Bennett played the opening sequence of *Scream* while declaring, "This is brought to you by Walt Disney."[9]

Following these hearings, the Senate, under the guidance of Orrin Hatch and Joseph Lieberman, approved a joint inquiry by the Federal Trade Commission and the Department of Justice into the entertainment industry's marketing practices. Over the course of the fifteen-month investigation, several different media forms were examined, and many different companies drew scrutiny. Though no Miramax films were cited as directly influencing the Columbine killers, nonetheless those discussing the marketing of violent content to teens brought up the company on quite a few occasions. Significantly, whereas in the past Miramax had largely benefited from the publicity it had gained from testing the limits of the rating system, it now became vilified for such practices. Ultimately, the FTC's report broadly attacked the entertainment industry's marketing practices but did not directly implicate any individual company.[10] Further, no specific regulatory or legislative action was recommended. Even so, the film industry implemented a series of self-regulatory acts, ranging from exhibitors more aggressively carding moviegoers to distributors modifying the marketing of violent content[11] to producers moving away from developing graphic material featuring teenagers in lead roles.[12] Cumulatively, these moves affected the types of teen films released both by the industry in general and Miramax in particular. For example, Miramax subsequently changed the name of the Kevin Williamson–directed *Killing Mrs. Tingle* to *Teaching Mrs. Tingle* (1999) and postponed the release of its violent high school drama *O* (2001, based on *Othello*). It also focused its efforts on distributing teen-oriented comedies (e.g., *Boys and Girls*, 2000; *Get Over It*, 2001) as opposed to horror films in the mold of *Scream*.

Miramax may have sidestepped trouble with regard to its marketing of violent content toward youth, but it could not avoid controversy as a result of its involvement with Kevin Smith's satire of Catholicism, *Dogma* (1999). Significantly, if not for Smith's participation, it is likely that Miramax would never have been involved with this religious-themed adventure fantasy-comedy in the first place. The company had long since moved away from releasing such explicitly controversial material or selling films based on controversy.[13] It had been four years since Miramax had sold off a film in its possession (*Kids*, 1995) or had been involved with religious content (*Priest*, 1995). Yet Smith was firmly ensconced in the Miramax stable of talent, especially after his surprising success with the ultra-low-budget *Chasing Amy* (1997). Further, *Dogma*'s all-star cast, which included Ben Affleck and Matt Damon (as two fallen angels), Chris Rock (as a thirteenth apostle, absent from the Bible because he is black), Linda Fiorentino (as an abortion clinic employee), and Alanis Morissette (as God), made it an attractive property for Miramax.

Disney was less than thrilled by Miramax's investment in the project.[14] As a result, even before the film had screened publicly, the Weinsteins decided to reacquire the North American rights from Miramax and sell them to a third-party distributor unaffiliated with Disney.[15] They made this decision after top Disney executives deemed the film "inappropriate for all our labels."[16] According to Harvey Weinstein, this was a preemptive decision: "What [Disney] said is, 'We have a problem.' . . . So we came up with a solution." From his perspective, "Disney is too easy a target."[17] Though Smith declared *Dogma* to be "a love letter to both faith and God almighty" and "a recruitment film for the Catholic Church," Disney executives expressed concern that the subject matter would adversely affect its brand and its bottom line.[18] Little information about the film's content had leaked to the public before the Weinsteins reacquired the rights in April 1999, but the mere fact that it critiqued aspects of Catholicism was enough to make Disney skittish. As *Variety* noted at the time that the initial news broke, "*Dogma* is said to include such hot-button material as a foul-mouthed apostle, a discussion of whether Joseph and Mary had sex and a descendant of Jesus who happens to work in an abortion clinic."[19]

Disney and the Weinsteins may have thought that by discarding the film before any controversy took place, they would avoid the negative media coverage that surrounded *Kids*. Yet though the story appeared in the *New York Times* after Miramax (and Disney) were no longer officially involved with the project, the mere fact that a Disney subsidiary had *ever* been involved was enough to prompt protests by certain religious organizations. The most vocal group, the Catholic League, mounted a large-scale attack against the company. Notably, in late June 1999, the league funded a full-page advertisement in the *New York Times* reading, "Appeal to Disney: Dumping *Dogma* took guts, now dump Miramax."[20] As one reporter covering this fracas observed, "This is the very holy war the Weinstein brothers were hoping to avoid when they purchased the film from their own company five weeks ago."[21] Ironically, at the same time that select groups attacked Miramax for producing sacrilegious content and marketing violent films to youth, others lambasted the company for failing to stand by its talent and for moving too far away from the types of "small hidden gems" it used to support. As a sign of how much times had changed, Miramax's primary goal at the 1999 Cannes festival was not to acquire films, but rather to sell the rights to *Dogma*.[22] In September 1999, Lions Gate officially announced that it had acquired the rights for the film from the Weinsteins.[23] As will be discussed further below, at this time Lions Gate was becoming the "go-to" company for "hot-button" films such as *Mr. Death: The Rise and Fall of Fred A. Leuchter, Jr.* (1999). The independent distributor's decision to acquire *Dogma* paid off; upon its release in November 1999, the film earned more than $30 million at the box office and became the company's highest-grossing film to date.[24]

The coverage of *Dogma*—in tandem with the coverage of *Happy, Texas, Shakespeare in Love*, and a variety of teen films—reaffirmed many of the anxieties repeatedly expressed by those involved in the production, distribution, and exhibition of low-budget films. Fears about the diminished space for independent filmmakers and specialized films became even more pronounced when Barry Diller's USA Networks acquired both October Films and Gramercy Pictures in early April 1999 from Seagram/Universal.[25] The size and scope of this newly formed company, USA Films, remained unclear for some time, which contributed to a growing sense of unease in the specialty business. At exactly the moment that October drew praise for the support it provided to such 1998 films as *Hilary and Jackie, High Art*, and the early Dogme 95 film *The Celebration*, its own future seemed increasingly tenuous.

As Diller's emerging multimedia empire absorbed October, the Weinsteins accelerated their efforts to craft their own media conglomerate. This was an odd situation, given that Miramax itself was a relatively small entity within a major media conglomerate. This fact did little to deter the brothers from forging ahead with a series of deals that took them ever further afield from their original emphasis on low-budget film distribution. Over the course of 1999–2000, Miramax joined with Hearst to launch a new general interest magazine, *Talk*, to be run by former *Vanity Fair* editor Tina Brown; announced plans to partner with Robert De Niro to develop soundstages at the Brooklyn Navy Yard; struck an eight-picture deal with MGM that included plans to coproduce such mid-range films as *Cold Mountain* (2003), *Bounce* (2000), *All the Pretty Horses* (2000), and *The Talented Mr. Ripley* (1999); coproduced its first Broadway play, *The Real Thing* (2000); launched the Kevin Williamson–created television drama *Wasteland* (1999) on ABC; and prepared an animated prime-time version of Kevin Smith's *Clerks* (2000), also to air on ABC.[26] The company further increased the size of its staff to handle these new activities; by this point, Miramax employed nearly five hundred people.[27] In addition, Miramax continued signing talent to multipicture deals. With approximately thirty production deals in place, Miramax's talent agreements matched the number in effect at several major studios.[28]

Perhaps these various ventures can be viewed in part as a response to shifting market conditions. The specialty business was now cluttered with companies competing for rights to the same films. From this purview, there is a certain logic behind Miramax's efforts to expand beyond its core business. Yet the expansion Miramax initiated in the late 1990s often seemed to defy marketplace realities. There existed ample evidence that, from an economic standpoint, so-called mid-range pictures were among the riskiest ventures. Yet here was Miramax making even more of these films. Further, the budgets for these projects continued to rise dramatically. In proceeding in such a fashion, the Weinsteins displayed their belief that their company was immune to—or maybe even capable of altering—broader structural conditions. Whereas in the previous decade they had thrived by exploiting cracks in the system, they now seemed hell-bent on making the system conform to their will. By renewing once again the brothers' contracts in May 2000, Disney in effect sanctioned such moves.[29] These seven-year contracts provided the brothers with greater financial support for both production and marketing.[30] Meanwhile, a rapidly expanding set of competitors proceeded to occupy the niches that Miramax had begun to neglect.

Hooray for Indiewood

> You know, when I started this job, we had about 200 films to look at in terms of submissions for competition, and now we're talking about 840 dramatic features, 360 docs, to say nothing of another 100 and something plus films that we're considering for premieres and other kinds of categories, and another 400–500 for international. It's a very different universe just in terms of the numbers of films being produced.
>
> Geoffrey Gilmore, Sundance Film Festival codirector, 1999

As the April 1999 acquisition of Gramercy and October by USA makes clear, at the end of the decade there continued to be adjustments to the name, size, and scope of those companies involved in the specialty business. This remained the case in the years to come. As one of the more extreme examples, Vivendi Universal reacquired USA Films, along with the other USA Networks properties, in 2001.[31] A year later, USA Films merged with Universal Focus (formed in 2000) and the specialty company Good Machine (acquired by Universal in 2002) to become Focus Features.[32] Though the specific companies shifted over time, by the end of the 1990s the viability of the indie business was largely unquestioned. The business model for indies stayed in place throughout most of the new decade. This business had particular practices, players, and products. An entire infrastructure had developed to support the production, distribution, and exhibition of specialty, or tier 2, films. What's more, the indie sector had matured to the point that those involved with it now began to reflect on both its present status and its historical development. As a sign of the mature stage of the indie business at the turn of the century, late in 1999 *indieWIRE* undertook a series of conversations with individuals who had played a central part in shaping the 1990s specialty scene.[33] During the course of one such interview, Miramax president Mark Gill challenged *indieWIRE* editors Eugene Hernandez and Mark Rabinowitz to find a better label than "mini-major" or "studio" to describe his company and its main competitors.[34] "If you guys can come up with something new," he observed, "you'll brand it for the new millennium." *indieWIRE* decided to do just that, forwarding a word they had been using off and on for nearly two years: "IndieWood."[35]

By late 1999, the newly christened IndieWood (or Indiewood, as it was more commonly spelled) had become entrenched, as every major studio had at least one specialty division. Though the films released by different indie divisions varied to some extent based on each company's resources, their executives' sensibilities, and their particular market orientation, broadly speaking their output included a blend of quality American indies, foreign-language films, English-language imports, and genre pictures. By the end of 1999, Paramount Classics was fully operational and had released a handful of films, including the romantic drama *Get Real*, the István Szabó–directed historical drama *Sunshine*, and the coming-of-age tale *The Adventures of Sebastian Cole*.[36] Many more, including *The Gift*, *The Virgin Suicides*, and *You Can Count on Me* (all 2000), were on their way. Also by that time MGM had further expanded its presence in the specialty business by relaunching United Artists as an indie division.[37] Meanwhile, Sony revived its decades-old Screen Gems label. Initially, the rebranded Screen Gems lacked a clear focus, releasing everything from the Jeff Bridges–Tim Robbins thriller *Arlington Road* to the John Sayles–directed *Limbo* (both 1999). Within a few years, however, Screen Gems established itself as a clear competitor to Dimension and increasingly came to dominate the genre business.[38]

As Screen Gems became more prominent in the distribution of low-budget genre films, New Line moved further away from such material.

Though it still promoted itself as an independent company, New Line increasingly looked and acted like a major, or tier 1, company. With growing frequency, New Line's releases resembled those put out by sibling Warner Bros. in terms of both budget and content. For every indie-style *American History X* (1998) or *Magnolia* (1999), there was an $80 million effects-driven science fiction film (*Lost in Space*, 1998) or broad comedy (*The Wedding Singer*, 1998). Films such as *Blade* (1998) and *Rush Hour* (1998) might as easily be found on the release slate of any of the majors. *The Lord of the Rings* trilogy (2001–2003) represented the most obvious sign of New Line's expanded ambitions. In 1998, New Line committed more than $130 million to finance the Peter Jackson–directed series. (The budget reportedly rose to close to $300 million by the time he completed the films.) New Line's decision to move ahead with *Lord of the Rings* was a poignant one for the Weinsteins, as they had originally optioned the rights to J. R. R. Tolkien's books and planned to make the films at Miramax.[39] They were forced to relinquish their option, however, when Michael Eisner balked at the high price tag and ambitious scope of the project.[40] While Disney might have permitted Miramax to move into producing mid-level films such as *Shakespeare in Love*, *The Cider House Rules* (1999), *Bounce*, and *Chocolat* (2000), it was not going to allow the division to produce big-budget, special effects–driven spectacles. Eisner's refusal to finance the production of *The Lord of the Rings* only added to the mounting tensions between the brothers and Disney executives.[41]

At the same time that New Line began to compete with the majors and Miramax started to release more mid-range films, Fox Searchlight maintained far more modest aims. In the process, Searchlight gained momentum in the indie sector. In 1998, this News Corp. subsidiary reproduced the surprise success of *The Full Monty* (1997) with *Waking Ned Devine* (1998). With $24.7 million in box office receipts, *Ned Devine* was one of the highest-earning limited releases throughout the first half of 1999. In general, limited releases performed quite well. As of May 1999, such releases had cumulatively earned more than $110 million at the box office, which translated to an increase of 27 percent over the previous year.[42] Another high-profile Searchlight release, *Boys Don't Cry* (1999), generated a great deal of critical attention and yielded Hilary Swank a Best Actress Oscar.

With so many specialty companies now in the fray, indie films packed the summer 1999 schedule. In total, well over fifty such films were released from May to August.[43] As *Variety*'s Leonard Klady observed of the "crowded" schedule, "It's a staggering, unprecedented number to those who toil in the niches, up about 20% from '98."[44] Ten years earlier, Miramax drew attention from the press for its decision to counterprogram *sex, lies, and videotape* against the studios' summer event films. In contrast, in the summer of 1999, specialty companies released more than a dozen niche-oriented films each month. Some media analysts expressed concern about whether the marketplace could sustain so many films. And, in fact, many of these movies came and went from theaters quickly and earned but a few thousand dollars in the process. Nonetheless, on the whole, business was up.

The rising returns obscured the ever more hit-driven nature of the specialty business. Though a growing number of films earned in excess of $5 million, a growing number also made only negligible amounts at the box office.[45] In this sense, the indie sector paralleled the studio sector of the film business in still another way. Yet, for two key reasons, this organizational structure proved desirable for conglomerates during the late 1990s and early 2000s: First, one hit could mean an influx of tens of millions of dollars as the film moved through its life cycle. With additional cable channels being launched, and more new technologies (and thus more distribution outlets) looming on the horizon, the potential life cycle for product continued to extend. Especially significant was the rapid increase in DVD sales and rentals starting in 1999.[46] As the DVD market began to boom, new money flowed into the indie film business. Second, executives viewed indie films as adding value to their parent companies' libraries.[47] Libraries gained value in part due to the expansion of the DVD business, and due to the widespread belief that there was substantial money to be earned once broadband became widely diffused and content could be more easily delivered over the Internet.[48] Since there were no longer many "freestanding" companies with large libraries available for purchase in toto, it became imperative to build libraries through acquisitions. Specialty companies could effectively accomplish this objective.

That specialty companies could target specific niches more effectively and efficiently than the studios was reaffirmed in 1999. Throughout the year, the majors released one indie-style film after another (e.g., *Go* [Sony]; *Rushmore* [Disney]; *Election* [Paramount]; *Three Kings* [Warner Bros.]) that, though critically acclaimed, underperformed at the box office. Commenting on *Go*, one journalist stated, "What Miramax, or any of its smaller competitors, probably could have done, say industry observers, was release the film more economically. Indie companies— and even studio specialized divisions—can put out small pix for less money than the majors for a number of reasons, marketing mavens say."[49] Because the majors released these films, it also became more difficult to position them discursively as independents. The value of having this cultural status should not be ignored.

The studios' inability to reap substantial returns from films such as *Go* and *Rushmore* reinforced the logic of the emergent three-tier system. Meanwhile, the stakeholders involved and invested in the specialty business extended well beyond the various divisions of the media conglomerates—these included festivals and markets, talent agents and producer's representatives, multiplexes and art houses, cable and satellite companies, journalists and critics, private investors, and government agencies around the world. A rapidly growing number of festivals were overrun with a plethora of agents, managers, publicists, and producer's reps. Talent agents became crucial to the smooth functioning of the specialty business; most of the major agencies, including CAA, William Morris, ICM, UTA, and Endeavor, now had independent film divisions. Though the income generated by talent involved with specialty films usually was modest at best, agents saw these films as both possible stepping stones for new talent and a way to keep A-list talent employed in between better-paying projects.[50] For festivals, indie films assisted in drawing tourists and also generated local, state, national, or international media coverage, especially as celebrities came to town in conjunction with their films' screenings. Of course, each stakeholder benefited from indie films in different ways. For critics, covering indies was often seen as offering a reprieve from reviewing the latest big-budget studio event pictures. For journalists, the films promised sexy stories—whether of the "little person/company makes good" or the "big star who believes in the little project" variety. For individual investors and institutions that had been seduced with tales of breakout hits like *Pulp Fiction* (1994) and *Chasing Amy*, there lingered the promise of a financial windfall.

Such fantasies were further fueled in the summer of 1999 when a company outside the major studios, Artisan, released a wildly successful ultra-low-budget horror film, *The Blair Witch Project*.[51] For many scholars and journalists writing in the late 1990s and early 2000s, *Blair Witch* was seen as significant for the ways it foreshadowed changes afoot in cinema in the new millennium.[52] That the film generated so much attention is not surprising. It fit the by now well-worn "little film that could" narrative perfectly: Initially produced for well under $100,000 (though completion costs[53] raised the budget by hundreds of thousands of dollars), and acquired by Artisan for $1.1 million after achieving favorable audience response at Sundance, *The Blair Witch Project* eventually grossed more than $248 million in theaters worldwide.[54] Shot by and starring unknowns and released by a company unaffiliated with the major conglomerates, few could have anticipated that it would become an industrial or cultural phenomenon. The film certainly surprised Artisan executives, who only weeks before it opened declared their hope that it would gross "at least $10 million" during its North American theatrical run.[55]

Even before its release in July 1999, the media coverage of *Blair Witch* rivaled that being attended on the latest *Star Wars* installment, *Episode I: The Phantom Menace,* which had come out only a couple of months earlier. Some envisioned *Blair Witch* as the future of cinema not only because of its "anyone can do it" digital video aesthetic, but also because of the extent to which it exploited its online extensions in creative ways.[56] Along with *The Matrix,* which Warner Bros. released a few months prior, *The Blair Witch Project* marked an early example of transmedia marketing and storytelling.[57] In particular, *The Blair Witch Project* was notable for how it used the Internet to enrich and expand on the narrative universe developed in the film itself. As *USA Today*'s Claudia Puig noted, though most movies had websites by the late 1990s, the *Blair Witch* website was distinctive both for its interactivity and for the depth of its content. The site included "extensive faux historical data, news interviews and police reports," as well as extra footage that did not appear in the mockumentary.[58] Though *The Blair Witch Project* might have been a harbinger of a new age in terms of its marketing,[59] the film itself was scarcely innovative either aesthetically or industrially. Aesthetically, *The Blair Witch Project* built on well-established traditions in independent horror (e.g., *Night of the Living Dead* (1968); *The Texas Chain Saw Massacre,* 1974), as well as reality television, direct cinema, and documentary.[60] Industrially, it replicated the exploitation strategies employed by so many other specialty companies over the decades. Indeed, rather than seeing *The Blair Witch Project* as signaling a new direction in independent production and distribution, it should instead be viewed as representing the culmination of well over a decade of indie production, marketing, and distribution practices—practices that Miramax played a central role in pioneering, and that have been outlined at length throughout this book. The film grew to be the indie blockbuster that it did due to a range of factors, including not only its effective exploitation of emerging media outlets, but also the skill with which it was targeted to a variety of niches in traditional media channels (e.g., television, print). Strong critical support and extensive media coverage, including the covers of both *Time* and *Newsweek,* also helped build early buzz.

As with *Pulp Fiction, The English Patient* (1996), and *Scream,* the commercial success of *The Blair Witch Project* reignited widespread debates about what constituted an independent film. After it emerged as a franchise in its own right, replete with a comic book, sequel, and trio of computer games, criticism of the film and challenges to its claims of independence became quite pronounced. In the process, the media backlash occurred even more rapidly for *The Blair Witch Project* and its filmmakers than it had for Miramax/Dimension or any of the films it released through the late 1990s. Considering that *The Blair Witch Project* assumed the title of "highest-grossing independent film of all time," it might come as little surprise that this backlash ensued as swiftly as it did.

For all the attention *Blair Witch* garnered after its release, it is stunning how little long-term influence the film had.[61] After *The Blair Witch Project*, Artisan tried too quickly to expand. An attempt at an initial public offering failed,[62] and a wave of expensive films disappointed at the box office (e.g., *Stir of Echoes* and *The Ninth Gate*, both 1999).[63] The $15 million *Blair Witch* follow-up, *Book of Shadows* (2000), brought in only $26 million domestically. Meanwhile, the talent affiliated with the films continued to work, but none emerged as breakout stars in their own right. Audiences did not witness a rush of first-person, digitally shot films, despite the fact that several experiments were attempted.[64] Though other companies tried to emulate its online marketing tactics, they usually did so with only limited success.[65] Thus *The Blair Witch Project* proved a relatively isolated incident, an exception that underscored the substantial structural constraints that faced most low-budget filmmakers and independent operations that remained unaffiliated with major conglomerates. By 2001, Artisan was one of only two high-profile tier 3 independents left in the marketplace.[66] The other was the Canadian company Lions Gate, which acquired the struggling Artisan in 2003.[67]

A New Type of Independent: Lions Gate

Lions Gate quickly became the front-runner for the position of "the next Miramax." In fact, the 1999 Oscar ceremony marked a turning point not only for Miramax but also for Lions Gate. Two of its 1998 releases, *Affliction* and *Gods and Monsters*, were nominated for a total of five Academy Awards. Each received one Oscar statue: *Gods and Monsters'* Bill Condon for Best Adapted Screenplay, and *Affliction's* James Coburn for Best Supporting Actor. Lions Gate executives Tom Ortenberg and Mark Urman readily acknowledged the impact that Miramax had on their own Oscar campaign. As Urman remarked, "It's fair to say that those of us who succeed in the independent arena learned a lot from Miramax."[68]

Lions Gate did more than simply model its awards-season campaign on Miramax's past successes. It also courted controversy in a way that Miramax had in the past but no longer could. This was particularly evident in the North American theatrical distribution of *Dogma*, which Lions Gate acquired from the Weinsteins. The wave of publicity surrounding *Dogma* benefited the film immensely; it ended up grossing more than $30 million theatrically, and thus became Lions Gate's biggest release to date by nearly $20 million. After Artisan started its downward spiral, Lions Gate increasingly became the go-to company for those films perceived to be too controversial for studio-based indies (e.g., the ultra-violent *American Psycho*, 2000; the Miramax discard *O*). That Lions Gate could thrive despite its lack of a major conglomerate parent indicates that there did remain some space for smaller companies in the media landscape. That it was the only such company to stay in business during much of the 2000s, however, underscores how limited a space this was.

In fact, as the decade continued, it became clear that Lions Gate was not the "next Miramax" at all. Though it dabbled in quality American indies (*Monsters Ball*, 2001; *Shattered Glass*, 2003; *Crash*, 2005), English-language imports (*The Golden Bowl*, 2001; *Danny Deckchair*, 2004), and foreign-language films (*The Widow of Saint-Pierre*, 2001; *Irréversible*, 2003), Lions Gate focused predominantly on genre fare that echoed those films released by New Line in the late 1980s. The company enthusiastically embraced the popular, the lowbrow, and the most easily exploitable material. By the mid-2000s, Lions Gate (which rebranded itself as Lionsgate in 2005) veered further and further away from the types of indies released by the studios' specialty divisions.[69] It increasingly emphasized extreme horror (especially "torture porn" films such as the *Hostel* and *Saw* series), broad, often raunchy comedies (*Waiting . . .*, 2005; *Larry the Cable Guy: Health Inspector*, 2006), and lower-budget and less effects-driven action films (*The Punisher*, 2004; *Crank*, 2006). The company also found success through its release of African American–targeted material, especially the films of Tyler Perry (*Madea's Family Reunion*, 2006; *Why Did I Get Married?*, 2007). In addition, television became a greater priority—and growing source of income and prestige—for Lions Gate than it ever was for Miramax. In 2006, Lions Gate heightened its investment in TV through its acquisition of the syndication distributor Debmar-Mercury.[70] The company also financed several high-profile and highly acclaimed cable television series, including *Weeds* (2005–) and *Mad Men* (2007–).

That Lions Gate's films deviated so dramatically from those released by the studio-based indies reinforces the types of opportunities available for true independents in the 2000s. It also points to the broader changes in the industry. Lions Gate would not become the "next Miramax" for a couple of key reasons. First, the indie divisions themselves now occupied that terrain. Lions Gate stood to benefit little financially by becoming another competitor in an already-overcrowded indie environment. Second, along with there being little economic value in being the next Miramax, there was also little cultural benefit to doing so. Both marketers and the press had overused the labels "independent" and "indie." The term's value as a source of distinction had diminished substantially since the 1990s. In addition, as Lions Gate released fewer American indies and more genre films, it stood to benefit little by exploiting the term in its own marketing materials. Meanwhile, as Lions Gate had minimal interest in promoting its status as an independent, Miramax had greater difficulty doing so with each passing year.

Remnant of Its Former Self

> On Miramax's future 10 years from now, [Harvey] Weinstein
> joked, "The company will probably be in Boise, Idaho, a remnant
> of its former self, and Bob and I will be alcoholics."
>
> Variety, *May 2003*

By the early 2000s, Miramax was in an increasingly perilous position. The Weinsteins were busting the indie business model that they played a lead role in forging more than a decade prior. In the process, they drove up costs for the entire industry, alienated Disney executives, and generated ample negative press. Miramax now had strayed far from its focus on quality American indies, English-language imports, and foreign-language films. Though these types of movies maintained a place on its release schedule, they were overshadowed by the company's expansion into other media (e.g., publishing, television) and its heightened emphasis on mid-range, star-driven "Oscar bait." With each year of the new decade, the Weinsteins shifted further away from their company's original mandate by Disney to produce high-quality, low-cost films.

The Weinsteins' growing disregard for their owners' demands led to mounting conflicts between Miramax and Disney executives.[71] Battles repeatedly occurred over Miramax's content, cost, autonomy, and scope of activities. These clashes paved the way for the brothers' departure from Disney in the fall of 2005. Numerous factors contributed to the escalating discord between Miramax and Disney. Struggles occurred over a range of topics: Eisner's refusal to let Miramax either launch its own cable channel or purchase Bravo or IFC;[72] the Weinsteins' excessive spending on both acquisitions and in-house productions; the company's oversized release slate; and high-profile failures such as *Talk* magazine and the Brooklyn Navy Yard venture. A string of costly releases—such as the $97 million *Gangs of New York* (2002), the $80 million *Cold Mountain* (2003), and the $116 million *The Aviator* (2004)—indicated that the company was headed in the wrong direction financially. With marketing costs factored in, the results were downright disastrous. Miramax was in effect producing mid-range product at event-film prices. This was simply not a practicable way to do business—at least if this business was about earning a profit.

Whereas in the 1990s Miramax adhered more closely to budget caps and sold many of its films as edgy indies or alternatives to bloated Hollywood product, by the early 2000s it no longer could do so. Of course, there were still critical and financial successes mixed in with the company's many missteps. Miramax repeatedly campaigned heavily for Oscars; in turn, it received Best Picture nominations for *The Cider House Rules, Chocolat, In the Bedroom* (2001), *Gangs of New York, Finding Neverland* (2004), and *The Aviator*. It even had another Best Picture winner in *Chicago* (2002). The company nurtured a number of lower-budget films to respectable box office returns, including the French import *Amélie* (2001, $33.2 million domestic) and the negative pickup and Sundance award winner *In the Bedroom* ($35.9 million domestic). Miramax's longstanding stable of talent provided it with several hits as well. Quentin Tarantino's *Kill Bill* films (2003, 2004) each earned more than $60 million in their North American theatrical releases. Robert Rodriguez's *Spy Kids* emerged as a lucrative children's franchise for Dimension (2001–2003), with the three films cumulatively earning more than $300 million in box office grosses in North America alone.[73] Meanwhile, the Ben Affleck–Matt Damon–Chris Moore–produced reality television series *Project Greenlight* became a modest hit (on HBO for the 2001–2002 and 2003 seasons; on Bravo for the 2005 season). *Project Greenlight*, in turn, paved the way for the Miramax-produced *Project Runway*, which premiered on Bravo in 2004 and immediately became a full-fledged success.[74] Dimension was perhaps the most reliable performer for Miramax. The impressive box office returns for the *Spy Kids* films were exceeded by those for a trio of *Scary Movie* releases (2000, 2001, 2003).[75] With $96 million in theatrical returns, the Nicole Kidman thriller *The Others* (2001) also surpassed expectations.

Alas, the critical acclaim and remarkable box office receipts yielded by these films often came at great cost to the company's image and its relationship with its Disney overseers. Miramax continued to "buy its way"

Select Miramax Big-Budget Disappointments (2000–2005)

Title	Budget (m)	Dom. box office (m)
All the Pretty Horses (2000)	$45	$15.5
Bounce (2000)	$35	$35.7
Reindeer Games (2000)	$36	$23.3
Captain Corelli's Mandolin (2001)	$57	$25.5
Kate and Leopold (2001)	$48	$47
Texas Rangers (2001)	$38	$0.6
The Shipping News (2001)	$35	$11.4
Gangs of New York (2002)	$97	$77.7
The Four Feathers (2002)	$35	$18.3
The Human Stain (2003)	$30	$5.3
Cold Mountain (2003)	$80	$95
Duplex (2003)	$40	$9.6
Jersey Girl (2004)	$35	$25.2
The Aviator (2004)	$110	$102
Ella Enchanted (2004)	$35	$22
Proof (2005)	$20	$7.5
An Unfinished Life (2005)	$30	$8.5
The Great Raid (2005)	$60	$10

Figures for this chart come from http://www.the-numbers.com/ and http://www.imdb.com/, accessed 5 June 2010. As with all publicly reported numbers, these are approximations at best. In terms of expenses, marketing costs are not included. In terms of returns, neither foreign nor ancillary income is accounted for. In addition, Miramax split the costs—and rights—for many of these projects.

to Oscars or box office through sizable marketing expenditures. In addition, the awards-driven films were often quite costly to begin with, so box office returns needed to be substantial for them to break even. Further, the hits had to pay for the failures. And for three out of five years from 2000 to 2004, they did not—a point that Michael Eisner reiterated on numerous occasions to the press as his relationship with the Weinsteins became even more acrimonious.[76]

Up through early 2003, the Weinsteins and Eisner largely maintained the public facade that their relationship was working. The Weinsteins initially denied that Eisner pressured them to make cutbacks.[77] As the Disney CEO came under attack from various quarters, however, the Weinsteins (especially Harvey) added to the cacophony of criticism.[78] For example, in December 2003, Harvey Weinstein told one interviewer that "all the great [Disney] executives have been driven from the company." Weinstein continued, "I think there is no camaraderie anymore, no great esprit de corps that I found earlier. I think there was more risk-taking, a more fun company. I don't know why, and it's sad that it is."[79] A week later, he underscored how strained the relationship had become when he told the *New York Times* that "there's always the case of Michael Eisner firing us, but that might be a cause for celebration in all quarters—ours included."[80] The breaking point finally occurred in May 2004, when Disney forced the Weinsteins to buy back the rights to Michael Moore's *Fahrenheit 9/11.*[81] (They subsequently sold the North American theatrical rights to Lions Gate.) Whereas in previous cases such as *Kids* and *Dogma* the two parties had been able to resolve their differences, this time it was not to be.[82]

Though *Fahrenheit 9/11* may have been the event that set off the media coverage about worsening relations between Miramax and Disney, a range of personal, financial, and creative reasons spurred their divorce.[83] One of the primary sources of tension involved Disney's threats to scale back Miramax's $700 million production fund.[84] At a time when the Weinsteins were becoming ever more reckless in spending on both their film projects and other media ventures, Disney wanted the company to behave more like it had in 1993.[85] These demands were made at precisely the moment that the Weinsteins' contracts were up for review.[86]

It is worth emphasizing that Eisner did not simply pursue these cutbacks because he was dissatisfied with how Miramax was operating. Rather, at this exact moment he was facing serious challenges to his management from "shareholder activists," led by Walt Disney's nephew, Roy Disney, and Pixar (and Apple) CEO Steve Jobs.[87] In *Disney War*, James B. Stewart chronicles the difficulties Eisner faced as CEO and board member at Disney. In the early 2000s, he came under criticism for a variety of reasons, including ABC's downward spiral, huge payouts that had to be made to both Jeffrey Katzenberg and Michael Ovitz, and his inability to renew Pixar's distribution deal with Disney.[88] Whereas the conflict with Jobs posed a substantive threat to Disney's balance sheet, the conflict with the Weinsteins added to Eisner's public humiliation. The rising hostilities between Eisner and the Weinsteins—as well as with Steve Jobs and Roy Disney—are striking for the extent to which they underscore the impact a select number of individuals had on the structure and content of a major media conglomerate. Significantly, Eisner's own contract with Disney was in peril at the same time that he haggled with the Weinsteins over theirs. The botched relationship with the Weinsteins became just one more reason behind calls for his resignation. Finally, on 13 March 2005, Eisner announced that he would leave the company after he helped newly appointed CEO Robert Iger transition into the position.[89] A few weeks later, the Weinsteins officially declared that they, too, would terminate their relationship with Disney when their contracts expired on 30 September 2005.[90]

The Weinsteins could leave Disney, but, much to their chagrin, they had to leave Miramax behind. After all, they were merely employees of Miramax, tied to the company via service contracts. Disney owned the Miramax brand name and its library.[91] Though the Weinsteins hoped to take the Miramax label with them upon their departure, Disney refused their request. But the Weinsteins did not leave empty-handed: Their settlement was estimated to total about $135 million.[92] They also took the Dimension brand name, although Disney retained the right to partner with them on any future Dimension films.[93] In addition, most of Miramax's high-profile talent stayed faithful to the Weinsteins: Robert Rodriguez, Kevin Smith, Quentin Tarantino, Anthony Minghella, and Rob Marshall, along with several executives, followed the Weinsteins to their new start-up, the Weinstein Company.[94]

Indie, Sink: The End of an Era

> Will there be a Miramax, like the one from the early 90s, for a new generation of adventurous moviegoers? I think the jury's still out.
>
> Eugene Hernandez, indieWIRE *editor in chief, 2009*

In the fall of 2005, Bob and Harvey Weinstein severed relations with the company they had launched twenty-seven years earlier.[95] At the time of their departure, Miramax was widely reported to be worth at least $2 billion.[96] On 1 October 2005, the Weinstein Company officially began business as an independent distributor; meanwhile, a "leaner" Miramax continued to operate at Disney for several more years. This post-Weinstein incarnation released far fewer films (between five and ten per year), had an annual budget of $350 million, and employed a smaller number of people.[97] Miramax's new president, Daniel Battsek, came from within the Disney ranks. That the "new" Miramax's releases still ran the gamut from American indie (*Gone Baby Gone*, 2007; *Smart People*, 2008) to English-language import (*The Queen*, 2006; *Eagle vs. Shark*, 2007) to foreign-language import (*Tsotsi*, 2005; *The Diving Bell and the Butterfly*, 2007) indicates both the long-term influence of the Weinsteins and the extent to which the practices of the specialty business had been institutionalized by this point.

Certainly many changes in the film and media industries occurred during the first decade of the 2000s, although crucial continuities between the 1990s and the 2000s can be found. Miramax, under the ownership of Disney, played an active part in reconstituting Hollywood throughout the 1990s; much of this structure remained in place into the early 2000s. For a time, specialty companies and low-budget films became an important way for conglomerates to reduce labor, production, and distribution costs and expand their libraries. These divisions offered a route for new talent to break in and for established talent to reinvent themselves or branch out. Along with the rise of indie subsidiaries came the growth of affiliated businesses and organizations, including film festivals, specialty cable channels, and indie-oriented talent agency divisions. In the process, marketers helped construct specific discourses around low-budget films. In the best of circumstances, specialty films appealed to varied demographic groups and taste cultures. Some even achieved indie blockbuster status.

Thus the history of Miramax involves far more than the incorporation and exploitation of independent cinema—a trite tale about a loss of autonomy or decline in quality. Rather, this case study reinforces the always-dynamic relationships among Hollywood, independent producers and distributors, film festivals, the press, and critics. The tale of Miramax is ultimately the tale of the reorganization and reconstitution of the film industry during the 1990s, and one company's active role in this process. Tapping into journalists' and critics' discourses about "independence," Miramax facilitated this industrial reorganization. Sometimes these efforts failed, sometimes they succeeded, but in the process, a wide range of American indie, foreign language, English-language, genre, and transnational prestige films were financed, produced, and made available to audiences at art houses, multiplexes, and at home. Though at its height of profitability approximately "4 to 6 percent of Disney's filmed entertainment division" income came from Miramax, its value cannot simply be measured by what it added to the company's bottom line.[98] Its broader creative and cultural impact must also be considered. On these counts, Miramax added far more. As *Entertainment Weekly's* Owen Gleiberman observed when the Weinsteins announced their departure in 2005, "Miramax had remade the world of movies, which is why that world can now go on without it."[99]

It is important to note that Gleiberman's statement is not entirely accurate. Miramax *did* remake the world of movies—for a time. But by the late 1990s it had gone too far, spent too much. The direction the company pursued contributed to its own destruction, along with the decimation of the very business it had played a central part in creating more than fifteen years prior. Indeed, Miramax executives assisted in putting in motion a set of conditions that adversely affected the entire industry. As the 2000s wore on, the business model for specialty divisions grew increasingly untenable. Too many companies spent too much money acquiring and producing too many films for which there was not a large enough market. More films did not in fact lead to more indie blockbusters. Though every year a handful of indie films broke out, dozens spent a week or two on a limited number of screens before making their way to video.

As long as the DVD market remained strong and libraries retained their value, conglomerates retained their indie divisions. Since 2008, however, a series of broader economic, technological, and cultural developments has contributed to the near collapse of the specialty sector. The growing economic crisis and the consequent reduction in available credit for investment has had an adverse effect as well. Other contributing factors included the decline in the DVD sell-through market and the inability of the industry to find a profitable replacement; the rise of Redbox and other "jukebox" video rental services that focused primarily on offering the biggest hits; a reassessment and subsequent devaluing of libraries; a heightened emphasis by cable channels on original series over motion pictures; the global growth of locally based film operations that produced and distributed more of their own material; and an overabundance of media options, many of which competed directly with indie films for time and money.[100]

In 2008, in a keynote speech at the Los Angeles Film Festival's Financing Conference, former Miramax Films president Mark Gill articulated in his title what many in the indie business already knew: "Yes, the Sky Really Is Falling."[101] Over the course of the next several minutes, Gill ticked off over a dozen reasons why the specialty business was in free fall. As a few examples of the dire conditions in which this business found itself, Gill cited the downsizing of New Line as well as the recent closure of Paramount Vantage, Time Warner's Picturehouse division, and Warner Independent.[102] His grim talk set off a chain reaction of discussion—and panic—among all those involved in producing and distributing indie films.

As bad as things were in 2008, they got worse for the indie sector in the ensuing years. A particularly notable low point occurred in January 2010 when Disney announced it was shutting down Miramax and exiting the specialty film business entirely.[103] Miramax did not fit into CEO Robert Iger's plan to emphasize products that best served Disney's family-friendly brand identity. Beyond Disney's heightened emphasis on franchises, the cost of sustaining the division hardly seemed worth the investment to Disney executives any longer. Though the Weinsteins tried to secure financing to regain control of Miramax when it went up for sale, ultimately they were unsuccessful in their bid. Thus, in December 2010, a consortium of investors led by the businessman Ron Tutor acquired what was left of Miramax for $663 million.[104] Included in the transaction were the indie's library of close to seven hundred titles along with the Miramax brand name and a handful of yet-to-be-released films. It seemed doubtful that the new investors would do much more than license and relicense old Miramax content for physical and digital distribution.[105]

As this book goes to press, it is unclear if a new generation of indie companies, films, and filmmakers can emerge, and if so, what form they might take. It is worth noting that there were still a limited number of studio-based indie divisions around as of early 2011, including Sony Pictures Classics, Screen Gems, Focus Features, and Fox Searchlight. Yet these subsidiaries exist in a far different landscape—one with fewer releases and fewer executives. They spend less on the films they acquire, and expect the films that they release to earn less than they might have in Miramax's heyday. Mid-range or prestige pictures have all but disappeared. The long-term prospects of these divisions, as well as the prospects of the tier 3 independents operating without conglomerate support, remain to be seen.[106] Meanwhile, the Weinstein Company has struggled to stay in business. Rather than learning from the missteps they made in the early 2000s and sticking to their core business of releasing low-budget, niche-oriented films, the brothers persisted in many of the detrimental practices they had employed during their time at Disney. Over the course of their first five years in business, they invested in everything from a fashion company to an Internet-based social media company.[107] Only after releasing a string of films that disappointed at both the box office and the Oscars (e.g., *Nine*, 2009; *The Road*, 2009) did they start to rethink their practices. This change of course led the Weinsteins to lean heavily on the films and filmmakers on whom they had built Miramax in the 1990s (e.g., Quentin Tarantino, Kevin Smith, the *Scream* franchise).[108] It is too early to determine whether Best Picture winner and quality indie blockbuster *The King's Speech* (2010) marked the start of a long-term reversal of fortune for the Weinstein Company or just a momentary upswing.

Despite the uncertain status of the contemporary indie business and the Weinsteins' place within it, it *is* certain that throughout the 1990s Miramax played a central role in reshaping Hollywood's structure and content. From launching the careers of dozens of executives and talent to crafting innovative marketing campaigns for a diverse slate of films, from forging one of the most prominent brand names for a motion picture company to dominating awards ceremonies, Miramax's impact was widely felt, both industrially and culturally. By exploiting gaps in the marketplace—and later using their extensive resources via Disney to their advantage—the Weinsteins and their staff released an impressive array of motion pictures that appealed to a diverse set of demographic groups. In the process, the company figured prominently in debates about corporate power, individual autonomy, and definitions of authenticity. Only time will tell if a similar operation—or perhaps even the Weinsteins' own company—can wield the same influence over the business and culture of film in the future.

Notes

Chapter 1

1. Amy Wallace, "'Shakespeare' Hit by Snipers," *Los Angeles Times*, 23 March 1999, F1. Please note that throughout the book, listed release dates are for North American theatrical distibution.

2. Miramax distributed these films theatrically in the United States and Canada. Many other distributors had an investment in these films globally and in aftermarkets such as home video and cable.

3. The exact amount Miramax was sold for was never made public, nor were the specific arrangements of the deal. Press figures vary, but the general consensus is that the purchase was for somewhere between $60 and $80 million. The entire deal, according to Lynn Hirschberg, was worth about $100 million. This amount includes $20 million in Disney stock options to the Weinsteins and $25 million in operating capital. "The Mad Passion of Harvey and Bob," *New York*, 10 October 1994, 48–57. Leonard Klady adds, "Disney was to pay increments of 20% per year up to the purchase price of around $60 million. That $60 million covered debt, liabilities, cash and exec salaries as well as about $20 million worth of Disney stock options." "Weinsteins Renegotiating Pact with Disney," *Variety*, 24–30 July 1995, 17.

4. As Barbara Wilinsky observes, the "art house" label is "ambiguous and flexible." It has shifted in meaning over time; as Hollywood has changed in structure, form, and content, so has art house cinema. She notes that art films can be considered in terms of their textual properties and industrial status. Wilinsky underscores the ways that the film industry cultivated particular discourses about art cinema as a means of product differentiation. Her study focuses on art films in the immediate post–World War II context, but many of the ideas remain applicable to this day. See *Sure Seaters: The Emergence of Art House Cinema* (Minneapolis: University of Minnesota Press, 2001), 12–13.

5. The name was changed to Focus Features in 2001.

6. Sony Pictures Classics was the first of the new generation of indie subsidiaries, but as will be discussed in chapter 7, it always remained a relatively small-scale enterprise in terms of resources, staffing, and scope. The names and activities of these divisions may have changed from 1993 to 2011, but they nonetheless remained a vital part of conglomerates throughout this period.

7. Jennifer Holt and Alisa Perren, eds., *Media Industries: History, Theory, and Method* (Malden, MA: Wiley-Blackwell, 2009).

8. Douglas Kellner, "Media Industries, Political Economy, and Media/Cultural Studies: An Articulation," in Holt and Perren, *Media Industries*, 95–107.

9. For example, see Janet Wasko, *How Hollywood Works* (Thousand Oaks, CA: Sage, 2003); Paul McDonald and Janet Wasko, eds., *The Contemporary Hollywood Film Industry* (Malden, MA: Wiley-Blackwell, 2008); Thomas Schatz, "New Hollywood, New Millennium," in *Film Theory and Contemporary Hollywood Movies*, ed. Warren Buckland

(New York: Routledge, 2009), 19–46; Jennifer Holt, *Empires of Entertainment: Media Industries and the Politics of Deregulation, 1980–1996* (New Brunswick, NJ: Rutgers University Press, 2011).

10. Grosses are a crude form of measurement, as approximately half this money goes to theaters. Nonetheless, these figures are useful for making a general comparison. "Box Office History for Distributor—Miramax," *The Numbers*, accessed 29 May 2010, http://www.the-numbers.com/market/Distributors/Miramax.php. For a discussion of the challenges of evaluating film industry financials, see Edward Jay Epstein, *The Big Picture: Money and Power in Hollywood* (New York: Random House, 2005).

11. "Box Office History for Distributor—Walt Disney Pictures," *The Numbers*, accessed 29 May 2010, http://www.the-numbers.com/market/Distributors/BuenaVista.php.

12. See Thomas Schatz, "The New Hollywood," in *Film Theory Goes to the Movies*, ed. Jim Collins, Hilary Radner, and Ava Preacher (New York: Routledge, 1993), 8–36; Justin Wyatt, *High Concept: Movies and Marketing in Hollywood* (Austin: University of Texas Press, 1994).

13. Geoff King places Indiewood within a "post-Fordist" context in *Indiewood, USA: Where Hollywood Meets Independent Cinema* (London: I. B. Taurus, 2009). Michael Curtin opts for the label "neo-network era" in "On Edge: Culture Industries in the Neonetwork Era," in *Making and Selling Culture*, ed. Richard Ohmann (Hanover, NH: Wesleyan University Press, 1996), 181–202.

14. David Hesmondhalgh challenges certain models of political economy in *The Cultural Industries*, 2nd ed. (Thousand Oaks, CA: Sage, 2007).

15. Michael Newman, "Indie Culture: In Pursuit of the Authentic Autonomous Alternative," *Cinema Journal* 48, no. 3 (Spring 2009): 16–34.

16. Newman and King both turn to Pierre Bourdieu's work on taste cultures in *Distinction: A Social Critique of the Judgment of Taste*, trans. Richard Nice (London: Routledge, 1984).

17. Newman, "Indie Culture."

18. I discuss these terms more fully in my essay "A Big Fat Indie Success Story? Press Discourses Surrounding the Making and Marketing of a 'Hollywood' Movie," *Journal of Film and Video* 56, no. 2 (Summer 2004): 18–31.

19. Gregory Goodell, *Independent Feature Film Production: A Complete Guide from Concept Through Distribution* (New York: St. Martin's Press, 1998).

20. Stephen Prince, *A New Pot of Gold: Hollywood Under the Electronic Rainbow, 1980–1989* (Berkeley: University of California Press, 2000); Justin Wyatt, "The Formation of the 'Major Independent': Miramax, New Line, and the New Hollywood," in *Contemporary Hollywood Cinema*, ed. Steve Neale and Murray Smith (London: Routledge, 1998), 74–90.

21. Douglas Gomery, *Shared Pleasures: A History of Movie Presentation in the United States* (Madison: University of Wisconsin Press, 1992).

22. Chuck Kleinhans, "Independent Features: Hopes and Dreams," in *The New American Cinema*, ed. Jon Lewis (Durham, NC: Duke University Press, 1998), 307–327.

23. Emanuel Levy, *Cinema of Outsiders: The Rise of American Independent Film* (New York: New York University Press, 1999).

24. Geoff King, *American Independent Cinema* (Bloomington: Indiana University Press, 2005).

25. In using this definition, Tzioumakis turns to Michel Foucault, who writes that discourses "bring cultural objects into being by naming them, defining them, delimiting their field of operation." Yannis Tzioumakis, *American Independent Cinema: An Introduction* (New Brunswick, NJ: Rutgers University Press, 2006), 11.

26. Also see Geoff Andrew, *Stranger Than Paradise: Maverick Film-Makers in Recent American Cinema* (New York: Limelight Editions, 1999); Donald Lyons, *Independent Visions: A Critical Introduction to Recent Independent American Film* (New York: Ballantine Books, 1994); Greg Merritt, *Celluloid Mavericks: A History of American Independent Film* (New York: Thunder's Mouth Press, 2000); John Pierson, *Spike, Mike, Slackers, and Dykes: A Guided Tour Across a Decade of American Independent Cinema* (New York: Hyperion/Miramax Books, 1995). In addition, Christine Holmlund and Justin Wyatt's edited collection *Contemporary American Independent Film* (London: Routledge, 2005) offers a range of industrial, formal-aesthetic, and cultural approaches to studying independent films released since the early 1970s.

27. John Berra, *Declarations of Independence: American Cinema and the Partiality of Independent Production* (Bristol, UK: Intellect, 2008). See also Levy, *Cinema of Outsiders*; King, *American Independent Cinema*.

28. Max Horkheimer and Theodor Adorno, "The Culture Industry: Enlightenment as Mass Deception," *Media and Cultural Studies: Keyworks*, 2nd ed., ed. Meenakshi Gigi Durham and Douglas Kellner (Malden, MA: Wiley-Blackwell, 2005), 41–72.

29. Peter Biskind, *Down and Dirty Pictures: Miramax, Sundance, and the Rise of Independent Film* (New York: Simon & Schuster, 2004). A recurring theme throughout Biskind's book is that the best independents maintained a strong "us versus them" stance.

30. Peter Biskind, *Easy Riders, Raging Bulls: How the Sex-Drugs-and-Rock-'n'-Roll Generation Saved Hollywood* (New York: Touchstone, 1998).

31. In his discussion of Tarantino, for instance, Biskind declares that "the price of short-circuiting the film school route was the sacrifice of film culture." *Down and Dirty Pictures*, 127.

32. Ibid., 79.

33. For example, in a discussion of the James Gray–directed *The Yards* (2000), Biskind writes that "as he has shown repeatedly, it's not the hacks [that Harvey] exploits, but the real filmmakers, the ones who are ready to make sacrifices for their art." Ibid., 396.

34. This statement is made in a discussion of the selection of *Reservoir Dogs* (1992) at Sundance. Biskind writes that "*Dogs* represented the return of the repressed, the revenge of the exploitation picture. By accepting Tarantino's film, [Sundance programmer Geoff] Gilmore gave the festival's imprimatur to a much different kind of indie feature, closer to the tastes of the barbarians (read, Americans) outside the gates of Park City and—most fraught for the direction of the movement—potentially commercial." Ibid., 121.

35. The full passage reads, "By the summer of 1996, Dimension was a veritable beehive—perhaps a roach motel is more accurate—of activity." Ibid., 250.

36. In a revealing statement, Biskind writes that "despite stiff competition later from *Chocolat*, [*Life Is Beautiful*] has to be considered the lushest bloom of Miramax's kitsch period, its largely successful campaign to inject glucose into the veins of middlebrow American culture. At one time, the spectrum of Miramax's releases was broad enough to include both a *Cinema Paradiso* and a film like *The Cook, the Thief, His Wife, and Her Lover*, and do well with each. But as American indies gobbled up a bigger share of the market at the expense of foreign films, only the sentimental, accessible ones survived." Ibid., 360. For examples of similar comments, see pp. 234, 423.

37. Article- or chapter-length discussions of Miramax's production, distribution, and marketing strategies have been offered in Wyatt, "The Formation of the 'Major Independent'"; Berra, *Declarations of Independence*; King, *Indiewood, USA*; Bradley Schauer, "Dimension Films and the Exploitation Tradition in Hollywood," *Quarterly Review of Film and Video* 26, no. 5 (2009): 393–405; and Paul McDonald, "Miramax, *Life Is Beauti-*

ful, and the Indiewoodization of the Foreign-Language Film Market in the USA," *New Review of Film and Television Studies* 7, no. 4 (December 2009): 353–375.

38. See Toby Miller, Nitin Govil, John McMurria, and Richard Maxwell, eds., *Global Hollywood* (London: BFI, 2001); Toby Miller, Nitin Govil, John McMurria, and Ting Wang, eds., *Global Hollywood 2* (London: BFI, 2005).

39. King relies on Biskind's vague comment that the label of Indiewood emerged around the mid-1990s. In fact, this is an example of how Biskind's reliance almost solely on interviews leads to historical inaccuracies. In his 1994–1995 chapter, Biskind notes in passing that "a phrase was coined, 'Indiewood,' to describe this new reality" (of studio and indie films converging). *Down and Dirty Pictures*, 194. Yet through a comprehensive search of trade publications and newspaper articles, the earliest time I found the term to be used was in Eugene Hernandez, "Hello Cleveland! A Report from the First Midwest Filmmakers Conference," *indieWIRE*, 7 April 1998, accessed 17 June 2011, http://www.indiewire.com/article/hello_cleveland_a_report_from_the_first_midwest_filmmakers_conference/#.

40. Biskind's study does not so much "end" as it trails off due to the book going to press.

41. John Pierson, *Spike Mike Reloaded* (New York: Hyperion/Miramax Books, 2004).

Chapter 2

A portion of this chapter was published previously as "sex, lies, and marketing: Miramax and the Development of the 'Quality Indie' Blockbuster." *Film Quarterly* 54, no. 2 (Winter 2001–2002): 30–39. © 2001 by University of California Press.

1. Pierson uses the term "indie blockbuster" on p. 336 of *Spike, Mike, Slackers, and Dykes: A Guided Tour Across a Decade of American Independent Cinema* (New York: Hyperion/Miramax Books, 1995) but does not define it or expand on its meaning.

2. Paul D. Colford, "Movies Are Their Game; Miramax Steers Small Films into the Public Consciousness," *New York Newsday*, 20 February 1990, 8.

3. I employ the word "quality" throughout in much the same way as it is used by Jane Feuer, Paul Kerr, and Tise Vahimagi in their edited volume *MTM: "Quality Television"* (London: BFI, 1984). Feuer, for example, writes that "the very concept of 'quality' is itself ideological. In interpreting an MTM programme as a quality programme, the quality audience is permitted to enjoy a form of television which is seen as more literate, more stylistically complex and more psychologically 'deep' than ordinary TV fare. The quality audience gets to separate itself from the mass audience and can watch TV without guilt, and without realising that the double-edged discourse they are getting is also ordinary TV." Quality independents function in a similar sense for theatrical features released by Miramax. See "The MTM Style," 56. At different moments, discourses of quality are used by critics and the press to describe Miramax as a company, many of the films it released, and the audiences that consumed those films. Further, Miramax frequently exploited such discourses in its marketing practices.

Television studies scholars have extensively explored the ways that media companies have deployed discourses of "quality." Such discussions could be more extensively applied to analyses of the film industry. For a more recent discussion of "quality" as it relates to contemporary television, see Janet McCabe and Kim Akass, eds., *Quality TV: Contemporary American Television and Beyond* (London: I. B. Taurus, 2007).

4. For example, see Justin Wyatt, "The Formation of the 'Major Independent': Miramax, New Line, and the New Hollywood," in *Contemporary Hollywood Cinema*, ed. Steve Neale and Murray Smith (London: Routledge, 1998), 74–90. The term "independent

shakedown" comes from Daniel Cerone, "Smaller Films Seek a Summer Place," *Los Angeles Times*, 14 June 1989, 1.

5. Justin Wyatt, "Economic Constraints/Economic Opportunities: Robert Altman as Auteur," *Velvet Light Trap* 38 (Fall 1996): 51–67.

6. For a thorough discussion of the development and diffusion of the videocassette recorder, see Frederick Wasser, *Veni, Vidi, Video: The Hollywood Empire and the VCR* (Austin: University of Texas Press, 2002).

7. See Janet Wasko's discussion of ancillary markets in *Hollywood in the Information Age: Beyond the Silver Screen* (Austin: University of Texas Press, 1994).

8. Selling off presale rights as protection is discussed in Debra Goldman, "Business for Art's Sake," *American Film* 12, no. 6 (April 1987): 44–48.

9. Alvin P. Sanoff, "The New Shape of Hollywood," *U.S. News and World Report* 100, no. 8 (3 March 1986): 67.

10. For an extensive discussion of mid-1980s marketing of independents, see David Rosen and Peter Hamilton, *Off-Hollywood: The Making and Marketing of Independent Films* (New York: Grove Weidenfeld, 1987).

11. Daniel Cerone, "Taking an Independent Path," *Los Angeles Times*, 3 May 1989, 1.

12. "Harvey and Corky in Buffalo Booking Contest with Vet Jerry Nathan," *Variety*, 16 July 1978, 93–94.

13. Cerone, "Taking an Independent Path," 1.

14. "Miramax Marries Movies and Music," *Billboard*, 28 August 1982, retrieved from the Miramax file at the Academy of Motion Picture Arts and Sciences' Margaret Herrick Library, Beverly Hills, CA, June 2002 (hereafter cited as the Herrick Library).

15. "Buffalo," *Box Office*, 21 July 1989, retrieved from the Herrick Library.

16. Lisa Gubernick, "We Don't Want to Be Walt Disney," *Forbes*, 16 October 1989, 109.

17. "Miramax' Mainstream Program Focuses on AFM as Its Tool," *Variety*, 25 February 1987, 158.

18. The sub-distributors were usually distributors located in a city in which the film was released; they would cover release costs in that particular city for a nominal fee. See "Buffalo," *Box Office*, 21 July 1989, retrieved from the Herrick Library.

19. "Miramax on the Lookout," *Variety*, 19 February 1986, 160; "Miramax Increases Staff at New Digs, as Distrib Arm Lengthens," *Variety*, 1 July 1987, 4, 18.

20. Justin Wyatt surveys many of the 1980s-era independent companies in "Independents, Packaging, and Inflationary Pressure in 1980s Hollywood," in Stephen Prince, *A New Pot of Gold: Hollywood Under the Electronic Rainbow, 1980–1989* (Berkeley: University of California Press, 2000), 141–159.

21. Cerone, "Taking an Independent Path," 1; Gubernick, "We Don't Want to Be Walt Disney," 109.

22. Gubernick, "We Don't Want to Be Walt Disney," 109.

23. Ibid.

24. Ibid.

25. "Miramax Duo Backing 'Marketing Strength,'" *Screen International*, 19 September 1987, retrieved from the Herrick Library.

26. Robert B. Frederick, "Weinstein Is Upbeat as 'Burning' Tries Rising from Ashes," *Variety*, 17 November 1982, 4, 34.

27. "Miramax Increases Staff at New Digs, as Distrib Arm Lengthens," *Variety*, 1 July 1987, 4, 18.

28. Ibid.

29. Ibid.

30. These figures refer to the amount earned via box office film rentals in theatrical release for the United States and Canada according to "In Winner's Circle: Miramax's *Crying Game* Paces Indies," *Daily Variety: Special Section—Independents in Entertainment*, 17 August 1993, retrieved 14 June 2010 from the LexisNexis database, http://www.lexisnexis.com/.

31. Because they had less leverage, independent distributors often received smaller rentals from exhibitors than did the studios. Whereas the studios guaranteed a steady stream of high-production-value, star-driven product, independents could rarely do this. Thus, not only were these smaller companies faced with less money coming in with a hit, they also had less ability to collect payments from exhibitors than did the majors.

32. Daniel Cerone, "Independent Film Makers, Marketers Confront Box-Office Crisis," *Los Angeles Times*, 15 September 1989, 4.

33. Anne Thompson, "US Film Festival Proves There's Still Hope for the Independent Filmmaker," *Orange County (CA) Register*, 19 February 1989, K10; Corie Brown, "New Breed of Independent Filmmakers Ready to Branch Out," *Chicago Tribune*, 12 January 1990, O; Aljean Harmetz, "Independent Films Get Better but Go Begging," *New York Times*, 1 February 1989, C17.

34. There was another strand of independents that succeeded in the 1980s that I am largely excluding from the discussion here. These were independent production-distribution companies such as Carolco and Cinergi. Such companies focused on producing big-budget "event" films that were predominantly financed through a combination of foreign presales, equity investment, and licensing of North American theatrical rights to the majors. A number of these companies struggled in the late 1980s as well, due largely to poor production choices and mismanagement. For example, Carolco thrived for much of the 1980s and early 1990s with movies such as *Rambo III* (1988) and *Total Recall* (1990), but went under following the failure of *Cutthroat Island* (1995).

35. It is worth noting that these two films were among the most financially successful independent releases of all time.

36. Wyatt, "The Formation of the 'Major Independent,'" 76–78.

37. Tom Matthews, "New Line's Hard-Line Formula," *Box Office*, September 1989, 14–17. See also Wyatt, "The Formation of the 'Major Independent.'"

38. Wyatt, "The Formation of the 'Major Independent,'" 76.

39. Ibid.

40. Chris Mitchell, "Shrewd Marketing Fuels Freddy Phenomenon," *Variety*, 10 August 1992, 36.

41. See Wasser, *Veni, Vidi, Video*.

42. Cerone, "Smaller Films Seek a Summer Place," *Los Angeles Times*, 14 June 1989, 1.

43. Brown, "New Breed of Independent Filmmakers Ready to Branch Out," O.

44. Charles Kipps, "N.Y.-Based Miramax Partners with Canadian S. C. Entertainment," *Variety*, 19 August 1987, 4, 32.

45. "Miramax to Rep Almi Film Library," *Variety*, 9 December 1987, 3.

46. "Miramax on the Prowl at Mart with 'Slingshot' to Bag Buyers," *Variety*, 24 February 1988, 240.

47. Terry Pristin and James Bates, "The Climbing Game; Miramax Film Corp. Is atop the Hollywood Heap, Thanks to *The Crying Game*," *Los Angeles Times*, 29 March 1993, A1. Biskind's figures differ somewhat. He states that Midland Montague bought a 45 percent interest in Miramax for $3.5 million, $2.5 million of which was a direct loan to the company. Due to this investment, Miramax got a $10 million line of credit from JPMorgan Chase. See *Down and Dirty Pictures: Miramax, Sundance, and the Rise of Independent Film* (New York: Simon & Schuster, 2004), 59.

48. "About Miramax Films," *Strapless* press kit, 1990, retrieved from the Herrick Library.

49. Gubernick, "We Don't Want to Be Walt Disney," 109.

50. "Miramax' Mainstream Program Focuses on AFM as Its Tool," *Variety*, 25 February 1987, 158.

51. Steven Soderbergh, *sex, lies, and videotape* (New York: Harper & Row, 1990), 214. In the decade between the release of *sex, lies, and videotape* and *The Blair Witch Project*, this attitude shifted: by the late 1990s, it became a means of product differentiation for a movie to be shot on digital video.

52. Pierson, *Spike, Mike, Slackers, and Dykes*, 131.

53. Harmetz, "Independent Films Get Bigger but Go Begging," C17. Whereas in 1989 Sundance might be a small feature in some publications, by 1999 it was gracing the cover of such mainstream publications as *Entertainment Weekly*.

54. Soderbergh, *sex, lies, and videotape*, 225.

55. Harmetz, "Independent Films Get Bigger but Go Begging," C17.

56. Bob Thomas, "Star Watch: A Tough Act to Follow," Associated Press, 21 February 1992, retrieved 28 February 2011 from the LexisNexis database, http://www.lexisnexis.com/.

57. Colford, "Movies Are Their Game," 8.

58. "*Time's* 25 Most Influential Americans: Harvey Weinstein," *Time*, 21 April 1997, accessed 14 June 2010, http://www.time.com/time/magazine/article/0,9171,986206-8,00.html.

59. Colford, "Movies Are Their Game," 8.

60. "About Miramax Films," *sex, lies, and videotape* press kit, 1989. Similar text appears in the *Strapless* press kit.

61. Cerone, "Taking an Independent Path," 1.

62. Ibid.

63. Justin Wyatt provides a specific definition of "high concept" in his book of the same name. He writes, "High concept can be conceived . . . as a product differentiated through the emphasis on style in production and through the integration of the film with its marketing." A simpler version of "high concept" is applicable in the case of *sex, lies, and videotape*. This version conforms to the definition provided by Steven Spielberg: "If a person can tell me the idea in 25 words or less, it's going to make a pretty good movie." *High Concept: Movies and Marketing in Hollywood* (Austin: University of Texas Press, 1994), 13, 20.

64. Soderbergh, *sex, lies, and videotape*, 244.

65. Ibid.

66. Ibid., 244–245

67. Colford, "Movies Are Their Game," 8.

68. Cerone, "Independent Film Makers, Marketers Confront Box-Office Crisis," 4.

69. Ibid.

70. "Stakes up at Sundance Film Festival," *San Diego Union-Tribune*, 27 January 1990, retrieved 8 February 2010 from the *San Diego Union-Tribune* website, http://www.signonsandiego.com/.

71. Jeff Gordinier and Chris Nashawaty, "Film's Next Frontier," *Entertainment Weekly*, 11 February 2000, 20.

72. On the "small is beautiful" mentality, see Colford, "Movies Are Their Game," 8. "Milestone in entertainment licensing" statement is from Jennifer Pendleton, "Manic Bat-Marketing Underway," *Variety*, 20 April 1992, 3.

73. Thomas Schatz, "The Return of the Hollywood Studio System," in *Conglomerates and the Media*, ed. Erik Barnouw et al. (New York: New York Press, 1997), 93.

74. Pierson extensively chronicles the process of selling *Roger & Me* in *Spike, Mike, Slackers, and Dykes.*

75. Cerone, "Smaller Films Seek a Summer Place," 1.

76. Wyatt, *High Concept.*

77. Kathleen Berry, "Movie Industry Growth Expected in International Markets," *Investor's Business Daily,* 25 March 1996, A3.

78. "MPAA Puts '88 B.O. at Peak of $4.46-Bil; Aud Gets Older," *Variety,* 15 February 1989, 1, 4.

79. Island Alive's *Kiss of the Spider Woman* is often cited as the first independent to be effectively counterprogrammed against the studio's event films in the summertime. See, for example, Richard Gold, "Specialty Distribs Claim Summer, Not Ceding to Majors' Films," *Variety,* 5 August 1984, 3, 9.

80. Richard Gold, "Miramax Pickup, 'Roger' Bidding Mark IFFM Opening," *Variety,* 11 October 1989, 17.

81. *Cinema Paradiso* earned $12 million in its North American theatrical release, while *My Left Foot* earned almost $15 million domestically.

82. Bruce Horovitz, "Marketing: Targeting Movie Ads Without Sticking Your (Left) Foot in Your Mouth," *Los Angeles Times,* 20 March 1990, D6.

83. Ibid.

84. Ibid.

85. Peter Biskind notes that Miramax used strategies in its campaigns for Oscar nominations that, for the most part, had previously only been employed by the major studios. Among the most notable of these tactics was sending out screener tapes and arranging small dinner parties with members of the Hollywood Irish community. See *Down and Dirty Pictures,* 98–99.

86. "American Moviegoers Shunning Foreign Fare," *Hollywood Reporter,* 1 September 1992, 11.

87. Tzioumakis provides an impressive survey of the rise and fall of Orion in the 1980s in *American Independent Cinema: An Introduction* (New Brunswick, NJ: Rutgers University Press, 2006).

88. Interestingly, *Cinema Paradiso* bombed in its initial release in Italy, according to Biskind, *Down and Dirty Pictures,* 86.

89. Their affection for the film was so strong that they supervised its rerelease in 2002 as a reedited "director's cut."

90. See Justin Wyatt, "The Stigma of X: Adult Cinema and the Institution of the MPAA Ratings System," in *Controlling Hollywood: Censorship and Regulation in the Studio Era,* ed. Matthew Bernstein (New Brunswick, NJ: Rutgers University Press, 1999), 238–264, for a discussion of the shifting value of the X rating during the 1960s and 1970s. For a history of the implementation and enforcement of the X rating, see Jon Lewis, *Hollywood v. Hard Core: How the Struggle over Censorship Saved the Modern Film Industry* (New York: New York University Press, 2002).

91. According to Biskind, Miramax (especially pre-Disney) tried to ensure that some of its movies would receive X ratings by intentionally cutting the films to be more scandalous. Miramax always intended to recut them to get an R in their theatrical release. See *Down and Dirty Pictures,* 60–63.

92. Richard Gold, "Indie Specialty: Marketing the Unconventional," *Variety,* 13 June 1990, 46.

93. Ronald Grover, "Crying All the Way to the Oscars," *Business Week,* 15 March 1993, 38.

94. Will Tusher, "'Up' Loses Fight; Judge Comes Down on MPAA," *Variety,* 25 July 1990, 5, 16.

95. Ibid.

96. Ibid.

97. Ibid.

98. Will Tusher, "Distrib Forfeits R on 'Numbers' Due to Ad Flak," *Variety*, 27 May 1991, 3, 8.

99. Larry Rohter, "Resistance to NC-17 Rating Develops," *New York Times*, 13 October 1990, 13. Universal's *Henry and June* (1990) was the first film to be released theatrically with the NC-17 rating.

100. Grover, "Crying All the Way to the Oscars," 38.

101. Ibid.

102. John Evan Frook, "Miramax Paradiso," *Variety*, 21 September 1992, 101, 106. Whereas grosses are the amount taken in at the box office, the term "rentals" refers to the amount that goes to the distributor after the exhibitor takes its cut.

103. "Miramax Expected to Tap Milstein as Prod'n Chief," *Variety*, 11 April 1990, 4.

104. Michael Fleming, "New Prestige Subsidiary to Keep Miramax in the Arthouse Game," *Variety*, 3 December 1990, 3.

105. Doris Toumarkine, "Prestige Picks up *Paris Is Burning*," *Hollywood Reporter*, 19 July 1991, retrieved 8 February 2010 from the *Hollywood Reporter* website, http://www.hollywoodreporter.com/.

106. Claudia Puig, "Christian Watchdog Group Calls for Boycott of *Paris*," *Los Angeles Times*, 8 August 1991, F2.

107. Ibid.

108. Lawrence Cohn, "Miramax, with More Pics, Execs, Strides into Its Second Decade," *Variety*, 28 January 1991, 16.

109. The Weinsteins repeatedly declared the importance of their library to the press. See, for example, ibid.

110. "HBO, Miramax Renew Ties," *Variety*, 18 March 1991, 25; Andrea King, "WB to Distribute Miramax Remakes," *Hollywood Reporter*, 20 May 1991, retrieved 8 February 2010 from the *Hollywood Reporter* website, http://www.hollywoodreporter.com/.

111. Marc Berman and John Evan Frook, "Par Scales 'K2' in Miramax Pact," *Variety*, 10 February 1992, 20, 93.

112. Lawrence Cohn, "Miramax, Bravo Ink Licensing Pact," *Variety*, 23 March 1993, 36.

113. "Miramax Films Launching Vid Label; Industry Vet Santrizos Will Be at Helm," *Billboard*, 4 January 1992, 45; Lawrence Cohn, "Miramax Films Unveils Foreign Division," *Variety*, 11 May 1992, 7, 34.

114. "BMG to Represent Music Catalogs of 3 Film Cos," *Billboard*, 29 August 1992, 79; Frook, "Miramax Paradiso," 101–106. Rich Zahradnik, "Rank, Miramax Ink $5 Mil Film Processing Deal," *Hollywood Reporter*, 29 September 1992, 15. According to Zahradnik, the $5 million was to be used toward film processing in Rank's Deluxe Film Laboratories.

115. Doris Toumarkine, "'Freddie' Widest Miramax Opener," *Hollywood Reporter*, 24 July 1992, retrieved 8 February 2010 from the *Hollywood Reporter* website, http://www.hollywoodreporter.com/.

116. The company did, however, limit its risk by coproducing the film with CBS; the network paid for much of the production. Kirk Honeycutt, "CBS to Fund Miramax 'Boys,'" *Hollywood Reporter*, 2 November 1992, retrieved 8 February 2010 from the *Hollywood Reporter* website, http://www.hollywoodreporter.com/.

117. Both Miramax and New Line distributed twenty-six films in 1991—a number that had both companies releasing the most films of *any* U.S. distributors that year. Lawrence Cohn, "Miramax, NL, WB Most Prolific Distribs in '91," *Variety*, 23 December 1991, 14.

118. New Line had increased its output as well, releasing approximately the same number of titles annually as Miramax in the early 1990s. Lawrence Cohn, "Fewer New Pix in '90, but More by Majors," *Variety*, 24 December 1990, 3, 8; Cohn, "Miramax, NL, WB Most Prolific Distribs in '91."

119. "Independent Miramax Mirrors the Majors; The Independent Company, Riding the Momentum of *sex, lies, and videotape*, Is Buying Up Films for Distribution," *Los Angeles Times*, 24 October 1989, F1.

120. Michael Fleming, "Miramax, Riding 'Sex' Wave, Storms on into the '90s," *Variety*, 31 January 1990, 16.

121. Bernard Weinraub, "The Talk of Hollywood: Everyone Has Heard; How Many Will See?," *New York Times*, 21 September 1992, C11.

122. According to Bob Weinstein, the Miramax label was "dealing with the more upscale, sophisticated literary type of genre, [and so Dimension] gives us a balance." Martin A. Grove, "Miramax Enters New Dimension in Features," *Hollywood Reporter*, 19 June 1992, retrieved 8 February 2010 from the *Hollywood Reporter* website, http://www.hollywoodreporter.com/.

123. Weinraub, "Talk of Hollywood," C11.

124. See, for example, Fleming, "Miramax, Riding 'Sex' Wave, Storms on into the '90s," 9, 16; "Miramax Seeking Universal Answer?," *Variety*, 1 August 1990, 87.

125. Anne Thompson, "Will Success Spoil the Weinstein Brothers?," *Film Comment* 24 (July/August 1989), 75.

126. Steven Rea, "Independent Filmmakers Need Parachutes to Break the Falls," *Orange County (CA) Register*, 29 October 1989, L9.

127. Pierson, *Spike, Mike, Slackers, and Dykes*, 151.

128. Deborah Young, "The U.S. Distribs: What Do They Buy?," *Variety*, 31 August 1992, 54.

129. Glenn Collins, "More Screens, but Fewer Choices to Choose From," *New York Times*, 18 March 1991, C11.

130. Pierson, *Spike, Mike, Slackers, and Dykes*, 151.

131. Andy Marx, "Sleeping Dogs; Even When You're Hot, Sometimes It's a Cold Town," *Los Angeles Times*, 16 February 1992, 25.

132. John Evan Frook, "Miramax Angling to Pick up 'Fiction,'" *Daily Variety*, 25 June 1993, 3.

133. Grover, "Crying All the Way to the Oscars," 38.

Chapter 3

1. Among the high-profile distributors that declared bankruptcy during this period were DEG, Film Dallas, Vestron, Cannon, Spectrafilm, New World, Island, Cineplex Odeon, Atlantic, Hemdale, Cinecom, Avenue, and Aries. The death of the mini-major Orion was particularly disappointing for many within the creative community, as the company had championed a number of more cutting-edge films during its heyday.

2. John Evan Frook, "Miramax Paradiso," *Variety*, 21 September 1992, 101–106.

3. Ibid.

4. Paul Noglows, "Indies' Success Splits Opinion on Wall Street," *Variety*, 12 August 1991, 57–58.

5. Ibid.

6. "Miramax Seeking Universal Answer?," *Variety*, 1 August 1990, 87; Andrea King, "WB to Distribute Miramax Remakes," *Hollywood Reporter*, 20 May 1991, retrieved 8 February 2010 from the *Hollywood Reporter* website, http://www.hollywoodreporter.

com/; Marc Berman and John Evan Frook, "Par Scales 'K2' in Miramax Pact," *Variety,* 10 February 1992, 20, 93.

7. Claudia Eller, "New Line Forms New Label for Specialty Releases," *Variety,* 10 December 1990, 5; Paul Noglows, "Can Freddy Steady New Line?," *Variety,* 9 November 1992, 1, 84.

8. Eller, "New Line Forms New Label for Specialty Releases."

9. John Evan Frook, "U.S. Indies Hit the Beach with Big-Budget Bang," *Variety,* 10 May 1993, C4, C134.

10. For a discussion of this see Judy Brennan, "Savvy Wags Say Savoy's the Indie to Watch," *Variety,* 4 January 1993, 5, 30.

11. Terry Ilott and Don Groves, "Cannes No 1-Nite Stand as Output Deals Get Serious," *Variety,* 13 May 1991, 1, 14.

12. Ibid.

13. Don Groves, "Much Has Changed at Market," *Variety,* 6 May 1991, C4.

14. Charles Fleming, "Risky Christmas Pix Top Tinseltown's Wish List," *Variety,* 9 November 1992, 1, 85.

15. Peter Bart, "Lowest Common Denominator Doesn't Work Anymore," *Variety,* 22 March 1993, 19.

16. "Sony Adds Classics Operation," *Variety,* 17 February 1992, 21.

17. Anita M. Busch and Doris Toumarkine, "Miramax, Dis in 'Sarafina!' Talks," *Hollywood Reporter,* 2 July 1992, 1.

18. Frook, "Miramax Paradiso," 106.

19. John Evan Frook, "BVHV Grabs 5 Miramax Pix," *Daily Variety,* 12 October 1992, 1.

20. Judy Brennan and Michael Fleming, "Miramax Markets Itself," *Daily Variety,* 26 April 1993, 12.

21. Ibid.

22. *Variety* editor-in-chief Peter Bart suggested Miramax was "cash-starved" in "No Room for Rumor," *Variety,* 27 July 1992, 3, 5.

23. "United Kingdom: Film Biz Is Looking Up," *Variety,* 15 February 1993, 40.

24. Jeongmee Kim outlines the diverse range of funding sources used to produce and distribute British cinema throughout the 1990s. This essay suggests some of the subtle ways that the influx of money from Europe and the United States affected content. Different notions of "Britishness" were constructed or emphasized, in part, as a means of differentiating select movies for global distribution. Kim also effectively calls attention to the complex interrelationship between the British television and film industries. For more, see "The Funding and Distribution Structure of the British Film Industry in the 1990s: Localization and Commercialization of British Cinema Towards a Global Audience," *Media, Culture & Society* 25, no. 3 (2003): 405.

25. Neil Watson notes this point in "Hollywood UK," in *British Cinema of the 90s,* ed. Robert Murphy (London: BFI, 1999), 83.

26. Robert Murphy, "Citylife: Urban Fairy-Tales in Late 90s British Cinema," in *The British Cinema Book,* ed. Robert Murphy (London: BFI, 2001), 292–300.

27. For a few different perspectives on this cinema of the "poor and oppressed," see Martin McLoone, "Internal Decolonisation? British Cinema and the Celtic Fringe," in Murphy, *British Cinema Book,* 184–190; Moya Luckett, "Image and Nation in 1990s British Cinema," in Murphy, *British Cinema of the 1990s,* 88–99; and Claire Monk, "Underbelly UK: The 1990s Underclass Film, Masculinity, and the Ideologies of New Britain," in *British Cinema, Past and Present,* ed. Justine Ashby and Andrew Higson (London: Routledge, 2000), 274–287.

28. Such an argument makes PolyGram (which was a division of the European company Philips until 1998)—and, by extension, Europeans—the "saviors" of the film industry at the same time that it vilifies North American companies. For further discussion of the role of PFE, see Robert Murphy, "A Path Through a Moral Maze," 1–16; Peter Todd, "The British Film Industry in the 90s," 17–26; and Geoffrey Macnab, "Unseen British Cinema," 135–144, all in Murphy, *British Cinema in the 90s*. See also former PolyGram president Michael Kuhn's autobiography of his experience at the company in *One Hundred Films and a Funeral: PolyGram Films—Birth, Betrothal, Betrayal, and Burial* (London: Thorogood, 2003).

29. This is also noted by Watson in "Hollywood UK," 83–84.

30. John Hill nicely captures the odd paradoxes of contemporary British cinema in observing that "while British cinema may depend upon international finance and audiences for its viability, this may actually strengthen its ability to probe national questions; that while cinema has apparently lost its 'national' audience in the cinemas, it may have gained a more fully 'national' audience via television; and that while the British cinema may no longer assert the myths of the 'nation' with its earlier confidence, it may nonetheless be a cinema which is more fully representative of national complexities than ever before." "British Cinema as National Cinema: Production, Audience and Representation," in Murphy, *British Cinema Book*, 212.

31. Jane Giles, *The Crying Game* (London: BFI, 1997), 25, 27.

32. Ibid., 27.

33. Ibid., 28.

34. For a discussion of this trend, see Don Groves, "Cannes Fever Fans Fire Under Indies," *Variety*, 18 May 1992, 1, 84.

35. John Evan Frook, "It's 'Crying' Time for Miramax," *Daily Variety*, 20 July 1992, 1, 10.

36. Giles, *The Crying Game*, 38.

37. Frook, "'Crying' Time." According to Michael Fleming and Leonard Klady, Miramax purchased the rights by settling some past bills with British Screen Finance and paying approximately $1.5 million. "'Crying' All the Way to the Bank," *Variety*, 22 March 1993, 1, 68–69.

38. Palace did not realize much of the financial windfall from *The Crying Game* because, according to Peter Biskind, Miramax purchased all the rights to the film from the British operation relatively early in its North American theatrical run. *Down and Dirty Pictures: Miramax, Sundance, and the Rise of Independent Film* (New York: Simon & Schuster, 2004), 145–147.

39. Giles, *The Crying Game*, 42–43.

40. Some critics have argued that *The Crying Game* also suffered in its UK release because of negativity directed toward Palace Pictures—a company that, according to Robert Murphy, "seemed to represent a daring, thrusting new generation of cine-literate film-makers," only to expire "amidst a cloud of acrimony in 1992." "A Path Through a Moral Maze," 1.

41. Giles, *The Crying Game*, 42–43.

42. Fleming and Klady, "'Crying' All the Way to the Bank."

43. "Crix' Picks," *Variety*, 30 November 1992, 41.

44. Fleming and Klady, "'Crying' All the Way to the Bank."

45. For an example of such a reference, see Todd McCarthy, "The Crying Game," *Variety*, 14 September 1992, 47–48.

46. Fleming and Klady, "'Crying' All the Way to the Bank."

47. Peter Stack, "Secret of 'Crying Game' Success," *San Francisco Chronicle*, 23 February 1993, D1.

48. David J. Fox, "No Tears at Box Office for 'Game,'" *Los Angeles Times*, 23 February 1993, F1.

49. Giles, *The Crying Game*, 46.

50. Anita M. Busch, "'Crying Game' Playing with Major Ad Push," *Hollywood Reporter*, 19 February 1993, retrieved 18 June 2010 from the LexisNexis database, http://www.lexisnexis.com/.

51. Giles, *The Crying Game*, 49.

52. Fleming and Klady, "'Crying' All the Way to the Bank."

53. Leonard Klady, "Where Have All the Independents Gone?," *Variety*, 23–29 January 1995, 13, 16.

54. Lawrence Cohn, "'Turtles' Tops, 'Born' Winner, 'Point' Steady," *Variety*, 5 April 1993, 12.

55. With its increasing popularity, Miramax was able to renegotiate its position from one of distributor to equity partner in the film, according to Fleming and Klady, "'Crying' All the Way to the Bank."

56. Eller and Frook, "Mickey Munches on Miramax," *Variety*, 3 May 1993, 1, 60, 62.

57. Disney and Warner Bros. played musical chairs for market share during much of the 1990s.

58. Aljean Harmetz, "Disney Expansion Set, Film Output to Double," *New York Times*, 2 December 1988, D1.

59. Leonard Klady, "Big Boys Anteing up to Get Library Cards," *Variety*, 13–19 May 1996, 13, 16.

60. These contracts guaranteed each an annual salary of $1.5 million.

61. Eller and Frook, "Mickey Munches," 62.

62. Dave McNary, "Disney Agrees to Buy Miramax," United Press International, 30 April 1993, retrieved 18 June 2010 from the LexisNexis database, http://www.lexisnexis.com/.

63. At the time of the deal, Miramax announced its intent to maintain the same level of output, releasing approximately twenty films per year, though this wound up fluctuating substantially over the years.

64. While this deal served the interests of both Miramax and Disney, allowing flexibility in both domestic and international distribution, it made matters more difficult for outsiders to evaluate. The existing set-up limited the ability for media analysts to determine the earnings of either company. Figures were combined at some points and separated at others. For example, in industry reports, Miramax typically remained separate from Disney. But it was Disney money—which went toward more prints and larger advertising campaigns—that helped Miramax raise its market share and profile both nationally and internationally.

65. Eller and Frook, "Mickey Munches," 61.

66. This hope was in fact realized, as Claudia Eller notes in "On-Screen Chemistry; The Synergy Between Unlikely Partners Miramax and Disney Has Surprised Many—Including Miramax and Disney," *Los Angeles Times*, 1 December 1995, D1.

67. Eller and Frook, "Mickey Munches," 61.

68. Leonard Klady, "Studio Deals Spark Indie Identity Crisis," *Variety*, 13 December 1993, 91.

69. Turner also acquired Castle Rock Pictures at this time. Geraldine Fabrikant, "Turner Moves to Purchase Studio," *New York Times*, 7 August 7, 1993, 39.

70. Sharon Waxman, "Independent Means . . . ," *Washington Post*, 6 February 1996, E7.

71. Frank Spotnitz, "Money Matters; The End of the Indies," *Washington Post*, 19 September 1993, G4.

72. Bernard Weinraub, "Business Match Made in Hollywood," *New York Times*, 1 May 1993, 39.

73. McNary, "Disney Agrees to Buy Miramax."

74. Klady, "Studio Deals Spark Indie Identity Crisis."

Chapter 4

1. Jeff Dawson, *Quentin Tarantino: The Cinema of Cool* (New York: Applause, 1995).

2. Peter Biskind gives the period from 1993 to 1999 the label of "Golden Age." He considers the time from 1979 to 1986 the company's "Bronze Age" and the time from 1987 to 1993 its "Silver Age." See *Down and Dirty Pictures: Miramax, Sundance, and the Rise of Independent Film* (New York: Simon & Schuster, 2004), 376.

3. Jay Greene, "Distribbers Hot on Trail of Indies; 'Piano' Changed Tune of Market," *Daily Variety*, 27 October 1994, retrieved 8 February 2010 from the *Variety* website, http://www.variety.com/.

4. Biskind, *Down and Dirty Pictures*, 153–154.

5. *Wuthering Heights* and *Jane Eyre* links made by Kenneth Turan in "'The Piano' Plays an Intoxicating Tune," *Los Angeles Times*, 19 November 1993, F1. The Brontë link is also noted in Harriet Margolis, "Introduction: 'A Strange Heritage': From Colonization to Transformation?," in *Jane Campion's "The Piano,"* ed. Harriet Margolis (Cambridge: Cambridge University Press, 2000), 20.

6. Roger Ebert called the film "haunting" in "Keys to Passion: 'The Piano' Finds Its Strong Voice in Subtle Refrains," *Chicago Sun-Times*, 19 November 1993, 42. Richard Corliss called it "dazzling," in "The Piano," *Time*, 22 November 1993, 79.

7. "Upscale" label from Leonard Klady, "Pix' Profit Picture Presents Surprises," *Variety*, 10–16 January 1994, 13–14. "Mature" label from John Brodie, "Old Niche Brings B.O. Gifts," *Variety*, 18–24 April 1994, 11, 14.

8. "Top 100 Grossers Worldwide, '93–'94," *Variety*, 17–23 October 1994, M56.

9. Dana Polan, *Jane Campion* (London: BFI, 2001), 17.

10. So labeled by Emanuel Levy in his review of the film, retrieved 23 January 2010 from http://www.emanuellevy.com/search/details.cfm?id=5934.

11. These materials can be found in *Variety*, 28 February–6 March 1994, 13–19.

12. Ibid.

13. Lucy Howard and Gregory Cerio, "Sour Notes on 'The Piano,'" *Newsweek*, 14 March 1994, 8.

14. David J. Fox, "Playing the Oscar Game Like a 'Piano'?," *Los Angeles Times*, 11 March 1994, F1.

15. "Lotta Scripts," *Variety*, 31 January–6 February 1994, 8. Miramax also published a novelization of the screenplay.

16. Claudia Eller, "On-Screen Chemistry; The Synergy Between Unlikely Partners Miramax and Disney Has Surprised Many—Including Miramax and Disney," *Los Angeles Times*, 1 December 1995, D1.

17. The rights to the soundtrack belonged to Virgin, not Miramax-Disney. Polan, *Jane Campion*, 168.

18. *Spotswood* has been classified at times as an Australian film as well, as its funding came in part from the Australian Film Commission and the Australian Film Finance Corporation. According to Biskind, however, the primary rationale behind this acquisition was the presence of the Brit Anthony Hopkins, whose profile had been raised significantly in the wake of his role as Hannibal Lecter in *Silence of the Lambs* (1991). See *Down and Dirty Pictures*, 139.

19. John Evan Frook, "Miramax Sounds 'Sirens,'" *Variety*, 10 May 1993, 9.

20. Don Groves, "Miramax Adds Oz Consultant," *Daily Variety*, 4 November 1994, 14.

21. Ibid.

22. According to http://www.imdb.com/, accessed 23 January 2010, *Priscilla* earned in excess of $11 million in the United States, and *Shine* earned more than $35 million.

23. Milo Bilbrough, "The Making of *The Piano*," in Jane Campion, *The Piano: Screenplay* (New York: Hyperion, 1993), 142. The same information appeared in the film's press kit. See "*The Piano*: Production Notes," *The Piano* press kit, 1993.

24. Ibid.

25. According to the producer-director Gaylene Preston, "The recipe for international success for films from the Antipodes was to create a film that is non-dialogue based, features stars from Hollywood, exploits the landscape, and has sex and violence. In the struggle to produce a film recognizably of this region yet able to crack the international market, Campion . . . 'solved a central problem—of dialect—and of central casting—by making one of them mute and one of them taciturn.'" Quoted in Margolis, "Introduction: 'A Strange Heritage,'" 7.

26. Polan, *Jane Campion*, 18.

27. Ibid.

28. This term is used with increasing frequency in trade publications from the 1990s into the early 2000s. For early examples, see James Ulmer, "Indie Financing Blooms with 'Cross-Pollination,'" *Hollywood Reporter*, 19 May 1994, retrieved 19 June 2010 from the LexisNexis database, http://www.lexisnexis.com/; Michael Williams and Adam Dawtrey, "Will Chunnel Vision Goose Pic Biz?," *Variety*, 26 January–1 February 1998, 1. Interestingly, *The English Patient* is celebrated by *Variety* for escaping the "Europudding" trap in "Zaentz Rewarded for Excellence," *Variety*, 23–29 June 1997, 48.

29. This trend is explored most thoroughly in the *Global Hollywood* books. See Toby Miller, Nitin Govil, John McMurria, and Richard Maxwell, eds., *Global Hollywood* (London: BFI, 2001); Toby Miller, Nitin Govil, John McMurria, Richard Maxwell, and Ting Wang, eds., *Global Hollywood 2* (London: BFI, 2005).

30. Mary Anne Reid, "Snapshot of the 90s," in *More Long Shots: Australian Cinema Successes in the 90s* (Sydney: Australian Film Commission, 1999), 8–32.

31. Data from "Top Grossing Foreign Imports for '92," *Variety*, 11 January 1993, 63; "Top Grossing Independent Films," *Variety*, 20–26 February 1995, A84; and the *Internet Movie Database*, retrieved 23 January 2010 from http://www.imdb.com/.

32. John Evan Frook, "Call Harvey Mickey Mouth," *Variety*, 29 November 1993, 75.

33. Kim Williamson, "The Buying Game," *Box Office*, August 1994, 18.

34. Brodie, "Old Niche Brings B.O. Gifts," 11.

35. Leonard Klady, "B.O. Bets on Youth Despite a Solid Spread," *Variety*, 10–16 April 1995, 13–14. A 1993 study reported that the over-40 audience doubled from 1983 to 1993. For more on this, see Klady, "Tracking a Lost Generation: Stunted Growth of Core Audience Frustrates Filmers," *Variety*, 29 November 1993, 1, 74.

36. As evident from discussion of sales figures in Eller, "On-Screen Chemistry."

37. Biskind, *Down and Dirty Pictures*, 136.

38. Tiiu Lukk, *Movie Marketing: Opening the Picture and Giving It Legs* (Los Angeles: Silman James Press, 1997), 21–22.

39. Dawson, *Cinema of Cool*, 173.

40. Betsy Sharkey, "The Brothers Miramax," *New York Times*, 24 April 1994, 2:1.

41. John Evan Frook, "Miramax Angling to Pick Up 'Fiction,'" *Daily Variety*, 25 June 1993, 3.

42. Ibid.

43. Ibid.

44. According to *Variety*, it became clear by the time of the Toronto Film Festival in September 1993 that "stateside acquisition has become extremely competitive, with anything of remote interest now often sold off at the script stage." See Leonard Klady, "Will Success Spoil the Toronto Fest?," *Variety*, 27 September 1993, 11, 19. Similarly, at the Cannes market in May 1994, many industry observers noted the lack of product available for acquisition compared to previous years. Festival favorites *Pulp Fiction*, the *Three Colors* trilogy, *A Simple Formality*, and *Caro Diaro* had already been acquired; of course, it was Miramax that had the rights to many of these acquired films. See Greg Evans, "Indie Distribs Hope for a Prize Inside Cannes," *Variety*, 2–8 May 1994, 13, 23.

45. Philip French, "Cannes '94: Pulping the Opposition," *The Observer* (London), 29 May 1994, 15.

46. Bernard Weinraub, "Filmmakers Discount Criticism by Dole," *New York Times*, 2 June 1995, A24. According to Jack Mathews of *New York Newsday*, "I've received more letters from readers about *Pulp Fiction* than any other film this year, most of them condemning *Newsday*'s sanguine critical coverage of it, and Hollywood insiders say its warped mix of humor and violence has taken it out of the running for the Oscar." "Can 200 Critics Be Wrong? (Maybe)," *New York Newsday*, 26 December 1994, F1.

47. Greg Evans, "Oscar Rings in New Era of Indie Chic," *Variety*, 20–26 February 1995, 1, 19.

48. So labeled by Richard Turner in "Will Big-Studio Sendoff for 'Pulp Fiction' Make It Big at the Box Office?," *Wall Street Journal*, 14 October 1994, B6.

49. Dana Polan says it "may well be that the appropriate comparison [for Tarantino] is not to film-makers . . . but to media performers." *Pulp Fiction* (London: BFI, 2000), 65.

50. According to Miramax, $5 million was spent on the film's launch. Outsiders placed the figure closer to $8–10 million. A range of numbers are presented in Turner, "Will Big-Studio Sendoff for 'Pulp Fiction' Make It Big at the Box Office?" The $5 million "ballpark" figure was also quoted in Richard Natale, "'Specialist,' 'Pulp' Duke It out over No. 1 Spot," *Los Angeles Times*, 17 October 1994, F1. In addition, see Evans, "Oscar Rings in New Era of Indie Chic."

51. Natale, "'Specialist,' 'Pulp' Duke It out over No. 1 Spot."

52. The precise box office performance of both films was the subject of much controversy following opening weekend, as Miramax claimed a victory with *Pulp Fiction* but was then forced to recant. See ibid.

53. Figures accessed 8 February 2010 from http://www.imdb.com/.

54. The $200 million gross figure was advertised in *Variety* on 22 May 1995. The *Internet Movie Database* reports a total global box office of $213 million.

55. Scott Hetrick, "'Pulp Fiction' Puts out Vid Hit: First Rental to Break 700,000-Unit Barrier," *Hollywood Reporter*, 30 August 1995, retrieved 8 February 2010 from the *Hollywood Reporter* website, http://www.hollywoodreporter.com/.

56. Ibid.

57. Kenneth Turan, "'Fiction': Quentin Tarantino's Gangster Rap," *Los Angeles Times*, 14 October 1994, F1.

58. Laurence Lerman, "Indies Big in Gotham," *Variety*, 18–24 September 1995, 17, 26.

59. For a discussion of the various stylistic connections to Tarantino, see Polan, *Pulp Fiction*; Paul A. Woods, ed., *Quentin Tarantino: The Film Geek Files* (London: Plexus, 2000); Dawson, *Cinema of Cool*.

60. The year 1992 was seen as the high point of "guerilla filmmaking." Filmmak-

ers who viewed themselves as "guerillas" would make movies by any means necessary. Favored practices included working without permits, employing no-name talent, shooting on 16mm film, and using only a handful of crew members. *Filmmaker* magazine, and in particular Next Wave Films executive Peter Broderick, wrote extensively about this phenomenon. See Broderick's "The ABC's of No-Budget Filmmaking," *Filmmaker Magazine*, Winter 1992, retrieved 19 June 2011 from http://www.peterbroderick.com/writing/writing/abcsofnobudgetfilmmaking.html; and "Learning from Low Budgets," *Filmmaker Magazine*, Winter 1993/1994, retrieved 19 June 2011 from http://www.peterbroderick.com/writing/writing/learningfromlowbudgets.html.

61. Ang Lee, Amy Heckerling, and Joel Coen can be considered as intersecting with this group to various degrees.

62. B. Ruby Rich, "The New Queer Wave," *Sight and Sound* 2 (September 1992): 30–34.

63. The year 1994 can be seen as both the high point and the beginning of the end for the micro-budget indie. In this year, seven of the sixteen features in the dramatic competition at Sundance were made on ultra-low budgets, including *Clerks*, *What Happened Was*, *Go Fish*, and *Grief*. Peter Broderick labels this the "off off Hollywood" phenomenon, and discusses it in "Recipe for a Low-Budget Success Story," *Los Angeles Times*, 6 January 1995, 20. After 1994, the budgets and production values at the festival continued to rise. Specialty companies' move away from such product paralleled Miramax's transition to higher-budget fare. *Clerks* has been seen as the "last hurrah" by Miramax in terms of its support of ultra-low budget product. According to John Pierson, "It was probably the last time in their [Miramax] corporate history that they ever would have gotten involved with that kind of film. So there does seem to be something resembling fate involved in things coming together at that moment." John Kenneth Muir, *An Askew View: The Films of Kevin Smith* (New York: Applause, 2002), 44.

64. James Schamus discusses the crucial nature of ancillary markets in "To the Rear of the Back End: The Economics of Independent Cinema," in *Contemporary Hollywood Cinema*, ed. Steve Neale and Murray Smith (London: Routledge, 1998), 91–105. Also, according to Marc Merry, director of corporate advertising at AMC Theaters, ancillary revenues were being factored into the increase in the number of films being made. See Klady, "Tracking a Lost Generation," 14.

65. In speculating that no new wave seemed on the horizon, Bart observed that "vast multinational companies are standing by, willing to lavish millions of dollars on the nurture of new talent, yet there doesn't seem to be anyone to nurture." See Peter Bart, "Waiting for the Wave," *Variety*, 13 January 1992, 12. Interestingly, *Pulp Fiction* producer Lawrence Bender around the same time stated (before the release of that film) that "I am one who absolutely believes that change is in the wind." Judy Brennan, "Weird or Wild? They Want It," *Variety*, 16 August 1993, 9, 13.

66. Dawson, *Cinema of Cool*, 26.

67. Robert Rodriguez, *Rebel Without a Crew* (New York: Plume, 1995), vii–xvi.

68. Muir, *An Askew View*, 9–21.

69. Ian Penman, "Don't Try This at Home," in Woods, *Quentin Tarantino*, 127.

70. Polan, *Pulp Fiction*, 65.

71. Richard Natale, "Indie Films No Longer Penny-Ante Affair," *Los Angeles Times*, 14 April 1995, F4.

72. Muir, *An Askew View*, 202.

73. *Pulp Fiction* is a perfect case in point here. According to Tiiu Lukk, who provides a case study of the marketing of *Pulp Fiction*, originally Miramax anticipated the primary audience for the film to be men between the ages of eighteen and twenty-four. Only

after a series of test screenings did they realize its appeal was much broader. Among the demographic groups that Miramax "found" enjoyed *Pulp Fiction* were twenty-five-to-thirty-four-year-olds, thirty-five-plus, urban audiences, and ethnic audiences. See Lukk, *Movie Marketing*, 21–31.

74. Michael Fleming, "Miramax, Riding 'Sex' Wave, Storms into the '90s," *Variety*, 31 January 1990, 18.

75. John Evan Frook, "Manhattan Moguls Vie for Big Pic Pacts," *Variety*, 24–30 January 1994, 8.

76. Frook, "Call Harvey Mickey Mouth," 75.

77. Claudia Eller and John Evan Frook, "Mickey Gets a New Mini: Miramax," *Daily Variety*, 3 May 1993, 13.

78. Frook, "Call Harvey Mickey Mouth," 75.

79. John Brodie, "Harvey's Hefty Cash Lends Fest Some Flash," *Variety*, 23–29 May 1994, 1, 63.

80. Ibid., 63.

81. Ibid.

82. So labeled in Frook, "Call Harvey Mickey Mouth."

83. Christina Lane addresses the ways that the consolidation of the film industry and the favoring of certain types of product by specialty companies led to the marginalization of many women filmmakers, including Anders and Holofcener. See "Just Another Girl Outside the Neo-Indie," in *Contemporary American Independent Film: From the Margins to the Mainstream*, ed. Christine Holmlund and Justin Wyatt (London: Routledge, 2005), 193–209.

84. Woods's deal was with both Hollywood Pictures and Miramax. John Evan Frook and Kathleen O'Steen, "'Girls' Goes to Miramax: Woods Shingle to Produce Rosenberg Script," *Daily Variety*, 20 April 1994, 3.

85. Tarantino's deal was a two-year first-look agreement; Rodriguez's was an overall exclusive arrangement. "Tarantino in New Miramax Deal," *Hollywood Reporter*, 2 May 1994, retrieved 8 February 2010 from the *Hollywood Reporter* website, http://www.hollywoodreporter.com/; "Miramax Pacts with Rodriguez," *Daily Variety*, 24 May 1995, 10, 14.

86. "Take Cover! Tarantino Forms Rolling Thunder," *Hollywood Reporter*, 14 July 1995, retrieved 8 February 2010 from the *Hollywood Reporter* website, http://www.hollywoodreporter.com/.

87. Michael Williams, "Disney Backs Miramax in French Pic Distrib'n," *Variety*, 10–16 October 1994, retrieved 8 February 2010 from the *Variety* website, http://www.variety.com/; Thomas R. King, "Disney's Miramax to Form Unit to Dub, Market, Distribute French Films in U.S.," *Wall Street Journal*, 10 October 1994, B5.

88. This was not the company's widest release; that honor goes to the animated *Freddie as F.R.O.7*, released in August 1992. John Evan Frook, "Miramax Films Goes Wide with 'Fortress,'" *Daily Variety*, 27 August 1993, 3.

89. Ibid.

90. Stephen Galloway, "Miramax Enter New Dimension," *Hollywood Reporter*, 22 May 1995, retrieved 19 June 2001 from the LexisNexis database, http://www.lexisnexis.com/; Leonard Klady, "'92 Box Office at Record Pace," *Hollywood Reporter*, 18 November 1992, 1.

91. Lee died in a freak accident on the set one week before shooting was completed. With the help of digital effects and a stunt double, the film was completed—albeit with a significant increase in its budget, from approximately $15 million to about $23 million. For more on the fallout from Lee's death, see Andy Marx and Kathleen O'Steen,

"Safety First—Again," *Variety*, 5 April 1993, 5, 10; Andy Marx, "'Crow' Flies with Computer Aid," *Variety*, 9 May 1994, 202.

According to the *Hollywood Reporter*, Paramount acquired domestic distribution rights in September 1993, but its distribution agreement was dependent on the delivery of a completed film. Producer Edward Pressman put up the money to finance the film and, after Paramount pulled out, made an agreement with Miramax for domestic distribution. Miramax was already involved in distributing the film internationally prior to Lee's death. See Anita M. Busch and Alex Ben Block, "'Crow's' Fate Still Not Clear," *Hollywood Reporter*, 2 April 1993; Anita M. Busch and Doris Toumarkine, "'Crow' Flying to Miramax?," *Hollywood Reporter*, 4 November 1993; "'Crow' Nest at Miramax/ Dimension Confirmed," *Hollywood Reporter*, 4 March 1994. All three sources retrieved 14 June 2010 from the LexisNexis database, http://www.lexisnexis.com/.

92. John Evan Frook, "'Crow' Flies in May," *Daily Variety*, 7 March 1994, 28.

93. A two-page advertisement placed by Miramax in *Variety* following *The Crow*'s opening reads, "$16,025,309 Opening Week. The #1 Movie in America. The Biggest Opening in Miramax/Dimension Films History." *Variety*, 23–29 May 1994, 4–5.

94. Greg Evans, "Indies Head for Genre Pic Middle Ground," *Variety*, 22 May 1995, 22.

95. Anne Thompson, "The Executive Life: Where Partnership Thrives in Filmdom," *New York Times*, 26 February 1995, 3:35.

96. Greg Evans and Anita M. Busch, "Gill Tops Miramax Marketing," *Variety*, 21–27 November 1994, 17.

97. Terry Pristin and James Bastes, "The Climbing Game: Miramax Film Corp. Is Atop the Hollywood Heap, Thanks to 'The Crying Game,'" *Los Angeles Times*, 29 March 1993, A1.

98. Some of the Weinsteins' early bad behavior is described in a 1992 article in *Spy* magazine. The piece discusses some of the ways Miramax mistreated other filmmakers and companies with which it did business. See Celia Brady, "Miramax, Miramax, on the Wall, Who's the Sleaziest of Them All?," *Spy* 6, no. 8 (June 1992): 14–15.

99. Harvey's reliance on "instinct" noted in Greg Evans and John Brodie, "Box Office Opens at Circus Miramaximus," *Variety*, 10–16 October 1994, 111. Just one of the instances of the Weinsteins being called moguls can be found in Peter Bart, "Miramax Gets Net for High-Wire Act," *Variety*, 19 December 1994–1 January 1995, 8. Meanwhile, Harvey declares his reliance on his "gut" in Lynn Hirschberg, "The Mad Passion of Harvey and Bob," *New York* 27, no. 40 (10 October 1994): 48–57.

100. John Brodie, "Miramax Pacts Cadre into Solid Niche Future," *Variety*, 6 November 1995, 7.

101. The conflict over *You So Crazy* discussed in "Disney's Miramax Loses Rights to Distribute Film," *Wall Street Journal*, 30 March 1995, B8; John Brodie, "Sex! Controversy! PR! Marketers Turn Ratings Battles into Positive Publicity," *Variety*, 29 August–4 September 1994, 7–8.

102. The hiring of Dershowitz is noted in Muir, *An Askew View*, 46. No cuts or changes were made to *Clerks* during the appeals process. Adam Sandler, "Miramax Duo Among 12 New R Pix," *Daily Variety*, 14 October 1994, 8; John Brodie, "'Kids' Causes Clamor: Miramax Pic Steals Limelight as Fest Winds Down," *Daily Variety*, 27 January 1995, 3, 34. There was also some conflict with the MPAA over an advertisement for Robert Altman's *Ready to Wear* (1994) featuring a scantily clad Helena Christensen. After Miramax heavily publicized the conflict, the MPAA approved a black-and-white version of the ad. See Peter Bart, "Miramax Gets Net for High-Wire Act," *Variety*, 19 December 1994–1 January 1995, 1, 8; Alex Ben Block, "Miramax OK'd to Bare 'Wear,'"

Hollywood Reporter, 20 December 1994, retrieved 19 June 2011 from the LexisNexis database, http://www.lexisnexis.com/.

103. For an example of such speculation, see Evans and Brodie, "Box Office Opens at Circus Miramaximus."

104. New Line's deal with Jim Carrey for *Dumb and Dumber* came right before he broke out and became the first actor to be paid $20 million, which he was offered for his role in Columbia's *The Cable Guy*. Dan Cox, "Carrey's $20 Mil 'Cable' Bill," *Daily Variety*, 14 July 1995, 1, 43.

105. Benedict Carver and Dan Cox, "New Line: Sibling Revelry," *Variety*, 9 March 1998, 1, 61.

106. Ibid.

107. Anita Busch, "Uni, PolyGram Setting Up Gramercy Pics Co-venture: Miramax's Schwartz Heads Stand-Alone Outfit," *Hollywood Reporter*, 21 May 1992, retrieved 8 February 2010 from the *Hollywood Reporter* website, http://www.hollywoodreporter.com/.

108. Ibid.

109. Doris Toumarkine, "Gramercy Slate Grows; So Does Its PR Corps," *Hollywood Reporter*, 17 November 1994, retrieved 8 February 2010 from the *Hollywood Reporter* website, http://www.hollywoodreporter.com/.

110. Busch, "Uni, PolyGram Setting Up Gramercy Pics Co-venture."

111. "Gramercy Finds Joy at 'Funeral'," *Hollywood Reporter*, 5 January 1995, retrieved 8 February 2010 from the *Hollywood Reporter* website, http://www.hollywoodreporter.com/.

112. Edwin Riddell and Jeffrey Jolson-Colburn, "PolyGram Net Surges 19 Percent to Record $483 Mil," *Hollywood Reporter*, 28 February 1994, retrieved 8 February 2010 from the *Hollywood Reporter* website, http://www.hollywoodreporter.com/.

113. Riddell, "PolyGram Plans Own U.S. Output," *Hollywood Reporter*, 6 September 1994, retrieved 8 February 2010 from the *Hollywood Reporter* website, http://www.hollywoodreporter.com/.

114. "Chronicling PolyGram's Foray into Film," *Hollywood Reporter*, 11 August 1992, retrieved 8 February 2010 from the *Hollywood Reporter* website, http://www.hollywoodreporter.com/.

115. Riddell and Jolson-Colburn, "PolyGram Net Surges 19 Percent to Record $483 Mil."

116. Ibid.

117. "Gramercy Finds Joy at 'Funeral'," *Hollywood Reporter*, 5 January 1995, retrieved 8 February 2010 from the *Hollywood Reporter* website, http://www.hollywoodreporter.com/. *Variety* labeled *Four Weddings and a Funeral* the "most profitable film" of 1994 on a "return-on-cost" analysis. *Pulp Fiction* was fifth in the chart; *Priscilla, Queen of the Desert* was seventh. Other releases by specialty companies to make the list were *Eat Drink Man Woman* at third (Goldwyn) and *The Mask* at sixth (New Line). From "World's Champs and Chumps," *Variety*, 13 February 1995, 7.

118. "'Lyric' Continues Gramercy's Streak," *Hollywood Reporter*, 7 October 1994, retrieved 19 June 2011 from the LexisNexis database, http://www.lexisnexis.com/.

119. Evans, "Oscar Rings in New Era of Indie Chic." In this year, more than a third of the seventy nominations went to "indie" companies.

120. Kirk Honeycutt, "PolyGram Film 100% Behind Gramercy Pics," *Hollywood Reporter*, 9 January 1996, retrieved 8 February 2010 from the *Hollywood Reporter* website, http://www.hollywoodreporter.com/.

121. Donna Parker, "Fox Searchlight on 'McMullen,'" *Hollywood Reporter*, 25 January 1995, retrieved 8 February 2010 from the *Hollywood Reporter* website, http://www.hollywoodreporter.com/.

122. Lea Saslav, "Indies: Some Hits but Few Heavy Hitters," *Hollywood Reporter*, 5 January 1996, retrieved 8 February 2010 from the *Hollywood Reporter* website, http://www.hollywoodreporter.com/.

123. Leonard Klady, "Studio Deals Spark Indie Identity Crisis," *Variety*, 13 December 1993, 1, 91.

124. Ibid.

125. Bravo and IFC at this time were owned by NBC, TCI, and Cablevision via their Rainbow Programming Services. Sundance was a coventure of Robert Redford's Sundance Corporation and Viacom's Showtime cable service. Jefferson Graham, "Sundance Goes Cable: Redford's Film Channel Flouts Formula," *USA Today*, 8 May 1995, 1D.

126. John Brodie, "Aliens Invade Hollywood!," *Variety*, 12–18 February 1996, 97.

127. Ibid.

128. Kirk Honeycutt, "Elwes to Head WMA Indie Unit," *Hollywood Reporter*, 4 March 1994, retrieved 8 February 2010 from the *Hollywood Reporter* website, http://www.hollywoodreporter.com/.

129. Ibid.

130. Saslav, "Indies: Some Hits but Few Heavy Hitters."

131. According to Leonard Klady, "The Spirit nominating committee has been given a mandate to consider such factors as 'economy of means,' 'uniqueness of vision' and 'original, provocative subject matter' when compiling the voting ballot." "New Spirit at IFP Awards Expands Eligibility, Prizes," *Daily Variety*, 27 October 1994, 5.

Chapter 5

1. Peter Bart, "Love for Sale," *Variety*, 18–24 September 1995, 5, 107.

2. Ibid., 5.

3. Adam Sandler, "Miramax Cries Foul over 'Crazy' Rating," *Variety*, 14–20 February 1994, 21.

4. "Disney's Miramax Loses Rights to Distribute Film," *Wall Street Journal*, 30 March 1994, B8.

5. Figures retrieved 19 June 2011 from http://www.imdb.com/.

6. John Brodie, "Sex! Controversy! PR! Marketers Turn Ratings Battles into Positive Publicity," *Variety*, 29 August–September 4 1994, 7–8; John Brodie, "'Clerks' Re-rated with an 'R,'" *Variety*, 17–23 October 1994, 23; Kirk Honeycutt, "'Advocate' Wins Its R Rating," *Hollywood Reporter*, 17 August 1994, retrieved 19 June 2011 from the Lexis-Nexis database, http://www.lexisnexis.com/.

7. *Natural Born Killers* did not immediately receive an R rating, however. According to *Time*, Stone had to cut approximately 150 shots in order to appease the MPAA. Richard Corliss and Martha Smilgis, "Murder Gets an R; Bad Language Gets an NC-17," *Time*, 29 August 1994, 68.

8. As discussed in chapter 4, there was some debate about *Pulp Fiction*'s violence and amorality. But to a large extent this was overshadowed by discussions about the film's style and Tarantino's status at the forefront of a new wave of 1990s auteurs.

9. Greg Evans, "'Priest' Foes Pass over Miramax, Boycott Disney," *Variety*, 3–9 April 1995, 24.

10. Greg Evans, "Miramax Shifts 'Priest's' Date," *Variety*, 27 March–7 April 1995, 25–26. *Priest* had already opened on screens in New York and Los Angeles on March 24. The protests only affected its wide release to about three hundred screens.

11. Evans, "'Priest' Foes Pass over Miramax, Boycott Disney."

12. Greg Evans and Todd McCarthy, "Will 'Kids' Be Too Hot for Harvey?," *Variety*,

6–12 April 1995, retrieved 19 June 2011 from the LexisNexis database, http://www.lexisnexis.com/.

13. Ibid.

14. See Peter Biskind, *Down and Dirty Pictures* (New York: Simon & Schuster, 2004), 201–202. In addition, in January 1995, *Variety* reported that "Miramax expects [*Kids*] to be one of the most controversial films of the year." Michael Fleming, "Sundance Sneak," *Variety*, 23 January 1995, 4.

15. Evans and McCarthy, "Will 'Kids' Be Too Hot for Harvey?"

16. Thomas R. King, "Miramax Film Heightens Clash with Disney," *Wall Street Journal*, 30 March 1995, B11.

17. Ibid.

18. Roger Ebert, "Cannes Rattled by 'Kids'; Depressing NC-17 Film Too Raw for Disney Banner," *Denver Post*, 25 May 1995, E3.

19. According to the *Hollywood Reporter*, "The Weinsteins say the Excalibur name is taken from the Arthurian legend because the brothers were enamored of the Camelot ideal as part of their admiration for late President John F. Kennedy." "Weinsteins Pay $3.5 Million for 'Kids' Custody," *Hollywood Reporter*, 29 June 1995, retrieved 8 February 2010 from the *Hollywood Reporter* website, http://www.hollywoodreporter.com/.

20. Elaine Dutka, "Miramax Circumvents 'Kids' Controversy," *Los Angeles Times*, 29 June 1995, F2.

21. "Weinsteins Pay $3.5 Million for 'Kids' Custody," *Hollywood Reporter*, 29 June 1995, retrieved 8 February 2010 from the *Hollywood Reporter* website, http://www.hollywoodreporter.com/.

22. Ibid.

23. "'Kids' Appeal Denied; To Be Released Without Rating," *Hollywood Reporter*, 13 July 1995, retrieved 8 February 2010 from the *Hollywood Reporter* website, http://www.hollywoodreporter.com/.

24. Other profitable pictures from 1995 were *Muriel's Wedding* (Miramax) and *The Brothers McMullen* (Fox Searchlight). See "Top Specialized Releases of 1995," *Variety*, 30 October–5 November 1995, 24; "Smartest Arthouse," *Variety*, 4–10 December 1995, 18.

25. It is worth noting the complete statement he made: "Creating this company was the perfect solution—unprecedented as far as I know. . . . It's the opposite of going head-on. Though we're at tremendous risk—losing Buena Vista's clout in the home video market and pay TV markets—if I were Disney, I'd have made the same decision. Especially in this political climate, they have a grand name and a reputation to protect." From Dutka, "Miramax Circumvents 'Kids' Controversy."

26. Scott Hettrick and Doris Toumarkine, "Trimark Vid Has 'Kids' Doing Darndest Things," *Hollywood Reporter*, 2 August 1995; Monica Roman, "Weinsteins Send 'Kids' to HBO," *Hollywood Reporter*, 9 August 1995. According to Roman, Encore had the rights to Miramax's films, but *Kids* was deemed "inappropriate for Encore's family-oriented fare." Both retrieved 8 February 2010 from the *Hollywood Reporter* website, http://www.hollywoodreporter.com/.

27. Cost cited in Elaine Dutka, "Miramax Circumvents 'Kids' Controversy." Bowles's statement appears in Greg Evans, "It's Lights out at Shining Excalibur," *Variety*, 16 October 1995, 8. Prints and advertising costs were estimated to be approximately $2 million, according to "Trimark Vid Has 'Kids' Doing Darndest Things," *Hollywood Reporter*, 2 August 1995, retrieved 8 February 2010 from the *Hollywood Reporter* website, http://www.hollywoodreporter.com/.

28. Evans, "It's Lights Out at Shining Excalibur."

29. Fleming, "Sundance Sneak"; Leonard Klady, "Where Have All the Independents Gone?," *Variety*, 23 January 1995, 13, 16.

30. Klady, "Where Have All the Independents Gone?," 13.

31. "Miramax: Profile of a Mini-Major," *Variety*, 26 August–1 September 1996, 28; "Spotlight on New Line Cinema," *Variety*, 14–20 October 1996, 27.

32. Klady, "Where Have All the Independents Gone?"

33. Ibid., 16.

34. Robert Koehler, "Beyond Niche: Specialty Auds' Tastes Still a Crap Shoop," *Daily Variety*, 25 July 1995, 6, 12.

35. Klady, "Where Have All the Independents Gone?," 16. Others cited by Klady as recently closed or on their way to closing include Avenue, New World, InterStar, Triton, Cinecom, Taurus, 21st Century, Vestron, Cineplex Odeon, and Cannon.

36. "Gilula Chief of Goldwyn's New Theatre Group," *Hollywood Reporter*, 4 February 1992, retrieved 8 February 2010 from the *Hollywood Reporter* website, http://www.hollywoodreporter.com/.

37. The company stated that competition from distributors with deeper pockets contributed to its troubles. To remain competitive, the Samuel Goldwyn Company "began taking unaccustomed risks that didn't pay off." Terry Pristin, "What Forced Goldwyn to Seek Sale?," *New York Times*, 31 July 1995, D7.

38. Martin Peers, "Goldwyn's 'For Sale' Sign," *Variety*, 10–16 July 1995, 7, 17. The article on *Kids* appeared on the same page: Paul F. Young, "Excalibur to Appeal NC-17 of 'Kids,'" *Variety*, 10 July 1995, 17.

39. Peter Bart, "The Goldwyn Age," *Variety*, 10 July 1995, 4.

40. Ibid.

41. Elaine Dutka, "Name of the Game Is Dependent Independence," *Los Angeles Times*, 21 June 1995, F1.

42. Ibid.

43. Biskind, *Down and Dirty Pictures*, 215.

44. One notable exception is Bradley Schauer's essay "Dimension Films and the Exploitation Tradition in Contemporary Hollywood," *Quarterly Review of Film and Video* 26, no. 5 (2009): 393–405. Schauer's case study of Dimension's production and marketing practices throughout the 1990s and 2000s is impressive, but his emphasis is on showing the continuities between Dimension and earlier exploitation companies, such as American International Pictures. As his essay spans the entire period of Dimension's existence under Disney, his emphasis is on thematic continuities as opposed to historical shifts. In contrast, I am emphasizing the distinctiveness of Dimension's activities during a particular historical moment: the mid-1990s.

45. Jeffrey Sconce defines "paracinema" as an "elastic textual category" that includes "entries from such seemingly disparate subgenres as 'badfilm,' splatterpunk, 'mondo' films, sword and sandal epics, Elvis flicks, government hygiene films, Japanese monster movies, beach-party musicals, and just about every other historical manifestation of exploitation cinema from juvenile delinquency documentaries to soft-core pornography." Significantly, these films are, for the most part, from previous decades and had minimal commercial viability at the time of their release but later developed "cinephilic subcultures" devoted to them. See "'Trashing' the Academy: Taste, Excess, and an Emerging Politics of Cinematic Style," *Screen* 36 (Winter 1995): 372.

46. Mark Jancovich discusses how *Scream*, in particular, was rejected by many cult movie fans because it was perceived as being too closely connected to mainstream, commercial Hollywood cinema. He notes how the film's big budget, its ties to the Hollywood studios, and its widespread popularity marked it as "inauthentic" to some horror

fans. The film was further perceived as not a "real" genre film because it featured television stars and was targeted to teenagers (teenage girls, no less). See "'A Real Shocker': Authenticity, Genre and the Struggle for Distinction," in *The Film Cultures Reader*, ed. Graeme Turner (London: Routledge, 2002), 469–480.

47. As early as October 1990, the horror film as it had developed for over a decade was seen to be in decline; as *Variety* notes, "This year represents a changing of the guard for horror films, as many of the long-running series pictures have been replaced by relatively new blood. For the first time in a long while, 1990 will have no theatrical entry bearing the *Friday the 13th, Halloween*, or *A Nightmare on Elm Street* brand name." See Lawrence Cohn, "Horrors! Hit Shocker Series on Hiatus," *Variety*, 22 October 1990, 3.

48. For a brief survey of the history of B movies and their status in the early 1990s, see Judy Brennan, "A-List B-Pics Adding More Sock to Schlock," *Variety*, 1 March 1993, 1, 78.

49. Leonard Klady, "Scary Future for Horror Pix," *Variety*, 11–17 April 1994, 13.

50. Ibid.

51. Roger Ebert, "Wes Craven's New Nightmare," *Chicago Sun-Times*, 14 October 1994, accessed 10 February 2010, http://rogerebert.suntimes.com/apps/pbcs.dll/article?AID=/19941014/REVIEWS/410140306/1023.

52. Ibid.

53. Janet Maslin, "Freddy Krueger Enters the Real World: Yikes!," *New York Times*, 14 October 1994, accessed 10 February 2010, http://www.nytimes.com/1994/10/14/movies/film-review-freddy-krueger-enters-the-real-world-yikes.html.

54. Budget data from "Wes Craven's New Nightmare," *The Numbers*, accessed 31 January 2010, http://www.the-numbers.com/movies/1994/0NOE7.php.

55. Leonard Klady, "H'W'D Pix up Pieces After Fall," *Variety*, 31 October–6 November 1994, 16.

56. Greg Evans, "Indies Head for Genre Pic Middle Ground," *Variety*, 22–28 May 1995, 7–22.

57. Roman, "Arthouse, Haunted House Buoy Miramax," *Daily Variety*, 10 January 1997, 58. The film's budget was high for Dimension, however. *The Numbers* estimates the production budget to be $20 million. Data available from "From Dusk Till Dawn," *The Numbers*, accessed 31 January 2010, http://www.the-numbers.com/movies/1996/0FDTD.php.

58. Roman, "Arthouse, Haunted House Buoy Miramax."

59. John Colapinto, "The Big Bad Wolves of Miramax," *Rolling Stone*, 3 April 1997, 46–49.

60. Monica Roman, "'Dusk' Prequel, Sequel Set," *Daily Variety*, 23 December 1996, 1, 17.

61. While this had long been a practice with horror titles, it was less common with other types of genre pictures. A few examples of non-horror straight-to-video "sequels" include *Bring It On: All or Nothing* (2006), *Cruel Intentions 2: Manchester Prep* (2003) and *Cruel Intentions 3* (2004), and *American Pie Presents Band Camp* (2005).

62. *Scream*'s budget is reported by Bob Weinstein as $14.8 million in Monica Roman, "Genre Pix Give Miramax an Added Dimension," *Variety*, 20–26 January 1997, 7. This does not include profit participation, which was offered to key talent involved.

63. Monica Roman, "College Sneaks for Miramax's 'Scream,'" *Daily Variety*, 4 December 1996, 35.

64. Roman, "Genre Pix Give Miramax an Added Dimension," 12.

65. This is an interesting point, considering the extent to which the film was later heralded by many scholars and cultural critics for its influence on the horror genre. See,

for example, Kathleen Rowe Karlyn, "'Scream,' Popular Culture, and Feminism's Third Wave: 'I'm Not My Mother,'" *Genders Online Journal* 38 (2003), accessed 20 June 2011, http://www.genders.org/g38/g38_rowe_karlyn.html; Davinia Thornley, "The 'Scream' Reflex: Meta-horror and Popular Culture," *Metro*, Spring 2006, 140–147; Valerie Wee, "Resurrecting and Updating the Teen Slasher," *Journal of Popular Film and Television* 34 (Summer 2006): 50–61.

66. Leonard Klady, "Film Review: *Scream*," *Daily Variety*, 11 December 1996, 31.

67. Ibid.

68. Janet Maslin, "Tricks of the Gory Trade," *New York Times*, 20 December 1996, C22.

69. Richard Corliss, "Scream," *Time*, 30 December 1996, 162.

70. Jay Carr, "'Scream' Gooses the Gore Genre," *Boston Globe*, 20 December 1996, E4.

71. David Ansen, "Scream," *Newsweek*, 23 December 1996, 68; Kevin Thomas, "Craven's 'Scream' a Bravura Sendup of Horror Pictures," *Los Angeles Times*, 20 December 1996, F14.

72. Bruce Orwall, "Baby Boomlet Boosts Teen Films into Hits," *Wall Street Journal*, 17 December 1997, B1. Despite increasing its number of screens by only thirty-seven in its second week in release, *Scream* showed an impressive 39 percent increase in box office grosses. See *Variety*'s box office chart, 6–12 January 1997, 13.

73. See Leonard Klady, "Studios Focus on Teen Stream," *Variety*, 13–19 January 1997, 11–12; Roman, "Genre Pix Give Miramax an Added Dimension."

74. Klady, "Studios Focus on Teen Stream," 12.

75. Ibid.

76. Roman, "Genre Pix Give Miramax an Added Dimension," 12.

77. Figures come from "Box Office/Business for Scream," *Internet Movie Database*, accessed 20 June 2011, http://www.imdb.com/title/tt0117571/business.

78. The international income was an added surprise, as historically horror films do not perform as well overseas. Claudia Eller, "On the Eve of 'Halloween: H2O's Release, Distributor Dimension Wonders . . . Will Lightning Strike Twice?," *Los Angeles Times*, 4 August 1998, D10. According to *Variety*, overseas performance of horror films is often small because many countries place bans on violent films. See Robert Koehler, "'Scream' Catalyst for New Horror Era," *Variety: MIFED '97 Special Section*, 13 October 1997, M5.

79. "Hollywood.com's Top 25 Highest Grossing Domestic Horror Films of All Time," Hollywood.com, accessed 15 July 2007, http://www.hollywood.com/feature/Hollywoodcoms_Top_25_Highest_Grossing_Domestic_Horror_Films_of_All_Time/3466506.

80. Ibid. Many journalists had difficulty deciding precisely what horror films could be cited and compared to *Scream*. Oft-cited titles included *The Exorcist*, *Psycho* (1960), *Rosemary's Baby* (1968), *Carrie* (1976), *Jaws* (1975), and *The Omen*. See also Leonard Klady, "Horror Pix Revival Scares up B.O. Gold," *Variety*, 25–31 August 1997, 9, 16.

81. Chris Petrikin, "Scribe's 'Scream': Two More," *Daily Variety*, 21 February 1997, 67.

82. Chris Vognar, "Scream Makes Horror Movies Hip Again," *Dallas Morning News*, 26 February 1997, D3.

83. Koehler, "'Scream' Catalyst for New Horror Era," M5.

84. Ibid.

85. Susan Wloszczyna, "Something to Scream About: Weinsteins Build New Empire," *USA Today*, 22 August 1997, 1D.

86. Ibid. This was one of only a handful of articles to appear during this period to express some skepticism about the company's substantial efforts to hide the corporate relationship between Miramax and Dimension. For example, the author notes at one point that journalists had been asked not to classify Dimension films as Miramax releases. But she quickly lets the Weinsteins "explain away" such behavior; ultimately, such practices are shown to be justified given the uphill battle that art house–oriented films face in the marketplace.

87. Elaine Dutka and John Clark, "Miramax Finds Success Breeds Admiration, Envy," *Los Angeles Times*, 30 January 1997, F1.

88. Also see Wloszczyna, "Something to Scream About."

89. Dan Cox and Monica Roman, "Bob Takes Mira to the Max: Genre Hits Lend Fiscal Heft to Arty Fare," *Variety*, 14–20 September 1998, 1.

90. Roman, "Genre Pix Give Miramax an Added Dimension," 12.

91. Ibid.

92. Wloszczyna, "Something to Scream About," 1D.

93. From Anthony Timpone, "To the Dawn and Beyond," in *Quentin Tarantino: The Film Geek Files*, ed. Paul A. Woods (London: Plexus, 2000), 136–137.

94. The precise label to apply to this group has been debated, as has the specific age range that belongs to this group. For a discussion of this demographic, and the development of teen media across platforms during the 1990s, see Valerie Wee, *Teen Media: Hollywood and the Youth Market in the Digital Age* (Jackson, NC: McFarland, 2010).

95. Orwall, "Baby Boomlet Boosts Teen Films into Hits," B1.

96. Unlike *Scream*, *Beavis and Butt-Head* was fading quickly by late January. Statistics from *Variety* box office charts, 3–9 February 1997, 8.

97. Klady, "Studios Focus on Teen Stream," 12.

98. This information courtesy of Dr. Valerie Wee, e-mail correspondence with the author. For a more extensive discussion of the teen media boom of the late 1990s and early 2000s, see Wee, *Teen Media*.

99. Rebecca Leung, "The Echo Boomers," *60 Minutes*, 11 February 2009, accessed 20 June 2011, http://www.cbsnews.com/stories/2004/10/01/60minutes/main646890.shtml?tag=currentVideoInfo;videoMetaInfo.

100. This article ran in conjunction with *Scream 2*'s $39 million opening weekend. The *San Diego Herald-Tribune* article is a reprint of Orwall, "Baby Boomlet Boosts Teen Films into Hits," originally in the *Wall Street Journal*. As Leonard Klady put it in another article, "Demos and statistics have been manipulated in a way that's worked against greenlighting pictures with strong youth appeal. While it's true the general population has been aging, the backbone of moviegoing remains late teens and early 20s. That is the segment with the most available leisure time, and filmgoing is one of the most affordable out-of-house entertainment activities." See "Studios Focus on Teen Stream," 12.

101. Valerie Wee indicates the importance of *Scream* to teen girls in particular. She suggests how *Scream* updated the horror film in a progressive fashion, speaking to and representing concerns of interest to teenage girls. See "Resurrecting and Updating the Teen Slasher: The Case of *Scream*," *Journal of Popular Film and Television* 34 (Summer 2006): 50–61.

102. Cox and Roman, "Bob Takes Mira to the Max," 93.

103. Petrikin, "Scribe's 'Scream.'" In this article, Williamson is described as making a "seven-figure deal."

104. The opening weekend numbers for *Scream 2* were the subject of a great deal of controversy. Miramax was accused of—and admitted to—inflating these figures by

more than $6 million. This brought the company negative publicity, as such a high degree of overstatement was extremely rare. The company claimed this was due to the understaffed and overworked distribution force at Dimension. See Bruce Orwall, "Miramax Admits It Overstated 'Scream 2' Ticket Sales," *Wall Street Journal*, 22 December 1997, B1, B8.

105. Foreign figures from "Foreign Language," *Box Office Mojo*, accessed 20 June 2011, http://www.boxofficemojo.com/movies/?page=main&id=scream2.htm.

106. Discussion about the publishing venture found in Monica Roman, "New Chapter Written for Miramax," *Variety*, 1–17 December 1997, 7, 17.

107. Petrikin, "Scribe's 'Scream.'" Williamson did not take a writing credit when the film was released; his only credit on the film was as "co-executive producer."

108. Figures from "I Know What You Did Last Summer," *Box Office Mojo*, accessed 20 June 2011, http://www.boxofficemojo.com/movies/?id=iknowwhatyoudidlastsummer.htm.

109. Williamson's name was so identifiable that Miramax reputedly paid a handsome sum to get him credit for a film he did not write. According to Patrick Goldstein, Miramax paid the original writers of *The Faculty* "roughly $100,000" in exchange for them agreeing to "take a story credit and waive their right to arbitration for a shared screenplay credit." This enabled Miramax to more prominently advertise Williamson's involvement in the film. See Patrick Goldstein, "Tenure Denied: 'Faculty' Withdraws Credit for Creative Writing," *Chicago Sun-Times*, 10 January 1999, 9.

110. At the time of the announcement of this deal, the film, based on a recently released documentary, was called *Fiddlefest*. Chris Petrikin, "Craven Pacts with Miramax," *Daily Variety*, 21 March 1997, 1, 50.

111. According to the *Hollywood Reporter*, the Wayans brothers' script, *Scream If You Know What I Did Last Halloween*, was merged with another horror parody script Miramax had in development at the time, *Last Summer I Screamed Because Friday the 13th Fell on Halloween*. The Wayans' participation in this project fulfilled the first part of their two-picture deal with Miramax. Zorianna Kit, "Wayans to Direct Horror Spoof," *Hollywood Reporter*, 10 February 1999, retrieved 14 June 2010 from the LexisNexis database, http://www.lexisnexis.com/.

112. One of the working titles for *Scary Movie*, in turn, was *Scream if You Know What I Did Last Halloween*.

113. Cox and Roman, "Bob Takes Mira to the Max," 1.

114. Because *Scream* came out at the end of the year, it does not fully factor into this total. Roman, "Genre Pix Give Miramax an Added Dimension," 12.

115. Bernard Weinraub, "Mavericks Adapting to Power of Studios," *New York Times*, 24 June 1996, C11.

116. Only *Scream 2*'s first few weeks in release factor into this total. *Operation Condor* was one of many Asian action films released by Dimension during the 1990s. For the most part, such films did not contribute significantly to the division's total box office at this time. For a discussion of the growing prominence of Asian action films—and Miramax/Dimension's place in this—see Peter Stein and Lisa Bannon, "Action Films from Hong Kong Knock out Hollywood," *Wall Street Journal*, 4 April 1996, B1, B8. The $190 million sum comes from Cox and Roman, "Bob Takes Mira to the Max," 93.

117. Dimension's numbers are all the more remarkable considering that, according to Tim Carvell, it was just five films that earned $172 million, while it took Miramax twenty releases to earn $250 million. "Dimension Films' Successful Scare Tactics: Studio-Sized Returns on Indie-Sized Budgets," *Fortune*, 29 December 1997, 27.

118. Cox and Roman, "Bob Takes Mira to the Max," 93.

119. Ibid. See also Klady, "Horror Pix Revival Scares up B.O. Gold."

120. Dennis Harvey, "Echo of a Scream, 'H2O' Holds Water," *Variety*, 3–9 August 1998, 35.

121. Don Groves and Rex Weiner, "Dealmakers, Heartbreakers," *Variety*, 3–9 March 1997, 13.

122. October previously had a label called Mad Dog, which had "a couple of service deals before Universal Pictures acquired a majority interest" in the specialty division in 1997. Monica Roman, "October Launches Genre Unit Rogue," *Variety*, 6–12 April 1998, 16.

123. Dan Cox, "Sony Finds Its Niche with New Screen Gems," *Daily Variety*, 7 December 1998, 1, 26.

Chapter 6

1. See, for example, Richard Natale, "'Lean' Indies Fatten Summer Boxoffice," *Variety*, 12 August 1991, 1, 61; Bob Strauss, "Indies Basking in Glow from Critics' Acclaim," *Variety*, 11 January 1993, 29, 44; David Ansen and Charles Fleming, "Hollywood: We Stink," *Newsweek*, 1 March 1993, 78; Greg Evans, "Oscar Rings in New Era of Indie Chic," *Variety*, 20–26 February 1995, 1, 191.

2. Monica Roman, "Weinstein Brothers Honored by IFP," *Variety*, 7 April 1997, 16; "Harvey Weinstein: Movie Mogul," *Time*, 21 April 1997, 52.

3. Todd McCarthy, "Fame Forces Sundance Fest to Turning Point," *Variety*, 29 January–4 February 1996, 13. The evolution of Sundance has been the subject of several publications. For more information about the festival's evolution from the late 1970s into the 2000s, see Lory Smith, *Party in a Box: The Story of the Sundance Film Festival* (Salt Lake City: Gibbs Smith, 1999); Kenneth Turan, *Sundance to Sarajevo: Film Festivals and the World They Made* (Berkeley: University of California Press, 2002); Peter Biskind, *Down and Dirty Pictures: Miramax, Sundance, and the Rise of Independent Film* (New York: Simon & Schuster, 2004).

4. Todd McCarthy, "Sundance Packed 'Em in but Pix Lacked Punch," *Variety*, 1 February 1993, 3, 5.

5. Ibid., 5.

6. John Brodie, "Sundance Gets Back to Independent Roots," *Variety*, 15–21 January 1996, 13–14.

7. Monica Roman and Leonard Klady, "B.O. Club Snubs Nouveau Niche: Indie Market Share Stalls Despite Hype," *Variety*, 3 February 1997, 1, 61.

8. Six hundred of the eight hundred were entered into the dramatic competition. Todd McCarthy, "Sundance Schusses Down Packed Slopes," *Variety*, 2–8 December 1996, 11, 24.

9. Brodie, "New Breed at Sundance," *Variety*, 30 January–5 February 1995, 13, 30.

10. McCarthy, "Indie Film Festival Grows up, Sundance Now Biz Hot Spot," *Daily Variety: Spotlight Utah Special Section*, 18 January 1995, 55–56.

11. Brodie, "Sundance Gets Back to Independent Roots."

12. McCarthy, "Fame Forces Sundance Fest to Turning Point," 25. See also Amy Taubin, "Hanging in Park City: Choked by Its Own Success, Sundance Plows On," *Village Voice*, 11 February 1997, 63.

13. John Brodie and Adam Dawtrey, "Great Art, Tough Mart," *Variety*, 20–26 May 1996, 1, 51. As this article indicates, it was not just at Sundance that these companies were competing for titles, but rather year-round at many different venues.

14. John Brodie, "Sundancers' Deals Hit Alpine Heights," *Variety*, 29 January 1996, 77.

15. In 1995, for example, twenty-five of the films playing at the festival already had distribution in place. In 1996, seventeen films had distribution before the start of the festival. See Brodie, "Sundance Gets Back to Independent Roots."

16. At least eight titles were acquired at Sundance in 1996, according to Brodie, "Sundancers' Deals Hit Alpine Heights."

17. Ibid.

18. McCarthy, "Sundance Schusses Down Packed Slopes." According to *Variety*, approximately 25 percent of the films submitted to Sundance for the 1997 festival had budgets of less than $100,000. See Roman and Klady, "B.O. Club Snubs Nouveau Niche," 61.

19. McCarthy, "Sundance Schusses Down Packed Slopes."

20. Rex Weiner, "Indies Translate in O'seas Coin," *Variety*, 27 January 1997, 5, 10. According to this article, the growth of the overseas television market "represents a 21% gain in total revenues over last year." Television was seen as starting to make up for the "disastrous slump of the home video market" overseas.

21. Reports did not specify what rights were included in the deal, though typically such numbers account for North American rights in all media. Degen Pener and Maggie Murphy, "An Ungodly Sum?," *Entertainment Weekly*, 6 September 1996, 14.

22. Ibid.

23. Ibid.

24. Domestic box office totals, as per http://www.boxofficemojo.com/ and http://www.imdb.com/, accessed 20 June 2011. Hundreds of thousands of dollars noted only for titles earning less than $5 million: *The English Patient*, $78m; *Sling Blade*, $24m; *Fargo*, $24m; *Emma*, $22m; *Trainspotting*, $16m; *Flirting with Disaster*, $14m; *Secrets & Lies*, $13m; *Lone Star*, $13m; *Marvin's Room*, $12m; *Big Night*, $12m; *Welcome to the Dollhouse*, $4.4m; *Breaking the Waves*, $4m; *Bound*, $3.8m; *Basquiat*, $3m; *When We Were Kings*, $2.7m; *I Shot Andy Warhol*, $1.8m; *Walking and Talking*, $1.2 million; *Dead Man*, $1m; *Manny & Lo*, $500,000; *Citizen Ruth*, $200,000; *Flirt*, $76,000. Often other companies handled distribution for these films outside the United States.

25. Rupert Widdicombe, "Small Is Bountiful," *Sunday Times* (London), 4 February 1996, retrieved 22 June 2011 from the LexisNexis database, http://www.lexisnexis.com/.

26. A discussion of the Sundance Channel's initial strategy can be found in Patricia Saperstein, "Indies Get Play on Sundance," *Variety*, 29 April–5 May 1996, 58. As Sundance Channel president Nora Ryan noted, "TV has become a business of brand names. . . . And our target audience is familiar with the Sundance name."

27. Ibid.

28. Robert Eberwein, "The IFC and Sundance: Channeling Independence," in *Contemporary American Independent Film: From the Margins to the Mainstream*, ed. Chris Holmlund and Justin Wyatt (New York: Routledge, 2005), 269.

29. Todd McCarthy, "Sundance Sports New Sidebar, Venues," *Variety*, 27 November–3 December 1995, 7.

30. John Pierson, *Spike, Mike, Slackers, and Dykes: A Guided Tour Across a Decade of American Independent Cinema* (New York: Hyperion/Miramax Books, 1995).

31. Brodie, "Sundance Gets Back to Independent Roots."

32. Leonard Klady, "Reality Bites Redford's Park City Picture Party," *Variety*, 30 January–5 February 1995, 30.

33. John Brodie, "Slamdance Soph Sesh Sets Dozen," *Variety*, 11–17 December 1995, 38.

34. *The Daytrippers* took home the festival's Jury Award. John Brodie, "Slamdance Fest Fetes Mottola's 'Daytrippers,'" *Variety*, 5 February 1996, 24.

35. Box office data retrieved 21 June 2011 from http://wwww.imdb.com/. Reports vary as to the precise budget for the film, but approximately $400,000 was paid back in "debts and deferred payments" once the film was licensed in select foreign territories. For a discussion of how the filmmakers cut costs, see Paula Span, "How to Make a Movie with Everything but Money," *Washington Post*, 28 March 1997, C1. The $700,000 figure comes from Desson Howe, "'The Daytrippers': You've Got a Good Reason," *Washington Post*, 28 March 1997, N51.

36. Examples of the ways Sundance was defined and redefined to different reporters include the following: Robert Redford saying "we're a bridge" between independents and the Hollywood studios in McCarthy, "Sundance Packed 'em in but Pix Lacked Punch," 5; Geoff Gilmore saying that festival programmers were cultivating a new definition of "mainstream independents" in Brodie, "New Breed at Sundance," 13; Redford speaking of Sundance being oriented toward supporting a "filmmaker's vision" regardless of whether films came from studios or independents in "Sundance's Hollywood Horizon: The Redford Festival Isn't Just for Independent Films Anymore," *Washington Post*, 28 January 1995, D1; and Gilmore declaring a shift away from "dark, heavily stylized, sometimes very violent films" in McCarthy, "Sundance Sports New Sidebar, Venues," 9.

37. "The Two Hollywoods: One Is a Global Blockbuster Business, the Other a Scrappy, Independent Cinema: Put Them Together and the Action Begins," *New York Times Magazine: A Special Issue*, 16 November 1997, cover. This issue featured over a dozen articles by journalists and prominent industry figures. Among the notable contributions: Neal Gabler, "The End of the Middle," 76–78; Art Linson, "The $75 Million Difference," 87–89; Janet Maslin, "Meeting Halfway," 101–103; Lynn Hirschberg, "The Man Who Changed Everything," 112–116.

38. For a couple of examples, see ibid.; Kathleen O'Steen, "Independents' Day . . . Anthony Minghella's Triumph over Hollywood," *Washington Post*, 22 November 1996, D1.

39. O'Steen, "Independents' Day"; Klady, "Indies Spiking Oscar's Punch: Studios Fear Losing Party to Crashers," *Variety*, 23 December–5 January 1996, 1, 58; James Bates and Claudia Puig, "Independents Day for Oscars," *Los Angeles Times*, 12 February 1997, A1; Richard Corliss, "Independents' Day," *Time*, 24 February 1997, accessed 22 June 2011, http://www.time.com/time/magazine/article/0,9171,985961,00.html.

40. Edward Helmore, "Secrets and Lies of a Hollywood Profit," *The Observer* (London), 2 February 1997, retrieved 18 October 2008 from the LexisNexis database, http://www.lexisnexis.com/.

41. This is just the tip of the iceberg in what proved to be a tumultuous year for the media industries. At the same time, Microsoft released Windows 95, the Senate and House passed the Telecommunications Act of 1996, Time Warner launched the WB broadcast network, and Paramount launched the UPN broadcast network.

42. Leonard Klady, "Hollywood Suffers Severe Sell Shock," *Variety*, 11–17 March 1996, 9, 12.

43. Leonard Klady, "Numbers Game at ShoWest," *Variety*, 10–16 March 1997, 7, 15.

44. Definition of "four quadrant" from Jonathan Bing, "Where Are All the Grown-Ups?," *Variety*, 3–9 November 2003, 10.

45. John Brodie and Anita M. Busch, "H'wood Pigs out on Big Pix: Are Huge Budgeters Hogging the Road?," *Variety*, 25 November–1 December 1996, 1, 87.

46. "Mid-range," "middle-class," and "mid-budget" all in ibid., 1; Leonard Klady, "Why Mega-Flicks Click," *Variety*, 25 November–1 December 1996, 1, 87; "middle-class" and "middle-range" discussed by 20th Century Fox studio chairman Bill Mechanic in John Cassidy, "Chaos in Hollywood," *New Yorker*, 31 March 1997, 41.

47. Klady, "Why Mega-Flicks Click." Klady adds, "Aside from mega-budgeted pics, the next cost range most likely to produce hits is $8 million–$15 million" (87).

48. Ibid., 87.

49. Brodie and Busch, "H'wood Pigs out on Big Pix," 1.

50. Leonard Klady, "B.O. Shows Slower Global Growth in '96," *Variety*, 20–26 January 1997, 12.

51. Cassidy, "Chaos in Hollywood," 41.

52. Klady, "Why Mega-Flicks Click." A little earlier in the year, Andrew Hindes placed this figure at $10 million. See "Low-Budget Niche Itch Hits Majors," *Variety: Spotlight AFM Special Section*, 26 February 1996, A2, A22.

53. For an example of the "polarization" discussion, see Peter Bart, "Lost in the Suck Zone," *Variety*, 20–26 May 1996, 3, 51.

54. Claudia Eller, "The Economics of Independents: Specialized Movies Are All the Rage These Days for Major Studios," *Los Angeles Times*, 31 January 1997, D4. According to Eller, "Sony Classics and most other specialty labels don't spend nearly as much to acquire or market their films."

55. The definition of a mid-range film was inconsistent, especially in early 1996. For example, the $15 million–$20 million figure was described as the most *desirable* budget range for indie companies by Michael Williams and Rex Weiner in "Small Pix Bear Fruit, Big Budgeters Rare at AFM," *Variety*, 11–17 March 1996, 9, 59. For additional discussions of preferred budgetary ranges, see also Eller, "Economics of Independents"; Leonard Klady, "Pix Get Ratio-Active," *Variety*, 10 February 1997, 1, 77.

56. John Brodie and Anita M. Busch, "Stars Breaking Bank While Megapix Tank," *Variety*, 4 March 1996, 1, 89.

57. The Independent Feature Project had an ongoing debate at mid-decade regarding what types of projects to fund. The organization remained uncertain whether to support more mainstream indie projects or those that were "more marginal" or "more funky." Some members of the group feared the organization would lose its edge if it made the "wrong" choices. See Ella Taylor, "The Cutting Room," *Village Voice*, 9 May 1995, 74.

58. Leonard Klady, "Indies No Longer on Cutting Edge," *Variety*, 26 February–3 March 1996, 30.

59. Joseph Steuer and Kirk Honeycutt, "October Revolution for Uni," *Hollywood Reporter*, 1 May 1997, retrieved 22 June 2011 from the LexisNexis database, http://www.lexisnexis.com/; Bruce Orwall, "Universal Pictures Gets Majority Stake in October Films," *Wall Street Journal*, 1 May 1997, B2.

60. According to Biskind, Harvey Weinstein found the fact that October was labeled the "new Miramax" a point of irritation. See *Down and Dirty Pictures*, 274.

61. Doris Toumarkine, "Schmidt Joins October Troika," *Hollywood Reporter*, 11 May 1992, retrieved 22 June 2011 from the LexisNexis database, http://www.lexisnexis.com/; Adam Dawtrey, "Oct. Films Comes in from the Cold," *Daily Variety*, 15 May 1992, 22.

62. Dawtrey, "Oct. Films Comes in from the Cold."

63. Ibid. Box office figure from *Life Is Sweet*, *Box Office Mojo*, accessed 22 June 2011, http://www.boxofficemojo.com/movies/?id=lifeissweet.htm.

64. Dawtrey, "Oct. Films Comes in from the Cold."

65. Ibid.

66. Service deals became increasingly popular among smaller distributors at this time as a means of increasing cash flow. For a discussion of this development, see Greg Evans and Adam Dawtrey, "Small Distribs Find Coin in Service Pacts," *Variety*, 22–28 January 1996, 15, 17; Monica Roman, "Second-String Indies Find Ways to Stay in Pix Game," *Variety*, 16–22 September 1996, 11, 16. A minimal theatrical release was still

desirable to the extent that it meant the film would be reviewed in major publications and begin building some initial buzz. In this sense, it was a loss leader, a form of marketing to help build awareness for the videocassette market.

67. Toumarkine, "Firms Banking on October Films," *Hollywood Reporter*, 28 October 1992, retrieved 22 June 2011 from the LexisNexis database, http://www.lexisnexis.com/.

68. So labeled in ibid.

69. Roman, "Second-String Indies Find Ways to Stay in Pix Game"; Rex Weiner and Andrew Hindes, "Indies' Lesson in '96: More May Mean Less," *Daily Variety*, 10 January 1997, 12, 64. Both LIVE and Trimark were trying to grow during this time and meeting with mixed success.

70. An acquisitions-driven approach was announced early in the company's career and sustained until 1996.

71. Wade Major, "Indies: The Big Squeeze," *Box Office*, August 1996, 28–31.

72. Laurence Lerman, "Smaller Indies Find Tough Going," *Variety*, 18–24 September 1995, 20.

73. Klady, "Indies No Longer on Cutting Edge," 30.

74. John Brodie and Monica Roman, "H'wood May Be Too Big for Its Niches," *Variety*, 10–16 June 1996, 57.

75. According to Leonard Klady, 3 to 4 percent was the average amount indies represented in box office income during the summer months. "Art Pix Whip Summer Bummer," *Variety*, 10–16 June 1996, 1, 59. Joseph Steuer showed even less optimism, pegging the art house audience at just 2 percent of the film-watching public in "The Indies: Too Much of a Good Thing," *Hollywood Reporter*, 9 January 1997, retrieved 22 June 2011 from the LexisNexis database, http://www.lexisnexis.com/. It is worth noting that many articles do not distinguish between independent and art house films, again showing the difficulty of using statistical data to accurately assess this environment. As a point of comparison, in 1995 the percentage of box office generated by independents was estimated to be approximately 5 percent as of October of that year. According to Klady, "While the profile for specialized product has grown considerably in the media, its commercial impact hasn't changed appreciably in the past decade. Thus far in 1995, those films represent 5.3% of the box office, about dead center of the high and low ends of their popularity during the past 10 years. It's still an impressive showing considering the fact that only about 400 of the market's approximately 26,000 screens are devoted year-round to arthouse movies." "Indie Niche Getting Packed with Product," *Variety*, 2–8 October 1995, 13.

76. Roman and Leonard Klady, "B.O. Club Snubs Nouveau Niche," 61.

77. For more on this topic, see Steuer, "The Indies."

78. Weiner and Hindes, "Indies' Lesson in '96."

79. Stephen Galloway, "October Fueled for Int'l Sales," *Hollywood Reporter*, 15 May 1996, retrieved 22 June 2011 from the LexisNexis database, http://www.lexisnexis.com/.

80. John Burman and Stephen Galloway, "October Toll for Lynch 'Highway,'" *Hollywood Reporter*, 13 May 1996, retrieved 22 June 2011 from the LexisNexis database, http://www.lexisnexis.com/.

81. According to Thom Geier, "October appears positioned to eventually challenge Disney's Miramax, which has earned its leadership position by handling the most films, using innovative marketing and earning the biggest boxoffice in the specialty market year after year." See "October Making Inroads to Become Next Miramax," *Hollywood Reporter*, 15 September 1998, retrieved 22 June 2011 from the LexisNexis data-

base, http://www.lexisnexis.com/. Universal acquired a majority state in October in the spring of 1997.

82. Rex Weiner and Anita M. Busch, "Studios Hunting for October," *Daily Variety*, 15 January 1997, 1; Eller, "Economics of Independents."

83. Godfrey Cheshire, "Restoration," *Variety*, 18–31 December 1995, 65.

84. Klady, "Cents and 'Sensibility,'" *Variety*, 18–31 December 1995, 7, 85.

85. Gavin Smith, "The Indie Year," *Film Comment* 32, no. 2 (March 1996): 65.

86. Ibid.

87. Eller, "On-Screen Chemistry," *Los Angeles Times*, 1 December 1995, D1.

88. Greg Evans, "Miramax Looks Ahead for Hits," *Daily Variety*, 4 January 1997, 36.

89. Eller, "On-Screen Chemistry."

90. Reports of the film's budget vary from source to source. An early report (as of 1995) places the amount at "roughly $30 million." See Beth Laski, "'Patient' to Miramax, BV Intl. for Distribution," *Daily Variety*, 14 August 1995, 3. A couple of years later, Dan Cox estimates the budget to be $27 million. "Marketeers Get to Work," *Variety*, 17–23 February 1997, 14. Claudia Eller places the figure at $33 million, of which $5.5 million came from producer Saul Zaentz. See "Miramax's 'Patient' Approach," *Los Angeles Times*, 21 March 1997, D4.

91. Leonard Klady, "Oscar Winners' B.O. Goes Bump Overnight," *Variety*, 31 March–6 April 1997, 9–10.

92. See Elaine Dutka and John Clark, "Miramax Finds Success Breeds Admiration, Envy," *Los Angeles Times*, 30 January 1997, F1; Ted Johnson and Dan Cox, "Patient's Rewarded: Best Pic Combined Best Elements of Indies, Studios," *Daily Variety*, 25 March 1997, 56; Bates, "An 'English Patient' Epic," *Los Angeles Times*, 25 March 1997, A1; Kenneth Turan, "A Return to Passion of Films Past," *Los Angeles Times*, 25 March 1997, A1; John Colapinto, "The Big Bad Wolves of Miramax," *Rolling Stone*, 3 April 1997, 46–49.

93. See Eller, "Miramax's 'Patient' Approach"; Mark Landler, "How Miramax Sets Its Sights on Oscar," *New York Times*, 23 March 1997, 2:17; Jack Matthews, "Patient's Oscars Frustrate the Studios," *Newsday*, 26 March 1997, B7.

94. Robert Koehler, "Producer Zaentz Rises to Lit Challenge," *Variety: Eye on the Oscars* supplement, 13 January 1997, 66–67.

95. Bates and Puig, "Independents Day for Oscars." According to this article, Zaentz forwarded $5.75 million of his own money, and crew deferrals totaled approximately $9.7 million.

96. Eller, "Miramax's 'Patient' Approach," D4.

97. Ibid.

98. Cox, "Marketeers Get to Work," 14.

99. Ibid.

100. *The English Patient* reached approximately five hundred screens by Thanksgiving. A week before the announcement of the Oscar nominations in February, Miramax expanded the film to approximately one thousand screens. More information on the film's release can be found in Eller, "Miramax's 'Patient' Approach."

101. Cox, "Marketeers Get to Work," 14.

102. Eller, "Miramax's 'Patient' Approach."

103. Scott Collins, "In the Campaign for Oscars, Independents Try Harder," *Los Angeles Times*, 11 March 1997, F1.

104. Eller, "Miramax's 'Patient' Approach," D4. According to Mark Landler in "How Miramax Sets Its Sights on Oscar," "Miramax's effort has included a huge advertising campaign in the industry's trade publications, *Variety* and *The Hollywood Reporter*, an

exhaustive schedule of screenings for academy members, a rash of television and radio shows about the making of Miramax movies, a series of cultural events tied to films and a telephone campaign in which Miramax employees called hundreds of academy members to plug lesser-known films like *Sling Blade*. The callers also poll academy voters to find out which movies and performances are getting the best reception; then Miramax coordinates its efforts to push those candidates."

105. Eller, "Miramax's 'Patient' Approach."

106. Landler, "How Miramax Sets Its Sights on Oscar."

107. Eller, "Miramax's 'Patient' Approach."

108. Klady, "Oscar Winners' B.O. Goes Bump Overnight," 9.

109. Klady, "Indies Spiking Oscars' Punch," 1.

110. Benjamin Svetkey, "Has Hollywood Lost It?," *Entertainment Weekly*, 14 March 1997, 22.

111. For instance, see Claudia Puig, "The 69th Academy Awards Nominations: The Indies' Fat Tuesday," *Los Angeles Times*, 12 February 1997, F1; Bernard Weinraub, "Studios Smarting from Oscars Snub of Hollywood Fare," *New York Times*, 17 February 1997, 1; Corliss, "Independents' Day." Of particular note, Johnson and Cox write in "Patient's Rewarded," "The point made by Zaentz and Minghella is that few major studios, caught up as they are today in marketing and merchandising blockbusters, would allow *Patient's* producer that degree of leeway with story and casting decisions. The Weinstein brothers bailed them out, and, as Zaentz noted in accepting the best pic Oscar, 'we had final cut'" (56).

112. For instance, trade writer Timothy M. Gray observes that "people are touting the triumph of independent companies, but few can agree what constitutes an indie." See "Oscar's 'English' Accent: Fresh Faces Rule," *Daily Variety*, 12 February 1997, 1. Similarly, Harvey Weinstein himself observes that "it's fashionable to say there's antagonism between independents and studios. . . . But studios are in the business of making big event movies, and it's actually more conservative for them to make those big movies. So they've left a piece of the real estate to the independents to follow projects that are a little riskier, less star-driven, more writer-oriented. As a result we can coexist peacefully." Puig, "The Indies' Fat Tuesday," F1.

113. Nick Higham, "Patient Marketing Reveals the Importance of Earning an Oscar," *Marketing Week*, 3 April 1997, 17.

114. Eller, "Miramax's 'Patient' Approach," D4.

115. Turan, "Return to Passion of Films Past," A1.

116. Johnson and Cox, "Patient's Rewarded," 56.

117. Michael Fleming, "Miramax Takes Heat for 'Blade's Big Bucks," *Variety*, 29 April–5 May 1996, 6.

118. John Dempsey, "Buena Vista TV Target: $150 Mil for Pic Package," *Daily Variety*, 4 February 1997, 3.

119. This claim is based on a survey of release schedules printed at the end of every summer in *Hollywood Reporter* for its annual independent film edition, as well as through a power search by distributor on http://*www.imdb.com*/, retrieved 12 July 2008.

120. Peter Bart, "Macho Moves of Miramax," *Variety*, 22–28 January 1996, 8, 115.

121. Dutka and Clark, "Miramax Finds Success Breeds Admiration, Envy."

122. As early as October 1994, *Variety* noted that between twenty and thirty-six projects were "either planned for release or well along the development route." See Greg Evans and John Brodie, "Box Office Opens at Circus Miramaximus," *Variety*, 10 October 1994, 111.

123. Brodie and Roman, "H'wood May Be Too Big for Its Niches," 57.

124. For examples of such proclamations, see Army Archerd, "Just for Variety," *Daily Variety*, 13 December 1996, 4; Dutka and Clark, "Miramax Finds Success Breeds Admiration, Envy"; Dan Cox and Monica Roman, "Hopeful Harvey Preps His Act II," *Variety*, 12–18 May 1997, 1, 78.

125. See Biskind, *Down and Dirty Pictures*, for an extensive discussion of this; see also Dutka and Clark, "Miramax Finds Success Breeds Admiration, Envy."

126. Turan, "Return to Passion of Films Past," A1.

127. Dutka and Clark, "Miramax Finds Success Breeds Admiration, Envy," F1.

128. Ibid. Dutka and Clark note that Harvey Weinstein was "as adept at quashing unfavorable stories as at spinning positive ones."

129. For example, see Corliss, "Independents' Day"; Andrew Pulver, "Players in a Reel World," *The Guardian* (London), 17 February 1997, T4. The label had been around for years by this point; it appears on occasion in publications dating back to the early 1990s.

130. Among the key individuals to depart were acquisitions executives Tony Safford and Mark Tusk, who went to Fox and New Line, respectively. Many more would follow shortly after. See Brodie and Roman, "H'wood May Be Too Big for Its Niches."

131. Dutka and Clark, "Miramax Finds Success Breeds Admiration, Envy."

132. Dan Cox, "Pix, Books on Same Page," *Variety*, 26 February 1996, 21, 30.

133. Cox and Roman, "Hopeful Harvey Preps His Act II."

134. Details on the original five-year contracts from Eller and Frook, "Mickey Gets a New Mini: Miramax," *Daily Variety*, 3 May 1993, 1, 13. Information on the new seven-year contracts from Greg Evans and John Brodie, "Miramax, Mouse Go for 7 More," *Daily Variety*, 10 May 1996, 1, 29. According to Evans and Brodie, these new contracts "essentially extend the brothers' previous ties to Disney by five years (their initial agreements expire in two)" (1).

135. Evans and Brodie, "Miramax, Mouse Go for 7 More," 1.

136. Ibid., 1, 29.

137. Ibid., 29.

138. Ibid. According to *Daily Variety*'s film production chart, *The Peacemaker* went into production in late May 1996. DreamWorks' other two 1997 releases, *Amistad* and *Mousehunt*, went into production early the following year. Production dates taken from "Film Production Chart," *Daily Variety*, 13 September 1996, 26 (for *Peacemaker*); "Film Production Chart," *Daily Variety*, 14 February 1997, 21 (for *Amistad* and *Mousehunt*).

139. Evans and Brodie, "Miramax, Mouse Go for 7 More," 29.

140. Corliss, "Independents' Day."

141. Cox and Roman, "Hopeful Harvey Preps His Act II."

142. Ibid.

Chapter 7

1. Adam Mayers, "Brokerage Whiz Kid Aims to Take on Tinseltown," *Toronto Star*, 5 September 1997, E1.

2. Monica Roman and Benedict Carver, "Ya Gotta Have Art: Indies Hike Output as Studios Scratch for Niches," *Variety*, 4–10 May 1998, 1, 103.

3. Thom Geier, "Indies Melt Down: Press and Product Get Blame," *Hollywood Reporter*, 10 September 1998, retrieved 22 June 2011 from the LexisNexis database, http://www.lexisnexis.com/.

4. These figures come from ACNielsen EDI, as reported in James Bates, "Big Profits Raise Profile of the 'Small Movie,'" *Los Angeles Times*, 23 March 1998, A1.

5. Both *The House of Yes* and *Next Stop Wonderland* generated a lot of press as a result of the high acquisition prices paid for them. *House of Yes* earned a little more than $600,000 at the box office, while *Next Stop Wonderland* barely broke $3 million. Figures retrieved 22 June 2011 from http://www.boxoffice.com/.

6. At the 1999 ceremony, Miramax took home its sixth screenplay award in seven years, a run that began with *The Crying Game* in 1993. In addition, *Shakespeare in Love's* Judi Dench became the fifth supporting actress win for Miramax in six years.

7. Daniel Lyons, "The Odd Couple," *Fortune*, 22 March 1999, 1. Another source reported that Miramax earned $100 million in 1998, compared to $18.1 million in 1994. These numbers came out during the course of Jeffrey Katzenberg's lawsuit against Disney. See Janet Shprintz and Martin Peers, "Disney Feels Katz Claws: Trial Could Trigger Further Fiscal Fisticuffs," *Variety*, 10–16 May 1999, 1, 44.

8. "Miramax, *Life Is Beautiful*, and the Indiewoodization of the Foreign-Language Film Market in the USA," *New Review of Film and Television Studies* 7, no. 4 (December 2009): 353–375.

9. This 5 percent figure is the one repeatedly cited; for example, see Leonard Klady, "Summer Drought Hits Specialized Fare," *Variety*, 9–15 June 1997, 7, 14; Jennifer Nix, "Indies Make Big Book Mark," *Variety*, 18–24 May 1998, 1, 89; Leonard Klady, "New Fix for Art Pix: Niche Houses Court Younger Audience," *Variety*, 28 September 1998, 1, 63. In "Summer Drought Hits Specialized Fare," Klady writes, "True specialized fare—pictures that play on a limited number of screens and have genuinely upscale appeal—has comprised about 5% of ticket sales for at least four decades. That should translate into $100 million during the current summer season. But it won't" (14).

10. Bates, "Big Profits Raise Profile of the 'Small' Movie."

11. Ibid. As Bates also notes, most films did less than $3 million at the box office.

12. Andrew Hindes, "Wave of Fiscal Woes Beaches Mart," *Variety*, 9–15 March 1998, 9, 14; Andrew Hindes, "Arthouses Face Empty Seats: Crowded Sked, High Costs Kill B.O.," *Variety*, 13–19 July 1998, 7.

13. Geier, "Indies Melt Down."

14. For example, see Adam Dawtrey and Dan Cox, "Indies Fasten Their Seatbelts," *Variety*, 27 October–2 November 1997, 9, 14; Monica Roman, "Indie Financing Hits Hurdles," *Daily Variety*, 21 September 1998, 16; Leonard Klady, "Niche Pix Rebuild Platform Planks," *Variety*, 9–15 November 1998, 5, 13.

15. Monica Roman and Benedict Carver, "Ya Gotta Have Art: Indies Hike Output as Studios Scratch for Niches," *Variety*, 4–10 May 1998, 1, 103.

16. Ibid., 103.

17. As an example of how unexpected this hit was, a preview of notable fall films in *Variety* in mid-October did not mention *Good Will Hunting* in the text (only listing it as one of the nearly fifty upcoming holiday releases). See Leonard Klady, "Studios Sharpen Santa Claws," *Variety*, 13–19 October 1997, 1, 108. Budget reported in Robert Dominguez, "Taking It to the Miramax," *New York Daily News*, 10 March 1998, 27. Figures retrieved 22 June 2011 from http://www.boxoffice.com/.

18. Dominguez, "Taking It to the Miramax," 27.

19. The story behind the film's development has generated some controversy. There has been debate about the extent to which the script was ghostwritten or doctored. Also, Affleck and Damon were not quite the "discoveries" that the publicity portrayed them to be: each had been building a solid resume in the business for several years before *Good Will Hunting* appeared in theaters.

20. Three seasons of this program aired, the first two on HBO and the last on Bravo.

21. "'Life' Finds Beautiful B.O.," *Variety*, 29 March–4 April 1999, 14.

22. "American Moviegoers Shunning Foreign Fare," *Hollywood Reporter*, 1 September 1992, I1.

23. "Breakthrough" label from Lawrence Cohn, "'Mediterraneo': '92's Most Moneyed Import," *Variety*, 11 January 1993, 63. The 0.75 percent figure comes from Leonard Klady, "Disney Takes 'Lion's' Share of '94 Boffo B.O.," *Variety*, 9–15 January 1995, 13, 20.

24. Leonard Klady, "Legions of Foreign-Lingo Pix Colonize Small Market Niche," *Variety*, 29 April–5 May 1996, 11, 27.

25. Ibid., 27.

26. Paul Gachot, "Stepping Stone: Non-English Nom Can Mean B.O. Gold," *Variety: Eye on the Oscars Special Section*, 21–27 December 1998, 41–42.

27. For a discussion of the globalization of Hollywood from the 1970s onward, see Toby Miller, Nitin Govil, John McMurria, and Richard Maxwell, eds., *Global Hollywood* (London: BFI, 2001). See also Tino Balio, "'A Major Presence in All the World's Important Markets': The Globalization of Hollywood in the 1990s," in *Contemporary Hollywood Cinema*, ed. Steve Neale and Murray Smith (London: Routledge, 1998), 58–73.

28. Frederick Wasser, "Is Hollywood America? The Trans-nationalization of the American Film Industry," *Critical Studies in Mass Communication* 12, no. 4 (1995): 423–437.

29. Michael Curtin, "Thinking Globally: From Media Imperialism to Media Capital," in *Media Industries: History, Theory, and Method*, ed. Jennifer Holt and Alisa Perren (Malden, MA: Wiley-Blackwell, 2009), 108–119.

30. Miramax placed a full-page "for your consideration" ad for *Il Postino* in the 1 January 1996 *Variety* in which the company declared, "Despite such unanimous acclaim, 'The Postman' is ineligible for Oscar consideration as Best Foreign Language Film because of one technicality—it was directed by an Englishman" (2). Thus, the company argued, the film needed to be celebrated for other awards, such as Best Actor, Best Director, Best Original Screenplay, and Best Picture.

31. Even Chan and Woo's films received only a limited theatrical release. Much of their popularity was gained through video distribution in the United States.

32. Though Miramax made some preliminary efforts to distribute Asian cinema in the United States during the 1990s, it accelerated its efforts after the success of *Crouching Tiger, Hidden Dragon* (which was distributed by SPC). See Lisa Dombrowski, "Miramax's Asian Experiment: Creating a Model for Crossover Hits," *Scope* 10 (February 2008), accessed 22 July 2008, *http://www.scope.nottingham.ac.uk/article.php?issue=10&id=988*.

33. Drawing from James English, Paul McDonald frames his discussion of foreign-language imports in terms of an "economy of prestige." According to McDonald, "Awards become a kind of currency in the specialty market, a tangible form of exchange which represents value." "Miramax, *Life Is Beautiful*, and the Indiewoodization of the Foreign-Language Film Market in the USA," 359–360.

34. Leonard Klady, "When Oscar Talks, the B.O. Listens," *Variety*, 4–10 April 1994, 7, 18.

35. See, for instance, "U.S. Imports: A Long Way Down from the '60s," *Variety*, 2 May 1990, S56. In one *Los Angeles Times* interview, October Films copresident Bingham Ray observed that "the subject matter of foreign films has been usurped by the American independents. The sexual frankness and aesthetic daring of foreign movies gave them an edge back in the '60s and '70s compared to American fare. But over the past decade, starting with breakout American independent hits like *sex, lies, and videotape* (1989), low-budget American movies (as well as British and Australian ones) have been

as daring—and sometimes more so—than foreign films, both in terms of content and style. These are the films that are likely to cross over into theaters in upscale suburban areas, some of which are hesitant to book anything but the most popular foreign titles." Richard Natale, "Subtitled Films Gaining in Fight for Share of Big-Screen Spotlight," *Los Angeles Times*, 8 January 1999, F2.

36. Peter Bart, "Oscar Snubs," *Variety*, 3 February 1992, 5, 9.

37. "American Moviegoers Shunning Foreign Fare."

38. Ibid., 11.

39. One version of this argument is offered in Miller et al., *Global Hollywood*.

40. Data from various issues of *Variety*, as well as "Foreign Language," *Box Office Mojo*, accessed 28 February 2011, http://www.boxofficemojo.com/genres/chart/?id=foreign.htm.

41. In his interview with Eugene Hernandez for *indieWIRE*, Bernard spoke of his respect for many 1980s-era filmmakers. From his perspective, the ability in the 1990s to make movies much more easily had led to a glut of subpar material: "So maybe you're someone that's got a script and you've got an uncle that's going to give you a million bucks, all of a sudden you have a movie that has great technical qualities, whereas in the 80's it was a much more interesting person who made an independent film, because not only did they have to find a good story, they had to really work their way through the production of it with really amateur technicians or actually take over a lot of those roles. . . . So I think you really had to be a determined person to make a movie in that time period. Whereas what I think has happened now is there's way too many movies with not much to say." Eugene Hernandez, "DECADE: Michael Barker and Tom Bernard—Another Ten Years in the Classics World, Part 2," *indieWIRE*, 1 December 1999, accessed 23 June 2011, http://www.indiewire.com/article/decade_michael_barker_tom_bernard_—_another_ten_years_in_the_classics_world/.

42. For a discussion of SPC, see Monica Roman and Andrew Hindes, "Classic Formula: But Sony Arthouse Arm Faces Friction," *Variety*, 3–9 August 1998, 7, 11. See also Leonard Klady, "Paucity of Pix Leaves Arthouse in Outhouse," *Variety*, 30 October–5 November 1995, 17, 24.

43. Eugene Hernandez, "DECADE: Michael Barker and Tom Bernard—Another Ten Years in the Classics World, Parts 1 and 2," *indieWIRE*, 20 December 1999, accessed 23 June 2011, http://www.indiewire.com/article/decade_michael_barker_tom_bernard_-_another_ten_years_in_the_classics_world/.

44. Ibid.

45. Roman and Hindes, "Classic Formula," 11.

46. It is unlikely that as many East Asian films would have been released theatrically in the United States during the 1990s were it not for the Tokyo-based Sony's interest.

47. Hernandez, "DECADE: Michael Barker and Tom Bernard—Another Ten Years in the Classics World, Part 2."

48. SPC releases, like those at the other indie companies, continued to reap profits for Sony in various aftermarkets such as video and cable after their theatrical release.

49. See, for example, Greg Evans, "Miramax Looks Ahead for Hits," *Daily Variety*, 4 January 1996, 34, 36.

50. For a discussion of Miramax's global strategies, see Adam Dawtrey, "Miramax Gets Global: Deals in Japan, Italy Part of 'Full-Service' Tack," *Daily Variety*, 28 February 1998, 1, 39; Rex Weiner, "Miramax Aims for China," *Daily Variety*, 7 March 1996, 1, 86; "Miramax Films to Fund New London-Based Firm," *Wall Street Journal*, 28 October 1997, B2; Adam Dawtrey, "Miracle at Miramax: Weinsteins Pull Off a Coup in London," *Variety*, 3–9 November 1997, 7, 8.

51. Miramax International was launched prior to Miramax's purchase by Disney but was significantly expanded after that deal was completed. For the announcement of the division's launch, see Jeffrey Jolson-Colburn, "Miramax Bows Int'l Sales Unit," *Hollywood Reporter*, 12 May 1992, retrieved 14 June 2010 from the LexisNexis database, http://www.lexisnexis.com/. See also Benedict Carver, "Miramax Intl. Inks Pacts, Adds Partners," *Variety*, 15–21 June 1998, 12.

52. Cesare Petrillo of *Variety* declared Tornatore "arguably the most powerful director in Italy and one of the few able to get expensive projects greenlighted by producers." See "Boffo Box Office Not a Given for Fest Winners," *Variety: Cannes Special Section*, 10 May 1993, C6.

53. McDonald, "Miramax, *Life Is Beautiful*, and the Indiewoodization of the Foreign-Language Film Market in the USA," 363.

54. See ibid.; Dombrowski, "Miramax's Asian Experiment."

55. Monica Roman, "'Life Is Beautiful' for Miramax," *Variety*, 23 February–1 March 1998, 38; David Rooney, "Native Films Top Italo B.O," *Daily Variety*, 28 January 1998, 14.

56. Roman, "'Life Is Beautiful' for Miramax," 38. *Titanic* label in Claudia Puig, "Foreign Films' Softer Side: Sensuality Is Out, Sentimentality Is In, Especially This Year," *USA Today*, 3 March 1999, 1D.

57. Roman, "'Life Is Beautiful' for Miramax."

58. Monica Roman, "Miramax Wraps 'Life' Deal," *Daily Variety*, 17 February 1998, 23; italics added.

59. Gachot, "Stepping Stone," 42.

60. Puig, "Foreign Films' Softer Side," 1D.

61. Ibid.

62. In one of the earlier examples, Miramax demanded extensive cuts and reediting of *Cinema Paradiso*. The "director's cut" ran more than fifty minutes longer than the version released in the United States in 1990.

63. Roger Ebert, "No-Holds Harvey; Miramax Exec Has More Bluster for Hollywood," *Chicago Sun-Times*, 18 May 1999, 37.

64. Ibid.

65. According to numerous reports, the film received a ten-minute standing ovation at its Cannes screening. For example, see discussion in Robert Ebert, "Daring Holocaust Comedy Is Controversial Hit," *Calgary Herald*, 20 May 1998, F5; Laura Winters, "An Indie Race at Film's Grand Prix," *Washington Post*, 24 May 1998, G4. Benigni provided one of his many over-the-top responses to the announcement at Cannes. *Variety* wrote of Benigni's dramatic acceptance, in which he went springing "to the stage, pick[ing] up the petite master of ceremonies, Isabelle Huppert, and [spinning] her around, lay[ing] prostrate at the feet of Scorsese, then proceed[ing] to kiss every member of the jury while shouting with glee." Todd McCarthy, "Angelopoulos 'Eternity' Takes Cannes Fest's Palme d'Or," *Variety*, 1–7 June 1998, 9. Ebert reported "cries of 'bravo!' rolling like waves across the auditorium"; Harlan Jacobson of *USA Today* heard one eager fan shouting, "You are Chaplin—better than Chaplin." "Benigni's 'Life' Stirs Passions," *USA Today*, 19 May 1998, 8B.

66. Richard Schickel of *Time* provided one of the most pointed attacks of the film: "Turning even a small corner of this century's central horror into feel-good popular entertainment is abhorrent. Sentimentality is a kind of fascism, too, robbing us of judgment and moral acuity, and it needs to be resisted. *Life Is Beautiful* is a good place to start." "Fascist Fable," *Time*, 9 November 1998, accessed 24 June 2011, http://www.time.com/time/magazine/article/0,9171,989504,00.html.

67. Favorable reactions to *Life Is Beautiful* can be found in Kenneth Turan, "The Improbable Success of 'Life Is Beautiful,'" *Los Angeles Times*, 23 October 1998, F1; Janet Maslin, "Giving a Human (and Humorous) Face to Rearing a Boy Under Fascism," *New York Times*, 23 October 1998, E1; Roger Ebert, "Playing the Role of His 'Life': Benigni Adds Humor, Humanity," *Chicago Sun-Times*, 30 October 1998, 31. More negative reactions can be found in David Sterritt, "'Life Is Beautiful': Too Heavy for Heavy Subject Matter?," *Christian Science Monitor*, 30 October 1998, B3; J. Hoberman, "Nazi Business," *Village Voice*, 27 October 1998, 135; Owen Glieberman, "Happy Camper; In the Bold—or Maybe Foolish—*Life Is Beautiful*, Roberto Benigni Sweets the Evils of the Holocaust," *Entertainment Weekly*, 6 November 1998, 54.

68. See, for example, Bob Ivry, "Tragic Clown; In 'Life Is Beautiful,' Roberto Benigni Moves from Slapstick to Fable, and Tells a Heartbreaking Story of the Holocaust," *Bergen (NJ) Record*, 18 October 1998, Y1; Daniel Kotzin, "A Clown in the Camps," *Jerusalem Report*, 26 October 1998, 40; Dana Thomas and Corie Brown, "The Death-Camp Game," *Newsweek*, 1 June 1998, 59.

69. Natale, "Subtitled Films Gaining in Fight for Share of Big-Screen Spotlight."

70. Klady, "Niche Pix Rebuild Platform Planks." Screen count from "Life Is Beautiful," *Box Office Mojo*, accessed 23 June 2011, http://www.boxofficemojo.com/movies/?page=weekend&id=lifeisbeautiful.htm.

71. "Chart: Specialized Pix Go Wider," *Variety*, 12–18 July 1999, 28.

72. The $171 million is for theatrical grosses outside North America. Including North American grosses, *Life Is Beautiful* earned approximately $229 million. Figures from "Life Is Beautiful," *Box Office Mojo*, accessed 23 June 2011, http://www.boxofficemojo.com/movies/?page=main&id=lifeisbeautiful.htm.

73. Roman, "Miramax Wraps 'Life' Deal," 23.

74. Benedict Carver, "Miramax Makes Chinese Debut with Benigni's 'Life,'" *Variety*, 26 July–1 August 1999, 12.

75. See Dombrowski, "Miramax's Asian Experiment."

76. Miramax International's Rick Sands described Miramax's deal with *Life Is Beautiful* as serving as a potential "model for the kinds of creative and business alliances with our family of primary distributors with whom Miramax Intl. is becoming increasingly involved." Roman, "Miramax Wraps 'Life' Deal," 23.

77. Before *Life Is Beautiful*, Costa-Gavras's *Z* (1969) was the only other film to be nominated for both Best Picture and Best Foreign-Language Film.

78. Timothy M. Gray, "Trends Are in the Details," *Variety*, 15 February 1999, 18.

79. With $48.7 million grossed in Italy, *Life Is Beautiful* overtook the former Italian box office leader, *The Cyclone* (1996), to become the highest-grossing Italian film of all time in Italy. Benedict Carver and David Rooney, "Vittorio's Gori Story: Top Italo Producer-Distribber Hits Speed Bumps," *Variety*, 21 June 1999, 93.

80. So labeled in Carrie Rickey, "'Life Is Beautiful' Hits Nerve at Cannes," *Philadelphia Enquirer*, 21 May 1998, E1; Susan Wloszczyna, "The Oscar Field of Combat," *USA Today*, 11 December 1998, 1E.

81. Greg Evans, "Miramax Looks Ahead for Hits," *Daily Variety*, 4 January 1996, 36–37.

82. Andrew Gumbel, "Tears and Joy from Death-Camp Film," *The Independent* (UK), 7 February 1999, 16.

83. McDonald, "Miramax, *Life Is Beautiful*, and the Indiewoodization of the Foreign-Language Film Market in the USA," 371.

84. Ibid., 372.

85. Ibid., 372–373.

86. "$100 Million Overseas Grossers," *Variety*, 16 August 1999, 1.

87. *Shakespeare in Love* was a coproduction with Universal Pictures. Universal had originally developed the film and then placed it in turnaround. Miramax took the film out of turnaround, but Universal retained certain rights to the project. For more backstory, see Claudia Eller, "Bard Not to Be for Savoy, U," *Daily Variety*, 23 October 1992, 1, 14; Adam Dawtrey and Monica Roman, "'Love' Triangle Times 3," *Variety*, 23–29 March 1998, 12.

88. Timothy M. Gray and Dan Cox, "Will Dark Horses Win Gold? Latecomers Press 'Ryan' in Oscar Derby," *Variety*, 4 January 1999, 1, 117. Though he did not yet know that *Shakespeare in Love* would be the film that would pose the greatest challenge to *Saving Private Ryan*, Harvey Weinstein began to jokingly attack Spielberg's film as early as August 1998. For example, one article reported that "while some consider Spielberg's *Saving Private Ryan* a shoo-in to sweep the Oscars, Harvey insists, 'Steven Spielberg is very worried.' Unlike his brother, he's not afraid to make jokes in print." Monica Roman, "Savvy Siblings Revitalize Art of the Indie Deal," *Variety: Deauville Special Section*, 31 August 1998, 85.

89. Leonard Klady, "Niche Pix Rebuild Platform Planks," *Variety*, 9–15 November 1998, 5, 13.

90. Peter Bart, "Hot Race Stokes Harvey's Hunger," *Variety*, 4–10 January 1999, 1.

91. As Richard Corliss of *Time* noted, "The irresistible rise of *Shakespeare in Love* can . . . be attributed to the quirk of an earlier award ceremony, the Golden Globes. . . . [Due to this] the combatants were now officially equal. Weinstein could declare war." "World War III for Oscar: It's a Foreign Battle for Hollywood," *Time*, 22 February 1999, 54.

92. Gray and Cox, "Will Dark Horses Win Gold?"

93. Keith Collins, "Walking Tall: Indies Stand Shoulder to Shoulder with Majors in Quest for Big Prize," *Variety: Eye on the Oscars Special Section*, 11–17 January 1999, 69.

94. Corliss, "World War III for Oscar," 54.

95. Shprintz and Peers, "Disney Feels Katz Claws"; Janet Shprintz, "Mouse Grouses over Bonus Onus: Product Value at Crux of Katzenberg Trial," *Variety*, 7–13 June 1999, 7, 14.

96. For more on the history of United Artists, see Tino Balio's *United Artists: The Company Built by the Stars* (Madison: University of Wisconsin Press, 1976); and *United Artists: The Company That Changed the Film Industry* (Madison: University of Wisconsin Press, 1987).

97. Eugene Hernandez and Mark Rabinowitz, "DECADE: Liz Manne—Understanding 'Independence' and Taking Risks, Part 2," *indieWIRE*, 1 December 1999, accessed 23 June 2011, http://www.indiewire.com/article/decade_liz_manne_—_understanding_independence_and_taking_risks_part_2/#.

98. Corliss, "World War III for Oscar," 54.

99. David Shaw, "Thumbs Up or Down on Movie Critics?," *Los Angeles Times*, 20 March 1999, A1.

100. See, for example, Richard Natale, "'Shakespeare' Ad Blitz Has 'Ryan' Returning Fire," *Los Angeles Times*, 8 March 1999, accessed 18 October 2009, http://articles.latimes.com/1999/mar/08/entertainment/ca-15060; Nikki Finke, "Much Ado About Oscar," *New York*, 15 March 1999, accessed 18 October 2009, http://nymag.com/nymetro/movies/columns/hollywood/167/.

101. *Life Is Beautiful* (and in particular Benigni) also came under attack, though not to the same extent as *Shakespeare in Love*.

102. See also Reed Johnson, "Has Success Spoiled Miramax?," *Cleveland Plain Dealer*, 17 March 1999, 1E.

103. "Miramax Fires Back," *Los Angeles Times*, 13 March 1999, F4.

104. Peter Bart, "The Bard's Big Night," *Variety*, 29 March 1999, 4.

Chapter 8

1. Peter Biskind speaks briefly of a "post-Miramax" era in the postscript for *Down and Dirty Pictures: Miramax, Sundance, and the Rise of Independent Film* (New York: Simon & Schuster, 2004), which ends with a discussion of the 2002–2003 period. But he does not elaborate on when precisely this era began, or on its exact characteristics. See p. 472.

2. Andrew Hindes and Chris Petrikin, "Getting Happy's Cost Is More Credibility Than Coin," *Variety*, 1–7 February 1999, 16.

3. Fox acquisitions executive and former Miramax employee Tony Safford told *Variety* in this same article, "I know for a fact that the movie was sold for north of $10 million. . . . But I believe Miramax must feel that such a high acquisition cost does not ultimately benefit the perception of the movie." In the same article, Miramax's Mark Gill responded, "As the entire industry knows, Tony is a disgruntled ex-Miramax employee with an ax to grind. I was in the room for the full 12 hours of negotiations, and not once did I see or hear Tony Safford. Clearly the man has a tremendous gift for imagination and spite." See Amy Wallace, "'Happy, Texas' Deal Spurs War of Words," *Los Angeles Times*, 29 January 1999, F1.

4. Hindes and Petrikin, "Getting Happy's Cost Is More Credibility Than Coin," 16.

5. "Take This Film and Shelve It," *Newsweek*, 22 February 1999, 12. As of May 1998, Miramax was estimated to have $50 million worth of unreleased films on its books, according to *Variety* in Monica Roman and Benedict Carver, "Ya Gotta Have Art," *Variety*, 4–10 May 1998, 1, 103.

6. Beverly Gray, "The Reel Deal: Miramax," *Hollywood Reporter: Indie Scene '98 Special Issue*, August 1998, 10, 12. In 1997 Miramax stated that acquisitions made up a third of its slate. See Bruce Orwall, "Disney Hopes to Cash in on Miramax Unit's Cachet," *Wall Street Journal*, 25 August 1997, B4. The target number varies from article to article, but when Miramax is placed on the defensive regarding its acquisitions, its executives tend to minimize the number of productions developed internally. For example, in December 1999 Mark Gill stated that "our ratio [of productions to acquisitions] has changed. . . . We're now about half and half. But we've reduced the number of films we release from about 47 a year when I started down to about 30. So if you want to run the numbers for a second, and let's say it's 48 for the sake of averaging, that meant that 36 films a year were getting acquired. You're now down to 30 films, half of those are acquisitions—so now it's about 15 films a year being acquired, so it's a substantial difference." Eugene Hernandez, "DECADE: Michael Barker and Tom Bernard—Another Ten Years in the Classics World, Parts 1 and 2," *indieWIRE*, 20 December 1999, accessed 23 June 2011, http://www.indiewire.com/article/decade_michael_barker_tom_bernard_-_another_ten_years_in_the_classics_world/.

7. Godfrey Cheshire, "She's All That," *Variety*, 1–7 February 1999, 55.

8. *Cop Land* (released August 1997) was the previous record holder for best opening weekend for the Miramax label, with $13.5 million. Andrew Hindes, "Teens Dig 'All That,' Rule Frame," *Daily Variety*, 1 February 1999, 1, 48.

9. According to this article, Miramax denied targeting *Scream* or *Scream 2* to viewers under the age of seventeen, and "had no comment when asked how they would respond if their marketing records were subpoenaed." Christopher Stern, "D.C. Thrusts, H'wood Parries," *Variety*, 10–16 May 1999, 46.

10. According to Jill Goldsmith and Pamela McClintock, following the FTC investigation, MPAA head Jack Valenti "got all the major studios and DreamWorks to sign off on a 12-point initiative curbing the marketing of violent, R-rated movies to kids. Early on in those negotiations, Disney's very public announcement that it would go beyond the MPAA initiative and adopt additional measures on its own drew a few barbed comments." "H'wood Bets Its Schmooze Can't Lose," *Variety*, 6 November 2000, 78. See also Pamela McClintock and Dade Hayes, "Jack's Concession Stand: Proposals to Limit Marketing to Kids May Not Mollify Pols," *Daily Variety*, 27 September 2000, 1, 25.

11. Movies now were required to have not only a rating but also a description of why they received that rating. The studios were also much more careful where and how they made trailers for R-rated films available. In addition, moviegoers under seventeen were no longer allowed into test screenings without an adult present.

12. The success of teen romantic comedies such as *She's All That* and *Can't Hardly Wait* (1998) already indicated a shift in the types of teen films being produced. The production of violent content—to teens or adults—was further diminished following 9/11.

13. Harvey Weinstein made his attitude clear in an interview with the *Hollywood Reporter* in August 1998: "Disney has given me the freedom to make the movies I want; they have let me grow. I have had to shy away from some controversial [pictures], but they have allowed me to make the other movies." Stephen Galloway, "Corporate *Jungle,*" *Hollywood Reporter: Indie Scene '98 Special Issue*, August 1998, 153.

14. It is worth noting that only a couple of weeks before the *Dogma* story broke, *Forbes* magazine ran an article that discussed at length the success of the Disney-Miramax relationship. In this article, titled "The Odd Couple," Daniel Lyons wrote about how "the Disney-Miramax marriage worked out so well." He continued, "Five years of Disney distribution and Weinstein will have made Miramax into a gold mine, with pretax profits of $125 million last year, up 18-fold in five years." "The Odd Couple: How Did the Disney-Miramax Marriage Work Out So Well?," *Forbes*, 22 March 1999, 52.

15. Benedict Carver and Oliver Jones, "Weinsteins Find Unorthodox Way 'Round 'Dogma' Dilemma," *Daily Variety*, 8 April 1999, 1, 16. Significantly, Miramax Intl. held on to the foreign rights, licensing them for overseas territories. Oliver Jones, "'Dogma' Goes to Lions Gate," *Daily Variety*, 9 September 1999, 5, 26. Precisely how much the Weinsteins spent to reacquire the rights is unclear. Initial reports placed the figures at between $10 million and $14 million. The $10 million figure comes from Carver and Jones, "Weinsteins Find Unorthodox Way 'Round 'Dogma' Dilemma." The $10 million–$14 million range comes from Kenneth Turan, "Having Faith in 'Dogma,'" *Los Angeles Times*, 22 May 1999, accessed 24 June 2011, http://articles.latimes.com/print/1999/may/22/entertainment/ca-39716. A later source, however, estimates the price at "north of $2 million." Jones, "'Dogma' Goes to Lions Gate," 5.

16. Bernard Weinraub, "Disney and Miramax Collide over Church Issues in Film," *New York Times*, 7 April 1999, C4. See also Bruce Orwall, "Miramax Co-chiefs to Buy Film That Parent Disney Won't Release," *Wall Street Journal*, 8 April 1999, B10; Eugene Hernandez, "Dispatch from IndieWood: Miramax Drops Kevin Smith's 'Dogma'; Indie Crowd Gets 'Slossed,'" *indieWIRE*, 9 April 1999, accessed 24 June 2011, http://www.indiewire.com/article/daily_briefs_dispatch_from_indiewood_—_miramax_drops_kevin_smiths_dogma_in/.

17. Weinraub, "Disney and Miramax Collide over Church Issues in Film," C4. It is likely that Disney was especially nervous because of the recent controversy between Seagram/Universal and its indie subsidiary, October Films, over the Todd Solondz–directed *Happiness* (1998). Seagram/Universal objected to the "lurid content" of the film, which included "pedophilia, violent gun slayings, masturbation and dismember-

ment of a human body." The film's North American distribution was subsequently assumed by the foreign sales company/production company Good Machine. See Dan Cox, "'Happiness' over at October Films," *Daily Variety*, 2 July 1998, 1.

18. Weinraub, "Disney and Miramax Collide over Church Issues in Film," C4; Turan, "Having Faith in 'Dogma.'"

19. Carver and Jones, "Weinsteins Find Unorthodox Way 'Round 'Dogma' Dilemma," 16.

20. Oliver Jones, "League, Miramax in 'Dogma' Dogfight," *Variety*, 21–27 June 1999, 4.

21. Ibid.

22. Todd McCarthy, "Smith Swings Oddly at Religion," *Variety*, 24–30 May 1999, 73.

23. Jones, "'Dogma' Goes to Lions Gate."

24. A full list of Lions Gate's highest-grossing films can be found at "Lionsgate All Time Box Office Results," *Box Office Mojo*, accessed 25 June 2011, http://www.boxofficemojo.com/studio/chart/?view2=allmovies&view=company&studio=lionsgate.htm.

25. Benedict Carver and Dan Cox, "October Board OKs Planned Sale to Diller," *Variety*, 5–11 April 1999; Martin Peers and Benedict Carver, "Swap Meet Feels the Heat: After Myriad Trades, Duo Must Turn Deals into $," *Variety*, 12–18 April 1999, 1, 78–79.

26. For discussion of the development of *Talk*, see Dan Cox, "Will Tina Become 'Max-ed Out?," *Variety*, 13–19 July 1998, 1, 69; Lisa Granatstein, "Hearst, Disney Talk It Up," *Mediaweek*, 15 February 1999, 4. For discussion of the Navy Yard venture, see Charles V. Bagli, "De Niro and Miramax Plan a Film Studio at the Brooklyn Navy Yard," *New York Times*, 29 April 1999, B1; David N. Herszenhorn, "De Niro and Partners Dispute Giuliani Version of Navy Yard Deal," *New York Times*, 15 October 1999, B2. For more on the MGM deal, see Benedict Carver, "The New Lion Kings: Weinstein Sibs Put Dibs on MGM's H'wood Lair," *Variety*, 12–18 July 1999, 1, 57. Information about *The Real Thing* from Cathy Dunkley, "Weinsteins Re-up at Disney," *Hollywood Reporter*, 9 May 2000, 74.

27. Miramax hit this peak in the spring of 2002, at which point it laid off 15 percent of its workforce. Laura Holson, "Miramax Films Cuts 75 Jobs After Some Recent Setbacks," *New York Times*, 16 March 2002, C1.

28. Benedict Carver and Andrew Hindes, "Mini-Majors Get Maxi Clout," *Variety*, 7–13 June 1999, 1, 54.

29. These contracts were to run through 2007. Dan Cox, "Miramax Climax: Weinsteins Reup with Disney," *Variety*, 8–14 May 2000, 4.

30. Dunkley, "Weinsteins Re-up at Disney."

31. Jonathan Bing and Elizabeth Guider, "Messier: Viv U Now 'Tier One' Conglom," *Daily Variety*, 19 December 2001, 1, 30.

32. Dana Harris and Carl DiOrio, "Good Machine Buy Alters Focus at U," *Daily Variety*, 3 May 2002, 1, 35.

33. Among those interviewed were Strand's Marcus Hu and Jon Gerrans, recently departed October cofounder Bingham Ray, producer's representative John Pierson, SPC cofounders Michael Barker and Tom Bernard, producer Christine Vachon, Sundance Film Festival codirector Geoff Gilmore, and Miramax president Mark Gill. The interviews were run throughout December 1999, and all can be retrieved from http://www.indiewire.com/.

34. Hernandez, "DECADE: Michael Barker and Tom Bernard—Another Ten Years in the Classics World, Parts 1 and 2."

35. Ibid. "IndieWood" first appeared in the publication as a label given by the filmmaker Sarah Jacobson, as reported in Eugene Hernandez, "Hello Cleveland!," *indieWIRE*, 7 April 1998, accessed 17 June 2011, http://www.indiewire.com/article/

hello_cleveland_a_report_from_the_first_midwest_filmmakers_conference/. The label first appears in *Variety* in July 1998; see Monica Roman, "Welcome to Indiewood: October Buy Signals New Era for Rocky Specialty Biz," *Daily Variety: The Independents Stand-Alone Issue*, 16 July 1998, 15.

36. Christian Moerk and Claude Brodesser, "Classic Startup: Par's Niche Division Builds from Slow Start," *Variety*, 29 November–5 December 1999, 7, 16.

37. Bill Higgins and Chris Petrikin, "New Pride for Lion: UA to Become MGM Specialty Unit; Doran Gets Deal," *Variety*, 14–20 June 1999, 5–6. MGM's first foray into the specialty business had been the reinvention of Samuel Goldwyn as a specialty division in the fall of 1997. See Rex Weiner, "Going for the Goldwyn, Again: Rivals Playing Name Game as Mogul Mounts New Venture," *Variety*, 6–12 October 1997, 9, 12.

38. Dan Cox, "Sony Dusts off Screen Gems," *Variety*, 14–20 December 1998, 19.

39. According to Benedict Carver, New Line "assumed Miramax's option, and, for about $10 million, reimbursed Miramax for all of its development and research costs." New Line also procured from Miramax the prequel rights for *The Hobbit*, which is due out in 2012. "Alliance of Rivals Lord over 'Rings,'" *Variety*, 31 August–6 September 1998, 11, 20.

40. Ibid., 11; Michael Fleming, "Helmer Scales 'Mountains,'" *Daily Variety*, 26 March 2002, 1, 27.

41. James B. Stewart, *DisneyWar* (New York: Simon & Schuster, 2006), 303–304, 530.

42. "Bigger B.O. for Limited Pix," *Variety*, 10–16 May 1999, 47.

43. Leonard Klady, "Indies Vie for Summer Toehold," *Variety*, 3–9 May 1999, 11, 14.

44. Ibid., 11.

45. Leonard Klady does note that "more films than ever are grossing in excess of $5 million, the money mark for hit status in niche play. However, unless one has a crossover success, it's rare for even the most potent American indie or upscale foreign picture to milk more than $10 million from the sector's screens." "Niche Pix at Midlife Crisis," *Variety*, 2–8 August 1999, 16.

46. The summer of 1999 marked a key turning point for the DVD business, a fact signaled by both Disney's decision to release the first of its classic titles, *Pinocchio* (1940), and the impressive DVD sales of *Titanic* (1997). Shortly thereafter, Blockbuster announced that it would substantially expand its stock of DVDs. Paul Sweeting, "Hungry Mouse Puts Toons on DVD Plate," *Variety*, 23–29 August 1999, 18, 26; Marc Graser, "'Titanic' DVD Sinks Record," *Variety*, 30 August–5 September 1999, 16. As of late August, Fox Home Video had shipped one million units of *Titanic* to retailers. For a discussion of Blockbuster, see Peter Bart, "Foibles of a Futurist," *Variety*, 18–24 October 1999, 4, 57.

47. Benedict Carver, "Indies Throw Cash at Pix Stash," *Variety*, 5 October 1998, 7, 10.

48. Venture capital was flowing into a variety of start-up enterprises throughout 1999 in anticipation of the day when content could be viewed online. Yahoo! Broadcast Services, AtomFilms, iFilm, DEN, Broadcast.com, and Pop.com were among the entities either in business or soon to launch as sites for accessing moving images. As noted by Martin Peers, this was the time when "Wall Street's mania for the Internet . . . infected the showbiz sector, sending entertainment company stocks into orbit." "Showbiz Exex Gird for Nerds," *Variety*, 25–31 January 1999, 1. See also Marc Graser, "Pop Stakes Online Reel Estate: D'Works, Imagine up Netcasting Profile," *Variety*, 1–7 November 1999, 7, 12.

49. Andrew Hindes, "Small Pix Perplex Big Studios: Distribs Flunk Marketing Test on Low-Budgeters," *Variety*, 31 May 1999, 8.

50. See Benedict Carver and Chris Petrikin, "WMA Indie Film Division to Fly Solo," *Daily Variety*, 12 August 1998, 1, 22; Benedict Carver, "Aguero, Endeavor Go Indie,"

Daily Variety, 24 August 1998, 1, 10; Leonard Klady, "New Fix for Art Pix: Niche Houses Court Younger Viewers," *Variety*, 28 September–4 October 1998, 1, 64.

51. As Sarah L. Higley and Jeffrey Andrew Weinstock note, the precise budget remains a matter of much dispute. See "Introduction: The Blair Witch Controversies," in *Nothing That Is: Millennial Cinema and the Blair Witch Controversies*, ed. Sarah L. Higley and Jeffrey A. Weinstock (Detroit: Wayne State University Press, 2004), 16.

52. The Higley and Weinstock collection is one of many indications of this.

53. Completion costs are the costs involved in mastering the sound and image during the postproduction phase of a project in order to get the film in appropriate shape for theatrical distribution. Everything from paying for quality transfers from videotape to higher-resolution film/video to covering the cost of hiring a composer/orchestra can be part of the completion costs. Filmmakers often fail to factor these figures into budgets and marketers/studios often downplay these costs when discussing films with the press.

54. "The Blair Witch Project," *The Numbers*, accessed 28 March 2010, *http://www.the-numbers.com/movies/1999/BLAIR.php*. The most commonly cited budget is $35,000. Artisan spent millions more on marketing.

55. Carver and Hindes, "Mini-Majors Get Maxi Clout," 54.

56. See, for example, Charles Lyons and Timothy M. Gray, "Spooked by 'Witch': Low-Budget Pic Turns Studio Mind-Set Upside Down," *Variety*, 9–15 August 1999, 7–8; Claudia Puig, "The Legacy of 'Blair Witch': With a Spin of the Web, a Hit Is Born," *USA Today*, 17 August 1999, 1D.

57. See, for example, Henry Jenkins, *Convergence Culture: Where Old and New Media Collide* (New York: New York University Press, 2006).

58. Puig, "The Legacy of 'Blair Witch.'" The site remains archived at http://www.blairwitch.com/main.html, accessed 24 June 2011.

59. For an example of discussion of *Blair Witch* in the trade papers, see Lyons and Gray, "Spooked by 'Witch.'"

60. Higley and Weinstock explore the film's roots in "Introduction: The Blair Witch Controversies," 22–27.

61. Artisan is notable not only for its release of *The Blair Witch Project*, but also because it was one of the first companies to experiment with showing a recent feature film online. In the spring of 1999, Artisan struck a deal with Sightsound.com in which it licensed the 1998 Darren Aronofsky feature *Pi* for streaming for a thirty-day window. The experiment was a stunning failure, as only about one hundred people viewed the film. This event led *Variety*'s Marc Graser to declare that "the future of mass audiences viewing entire pics online looks grim." Of course, dial-up was still the predominant means by which most people accessed the Internet during this time, constraining the ability to download video content efficiently. See Marc Graser, "B'cast.com, O'Seas Link for 'Netcast," *Variety*, 26 July 1999, 10.

62. Jonathan Bing, "Indie Overachievers Facing Dicey Days," *Variety*, 25 June–8 July 2001, 9, 14.

63. Dan Cox and Jill Goldsmith, "Can Artisan Spread 'Blair' Flair?," *Variety*, 27 March 2000, 1, 78.

64. Occasionally, nearly a decade later, other companies had hits with similar found footage–style horror films; *Cloverfield* (Paramount, 2008), *Quarantine* (Screen Gems, 2008), *Paranormal Activity* (Paramount/DreamWorks, 2009), and *The Last Exorcism* (Lions Gate, 2010) are key examples. The most financially successful of these films were supported with extensive marketing money from media conglomerates. Further, few of these films were produced for the low cost of *The Blair Witch Project* (e.g., *Clo-*

verfield was produced for $25 million, *Quarantine* for $12 million). In addition, press coverage and promotional materials called attention to these films' connections to key creative figures (e.g., J.J. Abrams with *Cloverfield*, Steven Spielberg with *Paranormal Activity*, Eli Roth with *The Last Exorcism*). Found footage films lacking in this type of corporate backing tended to attract limited media coverage—and minimal income at the box office (e.g., *August Underground's Mordum*, 2003). Financial data retrieved 25 June 2011 from http://www.boxoffice.com/.

65. The argument could be made that *Blair Witch* was well ahead of its time, especially in terms of its online extensions. It would take several years for its innovative transmedia storytelling and marketing strategies to begin to be replicated. See Jenkins, *Convergence Culture*, for more examples of transmedia storytelling and marketing.

66. The next tier of "true independents" included Arrow, Strand, Zeitgeist, and First Look. Most of their releases went out to only a handful of screens and earned well under $1 million at the box office.

67. In what would become an all-too-familiar tale for the Weinsteins in the ensuing years, Miramax reportedly wished to acquire Artisan's library as well, but Michael Eisner prohibited the company from doing so. Ian Mohr, "Band of Brothers: Part 2; Weinsteins and Disney Finalize Divorce, Part 2," *Daily Variety*, 30 March 2005, 1, 12.

68. Edward Guthmann, "Oscar Preview: The Pride of Lions Gate," *San Francisco Chronicle*, 14 March 1999, 39.

69. Pamela McClintock, "Extreme Makeover: Indie Studio Strikes up the Brand," *Daily Variety*, 16 December 2005, 5, 65.

70. Denise Martin, "Lean Lionsgate Roars Louder," *Variety*, 2 October 2006, 25, 139.

71. For discussion of the growing Disney-Miramax conflicts, see Sharon Waxman and Laura Holson, "The Split Between Disney and Miramax Gets a Little Wider," *New York Times*, 7 June 2004, C3; David Rooney, "The Brothers Grim: Weinsteins Bridle at Disney Dictates," *Variety*, 14–20 June 2004, 1, 57–58; Michael McCarthy, "Eisner Issues Tough Words for Miramax," *USA Today*, 25 June 2004, 2B; Sean Smith, "Life Isn't Beautiful," *Newsweek*, 11 October 2004, 54–55.

72. Mohr, "Band of Brothers."

73. *Spy Kids 4: All the Time in the World* was released by Dimension Films (now owned by the Weinstein Company) in August 2011.

74. Denise Martin, "'Runway' a Runaway Hit for Bravo," *Daily Variety*, 25 February 2005, 7, 18.

75. A fourth *Scary Movie* film was produced following the Disney divorce, as a joint venture between Disney's Miramax and the Weinstein Company's Dimension.

76. See, for example, McCarthy, "Eisner Issues Tough Words"; Smith, "Life Isn't Beautiful"; Mark Harris, "Breaking up Is Hard to Do," *Entertainment Weekly*, 18 March 2005, 19. The Weinsteins challenged such claims. According to David Rooney, they insisted that Miramax "was profitable four of the five" years alluded to by Eisner. But, as Rooney continues, "while those numbers were calculated according to Disney accounting methods, the Mouse counters that Miramax's numbers don't include such factors as distribution fees and the Weinsteins' salaries." See "Brothers Grim," 57.

77. Holson, "Miramax Films Cuts 75 Jobs After Some Recent Setbacks"; Laura Holson and Rick Lyman, "Miramax's Big Screen Test: More Than Ever, Harvey Weinstein Needs Holiday Hits," *New York Times*, 4 November 2002, C2.

78. For example, Eisner's battles with the Weinsteins over costs are noted in Laura Holson, "Surviving at Disney, Eisner Faces Difficult Year," *New York Times*, 17 March 2003, C1.

79. Sharon Waxman, "Bitter Parting Words from a Disney," *New York Times*, 2 December 2003, C8.

80. Laura Holson and Sharon Waxman, "Criticism of Disney Chief Grows Bolder," *New York Times*, 8 December 2003, C1.

81. Stewart, *DisneyWar*, 519–520; Laura Holson and Sharon Waxman, "The Split Between Disney and Miramax Gets a Little Wider," *New York Times*, 7 June 2004, C1.

82. Notably, at the same time that the *Dogma* controversy took place, the Weinsteins were involved in contract negotiations with Disney. Yet publicly, at least, relations were harmonious at this time. For example, see discussion in Lyons, "Odd Couple."

83. Laura Holson charts the breakdown of relations between Disney and the Weinsteins in "How the Tumultuous Marriage of Miramax and Disney Failed," *New York Times*, 6 March 2005, 1.

84. Rooney, "Brothers Grim."

85. Ibid.

86. "A Mouse Minus Miramax? Pic Partners Ponder Prospects as Eisner and Weinstein Haggle," *Variety*, 19–25 July 2004, 5.

87. Michael McCarthy, "Disney Strips Chairmanship from Eisner," *USA Today*, 4 March 2004, 1B.

88. Holson, "Pixar, Creator of 'Finding Nemo,' Sees End to Its Disney Partnership," *New York Times*, 30 January 2004, A1.

89. A year before his resignation, in March 2004, Eisner was stripped of his status as a board member, a position he had held since 1984. See "A New Mouseketeer," *The Economist*, 19 March 2005, 71.

90. Ray Bennett and Chad Williams, "Dis, Weinsteins Finalize Separation," *Hollywood Reporter*, 5 April 2005, 59.

91. The number of titles reported to be in the library varies from six hundred to eight hundred, depending on the source. Eight hundred is the number reported in Harris, "Breaking up Is Hard to Do." When Disney placed Miramax for sale in 2010, the number reported dropped substantially. Seven hundred was the number given by Brook Barnes and Michael Cieply in "Weinstein Brothers Said to Be Near Deal to Buy Miramax from Disney," *New York Times*, 16 April 2010, accessed 7 July 2010, http://www.nytimes.com/2010/04/17/business/media/17miramax.html?_r=1&partner=rss&emc=rss. Anne Thompson identified the number as six hundred and eleven in "Miramax Going Forward: What Will Happen?," *Thompson on Hollywood*, 9 July 2010, accessed 24 June 2011, http://blogs.indiewire.com/thompsononhollywood/2010/07/09/miramax_going_forward_what_will_happen/.

92. Bennett and Williams, "Dis, Weinsteins Finalize Separation." This figure did not include the amount deducted due to their decision to take certain titles with them.

93. Ronald Grover, "A Hollywood Split's Shrunken Assets," *Businessweek*, 9 March 2005, retrieved from Academic Search Complete.

94. Ian Mohr, "Going for the Max: Disney Opts for Miramax While Harvey Maxes Up," *Variety*, 3–9 March 2005, 1, 77.

95. Bennett and Williams, "Dis, Weinsteins Finalize Separation."

96. For example, see Rooney, "Brothers Grim"; McCarthy, "Eisner Issues Tough Words"; "A Mouse Minus Miramax?," *Variety*, 19 July 2004, 5. The division's value depreciated substantially by the time it was sold in 2010. See Dawn C. Chmielewski and Ben Fritz, "Disney Reaches Agreement in Principle to Sell to Ron Tutor–led Group," *Los Angeles Times*, 8 July 2010, accessed 12 July 2010, http://latimesblogs.latimes.com/entertainmentnewsbuzz/2010/07/disney-reaches-agreement-in-principal-to-sell-miramax-to-ron-tutor.html.

97. Paul Bond, "Smaller Battle for Dis?," *Hollywood Reporter*, 5 April 2005, 15; Mohr, "Going for the Max."

98. Harris, "Breaking up Is Hard to Do," 22.

99. Owen Gleiberman, "Why Miramax Mattered: A Critical Appreciation," *Entertainment Weekly*, 18 March 2005, 23.

100. Beginning in the mid-2000s, tier 3 independents began to experiment more aggressively with new modes of distribution. As theatrical distribution became less desirable and possible, companies such as IFC and Magnolia began "premiering" their product through video-on-demand services offered by cable operators and online retailers such as Amazon. As of this writing, however, the income from these platforms has been seen as too negligible to be of value for the conglomerates' film subsidiaries. For a survey of early online distribution efforts by both independents and studios, see Alisa Perren, "Business as Unusual: Conglomerate-Sized Challenges for Film and Television in the Digital Arena," *Journal of Popular Film and Television* 38, no. 2 (Summer 2010): 72–78. In addition, for a discussion of independent distribution in the "post-Miramax" era, see Chuck Tryon, *Reinventing Cinema: Movies in the Age of Media Convergence* (New Brunswick, NJ: Rutgers University Press, 2009).

101. Mark Gill, "Yes, the Sky Really Is Falling," *indieWIRE*, 22 June 2008, accessed 24 June 2011, http://www.indiewire.com/article/first_person_film_departments_mark_gill_yes_the_sky_really_is_falling/.

102. Time Warner created Warner Independent in 2003. Picturehouse was also a Time Warner subsidiary, launched as a joint venture by the company's New Line and HBO divisions. Paramount Vantage replaced Paramount Classics in 2006. All three indie subsidiaries were closed in 2008. See Cathy Dunkley and Jonathan Bing, "Classics Click at WB," *Daily Variety*, 8 August 2003, 1, 17; Dana Harris, "Picturehouse Unveiled with Exex, 9-Pic Slate," *Daily Variety*, 16 May 2005, 18; Pamela McClintock, "Par Takes New Vantage Point," *Daily Variety*, 19 May 2006, 5.

103. David Teather, "Last Reel for Miramax as Disney Closes Studio," *The Guardian* (London), 29 January 2010, accessed 28 February 2011, http://www.guardian.co.uk/business/2010/jan/29/weinsteins-miramax-studio-closed-disney.

104. Marc Graser and Rachel Abrams, "Ron Tutor Closes Miramax Deal," *Daily Variety*, 3 December 2010, accessed 28 February 2011, http://www.variety.com/article/VR11 18028439?refCatId=18&query=ron+tutor+closes+miramax+deal.

105. During its first several months under new ownership, Miramax repeatedly indicated that its top priority was exploiting its library. Early announcements involved the company's licensing of streaming rights to both Netflix and Hulu in the United States. Miramax also partnered with Lions Gate and StudioCanal to distribute 550 of its titles on DVD, video-on-demand, and electronic sell-through in Europe. The new owners seemed far less interested in financing or acquiring new productions; any fresh content would come from developing sequels or television series built off existing franchises. For example, late in 2010, Miramax announced that it would partner with the Weinstein Company to produce sequels to existing properties such as *Bad Santa*, *Rounders*, and *Shakespeare in Love*. Its investment amounted to a 5 percent gross stake. As this book goes to press, these projects have not moved beyond the development phase. See "Miramax and Hulu Announce Multi-year Agreement," *Miramax: Press*, 1 June 2011, retrieved 24 June 2011 from http://www.miramax.com/press/; Dylan Stableford, "Miramax, Weinstein Co. to Produce Sequels to 'Bad Santa,' 'Swingers,'" *The Wrap*, 16 December 2010, accessed 24 June 2011, http://www.thewrap.com/movies/article/miramax-weinstein-co-announce-pact-produce-sequels-23286?x=0.

106. Focus Features' fate was the topic of much speculation throughout 2010. For

example, see Claudia Eller, "Positive Cash Flow Through Hits and Misses Makes Focus Features an Attractive Asset," *Los Angeles Times*, 25 May 2010, accessed 5 June 2010, *http://articles.latimes.com/2010/may/25/business/la-fi-ct-focus-20100525*.

107. Sharon Waxman, "Weinstein Debt Wiped Clean in Deal with Goldman, Ambac," *The Wrap*, 24 June 2010, accessed 12 July 2010, http://www.thewrap.com/movies/column-post/weinstein-debt-wiped-clean-deal-goldman-ambac-18716.

108. Dimension's effort to reboot the *Scream* franchise yielded disappointing returns. The $40 million *Scream 4* opened in April 2011 and faded quickly, grossing only $38 million in its North American theatrical release. "Scream 4," *Box Office Mojo*, accessed 25 June 2011, http://www.boxofficemojo.com/movies/?id=scream4.htm.

Selected Bibliography

A wide range of newspaper and magazine articles, trade publications, press kits, and online databases were consulted during the writing of this book. The sources from which I drew most directly are cited in the chapter endnotes. The list below consists primarily of scholarly articles and book-length publications.

Andrew, Geoff. *Stranger Than Paradise: Maverick Film-Makers in Recent American Cinema.* New York: Limelight Editions, 1999.

Balio, Tino. "'A Major Presence in All the World's Important Markets': The Globalization of Hollywood in the 1990s." In *Contemporary Hollywood Cinema*, edited by Steve Neale and Murray Smith, 58–73. London: Routledge, 1998.

———. *United Artists: The Company Built by the Stars.* Madison: University of Wisconsin Press, 1976.

———. *United Artists: The Company That Changed the Film Industry.* Madison: University of Wisconsin Press, 1987.

Berra, John. *Declarations of Independence: American Cinema and the Partiality of Independent Production.* Bristol, UK: Intellect, 2008.

Biskind, Peter. *Down and Dirty Pictures: Miramax, Sundance, and the Rise of Independent Film.* New York: Simon & Schuster, 2004.

———. *Easy Riders, Raging Bulls: How the Sex-Drugs-and-Rock-'n'-Roll Generation Saved Hollywood.* New York: Touchstone, 1998.

Bourdieu, Pierre. *Distinction: A Social Critique of the Judgment of Taste.* Translated by Richard Nice. London: Routledge, 1984.

Coombs, Felicity, and Suzanne Gemmell. "Preface." In *Piano Lessons: Approaches to "The Piano,"* edited by Felicity Coombs and Suzanne Gemmell, vii–x. Sydney: John Libbey, 1999.

Curtin, Michael. "On Edge: Culture Industries in the Neo-network Era." In *Making and Selling Culture*, edited by Richard Ohmann, 181–202. Hanover, NH: Wesleyan University Press, 1996.

———. "Thinking Globally: From Media Imperialism to Media Capital." In *Media Industries: History, Theory, and Method*, edited by Jennifer Holt and Alisa Perren, 108–119. Malden, MA: Wiley-Blackwell, 2009.

Dawson, Jeff. *Quentin Tarantino: The Cinema of Cool.* New York: Applause, 1995.

Dombrowski, Lisa. "Miramax's Asian Experiment: Creating a Model for Crossover Hits." *Scope* 10 (February 2008). Accessed 22 July 2008. http://www.scope.nottingham.ac.uk/article.php?issue=10&id=988.

Eberwein, Robert. "The IFC and Sundance: Channeling Independence." In *Contemporary American Independent Film: From the Margins to the Mainstream*, edited by Chris Holmlund and Justin Wyatt, 231–247. New York: Routledge, 2005.

Epstein, Edward Jay. *The Big Picture: Money and Power in Hollywood*. New York: Random House, 2005.

Feuer, Jane, Paul Kerr, and Tise Vahimagi, eds. *MTM "Quality Television."* London: BFI, 1984.

Giles Jane. *The Crying Game*. London: BFI, 1997.

Goldman, Debra. "Business for Art's Sake." *American Film* 12, no. 6 (April 1987): 44–48.

Gomery, Douglas. *Shared Pleasures: A History of Movie Presentation in the United States*. Madison: University of Wisconsin Press, 1992.

Goodell, Gregory. *Independent Feature Film Production: A Complete Guide from Concept Through Distribution*. New York: St. Martin's Press, 1998.

Hesmondhalgh, David. *Cultural Industries*. 2nd ed. Thousand Oaks, CA: Sage, 2007.

Higley, Sarah L., and Jeffrey Andrew Weinstock. *Nothing That Is: Millennial Cinema and the Blair Witch Controversies*. Detroit: Wayne State University Press, 2004.

Hill, John. "British Cinema as National Cinema: Production, Audience, and Representation." In *The British Cinema Book*, edited by Robert Murphy, 207–212. London: BFI, 2001.

Hoberman, J. "The Non-Hollywood Hustle," *American Film* 6, no. 1 (October 1980): 54–56, 88–90.

Holmund, Christine, and Justin Wyatt. *Contemporary American Independent Film*. London: Routledge, 2005.

Holt, Jennifer. *Empires of Entertainment: Media Industries and the Politics of Deregulation, 1980–1996*. New Brunswick, NJ: Rutgers University Press, 2011.

Holt, Jennifer, and Alisa Perren, eds. *Media Industries: History, Theory, and Method*. Malden, MA: Wiley-Blackwell, 2009.

Horkheimer, Max, and Theodor Adorno. "The Culture Industry: Enlightenment as Mass Deception." In *Media and Cultural Studies: Keyworks*. 2nd ed., edited by Meenakshi Gigi Durham and Douglas Kellner, 41–72. Malden, MA: Wiley-Blackwell, 2005.

Jancovich, Mark. "'A Real Shocker': Authenticity, Genre, and the Struggle for Distinction." In *The Film Cultures Reader*, edited by Graeme Turner, 469–480. London: Routledge, 2002.

Jenkins, Henry. *Convergence Culture: Where Old and New Media Collide*. New York: New York University Press, 2006.

Karlyn, Kathleen Rowe. "'Scream,' Popular Culture, and Feminism's Third

Wave: 'I'm Not My Mother.'" *Genders Online Journal* 38 (2003). Accessed 20 June 2011. http://www.genders.org/g38/g38_rowe_karlyn.html.

Kellner, Douglas. "Media Industries, Political Economy, and Media/Cultural Studies: An Articulation." In *Media Industries: History, Theory, and Method*, edited by Jennifer Holt and Alisa Perren, 95–107. Malden, MA: Wiley-Blackwell, 2009.

Kim, Jeongmee. "The Funding and Distribution Structure of the British Film Industry in the 1990s: Localization and Commercialization of British Cinema Towards a Global Audience." *Media, Culture & Society* 25, no. 3 (2003): 405–413.

King, Geoff. *American Independent Cinema*. Bloomington: Indiana University Press, 2005.

———. *Indiewood, USA: Where Hollywood Meets Independent Cinema*. London: I. B. Taurus, 2009.

Kleinhans, Chuck. "Independent Features: Hopes and Dreams." In *The New American Cinema*, edited by Jon Lewis, 307–327. Durham, NC: Duke University Press, 1998.

Kuhn, Michael. *One Hundred Films and a Funeral: PolyGram Films—Birth, Betrothal, Betrayal, Burial*. London: Thorogood, 2003.

Lane, Christina. "Just Another Girl Outside the Neo-Indie." In *Contemporary American Independent Film*, edited by Christine Holmlund and Justin Wyatt, 193–209. London: Routledge, 2005.

Levy, Emanuel. *Cinema of Outsiders: The Rise of American Independent Film*. New York: New York University Press, 1999.

Lewis, Jon. *Hollywood v. Hard Core: How the Struggle over Censorship Saved the Modern Film Industry*. New York: New York University Press, 2002.

Luckett, Moya. "Image and Nation in 1990s British Cinema." In *British Cinema in the 1990s*, edited by Robert Murphy, 88–99. London: BFI, 1999.

Lukk, Tiiu. *Movie Marketing: Opening the Picture and Giving It Legs*. Los Angeles: Silman James Press, 1997.

Lyons, Donald. *Independent Visions: A Critical Introduction to Recent Independent American Film*. New York: Ballantine Books, 1994.

Macnab, Geoffrey. "Unseen British Cinema." In *British Cinema in the 90s*, edited by Robert Murphy, 135–144. London: BFI, 1999.

Margolis, Harriet. "Introduction: 'A Strange Heritage': From Colonization to Transformation?" In *Jane Campion's "The Piano,"* ed. Harriet Margolis, 1–41. Cambridge: Cambridge University Press, 2000.

McCabe, Janet, and Kim Akass, eds. *Quality TV: Contemporary American Television and Beyond*. London: I. B. Tauris, 2007.

McDonald, Paul. "Miramax, *Life Is Beautiful*, and the Indiewoodization of the Foreign-Language Film Market in the USA." *New Review of Film and Television Studies* 7, no. 4 (December 2009): 353–375.

McDonald, Paul, and Janet Wasko, eds. *Contemporary Hollywood Film Industry*. Malden, MA: Wiley-Blackwell, 2008.

McLoone, Martin. "Internal Decolonisation? British Cinema and the Celtic Fringe." In *The British Cinema Book*, edited by Robert Murphy, 207–213. London: BFI, 2001.

Merritt, Greg. *Celluloid Mavericks: A History of American Independent Film.* New York: Thunder's Mouth Press, 2000.

Miller, Toby, Nitin Govil, John McMurria, and Richard Maxwell, eds. *Global Hollywood*. London: BFI, 2001.

Miller, Toby, Nitin Govil, John McMurria, Richard Maxwell, and Ting Wang, eds. *Global Hollywood 2*. London: BFI, 2005.

Monk, Claire. "Underbelly UK: The 1990s Underclass Film, Masculinity, and the Ideologies of New Britain." In *British Cinema, Past and Present*, edited by Justine Ashby and Andrew Higson, 274–287. London: Routledge, 2000.

Muir, John Kenneth. *An Askew View: The Films of Kevin Smith.* New York: Applause, 2002.

Murphy, Robert. "Citylife: Urban Fairy-Tales in Late 90s British Cinema." In *The British Cinema Book*, edited by Robert Murphy, 292–300. London: BFI, 2001.

———. "A Path Through a Moral Maze." In *British Cinema in the 90s*, edited by Robert Murphy, 1–16. London: BFI, 1999.

Newman, Michael. "Indie Culture: In Pursuit of the Authentic Autonomous Alternative." *Cinema Journal* 48, no. 3 (Spring 2009): 16–34.

Penman, Ian. "Don't Try This at Home." In *Quentin Tarantino: The Film Geek Files*, edited by Paul A. Woods, 124–128. London: Plexus, 2000.

Perren, Alisa. "A Big Fat Indie Success Story? Press Discourses Surrounding the Making and Marketing of a 'Hollywood' Movie." *Journal of Film and Video* 56, no. 2 (Summer 2004): 18–31.

———. "Business as Unusual: Conglomerate-Sized Challenges for Film and Television in the Digital Arena." *Journal of Popular Film and Television* 38, no. 2 (Summer 2010): 72–78.

Pierson, John. *Spike Mike Reloaded.* New York: Hyperion/Miramax Books, 2004.

———. *Spike, Mike, Slackers, and Dykes: A Guided Tour Across a Decade of American Independent Cinema.* New York: Hyperion/Miramax Books, 1995.

Polan, Dana. *Jane Campion.* London: BFI, 2001.

———. *Pulp Fiction.* London: BFI, 2000.

Prince, Stephen. *A New Pot of Gold: Hollywood Under the Electronic Rainbow, 1980–1989.* Berkeley: University of California Press, 2000.

Rich, B. Ruby. "The New Queer Wave," *Sight and Sound* 2 (September 1992): 30–34.

Rosen, David, and Peter Hamilton. *Off-Hollywood: The Making and Marketing of Independent Films.* New York: Grove Weidenfeld, 1987.

Schamus, James. "To the Rear of the Back End: The Economics of Independent Cinema." In *Contemporary Hollywood Cinema*, edited by Steve Neale and Murray Smith, 91–105. London: Routledge, 1998.

Schatz, Thomas. "The New Hollywood." In *Film Theory Goes to the Movies*, edited by Jim Collins, Hilary Radner, and Ava Preacher, 8–36. New York: Routledge, 1993.

———. "New Hollywood, New Millennium." In *Film Theory and Contemporary Hollywood Movies*, edited by Warren Buckland, 19–46. New York: Routledge, 2009.

———. "The Return of the Hollywood Studio System," in *Conglomerates and the Media*, edited by Erik Barnouw et al., 73–106. New York: New Press, 1997.

Schauer, Bradley. "Dimension Films and the Exploitation Tradition in Hollywood." *Quarterly Review of Film and Video* 26, no. 5 (2009): 393–405.

Sconce, Jeffrey. "'Trashing' the Academy: Taste, Excess, and an Emerging Politics of Cinematic Style." *Screen* 36 (Winter 1995): 371–393.

Smith, Lory. *Party in a Box: The Story of the Sundance Film Festival*. Salt Lake City: Gibbs Smith, 1999.

Stewart, James B. *DisneyWar*. New York: Simon & Schuster, 2006.

Thornley, Davinia. "The 'Scream' Reflex: Meta-horror and Popular Culture." *Metro*, Spring 2006, 140–147.

Timpone, Anthony. "To the Dawn and Beyond." In *Quentin Tarantino: The Film Geek Files*, edited by Paul A. Woods, 136–137. London: Plexus, 2000.

Todd, Peter. "The British Film Industry in the 90s." In *British Cinema in the 90s*, edited by Robert Murphy, 17–26. London: BFI, 1999.

Tryon, Chuck. *Reinventing Cinema: Movies in the Age of Media Convergence*. New Brunswick, NJ: Rutgers University Press, 2009.

Turan, Kenneth. Sundance to Sarajevo: Film Festivals and the World They Made. Berkeley: University of California Press, 2002.

Tzioumakis, Yannis. *American Independent Cinema: An Introduction*. New Brunswick, NJ: Rutgers University Press, 2006.

Udovitch, Mim. "Tarantino and Juliette." In *Quentin Tarantino: The Film Geek Files*, edited by Paul A. Woods, 111–118. London: Plexus, 2000.

Wasko, Janet. *Hollywood in the Information Age*. Austin: University of Texas Press, 1994.

———. *How Hollywood Works*. Thousand Oaks, CA: Sage, 2003.

Wasser, Frederick. "Is Hollywood America? The Trans-nationalization of the American Film Industry." *Critical Studies in Mass Communication* 12, no. 4 (1995): 423–437.

———. *Veni, Vidi, Video: The Hollywood Empire and the VCR*. Austin: University of Texas Press, 2002.

Watson, Neil. "Hollywood UK." In *British Cinema of the 90s*, edited by Robert Murphy, 80–87. London: BFI, 1999.

Wee, Valerie. "Resurrecting and Updating the Teen Slasher." *Journal of Popular Film and Television* 34 (Summer 2006): 50–61.

———. *Teen Media: Hollywood and the Youth Market in the Digital Age*. Jackson, NC: McFarland, 2010.

Wilinsky, Barbara. *Sure Seaters: The Emergence of Art House Cinema*. Minneapolis: University of Minnesota Press, 2001.

Woods, Paul A., ed. *Tarantino: The Film Geek Files*. London: Plexus, 2000.

Wyatt, Justin. "Economic Constraints/Economic Opportunities: Robert Altman as Auteur." *Velvet Light Trap* 38 (Fall 1996): 51–67.

————. "The Formation of the 'Major Independent': Miramax, New Line, and the New Hollywood." In *Contemporary Hollywood Cinema*, edited by Steve Neale and Murray Smith, 74–90. London: Routledge, 1998.

————. *High Concept: Movies and Marketing in Hollywood*. Austin: University of Texas Press, 1994.

————. "Independents, Packaging, and Inflationary Pressure in 1980s Hollywood." In *A New Pot of Gold: Hollywood Under the Electronic Rainbow, 1980–1989*, in Stephen Prince, 141–159. Berkeley: University of California Press, 2000.

————. "The Stigma of X: Adult Cinema and the Institution of the MPAA Ratings System." In *Controlling Hollywood: Censorship and Regulation in the Studio Era*, edited by Matthew Bernstein, 238–264. New Brunswick, NJ: Rutgers University Press, 1999.

Index

Haynes, Todd, 10, 190–191
HBO, 22, 48, 162, 182, 226, 270n20, 283n102; *Kids* rights, 121
Hear My Song, 58–59, 125
Heavenly Creatures, 86, 88
Hellraiser, 39
Hellraiser III, 49, 125
Hellraiser IV, 7
Helmore, Edward, on Hollywood three-tier structure, 155
Hemdale, 76, 123; bankruptcy, 244n1
Henry V, 55, 68, 123
Henry: Portrait of a Serial Killer, 45
Hernandez, Eugene, 218, 272n41; on indies' future, 229; use of term "Indiewood," 238n39
Hero, 56, 200
Hess, Rick, on independent film press coverage, 163
Hewitt, Jennifer Love, 140
Hidden Assassin, 129
High Art, 216
High Heels, 58
High Spirits, 61, 64
high-concept film, 6, 18, 26, 29; and New Hollywood, 37, 56; global appeal, 38
Highlander, 104
Hilary and Jackie, 216
Hindes, Andrew, 211, 265n52
Hitchcock, Alfred, 66, 129, 136
Hoberman, J., on *Life is Beautiful*, 197
Hoffa, 68
Hollywood industry, three-tier structure, 154–160, 218
Hollywood Pictures, 51, 252n84; Disney, 71; lack of prestige, 71
Hollywood Renaissance, 10. *See also* New American Cinema
Hollywood Reporter, 108, 110, 154, 180
Holofcener, Nicole, 79, 103; marginalization, 252n83
Holt, Jennifer, 5
home video, 18–19, 21, 24, 220, 231, 235n2; decline, 263n20; digital distribution, 232, 283n100, 283n105; Disney, 71, 93, 121, 256n25; Miramax, 48, 139; New Line, 55; 1980s independents, 29; rental and B-grade films, 27, 29; stores and franchising, 29
Hong Kong action, 52

Hook, 53
Hoop Dreams, 55
Hopper, Dennis, 30
Horkheimer, Max, 9
horror film, 24, 27, 113, 126–127, 135, 154, 214; found-footage style, 221–224, 280n64; international reception, 259n78; Miramax, 132–140; New Line, 28–29, 55; *New Nightmare*, 128–129, 133; 1980s decline, 127, 258n47; *Scream*, 257n46, 258n65, 259n80, 260n101; straight-to-video, 258n61
House of Yes, The, 100, 177; press and earnings, 270n5
House Party, 28, 127
Howard's End, 56, 59, 81
Hughes, Allen, on Disney-Miramax deal, 54
Human Stain, The, 227
Hunter, Holly, 81–82
Hyperion Books, 85

I Am Curious [Yellow], 186
I Know What You Did Last Summer, 140, 212
I Shot Andy Warhol, 149–150; box office, 263n24
I Still Know What You Did Last Summer, 212
ICM, 110, 221
Iger, Robert, 228, 231
Il Postino, 3, 43, 89, 174, 189, 192, 195, 199; national affiliations, 185, 271n30
In the Bedroom, 226
In Love and War, 157
In the Name of the Father, 91
Independence Day, 144, 164, 167
independent distributors, 2, 4, 9–11; and major studios, 11, 15, 56–57; in the 1980s, 26–27, 29; international marketplace, 29
Independent Feature Project, 19, 94, 111, 146; funding concerns, 265n57
independent film, 1–4, 11; aesthetic, 16–17; as American, 8–14, 95, 169–170; classics divisions, 27, 57; commercialism versus artistic expression, 9, 121–122; critical response, 99; definition, 7–8, 76, 110; different from indie, 7–8, 76; and Hollywood conventions, 9; profitability, 7; rhetoric, 3–4, 7–9, 15
Independent Film Channel (IFC), 6, 110–111, 148, 225, 255n125; as indie specialty

channel, 150–151; as "premier" exhibitor, 283n100

Independent Pictures, 210

Indiana Jones series, 38, 95

Indiana Jones and the Last Crusade, 37

indie blockbuster, 16–53, 77, 79, 91, 108, 145, 149, 158, 163, 181, 191, 198–199, 222, 230–232, 238n1; definition, 16; foreign-language film challenge, 178–179, 200

indie film, 1, 3, 4, 11; and commercialism, 9, 88–89, 92; conventions, 95–99; critical response, 99, 149; definition, 7–8, 40, 76; different from independent, 7–8, 76, 92, 169; as global phenomenon, 11–12; in Hollywood structure, 154, 221; in 1990s, 148–149, 180–181, 220; profitability, 7; rhetoric, 3–4, 7–9, 15

indie divisions, 3, 6, 8, 13, 15; and Hollywood structure, 154–160. *See also* specialty divisions

Indie, Inc., 3, 8, 12–13, 15

Indiewood, 4, 15, 208, 217; and industrial structure, 218; term usage, 13, 178, 218, 236n13, 238n39, 278n35

Indiewood USA, 13

Indochine, 189

Interstar, 76, 257n35

Into the West, 103

Iron and Silk, 47

Irréversible, 224

IRS Media, 76

Island, 17, 20, 22, 24, 26, 50, 111; bankruptcy, 244n1

Island/Alive, 9, 24, 26–27, 242n79

Italian cinema, 43, 178, 185, 194–196

Jackie Brown, 92, 100, 171

Jacob, Gilles, 64, 197

Janet, Veronika, 84

Jarmusch, Jim, 10, 20, 94, 195

Jason's Lyric, 108

Jay and Silent Bob Strike Back, 141, 181

Jerry and Tom, 211–212

Jersey Girl, 181, 227

Jerusalem International Film Festival, 197

Jeunet, Jean-Pierre, 190

Jobs, Steve, 228

Joe Versus the Volcano, 38

Johnny Stecchino, 195

Jordan, Neil, 61, 63, 66, 91

Joy Luck Club, The, 51

Jurassic Park, 6, 82

K2, 48

Kafka, 58

Kaige, Chen, 81, 190

Kalifornia, 107

Kar-wai, Wong, 190

Kate and Leopold, 227

Katzenberg, Jeffrey, 2, 69–70, 78; Disney departure, 106, 114, 119, 155, 174, 203, 228, 270n7; on Disney-Miramax alliance, 54, 75

Keaton, Buster, 195

Keeper, The, 150

Keitel, Harvey, 52, 82, 84

Kentucky Fried Movie, The, 18

Kiarostami, Abbas, 162

Kidman, Nicole, 174, 226

Kids, 7, 12, 103, 112–114, 214–215, 228; critics, 114, 119–123, 125, 137; marketing and distribution, 120–121; ratings controversy, 114–125, 256n14, 256n26

Kika, 162,

Kill Bill, 92, 226

Killing Mrs. Tingle, 214

Killing Zoe, 100, 162

Kim, Jeongmee, on British cinema, 60, 245n24

Kindergarten Cop, 53

King of the Hill, 108

King, Geoff, 8, 13–14, 236n13; *American Independent Cinema*, 8; *Indiewood, USA*, 13

King's Speech, The, 232

Kino International, 76, 150, 162

Kiss of the Spider Woman, 24, 242n79

Klady, Leonard: on 1999 indie schedule, 219; on horror, 127; on independent autonomy, 122; on prestige pictures, 157; on *Scream*, 133

Knowles, Harry, 100

Kolya, 144, 168, 189, 192

Konrad, Cathy, 121

Krays, The, 50, 59

Krim, Arthur, 191

Krim, Don, 191, 204; on business conditions, 162

Krueger, Freddy, 28–29, 107, 128

Tribeca Film Center, 120

Trimark, 76, 120, 149, 154, 161, 180, 266n96

Trip to Bountiful, The, 24

TriStar, 52, 55, 79, 91

Triton Pictures, 73–74, 76

Triumph, 19

Troche, Rose, 14

Troisi, Massimo, 195

Truffaut, Francois, 43

Tsotsi, 229

Tucci, Stanley, 152

Turan, Kenneth, 84, 197; on Miramax Oscar campaigning, 171; on *Pulp Fiction,* 93

Turner Broadcasting System, 14, 74–75, 107, 122, 124, 155, 160, 247n69

Tutor, Ron, 232

20th Century-Fox International Classics, 9, 19

Twin Dragons, 201

Twist and Shout, 23

Twister, 6, 144, 167

Tykwer, Tom, 190

Tzioumakis, Yannis, 8, 236n25, 242n87; *American Independent Cinema,* 8

ultra-low-budget films, 14, 49, 94, 96, 147–148, 163, 169, 221, 251n63

Ulrich, Skeet, 133

Unapix, 161

Unbearable Lightness of Being, 42

Unfinished Life, An, 227

United Artists Classics, 9, 19

Universal Focus, 4, 19, 217

Universal Pictures, 4, 24–25, 38, 51–52, 55, 91, 105–109, 122, 145, 155, 160, 164, 175–176, 216–217, 243n99, 262n122, 266n8, 275n87, 277n17

Up Close and Personal, 156

UPN, 6, 139, 264n41

Urman, Mark, 223

USA Films, 216–217

U.S. Film Festival, 31–32. *See also* Sundance Film Festival

Usual Suspects, The, 98, 100, 108

UTA, 110, 221

V.I. Warshawski, 71

Vachon, Christine, 121, 278n33

Van Peebles, Mario, 108

Van Sant, Gus, 110, 121; as cinema of cool precursor, 95

Vanya on 42nd Street, 190

Variety, 40, 65, 76, 90, 127, 137, 144, 147, 153–154, 157, 180, 186, 202, 207, 210, 219; on Disney-Miramax, 72–73, 78, 166, 174, 210; *Dogma,* 215; *Kids,* 113, 118, 122–123; on indies, 56, 101; on Miramax, 51, 105–106, 225; on *New Nightmare,* 129, 133; on *Scream,* 113. See also *Daily Variety*

Vaughn, Vince, 97

Venice Film Festival, 18

Vertigo, 66

Very Brady Sequel, A, 156

Vestron, 17, 26, 50, 75, 244n1, 257n35

Viacom, 4, 110, 255n125

Victory, 102

View Askew, 100

Village Voice, 197

Virgin, 31, 248n17

Virgin Records, 85

Virgin Suicides, The, 218

Vivendi Universal, 4, 217

Vognar, Chris, 135

von Trier, Lars, 164

Waiting . . . , 224

Waiting for Guffman, 188

Wakeman, Rick, 21

Waking Ned Devine, 219

Walken, Christopher, 164

Walking and Talking, 103, 149–150, 169, 263n24

Wallace, Amy, 1; on *Happy, Texas* acquisition, 210

Wall Street Journal, 119, 260n100

Walt Disney Studios, 2, 70, 152

Wang, Wayne, 10, 51, 110

Warner Bros., 38, 48, 55, 69, 91, 117, 154, 164, 219, 222, 247n57

Warner Independent, 13, 231, 283n102

War Room, The, 162

Wasko, Janet, 5, 239n7

Wasser, Frederick, on globalization of Hollywood, 184

Wasteland, 140, 216

Waters, John, 28

Wayan brothers, 141, 261n111

WB, 139–140, 159, 264n41

Lightning Source UK Ltd.
Milton Keynes UK
UKOW040954080413

208849UK00001B/1/P